Perspectives in Neural Computing

Springer-Verlag London Ltd.

Roberto Tagliaferri and Maria Marinaro (Eds)

Neural Nets
WIRN Vietri-01

Proceedings of the 12th Italian Workshop on Neural Nets,
Vietri sul Mare, Salerno, Italy, 17-19 May 2001

Società Italiana Reti Neuroniche (SIREN)
•
International Institute for Advanced Scientific Studies
"E.R. Caianiello" (IIASS)
•
IEEE Neural Network Council
•
INNS - SIG Italia
•
Department of Mathematics and Computer Science,
University of Salerno
•
Department of Information Science, University of Milan
•
Department of Physics "E.R. Caianiello", University of Salerno
•
Istituto Italiano per gli Studi Filosofici (Naples)

 Springer

Roberto Tagliaferri, Associate Professor of Computer Science and Neural Nets
DMI, Università di Salerno, 84081 Baronissi (SA), Italy

Maria Marinaro, Full Professor in Theoretical Physics
Dipartimento di Scienze Fisiche "E.R. Caianiello", Università di Salerno, 84081 Baronissi (SA), Italy

Series Editor
J.G. Taylor, BA, BSc, MA, PhD, FInstP
Centre for Neural Networks, Department of Mathematics, King's College, Strand, London WC2R 2LS, UK

British Library Cataloguing in Publication Data
WIRN VIETRI-01 (2001)
   Neural Nets-WIRN Vietri-01 : proceedings of the 12th
   Italian workshop on Neural Nets, Vietri sul Mare, Salerno,
   Italy, 17-19 May 2001. - (Perspectives in neural computing)
   1.Neural networks (Computer science) - Congresses
   I.Title II. Tagliaferri, Roberto III. Marinaro, M.
   006.3'2

Library of Congress Cataloging-in-Publication Data
A catalog record for this book is available from the Library of Congress

ISSN 1431-6854

ISBN 978-1-4471-1096-5   ISBN 978-1-4471-0219-9 (eBook)
DOI 10.1007/978-1-4471-0219-9

Typesetting: Camera ready by contributors
34/3830-543210 Printed on acid-free paper SPIN 10837433

Preface

This volume contains the proceedings of the *12th Italian Workshop on Neural Nets WIRN VIETRI-01,* jointly organized by the International Institute for Advanced Scientific Studies "Eduardo R. Caianiello" (IIASS), the Società Italiana Reti Neuroniche (SIREN), the IEEE NNC Italian RIG and the Italian SIG of the INNS.

Following the tradition of previous years, we invited three foreign scientists to the workshop, Dr. G. Indiveri and Professors A. Roy and R. Sun, who respectively presented the lectures *"Computation in Neuromorphic Analog VLSI Systems", "On Connectionism and Rule Extraction", "Beyond Simple Rule Extraction: Acquiring Planning Knowledge from Neural Networks"* (the last two papers being part of the special session mentioned below).

In addition, a review talk was presented, dealing with a very up-to-date topic: *"Neurofuzzy Approximator based on Mamdani's Model".*

A large part of the book contains original contributions approved by referees as oral or poster presentations, which have been assembled for reading convenience into three sections: Architectures and Algorithms, Image and Signal Processing, and Applications.

The last part of the books contains the papers of the special Session "From Synapses to Rules". Our thanks go to Prof. B. Apolloni, who organized this section.

Furthermore, two sections are dedicated to the memory of two great scientists who were friends in life, Professors Mark Aizerman and Eduardo R. Caianiello.

The editors would like to thank the invited speakers, the review lecturers and all the contributors whose highly qualified papers helped with the success of the workshop.

Finally, special thanks go to the referees for their accurate work.

Maria Marinaro
Roberto Tagliaferri

Organizing - Scientific Committee:

B. Apolloni *(Univ. Milano)*, A. Bertoni *(Univ. Milano)*, N.A. Borghese *(CNR Milano)*, P. Campadelli *(Univ. Milano)*, D.D. Caviglia *(Univ. Genova)*, A. Colla *(ELSAG S.p.A. - Genova)*, A. Esposito *(IIASS)*, M. Frixione *(Univ. Salerno)*, C. Furlanello *(ITC - IRST - Trento)*,), M. Gori *(Univ. Siena)*, G.M. Guazzo *(IIASS)*, F. Lauria *(Univ. Napoli)*, M. Marinaro *(Univ. Salerno - IIASS)*, F. Masulli *(Univ. Genova)*, F.C. Morabito *(Univ. Reggio Calabria)*, P. Morasso *(Univ. Genova)*, G. Orlandi *(Univ. Roma "La Sapienza")*, T. Parisini *(Politecnico di Milano)*, E. Pasero *(Politecnico Torino)*, A. Petrosino *(CNR - Napoli)*, V. Piuri *(Politecnico di Milano)*, R. Serra *(CRA Montecatini - Ravenna)*, F. Sorbello *(Univ. Palermo)*, R. Tagliaferri *(Univ. Salerno)*.

Referees:

Acernese F., Andretta M., Apolloni B., Bertoni A., Borghese N.A., Burattini E., Burrascano P., Campadelli P., Caviglia D.D., Chella A., Ciaramella A., Colla A.M., Di Claudio E.D., Eleutieri A., Frattale Mascioli F.M., Giove S., Lauria F., Marinaro M., Masulli F., Morabito F.C., Morasso P., Palmieri F., Parisi R., Parisini T., Pasero E., Petrosino A., Salzano M., Serra R., Sessa S., Sperduti A., Staiano A., Tagliaferri R., Uncini A.

The sponsorship and support of:

- Società Italiana Reti Neuroniche (SIREN)
- International Institute for Advanced Scientific Studies "E.R. Caianiello" (IIASS)
- IEEE Neural Network Council
- INNS - SIG Italy
- Dept. of Mathematics and Computer Science, University of Salerno
- Dept. of Information Science, University of Milan
- Dept. of Physics "E.R. Caianiello", University of Salerno
- Istituto Italiano per gli Studi Filosofici (Naples)

are gratefully acknowledged.

Contents

x

Section 1
Invited Paper

Computation in Neuromorphic Analog VLSI Systems

Giacomo Indiveri

Institute of Neuroinformatics, University/ETH Zurich

Zürich, Switzerland

Abstract

In this paper we present an overview of basic neuromorphic analog circuits that are typically used as building blocks for more complex neuromorphic systems. We present the main principles used by the neuromorphic engineering community and describe, as case example, a neuromorphic VLSI system for modeling selective visual attention.

1 Neuromorphic Engineering

The term *"neuromorphic"* was coined by Carver Mead to describe very large scale integration (VLSI) systems containing electronic analog circuits that mimic neurobiological architectures present in the nervous system [18]. Neuromorphic computation is related to modeling and simulation of networks of neurons and systems using the same *organizing principles* found in real nervous system. In recent times the term "neuromorphic" has also been used to describe mixed *analog/digital* VLSI systems that implement computational models of real neural systems. These VLSI systems, rather than implementing abstract neural networks only remotely related to biological systems, in large part, *directly* exploit the physics of silicon (and of CMOS VLSI technology) to implement the physical processes that underlie neural computation.

Neuromorphic engineering is a new discipline at the boundary between engineering and neuroscience, but which crosses many other fields, including biology, physics, computer science, psychology, physiology, *etc.*

Analog VLSI Circuits

There are some direct analogies between biological neural systems and analog VLSI neuromorphic systems: conservation of charge, amplification, exponentiation, thresholding, compression, and integration. The parallels between these two worlds run from the level of device physics to circuit architectures:

- Diffusion mechanisms in membrane and transistor channels

- Function determined by the system's structure

To point out why studying natural neural systems and implementing models of these systems, using analog VLSI technology can be potentially instrumental for improving technological progress, consider the following arguments:

1. Biology has solved the problem of using loosely coupled, globally asynchronous, massively parallel, noisy and unreliable components to carry out robust and energy efficient computation.

2. CMOS VLSI technology has been continuously improving, following Moore's law, for almost 30 years, pushed by a hyper-competitive $300 billion global industry. But, as CMOS technology improves further and transistor's gate lengths drop below 0.10 microns

    - transistors start to behave like neurons
    - we have the ability to place millions of simple processors on a single piece of silicon
    - single chips start to have complexities that are too difficult to handle by the design tools
    - we need to begin to worry about power consumption and power dissipation issues

Computation and Power Consumption

The brain has on the order on 10^{11} neurons and 10^{14} synapses. It performs on average 10^{15} operations per second. The power dissipation of the brain is approximately 10^{-16} J per operation, which results in about a total mean consumption of **less than 10 watts**. By comparison today's silicon digital technology can dissipate at best 10^{-8} J of energy per operation at the single chip level. There is no way of achieving 10^{15} operations per second on a single chip, with today's technology. But even if this was possible, to do that amount of computation a digital chip would consume MegaWatts (the output of a nuclear power station).

Any serious attempt to replicate the computational power of brains must confront this problem. *Subthreshold* analog circuits are also no match for real neural circuits, but they are a factor of 10^4 more power efficient than their digital counterparts.

In the following Section we present some basic analog circuits that are most commonly used as elementary building blocks for constructing complex neuromorphic systems. In Section 3 we present a VLSI device containing a model of selective visual attention, that uses many of the circuits described in Section 2, as a case example. Finally in Section 4 we draw the conclusions.

2 Subthreshold Analog Circuits

Perhaps the most elementary computational element of a biological neural structure is the neural cell's membrane. The nerve membrane electrically separates the neuron's interior from the extra-cellular fluid. It is a very stable structure that behaves as a perfect insulator. Current flow through the membrane is mediated by special ion channels (*conductances*) which can behave as passive or active devices. In the passive case, ion channels selectively allow ions to flow through the membrane by the process of *diffusion*. In electronics, it is possible to implement the same physical process by using MOS transistor devices, operated in the *subthreshold* region (also referred to as *weak inversion*) [17, 20].

2.1 From subthreshold MOS transistors ...

MOS transistors operate in the subthreshold region of operation when their gate-to-source voltage is below the transistor threshold voltage. This mode of operation of a transistor has been largely ignored by the analog/digital circuit design community, mainly because the currents that flow through the source-drain terminals of the device under these conditions are extremely low (typically of the order of nanoamperes). In subthreshold, the drain current of the transistors is related to the gate-to-source voltage by an exponential relationship. Specifically, for an n-type MOS transistor, the subthreshold current is given by:

$$I_{out} = \frac{W}{L} I_0 e^{\left((1-\kappa)\frac{V_{BS}}{U_T}\right)} e^{\left(\kappa\frac{V_{GS}}{U_T}\right)} \cdot \left(1 - e^{\left(-\frac{V_{DS}}{U_T}\right)} + \frac{V_{DS}}{V_0}\right) \tag{1}$$

where W and L are the width and length of the transistor, I_0 is the zero bias current, κ is the subthreshold slope coefficient, U_T is the thermal voltage, V_0 is the Early voltage and V_{GS}, V_{DS} and V_{BS} are the gate-to-source, drain-to-source and bulk-to-source voltages respectively. Typical values for devices with $W = L = 4\mu m$ fabricated with standard $2\mu m$ technology are: $I_0 = 0.72 \cdot 10^{-18}$ A, $\kappa = 0.65$, $V_0 = 15.0$ V.

If the transistor operates in saturation region (*i.e.* if $V_{DS} \geq 4U_T$) and if $\mid V_0 \mid \gg \mid V_{DS} \mid$ the above equation can be simplified to yield:

$$I_{out} = \frac{W}{L} I_0 e^{\left(\frac{\kappa V_G - V_S}{U_T}\right)} \tag{2}$$

The diffusion of electrons through the transistor channel is mediated by the gate-to-source voltage difference. As the input/output characteristic of a subthreshold transistor is an exponential function, circuits containing these devices can implement the "base functions" required to model biological processes: logarithms and exponentials.

2.2 ... to the Transconductance Amplifier

On of the most common tricks used both by biological and engineered devices for computing measurements insensitive to absolute reference values and robust to noise, is the one of using *difference* signals. The differential pair is a compact circuit comprising only three transistors that is widely used in many neuromorphic systems (see Fig. 1). It has the desirable property of accepting a *differential voltage* as input and providing in output a differential current with extremely useful characteristics: if the bias transistor is operated in the subthreshold domain and if we assume that all the

6

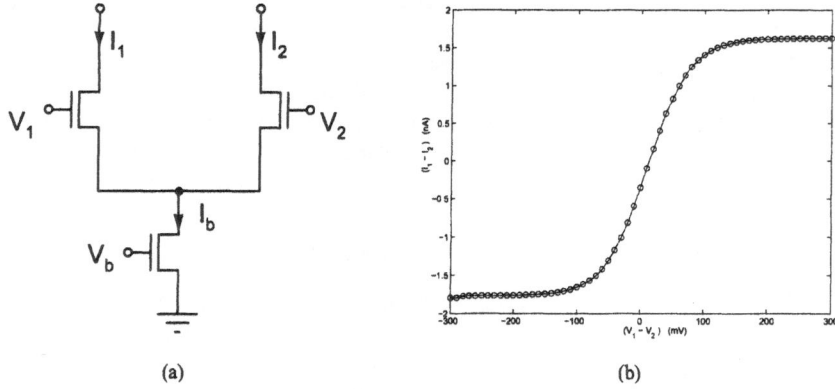

(a)   (b)

Figure 1: (a) Circuit diagram of the differential pair. The differential output current $I_1 - I_2$ is controlled by the differential input voltage $V_1 - V_2$ and scaled by a constant factor set by the bias voltage V_b. (b) Experimental data obtained from a differential transconductance amplifier with a bias voltage set to $V_b = 0.6V$.

transistors are in saturation (so that equation 2 holds), the transfer function of the circuit is:

$$I_1 - I_2 = I_b \tanh \frac{\kappa (V_1 - V_2)}{2U_T} \tag{3}$$

The beauty of this transfer function lies in the properties of the hyperbolic tangent present in it: it passes through the origin with unity slope, it behaves in a linear fashion for small differential inputs and it saturates smoothly for large differential inputs.

To provide in output the differential term $I_1 - I_2$ using a single terminal, one needs simply to connect a *current mirror* of complementary type to the differential pair output terminals (*e.g.* a current mirror of p-type MOS transistors in the case of Fig. 1). The circuit thus obtained would then be the famous *differential transconductance amplifier* [17]. For small differential voltages this circuit's transfer function (eq. (3)) is approximately linear:

$$I_{out} \approx I_b \frac{\kappa}{2U_T} (V_1 - V_2) =: g_m (V_1 - V_2), \tag{4}$$

The reason for this name is the fact that g_m has the dimensions of a conductance, but that the input voltage is applied between two terminals and the current is measured at a different terminal. A conductance in the straightforward sense can be measured at the input and output nodes.

The transconductance amplifier is widely used in many of the neuromorphic systems that have been designed up to today. More generally, using the basic circuits described in these sections it is possible to implement most of the circuits present in

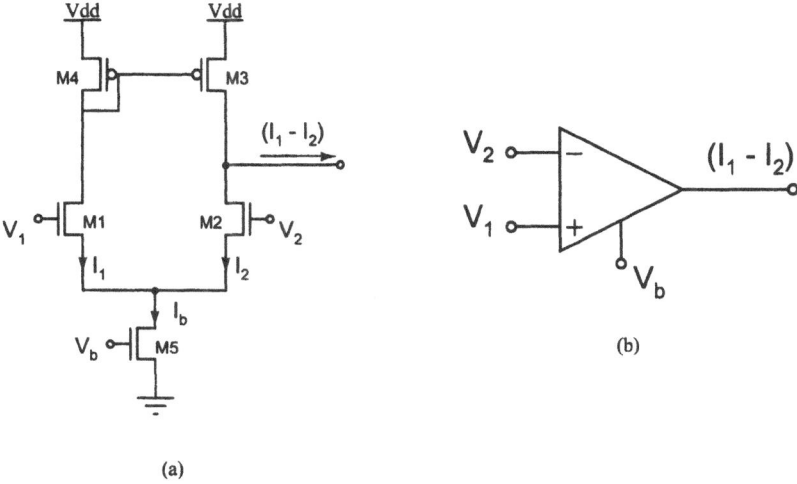

Figure 2: (a) Schematic diagram of the transconductance amplifier. (b) Transconductance amplifier's symbol

today's neuromorphic systems. In the following section we will see an example in which we use the transconductance amplifier, in conjunction with inverting amplifiers and single transistors to implement a silicon neuron.

2.3 Silicon Neurons

By silicon neurons we refer to circuits that emulate the electrical properties of biological neurons at different levels of abstractions. At high levels of abstractions it is possible to model a neuron's response by using a transfer function that maps the input current it receives into the frequency of the spikes it generates. If the mapping is linear even a single transistor can implement such a model. Neurons of this type are called *linear threshold units* [16]. If the mapping is *sigmoidal*, we can implement models of neurons using the transconductance amplifier described in Section 2.2. If we want to model the neuron's response in more detail, we have to take into account their spike-generating mechanism and implement circuits that generate spikes. The are two main classes of spiking silicon neurons: integrate-and-fire neurons and conductance based neurons. Neurons of the first class implement simplified models of real neurons, but can be a useful abstraction for designing dense networks of neurons and for studying neural network properties. Neurons of the second class implement a much more realistic model of biological neurons and can be used as a modeling tool for simulating/understanding properties of single neurons, or for implementing small neural networks. The conductance based silicon neurons emulate in great detail the electro-physiological behavior of biological neurons. They can also be used to model the continuous neuronal membrane properties of the dendrite and soma by interfacing

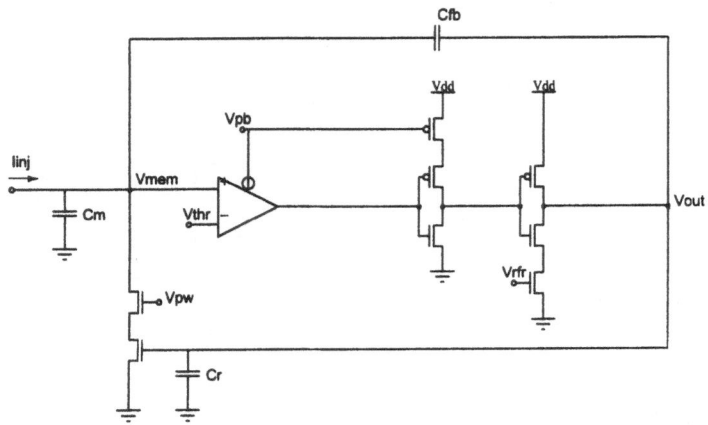

Figure 3: Circuit diagram of the integrate-and-fire neuron.

different circuits that represent homogeneous, isopotential *compartments* [11].

As we are mainly interested in analyzing the computational properties of networks of neurons, we will consider in this section circuits that implement integrate-and-fire neurons. The specific circuit that we will take into account is shown in Fig. 3.

Input is applied to this circuit by injecting the current I_{inj} into the membrane capacitance C_m. A comparator circuit compares the membrane voltage V_{mem} (which increases linearly with time if the injection current is applied) with a fixed threshold voltage V_{thr}. As long as V_{mem} is below V_{thr}, the output of the comparator is low and the neuron's output voltage V_{out} sits at 0V. As V_{mem} increases above threshold though, the comparator output voltage rises to the positive power supply rail and, via the two inverters, also brings V_{out} to the rail. A positive feedback loop, implemented with the capacitive divider C_{fb} C_m, ensures that as soon as the membrane voltage V_{mem} reaches V_{thr}, it is increased by an amount proportional to $V_{dd} \frac{C_{fb}}{C_m + C_{fb}}$ [17]. In this way we avoid the problems that could arise with small fluctuations of V_{mem} around V_{thr}. When V_{out} is high, the reset transistor at the bottom-left of Fig. 3 is switched on and the capacitor C_m is discharged at a rate controlled by V_{pw}, which effectively sets the output pulse width (the width of the spike). The membrane voltage thus decreases linearly with time and as soon as it falls below V_{thr} the comparator brings its output voltage to zero. As a consequence the first inverter sets its output high and switches on the n-type transistor of the second inverter, allowing the capacitor C_r to be discharged at a rate controlled by V_{rfr}. This bias voltage controls the length of the neuron's *refractory period*: the current flowing into the node V_{mem} is discharged to ground and the membrane voltage does not increase, for as long as the voltage on C_r (V_{out}) is high enough.

Figs. 4(a) and (b) shows traces of V_{mem} for different amplitudes of the input injection current I_{inj} and for different settings of the refractory period control voltage V_{rfr}. The threshold voltage V_{thr} was set at 2V and the bias voltage V_{pw} was set at 0.5V, such that the width of a spike was approximately 1ms. Figs. 4(c) and (d) show

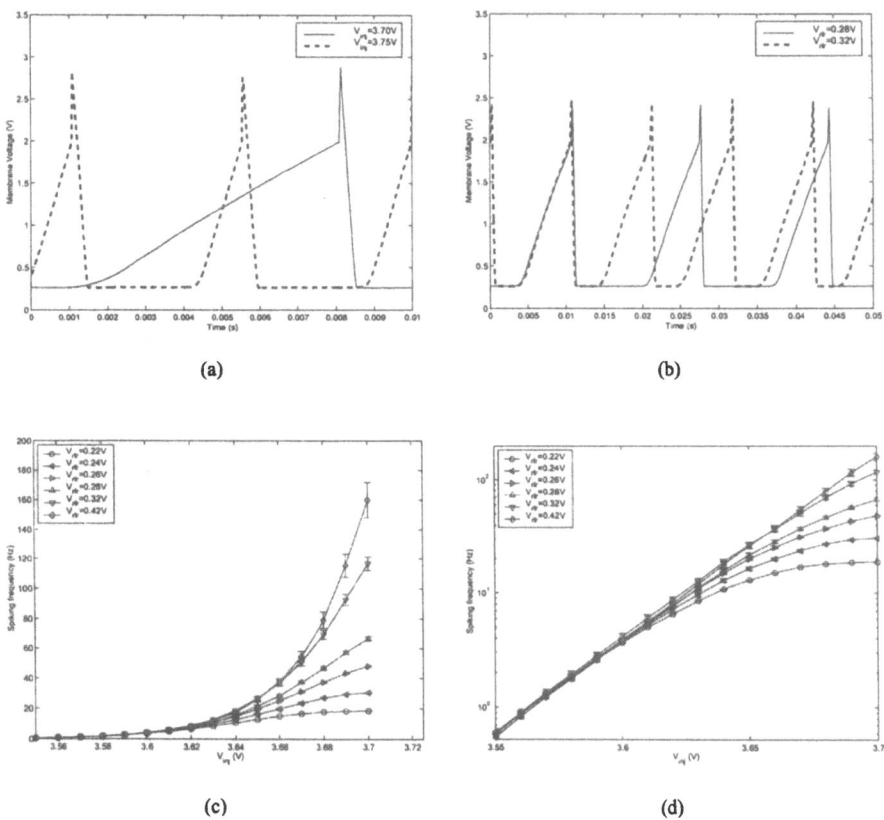

Figure 4: Integrate-and-fire neuron characteristics. (a) Membrane voltage for two different DC injection current values (set by the control voltage V_{inj}). (b) Membrane voltage for two different refractory period settings. (c) Firing rates of the neuron as a function of current-injection control voltage V_{inj} plotted on a linear scale. (d) Firing rates of the neuron as a function of V_{inj} plotted on a log scale (the injection current increases exponentially with V_{inj}).

how the firing rate of the neuron depends on the injection current amplitude. These plots are typically referred to as FI-curves. We can control the saturation properties of the FI-curves by changing the length of the neuron's refractory period. The error bars show how reliable the neuron is, when stimulated with the same injection current. We changed the injection current amplitude by modulating a control voltage V_{inj}. As the injection current changes exponentially with the control *voltage* V_{inj}, the firing rate of the neuron follows the same relationship. To verify that the firing rate is linear with the injection *current* we can view the same data using a log-scale on the ordinate axis (Fig. 4(d)).

2.4 Silicon Synapses

To implement networks of integrate-and-fire neurons we can connect the circuits described in Section 2.3 among each other with silicon synapses. To provide the proper input signal to an integrate-and-fire neuron, synaptic circuits need to convert the (digital) voltage pulses V_{out} of the neuron to an injection current I_{inj}. An *integrator* circuit implements a simplified model of a real biological synapse: as input pulses arrive at the synapse, they are integrated such that the circuit's output current encodes the frequency of the input spike train. Synapses can be *excitatory* or *inhibitory*. In the first case, given the silicon neuron of Fig. 3, they *source* current into the neuron's membrane capacitor. In the second case they *sink* current from the neuron's membrane capacitor. Using excitatory and inhibitory synaptic circuits, interfaced to silicon neurons, it is possible to design neural networks of arbitrary complexity. The size of the silicon neural network is only limited by the chip's surface. Using a low-cost technology and small chip sizes it is already possible to fabricate networks with thousands of neurons (and synapses). Using more aggressive technologies (such as the ones used to design the latest Pentium processors) it would be possible to fabricate networks containing millions of elements. The architecture of the (analog, silicon) neural network, its connectivity patterns and the synaptic circuit parameters (such as the synaptic weight) determine the computational properties of the neural network. Although it is possible in principle to implement learning algorithms using these circuits, in this section we will consider synaptic circuits with constant weights (that don't have the capability of "learning"). Learning and adaptation could be implemented by simply including additional circuits that automatically set/update the synaptic weights. These type of circuits make use of a new technology that allows us to store *analog* values on chip *permanently*: floating-gate technology [6].

A circuit that integrates digital voltage pulses into an *excitatory* analog output current is shown in Fig. 5. This circuit uses only 4 transistors and one capacitor. The input pulse is applied to transistor M1, which acts as a digital switch. Transistor M2 is biased by the analog voltage V_w to set the weight of the synaptic strength. Similarly, the voltage V_e on the source of transistor M3 can be used to set the time constant of the synapse. With each input pulse, a fixed amount of charge is sourced on the capacitor and the amplitude of the output current I_{ex} is increased. If no input is applied (*i.e.* no current is allowed to flow through M3), the output current I_{ex} decays with a $\frac{1}{t}$ profile.

We characterized the excitatory synapse of Fig. 5 by applying single pulses (see Fig. 6(a,b)) and by applying sequences of pulses (spikes) at constant rates (see Fig. 6(c,d)).

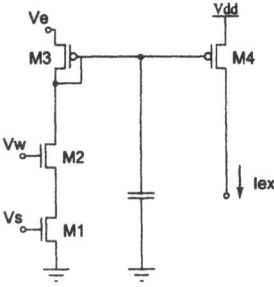

Figure 5: Excitatory synapse circuit. Input spikes are applied to M1, and transistor M4 outputs the integrated excitatory current I_{ex}.

Figure 6(a) shows the response of the excitatory synapse to a single spike for different values of V_w. Similarly, Fig. 6(b) shows the response of the excitatory synapse for different values of V_e. Changes in V_e modify both the gain and the time constant of the synapse. To better visualize the effects of V_e on the time evolution of the circuit's response, we normalized the different traces, neglecting the circuit's gain variations. Figure 6(c) shows the response of the excitatory synapse to a constant 50Hz spike train for different synaptic strength values. As shown, the circuit integrates the spikes up to a point in which the output current reaches a mean steady-state analog value, the amplitude of which depends on the frequency of the input spike train, on the synaptic strength value V_w and on V_e. Figure 6(d) shows the response of the circuit to spike train sequences of four different rates for a fixed synaptic strength value.

2.5 Silicon Retinas

The outer plexiform layer (OPL) of the vertebrate retina has attracted the interest of neuromorphic engineers because it performs some highly optimized image processing operations using just three layers of neurons; photoreceptors, horizontal cells, and bipolar cells.

In natural environments, the pattern of luminance reaching the receptor array results from the variable reflection of an illuminant by the surfaces of objects in the environment. Typically, the reflectivity of objects in any one scene ranges over only about one decade. Optimally, the operating range of the photoreceptors should be set to cover only this range of luminance. If the operating range of the photoreceptors is less than that of the scene, then luminance information will be lost due to thresholding or saturation. Whereas, if the operating range of the photoreceptors exceeds that of the scene, then the photodetectors will encode the luminance pattern at suboptimal resolution.

n the other hand, different scenes are subject to widely different illumination. The illumination varies by over 6 decades from bright sunlight to starlight. So, while the operating range of the retina should be optimized for any particular scene, the operating range should also adapt over 5-6 orders of magnitude to ensure that its response conforms to the prevailing illumination.

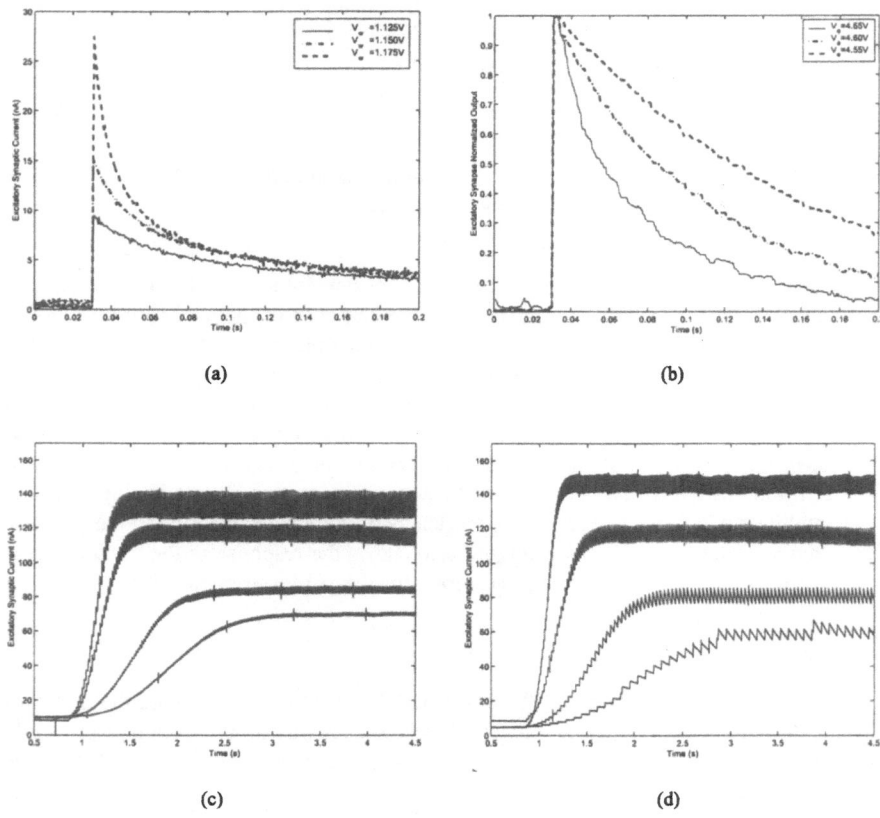

(a)

(b)

(c)

(d)

Figure 6: (a) Response of an excitatory synapse to single spikes, for different values of the synaptic strength V_w (with $V_e = 4.60$V). (b) Normalized response to single spikes for different time constant settings V_e (with $V_w = 1.150$V). (c) Response of an excitatory synapse to a 50Hz spike train for increasing values of V_w (0.6V, 0.625V, 0.65V and 0.7V from bottom to top trace respectively). (d) Response of excitatory synapse to spike trains of increasing rate for $V_w = 0.65V$ and $V_e = 4.6V$ (12Hz, 25Hz, 50Hz and 100Hz from bottom to top trace respectively).

It would be useful if the retina responded to some invariant characteristic of the luminance pattern, so that the intensity relationship between objects was invariant to illumination. Biological photoreceptors do this by reporting the contrast of the image rather than than its luminance pattern. They do this by reporting the logarithm of the luminance, so that the contrast, $\frac{\Delta L}{L}$, is invariant with illumination.

2.6   The Basic Pixel

During the last few years a number of single chip aVLSI 'silicon retinas' have been developed [14, 2] that capture these important OPL properties. Typically, these circuits consist of an array of pixels that implement adaptive contrast encoding. The pixels drive the nodes of an hexagonal resistive grid, which provides spatiotemporal filtering.

There are two families of retinal circuits; those that operate in voltage mode [14, 4], and those that operate in current mode [2].

2.6.1   Voltage Mode

The original silicon retina photoreceptor, developed by Mead and Mahowald, was a voltage mode circuit that embedded a logarithmic photodiode in a high gain amplifier. The original design has been greatly improved and characterized by Delbrück and Mead [4]. Their 5 transistor receptor [4]. Their 5 transistor receptor (Fig. 7) has a logarithmic response with a dynamic range of 1-2 decades at a single adaptation level, and a total dynamic range (including adaptation) of more than 6 decades.

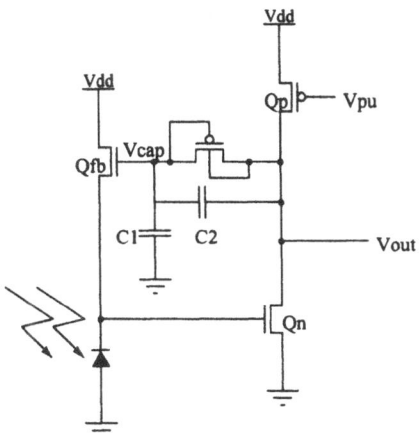

Figure 7: Circuit diagram of a pixel of the voltage-mode silicon retina. The photo-diode generates light-induced current. The voltage at the photo-diode node, logarithmically related to the light-induced current, is amplified by an adaptive high-gain amplifier (see text for details).

In the original receptor circuit, the Delbrück receptor embeds a photo-diode in a high-gain inverting amplifier. The output of this amplifier applies negative feedback to an N-FET transistor in series with the photo-diode. The effect of the feedback is to clamp the output of the photodiode (or equivalently, the input to the high-gain amplifier), thereby speeding up the response of the receptor circuit. The small-signal gain of the circuit depends on the capacitor ratio $\frac{C_1+C_2}{C_1}$, and the operating point of the the circuit depends on the voltage V_{cap}, which is proportional to the charge on the gate of Q_{fb}. Charge can accumulate or decay away from the gate via the adaptive element placed between the gate and the output of the receptor. For example, if the output voltage of the circuit remains high relative to the voltage V_{cap}, then current will flow through the adaptive element, gradually charge the gate, and thereby restore the output voltage of the photoreceptor amplifier.

This high gain photoreceptor can be used in connection with other circuits to provide early visual processing. Typically, applications involve large arrays of these photoreceptors, often with hexagonal nearest-neighbor coupling. Thus, the photoreceptors drive the nodes of an hexagonal resistive-capacitive grid that provides local spatio-temporal smoothing of the photoreceptor outputs. In this case the the output of any pixel of the retina is the difference between the photoreceptor signal, and the weighted spatio-temporal average of the neighboring photoreceptors.

Because of the technical difficulties of interchip communication present silicon retinae contain all their photodetection and processing circuitry on a single chip. Their outputs are sampled by a raster-scan mechanism, and after suitable conversion, displayed on a monitor screen. More recently, variants of the scanning circuitry have been developed that permit the silicon retina to be interfaced to a standard PC so that the neuromorphic retinae can be used for computer vision in place of commercial digital (CCD) cameras. There are also variants of the silicon retina that provide event outputs suitable for incorporation in multichip neuromorphic systems that use the Address Event Protocol for interchip communication [15, 7].

2.6.2 Current Mode

An alternative retinal design has been provided by [2]. Their retina is based on translinear circuits. The photo-sensitive element is a vertical bipolar transistor, whose emitter current is proportional to the intensity of the incident light. The circuit allows the photo current to diffuse in time and space. The diffusion takes place through two networks of horizontal diffusor elements (Fig. 8) which are implemented by N-FET transistors. The first (lower) layer of spreading emulates the lateral excitatory coupling between cone photoreceptors in biological retinae. The output of this layer excites the second (upper) layer of diffusors, which emulates the excitatory lateral coupling between the horizontal cells of the OPL. This second layer then feeds back to inhibit the first layer where it is used to control light sensitivity. The result is local automatic gain control.

The Boahen-Andreou silicon retina is a remarkable example of neuromorphic engineering. Each of its pixels comprises only 4 transistors (Fig. 8). Andreou has calculated that a 210x230 pixel version of their retina performs 10^{12} low precision calculations per second. Under these conditions the power consumption of the chip is 50mW. Thus the energy dissipated per operation is 0.05 pJ/op. This small dissipation should be compared to the much larger 10^5 pJ/op consumed by state of the art dig-

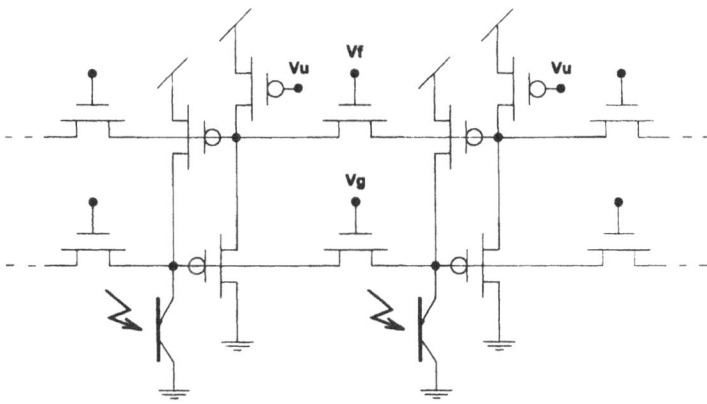

Figure 8: Circuit diagram of a pixel of the current-mode silicon retina. Photo-transistors generate light-induced current at each location. The current is then diffused laterally to neighboring pixels to create the center-surround type of response. V_u, V_f and V_g are control voltages that allow the user to set the amount of lateral spreading thus controlling the width of the pixel's receptive field

ital processors, which must switch the states of many transistors to perform any one operation.

3   A neuromorphic device for modeling selective attention

Selective attention is a mechanisms used to sequentially select the spatial locations of salient regions in the sensor's field of view. This mechanism overcomes the problem of flooding limited processing capacity systems with sensory information. It is found in many biological sensory systems and can be a useful engineering tool for artificial visual systems.

In this Section we present a hardware architecture that implements a real-time model of the stimulus-driven form of selective attention, based on the *saliency map* concept, originally put forth by Koch and Ullman [12]. This hardware architecture has been designed as the central part of a multi-chip system, able to receive input signals from different types of sensory devices. Input signals may arrive from visual sensors, but also from other neuromorphic sensors representing a wide variety of sensory stimuli obtained from different sources. In this framework, sensory signals are sent to (and from) the selective attention chip in the form of asynchronous binary pulses of fixed height, but with variable inter-pulse intervals (similar to neural spike trains), conforming to the *Address-Event Representation* (AER) [13, 3].

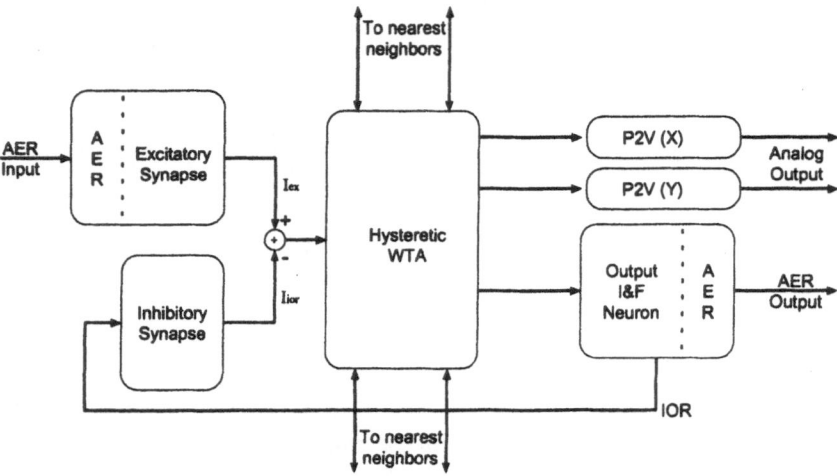

Figure 9: Block diagram of a basic cell of the 8 × 8 selective attention architecture.

3.1   The Selective Attention Chip

The selective attention chip described in this paper was fabricated using a standard $2\mu m$ CMOS technology. Its size is approximately 2mm×2mm and it contains of an array of 8×8 cells. The chip's architecture, easily expandable to arrays of arbitrary size, is laid out on a square grid, with input and output AER interfacing circuits. The AER communication protocol allows the chip to exchange data while processing signals in parallel, in real time. In this protocol input and output signals are transmitted as asynchronous binary data streams which carry the analog information in their temporal structure. Each event is represented by a binary word encoding the address of the sending node. The address of the sending element is conveyed in parallel along with two handshaking control signals [13, 1]. Systems containing more than two AER chips can be constructed implementing additional special purpose off-chip arbitration schemes [3, 9].

In a system containing AER sensors interfaced to the selective attention chip, address events would reach, at the input stage of each cell of the 8 × 8 array, excitatory synaptic circuits that convert the voltage pulses into an analog input currents. Figure 9 shows the block diagram of one of the 64 architecture's cells. The input current integrated by the excitatory synapse (see I_{ex} in Fig. 9) is sourced into a neuromorphic analog circuit that, connected with its neighbors, implements a hysteretic winner-take-all (WTA) network [10]. The output current of each WTA cell is used to activate both an integrate and fire (I&F) neuron and two position to voltage (P2V) circuits [5]. The P2V circuits encode the x and y coordinates of the winning WTA cell with two analog voltages, while the I&F neurons generate pulses that are used by the AER interfacing circuits to encode the position of the winning WTA cell with address-events. The neuron's spikes are also integrated by the local inhibitory synapse connected to it to generate a current I_{ior} that is subtracted from the current I_{ex} (see Fig. 9). The sum of the currents $(I_{ex} - I_{ior})$ is sourced into the input node of the hysteretic WTA cell. Each cell is connected to its four nearest neighbors, both with lateral excitatory connections and lateral inhibitory connections.

When a WTA cell is selected as a winner, its output transistors source DC currents into the two P2V row and column circuits. The winning WTA cell also sources a DC current into the input node of the local inhibitory neuron connected to it. The amplitude of the injection current is independent of the input current $(I_{ex} - I_{ior})$. This current allows the neuron to spike at a frequency proportional to the input current. Each spike produces an address-event. Next to transmitting their address events off chip, the output neurons, together with the local inhibitory synapse connected to them, implement the inhibition of return (IOR) mechanism (a key feature of many selective attention systems) [8, 19]. The spikes generated by the winning cell's output neuron are integrated by its corresponding inhibitory synapse, and gradually increase the cell's inhibitory post-synaptic current I_{ior}. As the neuron keeps on firing, the net input current to that cell $(I_{ex} - I_{ior})$ decreases until a different cell is eventually selected as the winner. When the previous winning cell is de-selected its corresponding local output neuron stops firing and its inhibitory synapse recovers, decreasing the inhibitory current I_{ior} back to zero.

The IOR mechanism forces the WTA network to switch from selecting the cell receiving the strongest input to selecting cells receiving inputs of decreasing strength, effectively enabling the system to "attend" sequentially the salient regions of the input space. Depending on the dynamics of the IOR mechanism, the WTA network will continuously switch the selection of the winner between the two strongest inputs, or between the three strongest, or between all inputs above a certain threshold, generating focus of attention *scanpaths* similar to the ones observed for human eye movements [21].

To characterize the behavior of selective attention chip with well controlled input signals we interfaced it to a workstation, via a National Lab-PC+ I/O card, and stimulated it using the AER communication protocol. With this setup we were able to stimulate all the 64 pixels of the network with voltage pulses (*i.e.* address-events) at a maximal rate of 500Hz. As the input synapses were set to have time constants of the order of milliseconds, each cell appeared to receive input spikes virtually in parallel. The handshaking between the chip and the PC was carried out at run time by the hardware present in the National I/O card. The chip's input stimuli consisted of patterns of address-events being generated by the workstation at uniform rates of different frequencies. In the experiment presented in ths paper we used a test stimulus that excited cells (2,2) (2,7) (7,2) and (7,7) of the selective attention chip with 30Hz pulses, and cell (5,5) with 50Hz pulses. Figure 10(a) shows the analog output of the P2V circuits in response to 300ms of stimulation with the input "saliency map" described above. The system initially selects the central cell (5,5). But, as the IOR mechanism forces the WTA network to switch the selection of the winner, the system cycles through all other excited cells as well. Figure 10(b) shows the histogram of the address-events generated by the output I&F neuron in response to the same stimulus pattern.

The details of the switching dynamics can be controlled by setting appropriately the bias voltages of the excitatory and inhibitory synaptic circuits and the neuron's firing rate. These bias voltages, together with the other ones controlling the hysteretic

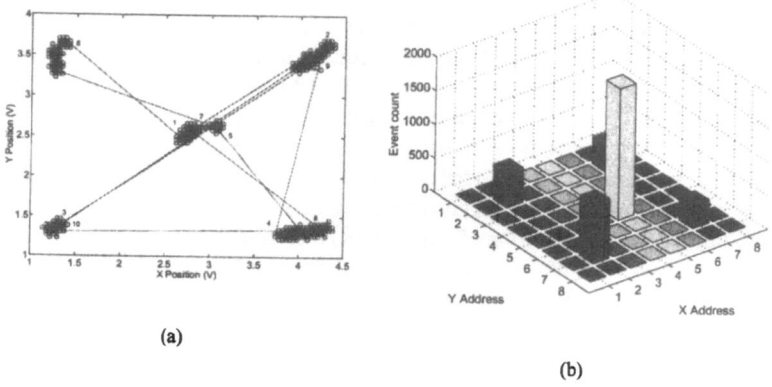

(a)

(b)

Figure 10: (a) Output of the P2V circuits of the selective attention architecture measured over a period of 300ms, in response to a test stimulus exciting four corners of
the input array at a rate of 30Hz and a central cell at a rate of 50Hz; (b) Histogram of
the chip's output address-events, captured over a period of 13.42s in response to the
same input stimulus.

WTA network's behavior endow the system with a sufficient amount of flexibility to
be able to use the same chip in different types of selective attention tasks.

4   Conclusion

During the last decade CMOS aVLSI has been used to construct a wide range of
neural analogs, from single synapses to sensory arrays, and simple systems. These
circuits are not general processors. They simply exploit the inherent physics of analog
transistors to produce an efficient computation of a particular task.

We demonstrated a case example that uses many of the circuital blocks described in
the paper to implement a real-time model of selective attention systems. This system
can be used both for scientific investigation of selective attention system properties
and for the development of potential engineering applications.

The system presented was a demonstration that these types of neuromorphic circuits have the advantage of emulating biological systems in real time. To the extent
that the physics of the transistors matches well the computation to be performed, and
digital communication between chips is small, the analog VLSI circuits use less power
and silicon area than would an equivalent digital system. This is an important advantage, because any serious attempt to replicate the computational power of brains must
use resources as effectively as possible.

References

[1] K.A. Boahen. Multiple pathways: Retinomorphic chips that see quadruple images. In *Proceedings of the Seventh International Conference on Microelectronics for Neural, Fuzzy and Bio-inspired Systems; Microneuro'99*, pages 12–20, Los Alamitos, CA, April 1999. IEEE Computer Society.

[2] K.A. Boahen and A.G. Andreou. A contrast sensitive silicon retina with reciprocal synapses. In D.S. Touretzky, M.C. Mozer, and M.E. Hasselmo, editors, *Advances in neural information processing systems*, volume 4. IEEE, MIT Press, 1992.

[3] S. R. Deiss, R. J. Douglas, and A. M. Whatley. A pulse-coded communications infrastructure for neuromorphic systems. In W. Maass and C. M. Bishop, editors, *Pulsed Neural Networks*, chapter 6, pages 157–178. MIT Press, 1998.

[4] T. Delbrück. Analog VLSI phototransduction by continuous-time, adaptive, logarithmic photoreceptor circuits. Technical report, California Institute of Technology, Pasadena, CA, 1994. CNS Memo No. 30.

[5] S. P. DeWeerth. Analog VLSI circuits for stimulus localization and centroid computation. *Int. J. of Comp. Vision*, 8(3):191–202, 1992.

[6] C. Diorio, P. Hasler, B.A. Minch, and C. Mead. A single-transistor silicon synapse. *IEEE Trans. Electron Devices*, 43(11):1972–1980, 1996.

[7] R. Douglas, M. Mahowald, and C. Mead. Neuromorphic analogue VLSI. *Annu. Rev. Neurosci.*, 18:255–281, 1995.

[8] B. Gibson and H. Egeth. Inhibition of return to object-based and environment-based locations. *Percept. Psychopys.*, 55:323–339, 1994.

[9] C. Higgins and C. Koch. Multi-chip motion processing. In *Proc. Conf. Advanced Research in VLSI*, Atlanta, GA, 1998.

[10] G. Indiveri. A current-mode analog hysteretic winner-take-all network, with excitatory and inhibitory coupling. *Jour. of Analog Integrated Circuits and Signal Processing*, 2001. In Press.

[11] C. Koch and I. Segev. *Methods in Neural Modeling*. MIT Press, 1989.

[12] C. Koch and S Ullman. Shifts in selective visual-attention – towards the underlying neural circuitry. *Human Neurobiology*, 4(4):219–227, 1985.

[13] J. Lazzaro, J. Wawrzynek, M. Mahowald, M. Sivilotti, and D. Gillespie. Silicon auditory processors as computer peripherals. *IEEE Trans. on Neural Networks*, 4:523–528, 1993.

[14] M. Mahowald and C. Mead. *Analog VLSI and Neural Systems*, chapter Silicon Retina, pages 257–278. Addison-Wesley, Reading, MA, 1989.

[15] M.A. Mahowald. *VLSI analogs of neuronal visual processing: a synthesis of form and function*. PhD thesis, Department of Computation and Neural Systems, California Institute of Technology, Pasadena, CA., 1992.

[16] W.S. McCulloch and W. Pitts. A logical calculus of the ideas immanent in nervous activity. *Bull. Math. Biophys.*, 5:115–133, 1943.

[17] C.A. Mead. *Analog VLSI and Neural Systems*. Addison-Wesley, Reading, MA, 1989.

[18] C.A. Mead. Neuromorphic electronic systems. *Proceedings of the IEEE*, 78(10):1629–1636, 1990.

[19] Y. Tanaka and S. Shimojo. Location vs feature: Reaction time reveals dissociation between two visual functions. *Vision Research*, 36(14):2125–2140, July 1996.

[20] E.A. Vittoz. Micropower techniques. In J.E. Franca and Y.P. Tsidivis, editors, *Design of VLSI Circuits for Telecommunications and Signal Processing*. Prentice Hall, 1994.

[21] A. L. Yarbus. *Eye movements and vision*. Plenum Press, 1967.

Section 2
Review Paper

Neurofuzzy Approximator based on Mamdani's Model

F. M. Frattale Mascioli, A. Mancini, A. Rizzi, M. Panella, and G. Martinelli

INFOCOM Dpt. University of Rome "La Sapienza"
Via Eudossiana 18, 00184 Rome, Italy
mascioli@infocom.uniroma1.it

Abstract

Neurofuzzy approximators can take on numerous alternatives, as a consequence of the large body of options available for defining their basic operations. In particular, the extraction of the rules from numerical data can be conveniently based on clustering algorithms. The large number of clustering algorithms introduces a further flexibility. Neurofuzzy approximators can treat both numerical and linguistic sources. The analysis of approximator sensitivity to the previous factors is important in order to decide the best solution in actual applications. This task is carried out in the present paper by recurring to illustrative examples and exhaustive simulations. The results of the analysis are used for comparing different learning algorithms. The underlying approach to the determination of the optimal approximator architecture is constructive. This approach is not only very efficient, as suggested by learning theory, but it is also particularly suited to combat the effect of noise that can deteriorate the numerical data.

1. Introduction

Neurofuzzy networks show a considerable efficiency in a wide range of application fields, mainly due to their capability of treating complementary information given by numerical data and linguistic rules. In the present paper, we focus our attention to a very important and general category of neurofuzzy networks; namely, we consider those nets capable of approximating an input-output mapping generated by an unknown process. Only a training set constituted by input-output pairs and linguistic rules, given by experts, are available. Moreover, we assume that the reliability of the numerical data could be impaired by the presence of noise. On the basis of this information, the neurofuzzy approximator should be determined at its best.

A large number of neurofuzzy networks can be defined, since there are many types of models and each of them is characterized by several configurations. The models to be used, as a basis of the neurofuzzy approximator, can be purely fuzzy, as

Mamdani's model [1], or characterized by a crisp output, as Sugeno's model [2]. From the previous models two architectures are derived: the FBF (fuzzy basis functions) net [3, 4] and the ANFIS (adaptive neurofuzzy inference system) net [5] respectively. There are, moreover, several other neurofuzzy architectures [6, 7, 8, 9]. In the following we will consider only the nets based on Mamdani's model (FBF). They are particularly flexible to be tailored to specific tasks required by the diverse applications and can easily incorporate linguistic information.

The main goal pursued in this paper concerns the investigation of the several options available for implementing FBF neurofuzzy approximators. In particular, the following topics are examined in relation to their influence on the net performance:

1) modeling of the membership functions (MFs) involved in the rules
2) fuzzy operations and reasoning
3) fuzzification, defuzzification
4) extraction of fuzzy rules from numerical data
5) use of linguistic information
6) optimization of the architecture
7) treatment of noisy numerical data

Several options can be adopted with regard to the previous topics. Depending on them, there are a large number of alternatives for the resulting approximator. Some of them will be considered in Sect. 2 with particular emphasis on the property of universal approximation, i.e. the capability of the net of approximating the mapping with any required accuracy.

The effect of choosing a particular option has a strong impact on the performance of the resulting net. An interesting example at this regard is the net proposed in [10]. Its performance is considerably enhanced by simply introducing an adaptive compensatory parameter in the usual fuzzy reasoning. Another example will be illustrated in Sect. 3 by showing how a simple modification of the MFs shape can strongly improve the accuracy of the neurofuzzy net proposed in [4].

An appropriate choice for shaping and locating the MFs is based on tailoring them directly to the data distribution in the conjunct input-output space. Namely, this strategy can be easily pursued by clustering data and by associating MFs to clusters. Since there are a large arsenal of clustering algorithms, the number of possible alternatives to the MFs modeling techniques explodes. In Sect. 4, we will limit our attention to only two clustering algorithms: the FCM (fuzzy-c-means) [11] and a modified version of MIN-MAX [12] proposed in [13]. Furthermore, due to the importance of the clustering algorithms, a concise survey of them will be provided in the appendix.

The input-output mapping implemented by the net can be interpreted in a significant and useful way. Namely, it is considered as the expansion of the unknown mapping in a basis of functions [3]. The basis functions originate from both numerical and linguistic data. The coefficients of the expansion depend on the several options undertaken with regard to the MFs related to rule consequents, the fuzzy operators and reasoning, and the reliability of the rules. The latter is considered in Sect. 5. In particular, it is possible to assign the same weight to all the rules of the same nature (linguistic or numerical), by assuming the reliability of the rules strictly connected to the data origin.

The complexity of the net architecture is proportional to the number of the rules derived by the training algorithm and suggested by experts. It affects the generalization capability of the net, as known from learning theory. The several criteria suggested by this theory (Vapnik [14], Rissanen [15], etc.) are difficult to be actually applied. A simple way to improve the generalization capability is the cross-validation technique. It consists in the most simple case in splitting the training set in two subsets: the validation set and the sub-training set. These two sets must be disjointed and must cover uniformly the input domain. An optimal procedure for carrying out the splitting operation exists only in the asymptotic case [16]. Since in actual applications the training set cardinality is far from this situation, it is necessary to follow a rule of thumb, as it will be done in Sect. 6. The learning theory is further applied in the present paper under the constructive approach, i.e. the final architecture of the net is obtained starting from a minimal structure and then increasing step-by-step its size.

The constructive approach is important not only for improving generalization but also for combating noise. The presence of noise reduces the information content of the numerical data and apparently renders more complex the model to be fitted by the net. Consequently, the search for a simpler model (that is the goal of learning theory) is also beneficial for combating noise. Furthermore, when linguistic data are available, a combination of the constructive approach and the use of linguistic rules can improve the robustness of the net. In Sect. 6, we will illustrate this topics by detailed examples.

The several aspects discussed in this introduction will be dealt in the paper both by proposing ad-hoc algorithms and by illustrating them with specific examples.

2. Mamdani's neurofuzzy approximator

The core of Mamdani's model is a set of N rules having the following structure:

$$\text{k-th rule: IF } z_1 \text{ is } A_1^{(k)} \text{ and ... and } z_n \text{ is } A_n^{(k)} \text{ THEN } w \text{ is } B^{(k)} \qquad (1)$$
$$\text{(antecedents)} \qquad\qquad \text{(consequent)}$$

where z_i and w are the linguistic variables defined by suitable membership functions, respectively $\mu_{A_i^{(k)}}(z_i)$ and $\mu_{B^{(k)}}(w)$. The rules can be extracted from the numerical training set (TS) or suggested by experts. Each rule yields a fuzzy output characterized by an appropriate MF $\mu_{B*^{(k)}}(w)$, when it is activated by a fuzzy input z_i defined by a MF $\mu_{A_i*}(z_i)$, $i = 1...n$. The outputs of the N rules are combined together yielding a final MF $\mu_{B*}(w)$ as the response of the model to the input.

Mamdani's model is the heart of the neurofuzzy approximator (NFA). The further components of NFA are: the fuzzifier, which converts the crisp input to the fuzzy form required by the model, and the defuzzifier, having the opposite role.

The overall input-output mapping, implemented by the net, can be represented by

$$y = \sum_{k=1}^{N} y^{(k)} \alpha^{(k)}(\underline{x}) \tag{2}$$

where: $\underline{x} = [x_1 \ldots x_n]$ is the crisp input and y the crisp output; $\alpha^{(k)}(\underline{x})$ is the k-th fuzzy basis function (FBF), that corresponds to the k-th rule; $y^{(k)}$ is the weight of the k-th FBF in the current mapping. The basis functions $\alpha^{(k)}(\underline{x})$ take on a form which is determined by all the options chosen in the steps required for passing from $\underline{x}$ to y; these steps are: fuzzification, MF modeling of the antecedents and consequents of the rules, fuzzy operators, fuzzy reasoning for deriving conclusions from premises and rules, defuzzification. In the following, we will describe three cases (out of the numerous alternatives) which can be obtained. Each of them constitutes a NFA.

NFA1

- Fuzzification: singleton.
  The linguistic variable z_i corresponding to the crisp input x_i is characterized by the following MF:

$$\mu_{A_i^*}(z_i) = \begin{cases} 1 & \text{if } z_i = x_i \\ 0 & \text{elsewhere} \end{cases} \tag{3}$$

- Model of MF for the antecedents: Gaussian.
  The shape is

$$\mu_{A_i^{(k)}}(z_i) = \exp\{ -\tfrac{1}{2}[(z_i - x_i^{(k)}) / \sigma_i^{(k)}]^2 \}, \quad i = 1 \ldots n, \quad k = 1 \ldots N \tag{4}$$

Remark: at the boundary of the range of interest the Gaussian shape is often replaced by an open sigmoid. Depending on the specific side (right or left), there are two expressions:

$$\text{open left sigmoid: } \exp\{ -\tfrac{1}{2}[\text{MAX}(z_i - x_i^{(k)}, 0) / \sigma_i^{(k)}]^2 \} \tag{5}$$
$$\text{open right sigmoid: } \exp\{ -\tfrac{1}{2}[\text{MIN}(z_i - x_i^{(k)}, 0) / \sigma_i^{(k)}]^2 \} \tag{6}$$

- Model of MF for the consequents: any symmetrical MF.
  Usual options are the Gaussian itself and the generalized bell. The latter is characterized by

$$\mu_{B^{(k)}}(w) = \frac{1}{1 + \left| \dfrac{w - d^{(k)}}{a^{(k)}} \right|^{2b^{(k)}}}, \quad k = 1 \ldots N \tag{7}$$

- Combination of the antecedents: product.

$$\mu_{\underline{A}^{(k)}}(\underline{z}) = \prod_{i=1}^{n} \mu_{A_i^{(k)}}(z_i), \quad k = 1...N \tag{8}$$

- Fuzzy reasoning ingredients: max-product composition and product implication.

$$\mu_{B^{\bullet(k)}}(w) = \underset{\underline{z}}{Max}\left[\mu_{\underline{A}^{(k)}}(\underline{z})\mu_{B^{(k)}}(w)\mu_{\underline{A}^{\bullet}}(\underline{z})\right] \tag{9}$$

where $\mu_{\underline{A}^{\bullet}}(\underline{z})$ is given by (8) with $\mu_{A_i^{\bullet}}(z_i)$ in place of $\mu_{A_i^{(k)}}(z_i)$

- Reliability of the rules: uniform.

- Defuzzification: center average.

With the previous choices and in the case of Gaussian MFs, $\alpha^{(k)}(\underline{x})$ and $y^{(k)}$ are given by

$$\alpha^{(k)}(\underline{x}) = \frac{\prod_{i=1}^{n}\exp\{-\frac{1}{2}[(x_i - x_i^{(k)})/\sigma_i^{(k)}]^2\}}{\sum_{j=1}^{N}\prod_{i=1}^{n}\exp\{-\frac{1}{2}[(x_i - x_i^{(j)})/\sigma_i^{(j)}]^2\}}; \quad y^{(k)} = c^{(k)} \tag{10}$$

where $c^{(k)}$ is the centroid of $B^{(k)}$

$$c^{(k)} = \frac{\int w\mu_{B^{(k)}}(w)dw}{\int \mu_{B^{(k)}}(w)dw} \tag{11}$$

NFA2

- Fuzzification: singleton.

- Model of MF for the antecedents and the consequents: gaussian as in (4).

- Combination of the antecedents: compensatory product.

$$\mu_{\underline{A}^{(k)}}(\underline{z}) = (u^{(k)})^{1-\gamma}(v^{(k)})^{\gamma}, \quad k = 1...N \tag{12}$$

where: $u^{(k)}$ coincides with (8) and $v^{(k)}$ is given by

$$v^{(k)} = (u^{(k)})^{1/n} \tag{13}$$

The two combinations $u^{(k)}$ and $v^{(k)}$ are significantly denoted as pessimistic and optimistic product [10]. The parameter $\gamma \in [0, 1]$ is the compensatory coefficient.

- Fuzzy reasoning ingredients: max-product composition and product implication.

- Reliability of k-th rule: $\delta^{(k)}$.
  $\delta^{(k)}$ is the variance of the Gaussian MF of the k-th rule consequent.

- Defuzzification: center average.

The resulting $\alpha^{(k)}(\underline{x})$ and $y^{(k)}$ are

$$\alpha^{(k)}(\underline{x}) = \frac{\delta^{(k)}\left[\prod_{i=1}^{n} \exp\{-\tfrac{1}{2}[(x_i - x_i^{(k)})/\sigma_i^{(k)}]^2\}\right]^{1-\gamma+\gamma/n}}{\sum_{j=1}^{N}\delta^{(j)}\left[\prod_{i=1}^{n} \exp\{-\tfrac{1}{2}[(x_i - x_i^{(j)})/\sigma_i^{(j)}]^2\}\right]^{1-\gamma+\gamma/n}} ; \quad y^{(k)} = c^{(k)} \tag{14}$$

NFA3

- Fuzzification: singleton.

- Model of MF for the antecedents and the consequents: gaussian as in (4).

- Combination of the antecedents: minimum.

$$\mu_{\underline{A}^{(k)}}(\underline{z}) = \underset{i=1...n}{\text{MIN}} \{\mu_{A_i^{(k)}}(z_i)\}, \quad k = 1...N \tag{15}$$

- Fuzzy reasoning ingredients: max-product composition and min implication.

- Reliability of the rules: uniform.

- Defuzzification: center average.

The resulting $\alpha^{(k)}(\underline{x})$ and $y^{(k)}$ are

$$\alpha^{(k)}(\underline{x}) = \frac{\underset{i=1\ldots n}{MIN}\left\{\exp\{-\tfrac{1}{2}[(x_i - x_i^{(k)})/\sigma_i^{(k)}]^2\}\right\}}{\sum_{j=1}^{N} \underset{i=1\ldots n}{MIN}\left\{\exp\{-\tfrac{1}{2}[(x_i - x_i^{(j)})/\sigma_i^{(j)}]^2\}\right\}} ; \qquad y^{(k)} = c^{(k)} \qquad (16)$$

It is interesting to note that the basis considered in (2) could be very heterogeneous, since some of its functions could be originated from numerical data (produced by an unknown process) and others from linguistic information (proposed by experts). When these different sources of information (which correspond to different level of knowledge) are available, the NFA should be able to match better the unknown process.

The use of one of the several alternative NFAs is conditioned by its ability to operate as a universal approximator, i.e. to have the capability of approximating an unknown mapping with any required accuracy. The verification of this property is carried out by different techniques [17, 4, 10]. A simple method is based on the application of Stone-Weierstrass theorem, which establishes the sufficient conditions for the universal approximation property. By following this approach it is easy to prove that NFA1 and NFA2 are universal approximators. NFA3, instead, does not meet all the conditions of the theorem and it is therefore not guaranteed to satisfy the said property.

3. MFs modeling

The MFs play a very important role in the realization of the mapping of the neurofuzzy approximator. In fact, simple modifications of their shape cause large variations in the net behavior. We illustrate this point by an example regarding the NFA proposed in [4]. This NFA is based on the preliminary extraction of one rule from each numerical pattern of the training set (TS). Also the entire set of the FBFs (expressed by (10)) has the same cardinality of TS. The MFs of the antecedents, extracted from the TS pairs $(\underline{x}_t^{(k)}, y_t^{(k)})$, $k = 1\ldots N_t$, are chosen as follows:

$$\mu_{A_i^{(k)}}(z_i) = \exp\{-\tfrac{1}{2}[(z_i - x_i^{(k)})/\sigma_i]^2\} , \quad i = 1\ldots n, \quad k = 1\ldots N_t \qquad (17)$$

with

$$\sigma_i = \frac{\underset{k}{MAX}(x_{ti}^{(k)}) - \underset{k}{MIN}(x_{ti}^{(k)})}{N} \qquad (18)$$

The learning approach followed in [4] requires to choose arbitrarily the cardinality N of the basis used in (2), and to select the best N FBFs with the corresponding weight by applying an orthogonal least-squares (OLS) algorithm. In this way, only the FBFs yielding the best match between the data and the mapping realized by the net are retained.

The MF shape defined in [4] is however not satisfactory because of the poor covering of the input space, due to the particular choice of σ_i, as given in (18). A new empirical formula was determined through an extensive simulation. It is

$$\sigma_i = \frac{\text{MAX}_k(x_{ti}^{(k)}) - \text{MIN}_k(x_{ti}^{(k)})}{N^{1/n}} \tag{19}$$

The effect of this simple modification of the algorithm proposed in [4] is noticeable, as evidenced by the following example. Let us consider the bidimensional function

$$y(\underline{x}) = (x_1 - 0.5)^2 - (x_2 - 0.5)^2 \tag{20}$$

defined in the domain $I = [0\ 1] \times [0\ 1]$ and shown in Fig. 1. It operates as the unknown mapping. We consider 50 points of I, as shown in the figure, and the corresponding values of y for the TS. Then, we apply the algorithm [4] with $N = 20$ and by using for σ_i both (18) and (19). The result of the mappings realized by the NFA in the two cases is shown in Fig. 2. Moreover, the performance of the NFA is measured by computing the MSE (mean squares error) in correspondence of a test set constituted by 196 points uniformly located in domain I. In the two cases, the resulting MSE is respectively equal to -25.3 dB and -41.1 dB ($dB = 10\log_{10}$). The effect of the previous simple modification of the MFs variances on the net accuracy is evident from the figure and the MSE. It is moreover necessary to point that all the remaining options and steps of the algorithm were unaltered.

The previous example suggests quite naturally the necessity for tailoring the MFs strictly to the distribution of the points representing the TS in the conjunct input-output space. It is in fact reasonable to assume that the regions, where the representative points are denser, correspond to the rules. The shape of these regions are directly connected to the MFs. Consequently, the extraction of the rules and the modeling of the MFs can be conveniently faced together by clustering the data. Each cluster denotes a rule and its shape determines the MFs involved in the rule.

The clustering algorithms are very numerous as pointed out in the appendix. Therefore, the use of clustering increases considerably the number of possible alternatives to NFA learning algorithms. In Sect. 4, we will consider only two of them, selected for their efficiency and low computational cost.

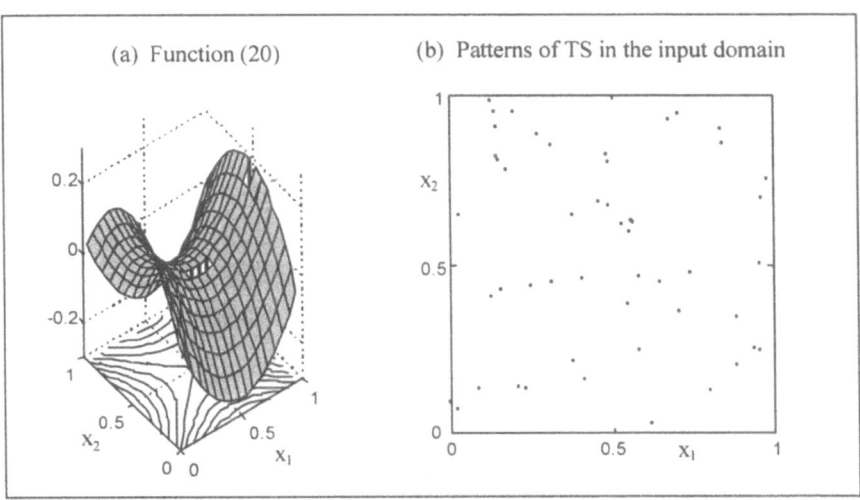

Figure 1.

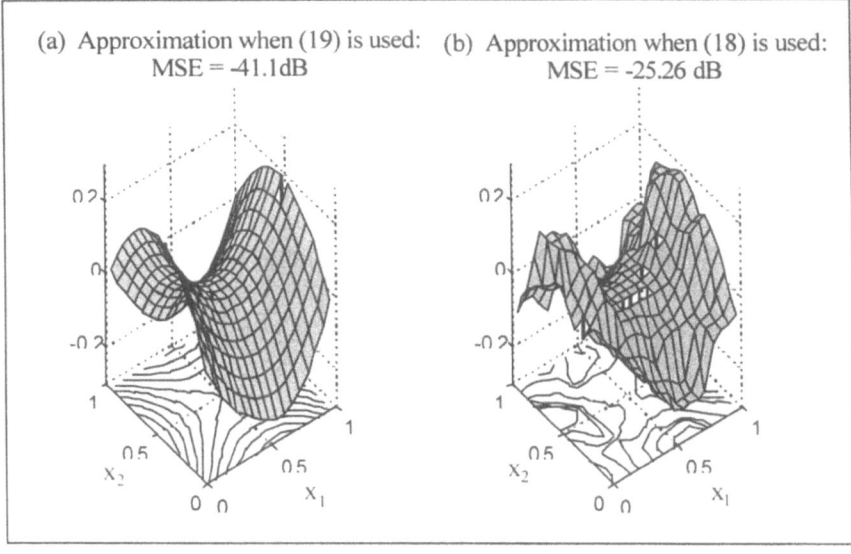

Figure 2.

4. Rules extraction and MFs modeling by clustering

Numerical information is available under the form of a data set of examples of the unknown input-output mapping. Each example is constituted by a couple of values (input, output) and can be represented as a point in a suitable space. There are possible 3 types of spaces: input, output and conjunct input-output space. Each rule manifests itself in these spaces by means of a structured set of points. Consequently, the determination of the rules from the available data set can be based on clustering it in one of the previous spaces.

Several alternative algorithms for carrying out clustering are available. They depend on the specific strategy followed for attaining the optimal partition of the available data set in the chosen space. The optimality is measured either by considering the compactness-separation of the clusters or the persistence of the partition when the clustering algorithm is hierarchical and guided by a scale parameter. The most used clustering approaches, besides the classical c-means with its fuzzy version, can be classified in 3 classes, as described in the appendix.

The clustering algorithms are therefore used for extracting the rules and modeling the MFs. In the present case we will limit our attention only to two algorithms chosen for illustrating how clustering algorithms can be used. They are the fuzzy-c-means (FCM) [11] and the MIN-MAX [12] in the γ-version proposed in [13], where a parameter γ controls the cluster formation. The methods described in the appendix can be also used, and any of them could be more convenient in specific problems. However there is not a general criteria to establish a-priori which clustering algorithm is the best in relation to a given data set.

A preliminary question preceding the choice of the clustering algorithm regards the space more convenient to be considered (the input, the output or the conjunct input-output space). The conjunct space has yielded better results in several tests carried out at this regard. Some of them will be presented in Sect. 4.1 for illustrating this point. The NFA learning algorithm is structured as follows:

1) apply the chosen clustering algorithm to the TS in the conjunct input-output space. The TS is represented by N_t points $(\underline{x}^{(k)}, y_t^{(k)})$, $k = 1...N_t$. Determine the centroids of the resulting N clusters $\underline{p}_c^{(j)}$, $j = 1...N$. The value of N is fixed a priori in the case of FCM or depends on γ in the γ-MIN-MAX case;

2) each cluster corresponds to a rule. The MFs of the antecedents of the j-th rule are determined with

$$\mu_{A_i^{(j)}}(z_i) = \exp\{-\tfrac{1}{2}[(z_i - x_{ci}^{(j)})/\sigma_i]^2\}, \quad i = 1...n \qquad (21)$$

where: $x_{ci}^{(j)}$ is the i-th component of the projection of $\underline{p}_c^{(j)}$ in the input space; σ_i is given by

$$\sigma_i = \frac{\underset{k}{MAX}(x_{ti}^{(k)}) - \underset{k}{MIN}(x_{ti}^{(k)})}{N^{1/n}}, \quad i = 1...n \qquad (22)$$

3) determine the FBFs $\alpha^{(j)}(\underline{x})$ and the weights $y^{(j)}$ by (10) and (11);

4) consider the vectors

$$\underline{q}_j = [\alpha^{(j)}(\underline{x}^{(1)}) \ldots \alpha^{(j)}(\underline{x}^{(Nt)})]^t , \quad j = 1 \ldots N \tag{23}$$

5) minimize the error between the mapping implemented by the NFA, expressed in (2), and the TS target given by

$$\mathbf{d} = [y_t^{(1)} \ldots y_t^{(Nt)}]^t \tag{24}$$

In the case of a minimization using the Least Squares Estimate (LSE) procedure, the coefficients of expression (2) are given by

$$[y^{(1)} \ldots y^{(N)}]^t = \mathbf{Q}^+ \mathbf{d} \tag{25}$$

where the symbol + denotes pseudo-inverse and

$$\mathbf{Q} = [\underline{q}_1 \ldots \underline{q}_N] \tag{26}$$

The above procedure will be denoted as FCM-ALG or γMM-ALG in the case of FCM or γ-MIN-MAX respectively. Steps 4 and 5 could be omitted with a consequent reduction in computational cost and deterioration of accuracy. Let us illustrate this point by the application of the two algorithms to the simple benchmark proposed in [18]. It concerns the unidimensional function

$$f(x) = \frac{(x-2)(2x+1)}{1+x^2} \tag{27}$$

defined in the domain $I = [-5 \ 5]$. The mappings obtained with the two algorithms are shown in Figs. 3 and 4. In the case of γMM-ALG a further option is the presentation order of the TS data. We have investigated two alternatives: random and radial. The latter consists in ordering the data on the basis of their distance from the gravity center of the whole data set. Since it yields better results in actual applications, we use it.

The two figures regard a different choice for the values of the coefficients $y^{(j)}$ of (2). Namely, in Fig. 3 we use the projections of the centroids $\underline{p}_c^{(j)}$ onto the output space. In Fig. 4 we use the values given by (25). Consequently, the latter corresponds to the complete procedure, i.e. including steps 4-5. We note from the figures that FCM-ALG is more accurate than γMM-ALG without steps 4-5. The use of these steps improves the accuracy in both cases, as expected.

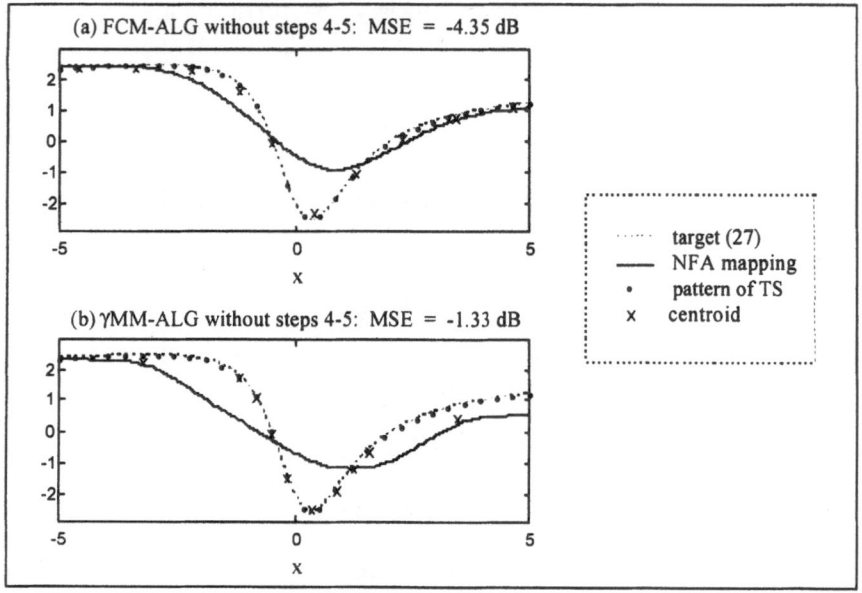

Figure 3.

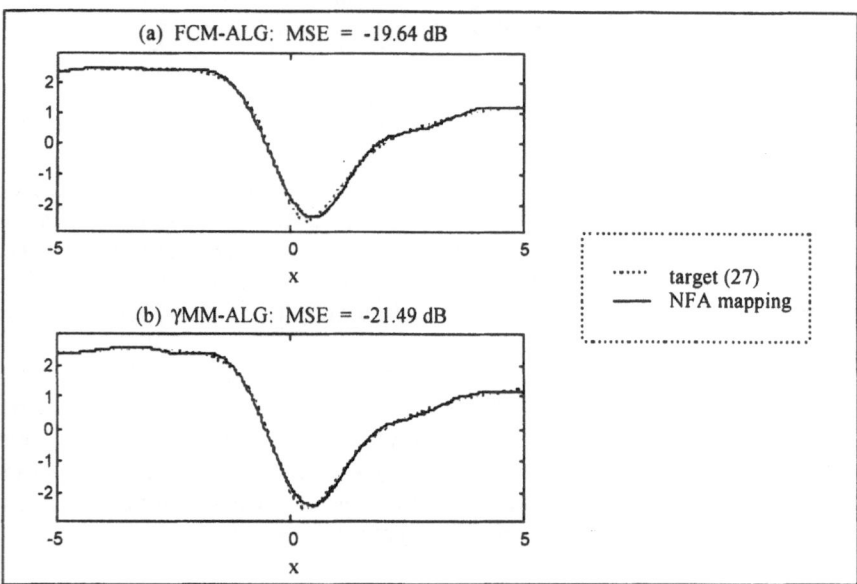

Figure 4.

This remark points out an important property, i.e. γMM-ALG yields a better basis than FCM-ALG. This is confirmed by several other simulation tests summarized in Tab. 1. They concern with the following examples of dimensions n = 1, 2, 3:

n = 1   function (27) with the same domain I

n = 2   function proposed in [19]
$$y(\underline{x}) = \sin(2\pi x_1) + 4(x_2 - 0.5)^2 \tag{28}$$
       defined in the domain $I = [-1\ 1] \times [-1\ 1]$

n = 3 $$y(\underline{x}) = (1 + x_1^{-2} + x_2^{-1.5} + x_3^{-1})^2 \tag{29}$$
       defined in the domain $I = [1\ 3] \times [1\ 3] \times [1\ 3]$

In the first row of Tab. 1 there are reported the mean and the variances of MSE obtained in 50 independent trials by changing randomly the initial centroids of the clusters. In the second row there are the values of MSE obtained by using the radial presentation of the TS data. The two algorithms FCM-ALG and γMM-ALG yield a basis that is reasonable but susceptible of further improvement, as it will be discussed and illustrated in Sect. 4.2.

Algorithm	n = 1 (function (27))		n = 2 (function (28))		n = 3 (function (29))	
	MSE (dB)	σ_{MSE}	MSE (dB)	σ_{MSE}	MSE (dB)	σ_{MSE}
FCM-ALG	- 27.4	1.67	- 6.23	1.27	- 8.39	0.71
γMM-ALG	- 32.46	-	- 8.33	-	- 8.7	-

Table 1.

4.1. Advantages of conjunct space clustering

The best choice of the space where the clustering of TS must be carried out is suggested by the results of a numerical investigation and corresponds to the conjunct input-output space. We will illustrate this point by the results of a simulation test concerning function (28) and the application of γMM-ALG with radial presentation.

The TS is constituted by $N_t = 80$ points non-uniformly distributed in the domain I: they are denser where the surface slope is steeper. The test-set is constituted by 196 points uniformly distributed in domain I. The parameter γ is set to 2.8, which determines 36 clusters. The resulting centroids in the input space are different in the two cases, as shown in Fig. 5 (input space clustering) and in Fig. 6 (conjunct space clustering). In the latter, the resulting mapping is improved of about 2.5 dB for the MSE.

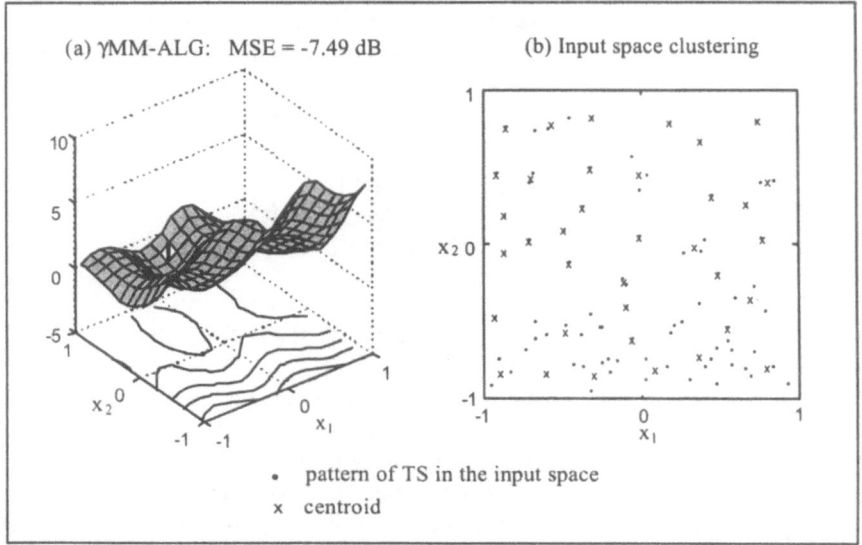

Figure 5.

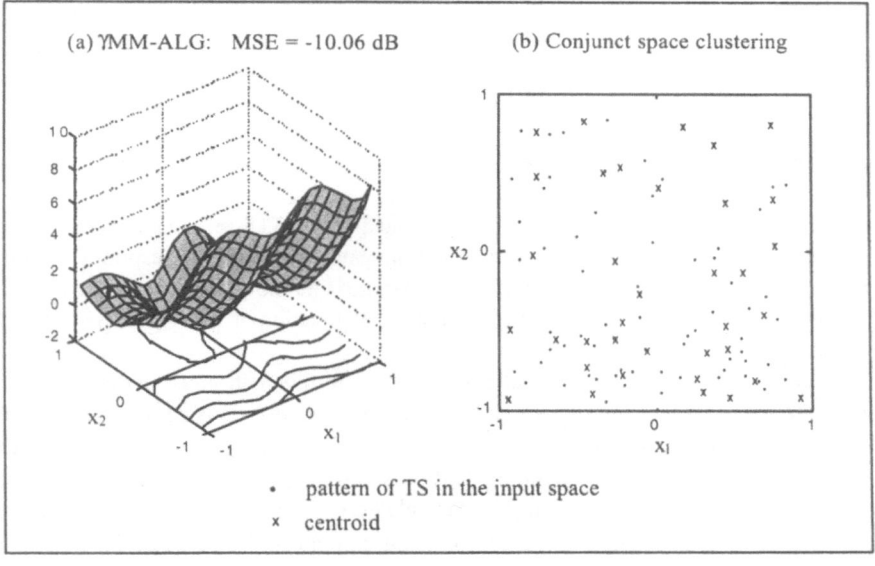

Figure 6.

4.2. Improving the mapping accuracy

The FBFs obtained with the previous FCM-ALG and γMM-ALG can be improved by increasing the accuracy of the cluster modeling. In the following, we will limit our attention to γMM-ALG. The clusters obtained by a MIN-MAX technique are hyperboxes, defined by two vertices. In the cases of the j-th cluster, we denote by $\underline{V}^{(j)} = [V_1^{(j)} \ldots V_n^{(j)}]$ and $\underline{v}^{(j)} = [v_1^{(j)} \ldots v_n^{(j)}]$ the two MAX and MIN vertices. There are numerous alternatives for modeling the hyperbox. We describe two of them, which give the more satisfactory performance:

A) modification of formula (22), by introducing a term depending on the hyperbox size:

$$\sigma_i^{(j)} = \frac{\underset{k}{MAX}(x_{ti}^{(k)}) - \underset{k}{MIN}(x_{ti}^{(k)})}{(4N)^{1/n}} + \frac{V_i^{(j)} - v_i^{(j)}}{4} , \quad i = 1 \ldots n, \quad j = 1 \ldots N+1 \quad (30)$$

()

B) use of a generalized bell for modeling the cluster

$$\mu_{A_i^{(j)}}(z_i) = \frac{1}{1 + \left| \dfrac{z_i - x_i^{(j)}}{a_i^{(j)}} \right|^{2b_i^{(j)}}} \quad (31)$$

with

$$x_i^{(j)} = \frac{V_i^{(j)} + v_i^{(j)}}{2}$$

$$b_i^{(j)} = \frac{\log\left[\dfrac{k_1(1 - k_2)}{k_2(1 - k_1)}\right]}{2\log\left(\dfrac{r_{2i}^{(j)}}{r_{1i}^{(j)}}\right)} ; \quad a_i^{(j)} = \frac{r_{2i}^{(j)}}{\left(\dfrac{1 - k_2}{k_2}\right)^{1/(2b_i^{(j)})}}$$

$$r_{1i}^{(j)} = \frac{V_i^{(j)} - v_i^{(j)}}{2} ; \quad r_{2i}^{(j)} = r_{1i}^{(j)} + q$$

where the parameters k_1, k_2, and q allow to tailor the MF to the hyperbox. Reasonable values for k_1 and k_2 are $k_1 = 0.95$, $k_2 = 0.1$. The parameter q controls the slope of the MF, i.e. the fuzziness.

The two previous options originate two new versions of γMM-ALG. A final aspect to be taken into account regards the possibility of improving the overall accuracy of the mapping by a fine-tuning of all the parameters involved in the expansion (2). A simple approach for pursuing this goal is to rely on a gradient based optimization. The advantage of this approach is the possibility of implementing a cost-effective procedure, similar to the well-known backpropagation algorithm used in connection with multilayer perceptron. For reason of space, we omit the resulting formulas and only illustrate, with an example, the gain in accuracy obtained by this final step.

The example regards the benchmark (27) with a TS of $N_t = 30$ points uniformly located in the corresponding definition domain I. The results of the simulation test is summarized in Tab. 2. The effects on the accuracy of the successive steps carried out with γMM-ALG are shown in the table. Three situations are evidenced; in each of them the options A and B for the MF are considered:

1) the algorithm is applied by using only the basis functions obtained without steps 4-5; the coefficients $y^{(j)}$ of expansion (2) are considered as the projections of the clusters centroids onto the output space.
2) the algorithm is applied in the complete version with all the 5 steps.
3) the algorithm is applied as in 2); successively all the net parameters are tuned by the backpropagation technique (learning rate = 0.1, number of epochs = 50).

The values of the parameters used in the procedure are: $\gamma = 1.51$, with resulting N=6 (case A); $\gamma = 1.46$, with resulting N = 5, and q = 2 (case B). The number of the NFA parameters is equal to 18 and 20 respectively.

MSE (dB)

option \ situation	1 without steps 4, 5	2 all the 5 steps	3 BP tuning
A	- 3.47	- 12.4	- 28.24
B	- 0.89	- 13.76	- 30.76

Table 2.

5. Neurofuzzy approximator with numerical and linguistic information

NFA accepts both numerical and linguistic information. The former is given as a set of N_t pairs $(x^{(k)}, y_t^{(k)})$. The latter is expressed by a set of P_L linguistic rules suggested by experts. The numerical data are converted to P_N linguistic rules by the methods discussed in the previous sections. Both the types of rules are then processed in a similar way yielding the FBFs to be used for approximating the unknown mapping. There are several alternatives for combining the two sets of rules.

The most important aspect to be taken into account regards the different reliability that can be attributed to the two information sources. In the following, we suggest two ways for handling this topic by introducing a reliability parameter $\lambda \in [0, 1]$.

- *Weak coupling of the sources*

    The two sources are treated separately. Their contribution is then combined together by weighting them on the basis of λ The expression of expansion (2) is replaced by

$$y(\underline{x}) = \lambda \sum_{j=1}^{P_N} y_N^{(j)} \alpha_N^{(j)}(\underline{x}) + (1-\lambda) \sum_{j=1}^{P_L} y_L^{(j)} \alpha_L^{(j)}(\underline{x}) \tag{32}$$

    The subscripts N and L stand for numerical and linguistic. The functions $\alpha_N^{(j)}(\underline{x})$ and $\alpha_L^{(j)}(\underline{x})$ are derived independently from the respective rules and following different algorithms. For instance, for the combination of the rules antecedents, we can adopt the product in the numerical case and the MIN operator in the other case. We have

$$\alpha_N^{(j)}(\underline{x}) = \frac{\prod_{i=1}^{n} \mu_{A_{N,i}^{(j)}}(x_i)}{\sum_{h=1}^{P_N} \left(\prod_{i=1}^{n} \mu_{A_{N,i}^{(h)}}(x_i) \right)} \tag{33}$$

$$\alpha_L^{(j)}(\underline{x}) = \frac{\underset{i=1..n}{MIN}\left\{ \mu_{A_{L,i}^{(j)}}(x_i) \right\}}{\sum_{h=1}^{P_L} \left(\underset{i=1...n}{MIN}\left\{ \mu_{A_{L,i}^{(h)}}(x_i) \right\} \right)} \tag{34}$$

    The reliability parameter is chosen on the basis of subjective considerations, regarding the experience and the knowledge of the mechanism originating the numerical data.

- *Strong coupling of the sources*

    The combination of the two sources can be made stronger when the net normalization layer involves both the "numerical" and "linguistic" MFs. The reliability parameter affects the weighting of the two sets of rules in correspondence to the normalization. As in the previous case, the MFs of the rules can be computed independently. If we adopt the same choice considered in the previous case, we obtain the following expressions:

$$y(\underline{x}) = \sum_{j=1}^{P_N} y_N^{(j)} \alpha_N^{(j)}(\underline{x}) + \sum_{j=1}^{P_L} y_L^{(j)} \alpha_L^{(j)}(\underline{x}) \tag{35}$$

with

$$\alpha_N^{(j)}(\underline{x}) = \frac{\lambda \prod_{i=1}^{n} \mu_{A_{N,i}^{(j)}}(x_i)}{\lambda \sum_{h=1}^{P_N} \left(\prod_{i=1}^{n} \mu_{A_{N,i}^{(h)}}(x_i) \right) + (1-\lambda) \sum_{h=1}^{P_L} \left(\underset{i=1\dots n}{MIN} \left\{ \mu_{A_{L,i}^{(h)}}(x_i) \right\} \right)} \tag{36}$$

$$\alpha_L^{(j)}(\underline{x}) = \frac{(1-\lambda) \underset{i=1\dots n}{MIN} \left\{ \mu_{A_{L,i}^{(j)}}(x_i) \right\}}{\lambda \sum_{h=1}^{P_N} \left(\prod_{i=1}^{n} \mu_{A_{N,i}^{(h)}}(x_i) \right) + (1-\lambda) \sum_{h=1}^{P_L} \left(\underset{i=1\dots n}{MIN} \left\{ \mu_{A_{L,i}^{(h)}}(x_i) \right\} \right)} \tag{37}$$

Expansions (32) and (35) can be used at successive levels of accuracy, since the discussion at the end of the previous section holds also in the present situation. Therefore: we may use, for the coefficients $y_N^{(j)}$, $y_L^{(j)}$, the quantities obtained by defuzzifying the rules (point 1); we may determine them by a LSE technique without modifying the basis functions (point 2); we may modify all the parameters by fine tuning them with a backpropagation algorithm (point 3).

We conclude this section with an example that illustrates the efficacy of the linguistic information, when available. The numerical data are handled with γMM-ALG. The MFs of the linguistic rules are Gaussian and open sigmoidal. The product is adopted for combining the antecedents of the rules, both in the numerical and linguistic case. The coupling between the two sources is strong.

Example 1

The unknown mapping is given by

$$y(\underline{x}) = 0.5 \left[F((x_1 + 0.35)/2) + F((x_2 + 0.35)/2) \right]$$
$$F(w) = 0.01 \, h(4(w - 1.2))$$
$$h(\rho) = 1/[(0.5\rho - 0.2)^2 + 0.01] + 1/[(0.5\rho - 0.8)^2 + 0.03] - 6 \tag{38}$$

It is shown in Fig. 7 in the domain $I = [0\ 1] \times [0\ 1]$. The TS is constituted by N_t=100 pairs randomly located in the domain I and by 7 linguistic rules. The latter qualitatively characterize the behavior of the mapping. In Tab. 3, the antecedents of these rules are summarized. The consequents are not reported, since the coefficients $y_N^{(j)}$ and $y_L^{(j)}$ are determined by the LSE technique when γMM-ALG is applied. The types of MFs reported in the tables are labeled with G (Gaussian), LS (left open sigmoid), RS (right open sigmoid).

The mapping realized by the NFA, when using only the numerical data with γMM-ALG, is shown in Fig. 8. The γ-MIN-MAX algorithm determines N = 19 clusters. In this case, the MSE attained by the NFA is -17.3 dB; it is computed on a test set constituted by 400 points located uniformly in I.

The use of the complete sources of information is then considered. The coefficients are determined by the LSE technique and the coupling is strong with λ=0.2. The resulting mapping realized by NFA is shown in Fig. 9. It achieves an MSE of -28.2 dB on the same test set.

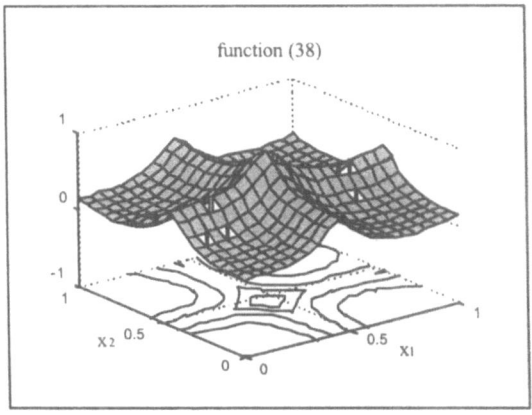

Figure 7.

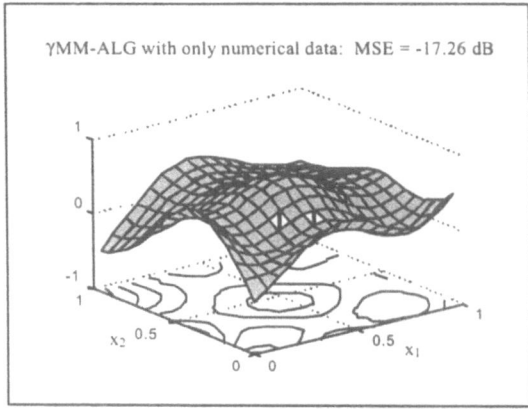

Figure 8.

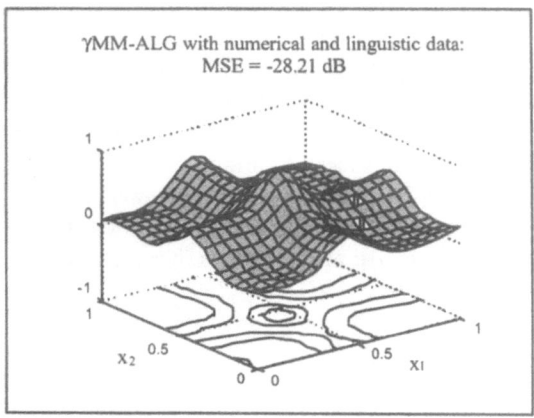

Figure 9.

rule	MF (z_1)	MF (z_2)
1	G: $x_1^{(1)} = 0.45$, $\sigma_1^{(1)} = 0.06$	G: $x_1^{(1)} = 0.45$, $\sigma_2^{(1)} = 0.06$
2	G: $x_1^{(2)} = 0.45$, $\sigma_1^{(2)} = 0.1$	-
3	-	G: $x_2^{(3)} = 0.45$, $\sigma_2^{(3)} = 0.1$
4	LS: $x_1^{(4)} = 0$, $\sigma_1^{(4)} = 0.1$	LS: $x_2^{(4)} = 0$, $\sigma_2^{(4)} = 0.1$
5	RS: $x_1^{(5)} = 1$, $\sigma_1^{(5)} = 1$	RS: $x_2^{(5)} = 1$, $\sigma_2^{(5)} = 1$
6	LS: $x_1^{(6)} = 0$, $\sigma_1^{(6)} = 1$	RS: $x_2^{(6)} = 1$, $\sigma_2^{(6)} = 1$
7	RS: $x_1^{(7)} = 1$, $\sigma_1^{(7)} = 1$	LS: $x_2^{(7)} = 0$, $\sigma_2^{(7)} = 1$

Table 3.

This simple example points out an important feature of NFA: when the numerical data are poor of information, a set of well defined linguistic rules can supply the loss of information and yields a large improvement on the mapping realized by the NFA. This feature, together with the constructive approach, can be conveniently used in actual situations when numerical data set is affected by noise. At the end of the next section we will illustrate this topics by a detailed example.

6. Noisy data and constructive NFA

The numerical data of the TS are usually affected by noise, since they are obtained by measurements carried out in the actual applications of interest. Due to noise, the TS appears to NFA as it was produced by an underlying process much more complex than the original one. NFA is not aware of this masking effect undertaken by the noise. Consequently, it looks for a model more complex than the unknown process.

An efficient way for combating noise is to constrain NFA to converge to a simpler solution, also if this strategy reduces the accuracy attained in matching the TS. The previous strategy is exactly what is required by learning theory for achieving the best possible generalization. Consequently, we can follow the methods here suggested, which require the minimization of an objective function constituted by two terms, measuring respectively the NFA accuracy and complexity. The minimum can be pursued either by a constructive or a pruning approach. In the following, we will apply the former, since less computational intensive.

The several methods proposed for determining the objective function [14, 15] are difficult to apply. For this reason, it is usual to follow another method: the cross-validation. The objective function is simply replaced by the approximation error of the NFA in connection with a data set not used during training. This set is called validation set. When this technique is applied, the numerical data of the TS are partitioned in two subsets: 1) a set effectively used for training; 2) a set used for validation. The optimal partition of the original TS in the mentioned two parts is known in the asymptotic case [16]. When the available TS is far from this situation, a rule of thumb suggests to partition it in two parts of equal cardinality and similar covering of the input space.

The constructive approach can be used in connection with each of the previous algorithms and variants. It requires the repeated application of the chosen algorithm for determining the optimal number of rules, i.e. the optimal NFA. Starting from a low value of N, we increase it up to the optimum. In correspondence to the current value of N, we consider the error of the corresponding NFA on the validation set. Namely, if $\{(\underline{x}_t^{(k)}, y_t^{(k)}), k=1...N_t\}$ is the TS, we initially split it in two disjointed sets: sub-training set STS = $\{(\underline{x}_{st}^{(k)}, y_{st}^{(k)}), k=1...N_{st}\}$ and validation set VS = $\{(\underline{x}_v^{(k)}, y_v^{(k)}), k=1...N_v\}$.

The objective function is therefore

$$E(N) = \frac{1}{N_v} \sum_{k=1}^{N_v} \left[net(\underline{x}_v^{(k)}, \Theta) - y_v^{(k)} \right]^2 \tag{39}$$

where net($\cdot$) is the output of NFA; Θ is the set of its parameters. These parameters are determined by the chosen algorithm (FCM-ALG, γMM-ALG and its variants). A value of E(N) will result. Then, N is augmented and the previous computation is again performed. The optimal N*, which yields the minimum value for E(N), is obtained by a unimodal search. The simple procedure of increasing step by step N does not work, since E(N) is subjected to an irregular behavior. What is guaranteed is only the general trend characterized by an initial decrease with N and then an increase. The actual behavior oscillates around this trend. After the unimodal search is concluded, we have the optimal number N* of rules and a good set of values for the NFA parameters. In spite of this, the parameters related to the consequents of the rules, i.e. the coefficients $y^{(j)}$, are tailored again, in order to improve the net performance. This goal can be achieved by carrying out the LSE minimization with the entire TS. The benefit of this final tuning will be illustrated in the following two examples.

The previous procedure applies in general. With specific algorithms, better results can be obtained by tailoring the procedure to their characteristics. In the following, we develop this point with reference to the algorithm γMM-ALG. Due to γ-MIN-MAX mechanism, the minimization with respect to N is controlled by the parameter γ. It is convenient to minimize E with respect to the quantity $\phi = 1/\gamma$. In fact, ϕ has a physical meaning in the clustering procedure, since it measures the fuzziness of the MFs defined in connection with the hyperboxes used during clustering. The range of ϕ to be explored should be limited between two values ϕ_m and ϕ_M ($\phi_m < \phi_M$) such that $N(\phi_M)$ be close to 1 and $N(\phi_m)$ to N_{st}. A practical method for determining them can be simply derived [13].

The proposed algorithm starts from $\phi = \phi_M$ and then diminishes it looking for the minimum of E in the said range by a unimodal search. In correspondence to each value of ϕ we apply γMM-ALG, determining the NFA parameters Θ and the function E value.

In the next examples, we will illustrate the previous procedure, based on γMM-ALG.

Example 1: approximation of function (27)

The test is carried out by considering two types of noise and two orders of presentation of the STS data during the clustering. The two types of noise are:
- impulsive noise: is constituted by a sequence of impulses having magnitude uniformly distributed in the range [-1 1] and probability equal to 0.3;
- Gaussian noise: the samples are due to a Gaussian process with zero mean and variance equal to 0.3.

The order of presentation is also of two types:
- random: the patterns of STS are ordered randomly;
- radial: the patterns are ordered on the basis of their distance from the gravity center of the STS.

The TS is obtained by considering 100 samples of the input space uniformly distributed in domain I, by determining the corresponding values of the output through (27), and then by superimposing to them the selected noise. The two subsets STS and VS are obtained by alternating their patterns between them. The test set is constituted by 200 patterns uniformly distributed and disjointed by the TS.

Let us consider firstly the Gaussian noise. The deteriorated TS is shown in Fig. 10 together with function (27). It is evident from the figure that the TS could correspond to a function much more complex than (27). The application of the previous constructive version of γMM-ALG yields the behavior shown in Fig. 11 for E in function of ϕ. The minimum is achieved at $\phi^* = 0.6$, where the corresponding optimal number of rules is $N^* = 12$. The MSE decreases with N (that is when ϕ decrease) in the case of training, as shown in Fig. 12. In the same figure, we see instead that the MSE on the test set has a trend similar to $E(\phi)$; its minimum value, achieved also at ϕ^*, is equal to 0.0128 (-18.91 dB). The efficiency of the constructive version of γMM-ALG is further confirmed by Fig. 13, where there are shown the mappings realized by NFA when N is equal to 12 (optimum), N = 8 and N = 17. The performance in the case N* clearly overcomes that obtained in the other cases; this is also proved by the values of MSE.

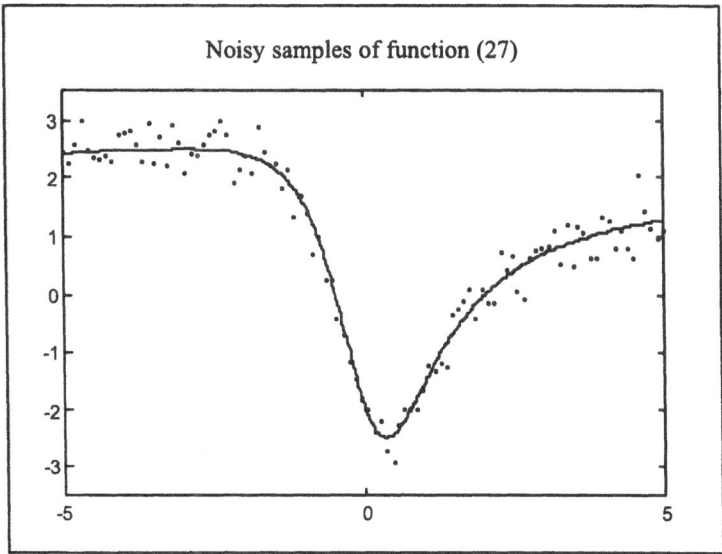

Figure 10.

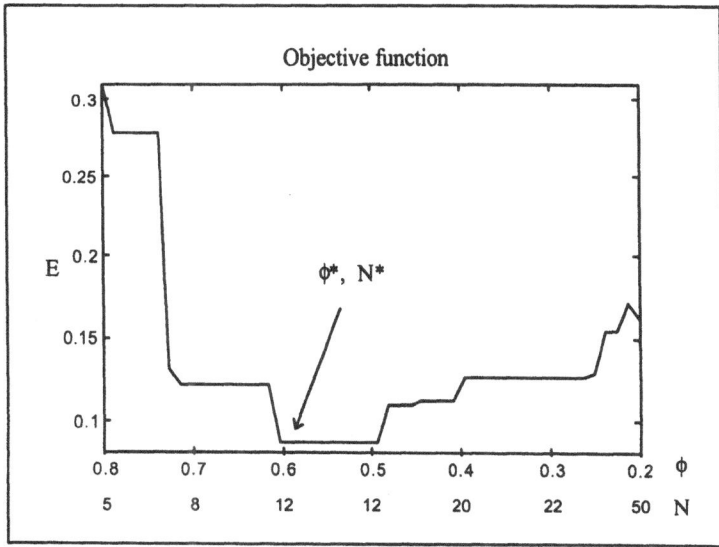

Figure 11.

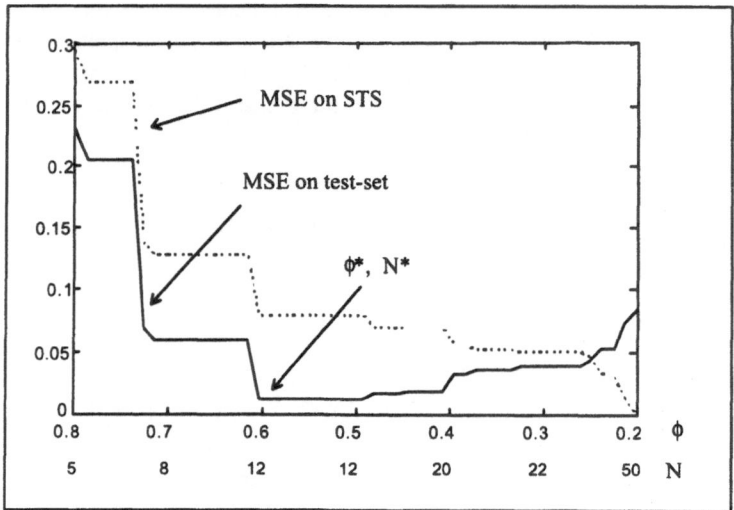

Figure 12.

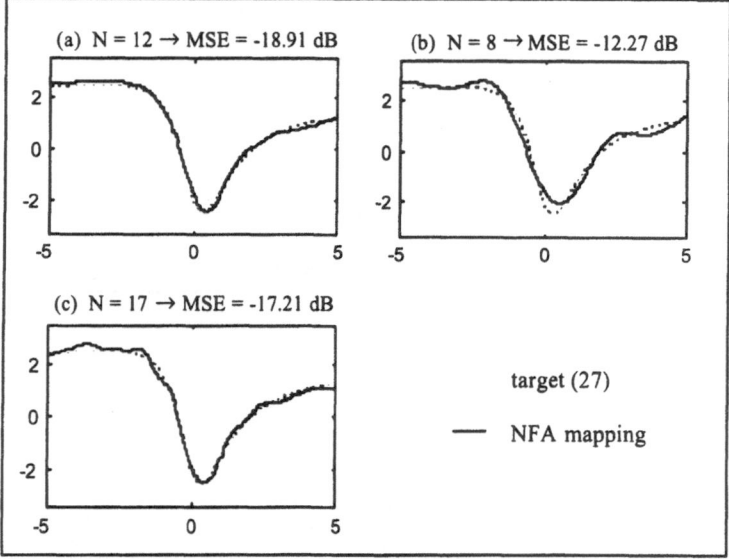

Figure 13.

The complete results of the experiments carried out with function (27) are reported in Tab. 4. The results regard 6 different cases. In 4 cases, reported in the first 2 rows of the table, the constructive procedure based on γMM-ALG is applied by considering the two types of noise and the two orders of presentation of the STS patterns. The remaining 2 cases, reported in the last row, concern the application of the procedure based on FCM-ALG, in the case of impulsive and Gaussian noise. The values reported in rows 2 and 3 correspond to the mean and the variance of N and MSE obtained in 20 independent trials, by changing randomly the order of presentation of the STS patterns (in the case of γMM-ALG) and the initial centroids of the clusters (in the case of FCM-ALG). It is also reported (in brackets) the values regarding the MSE obtained before the final tuning of the consequent parameters of NFA with the entire TS.

Algorithm	impulsive noise				gaussian noise			
	N^*	σ_{N}	MSE (dB)	σ_{MSE}	N^*	σ_{N}	MSE (dB)	σ_{MSE}
γMM-ALG (radial)	11	-	-21.88 (-17.93)	-	12	-	-22.18 (-18.91)	-
γMM-ALG (random)	10.35	1.19	-18.5 (-16.76)	1.2 (0.75)	11.2	0.81	-20.95 (-18.34)	1.27 (0.78)
FCM-ALG	10.55	0.74	-19.4 (-17.34)	1.26 (0.77)	11.4	0.49	-21.83 (-18.88)	0.46 (0.77)

Table 4.

Example 2: approximation of a bidimensional function

The function to be approximated is

$$y(\underline{x}) = \frac{(x_1 - 0.5)(x_2 - 0.5)(10x_1 - 2.5)}{(x_1 - 0.5)^2 + (x_2 - 0.5)^2 + 0.01} \tag{40}$$

defined in the domain I = [0 1] × [0 1]. The TS is constituted by 169 pairs uniformly distributed in I. It is corrupted by noise of the same types considered in the previous example, with the only difference of the range of the impulse noise and the variance of the Gaussian noise, respectively equal to [-1.5 1.5] and 0.5. The partition of TS (in the two subsets STS and VS) is obtained by alternating uniformly the patterns between them. Their cardinalities are respectively 85 and 84. The test set is constituted by 441 points. The application of the constructive versions of FCM-ALG and γMM-ALG yields the results summarized in Tab. 5. The experiment has been conducted as in the case of example 1. In all the tests, the algorithm γMM-ALG with radial order of presentation furnishes the best results in terms of MSE.

Algorithm	impulsive noise				gaussian noise			
	N^*	σ_{N}	MSE (dB)	σ_{MSE}	N^*	σ_{N}	MSE (dB)	σ_{MSE}
γMM-ALG (radial)	26	-	-14 (-11.11)	-	24	-	-13.64 (-11.3)	-
γMM-ALG (random)	24.45	3.37	-13.79 (-11.55)	0.6 (0.52)	24.45	5.32	-13.49 (-10.59)	0.73 (0.23)
FCM-ALG	23.8	5.12	-13.42 (-11.17)	0.66 (0.33)	21.85	3.84	-13.55 (-11.19)	0.7 (0.69)

Table 5.

Example 3: neurofuzzy controller (NFC) for the system "Ball & Beam"

The problem under consideration regards the approximation of the control law of a ball on a beam (Fig. 14). The beam is able to rotate in a vertical plane by applying a torque at the center of rotation and the ball is free to roll along the beam. The control u(t) is the acceleration, i.e. $\ddot{\theta}$. The problem under consideration is to design u(t) so that the ball can converge asymptotically into the origin, regardless the initial position of the beam and the initial position of the ball. The system is nonlinear and described by the following four state variables

$$x_1 = r , \quad x_2 = \dot{r} , \quad x_3 = \theta , \quad x_4 = \dot{\theta}$$

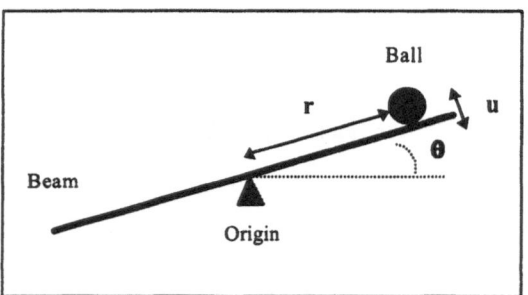

Figure 14.

The control law which achieves the said result can be determined via analytical tools. It is also obtainable by using a limited number of numerical examples and four high-level common sense rules, as shown in [20]. In the present case we furthermore consider the numerical data set affected by noise in order to cope more realistically with actual situations. The information available in this problem is constituted by :

- a numerical data set DS1 containing 100 samples of the control law u(t) analytically determined and located in the same range considered in [20];

- a noisy numerical data set DS2, obtained by superimposing to DS1 a Gaussian noise with zero mean and variance equal to 0.5;

- four common sense linguistic rules coincident with those used in [20], but with different MFs. The four rules are listed in Tab. 6, while the MFs presently adopted are listed in Tab. 7.

If r is positive and $\dot{r}$ is near zero and θ is positive and $\dot{θ}$ is near zero, then u is negative	
If r is negative and $\dot{r}$ is near zero and θ is negative and $\dot{θ}$ is near zero, then u is positive	
If r is positive and $\dot{r}$ is near zero and θ is negative and $\dot{θ}$ is near zero, then u is positive-big	
If r is negative and $\dot{r}$ is near zero and θ is positive and $\dot{θ}$ is near zero, then u is negative-big	

Table 6.

positive x_1	$\exp[-0.5\,(\min((x_1 - 3)/2,0))^2]$
negative x_1	$\exp[-0.5\,(\max((x_1 + 3)/2,0))^2]$
positive x_3	$\exp[-0.5\,(\min((x_3 - 0.6)/0.4,0))^2]$
negative x_3	$\exp[-0.5\,(\max((x_3 + 0.6)/0.4,0))^2]$
quasi-zero x_2 and x_4	$\exp[-0.5\,(x)^2]$
positive consequent	$\exp[-0.5\,(u - 0.5)^2]$
negative consequent	$\exp[-0.5\,(u + 0.5)^2]$
positive-big consequent	$\exp[-0.5\,(u - 2)^2]$
negative-big consequent	$\exp[-0.5\,(u + 2)^2]$

Table 7.

The synthesis of the NFC is carried out in 5 different situations in order to better understand the properties of the procedure.

Case 1: we only use DS1. The synthesis procedure is applied without optimizing φ. The number of rules is consequently not optimal; it is equal to 20. However, the resulting NFC is able to determine the correct control law. This result is illustrated in Fig. 15. In Fig. 15(a) there are shown the trajectories of the ball for four different starting conditions under the action of the controller analytically determined. Fig. 15(b) shows the trajectories due to the resulting NFC.

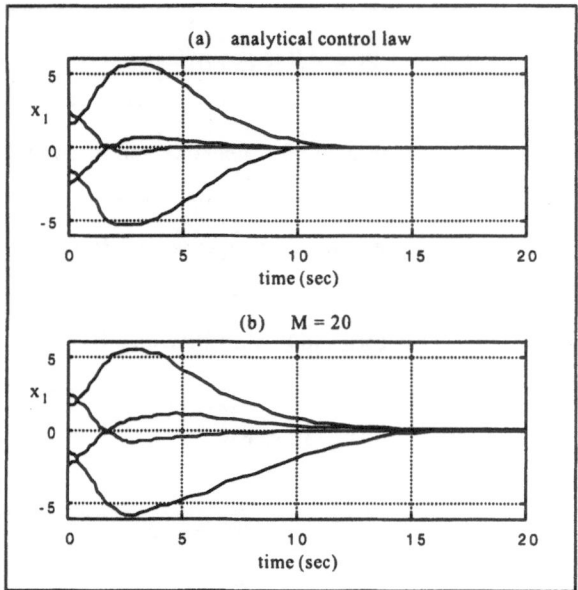

Figure 15.

Case 2: as in the previous case, but with DS2 in place of DS1. The resulting NFC is unable to attain the correct control law. The trajectories of the ball are now divergent, as shown in Fig. 16. The noise causes an information loss such that the remaining one is not sufficient for attaining the goal.

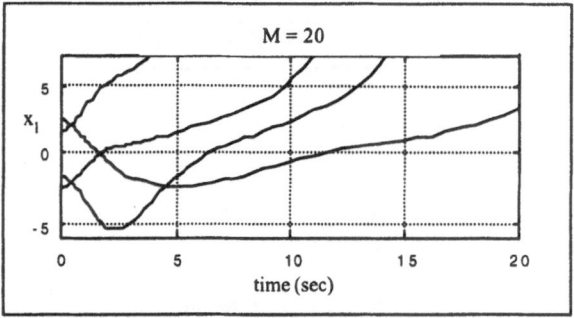

Figure 16.

Case 3: as in the case 2 but with the addition of the linguistic information. The resulting NFC is able to recover the correct control law with λ in the range [0.2, 0.5]. In this range the linguistic information is more important than the numerical one. It is interesting to note that the smoothness of the trajectories is directly related to the value of λ. The larger is λ, the smoother are the resulting trajectories. In Fig. 17(a) they are shown when λ = 0.5, i.e. when λ attains the maximum permissible value. In this situation we have the maximum of smoothness.

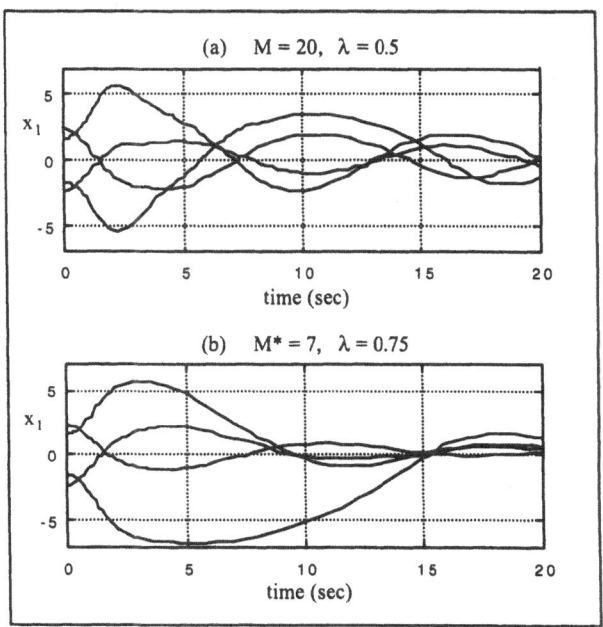

Figure 17.

Case 4: as in the case 2 but by applying the proposed constructive synthesis procedure. The optimal number of rules is M* = 7. Only one of the trajectories of the ball is still divergent, as shown in Fig. 18. Comparing this figure with Fig. 16, we see the improvement caused by the constructive mechanism.

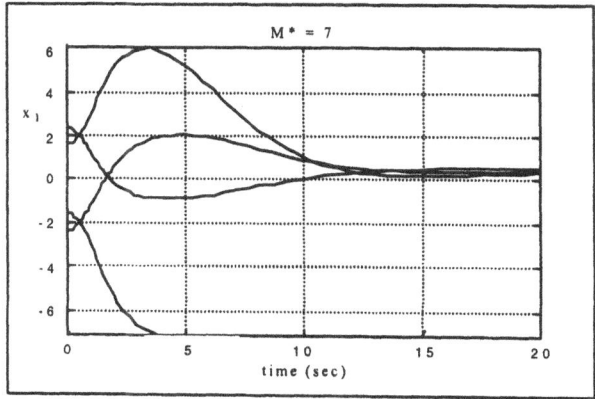

Figure 18.

Case 5: as in the case 4 but with the addition of linguistic information. The range of λ, where the resulting NFC is able to recover the correct control law, is much larger than in the case 3. We can use a value of λ greater than 0.5. With large values of λ, the contribution of the linguistic information is reduced and smoother trajectories result. This is illustrated in Fig. 17(b), which refers to $\lambda = 0.75$.

7. Conclusion

The possibility of using linguistic and numerical sources of information is a very important characteristic of the neuro-fuzzy approximators. We have illustrated with examples how few linguistic rules can replace numerical information and are equivalent to a suitable number of numerical data. Moreover, the linguistic information is not subjected to noise, as it happens to numerical data.

The paper has considered several aspects of the procedure for determining NFA from the TS. They can be deepened, since we often developed the topics by using illustrative examples and by introducing empirical formulas, obtained by exhaustive simulations. In particular, with regard to the proposed algorithm γMM-ALG, we have noted an irregular behavior of the number of clusters in function of the fuzziness parameter. This effect is due to the nature of the clustering algorithm used in γMM-ALG, i.e. the γ-MIN-MAX. Even if such a behavior is in agreement with the geometrical characteristics of the TS, in some cases an excessive discontinuity has caused a deterioration of performance. It is consequently useful to improve such type of clustering [21]. Improved clustering algorithms, when combined with an LSE final step, could yield a valid alternative to the constructive methods for optimizing the architecture and the parameters of the resulting neurofuzzy approximator. The optimal number of the rules could be directly provided by the clustering algorithm.

With regard to the modeling of the MFs, we have adopted formulas often derived empirically and on the basis of the best results obtained in several experiments. Further research at this regard is however necessary, since these MFs have a very strong impact on the performance of the approximator.

A final aspect to be deepened regards the use of weights for evaluating the reliability of the rules. We have introduced a "coarse" weighting in the case of linguistic and numerical rules. A fine-tuning of this criterion would require to associate a suitable weight to each rule on the basis of supplementary information regarding the problem domain.

References

[1] E.H. Mamdani, "Applications of fuzzy. algorithms for simple dynamic plant", *Proc. IEE*, Vol. 121, No. 12, 1974, pp. 1585-1588.

[2] T. Takagi, and M. Sugeno, "Fuzzy identification of systems and its application to modelling and control", *IEEE Trans. Syst. Man Cybern.*, Vol. 15, 1985, pp. 116-132.

[3] J.M. Mendel, "Fuzzy logic systems for engineering: a tutorial", *Proc. IEEE*, Vol. 83, No. 3, 1995, pp. 345-377.

[4] L.X. Wang, *Adaptive fuzzy systems and control*, Prentice-Hall, Englewood Cliffs, NJ, 1994.

[5] J.S.R. Jang, C.T. Sun, and E. Mizutani, *Neuro-fuzzy and soft computing*, Prentice-Hall, NJ, USA, 1997.

[6] G.A. Carpenter, S. Grossberg, et al., "Fuzzy ARTMAP: a neural network architecture for incremental supervised learning and analog multidimensional maps", *IEEE Trans. on Neural Networks*, Vol. 3, 1992, pp. 698-713.

[7] Ishibuchi, K. Kwon, and H. Tanaka, "Learning of fuzzy neural networks from fuzzy inputs and fuzzy targets", *Proc. of 5th IFSA World Conference*, Vol. I, 1993, pp. 147-150.

[8] C.T. Lin, "A neural fuzzy control system with structure and parameter learning", *Fuzzy Sets Syst.*, Vol. 70, 1995, pp. 183-212.

[9] I.Rojas, H. Pomares, J. Ortega, and A. Prieto, "Self-organized fuzzy system generation from training examples", *IEEE Trans. on Fuzzy Systems*, Vol. 8, No. 1, 2000, pp. 23-36.

[10] Y.Q. Zhang, and A. Kandel, "Compensatory neurofuzzy systems with fast learning algorithms", *IEEE Trans. on Neural Networks*, Vol. 9, No. 1, 1998, pp. 83-105.

[11] J.C. Bezdeck, *Pattern recognition with fuzzy objective function algorithms*, Plenum Press, New York, 1981.

[12] P.K. Simpson, "Fuzzy min-max neural networks–Part. 2: clustering", *IEEE Trans. on Fuzzy Syst.*, Vol. 1, No. 1, 1993, pp. 32-45.

[13] F.M. Frattale Mascioli, A. Mancini, A. Rizzi, and G. Martinelli, "Function approximation with noisy training data using FBF neural networks", *Proc. of NC'98*, Vienna, Sept. 1998, pp. 900-906.

[14] V.N. Vapnik, *The nature of statistical learning theory*, Springer-Verlag, 1995.

[15] J. Rissanen, "Modelling by shortest data description", *Automatica*, Vol. 14, 1978, pp. 465-471.

[16] S. Amari, et al., "Asymptotic statistical theory of overtraining and cross-validation", *IEEE Trans. on Neural Networks*, Vol. 8, No. 5, 1997, pp. 985-996.

[17] G.C. Mouzouris, and J.M. Mendel, "Nonsingleton fuzzy logic systems: theory and application", *IEEE Trans. on Fuzzy Systems*, Vol. 5, No. 1, 1997, pp. 56-71.

[18] M.H. Hassoun, *Fundamentals of artificial neural networks*, MIT Press, Cambridge, Mass., 1996.

[19] Poggio, and F. Girosi, "Networks for approximation and learning", *Proc. of IEEE*, Vol. 78, Sept. 1990, pp. 1481-1497.

[20] L.X. Wang, and J.M. Mendel, "Fuzzy basis functions, universal approximation and orthogonal least squares learning", *IEEE Trans. on Neural Networks*, Vol. 3, No. 5, 1992, pp. 807-814.

[21] A. Mancini, F.M. Frattale Mascioli, A. Rizzi, and G. Martinelli, "Improving FBF neurofuzzy approximator by optimised input space covering", *Electronics Letters*, Vol. 35, No. 4, 18 Feb. 1999, pp. 312-313.

[22] T. Kohonen, *Self-organizing maps*, Springer, 1995.

[23] T. Kohonen, E. Oja, O. Simula, A. Visa, and J. Kangas, "Engineering applications of the self-organizing maps", *Proc. of IEEE*; October 1996, pp. 1358-1384.

[24] F.M. Frattale Mascioli, A. Rizzi, G. Scrocca, and G. Martinelli, "Scale-based clustering via gravitational law imitation", *WIRN-99*, Springer, 1999, pp. 256-265.

[25] F.M. Frattale Mascioli, A. Rizzi, and G. Martinelli, "Compactness-separability optimization of fuzzy clusters", *Proc. of ISIS'97*, Reggio Calabria, Italy, Sept. 1997, pp. 452-457.

[26] F.M. Frattale Mascioli, A. Rizzi, M. Panella, and G. Martinelli, "Clustering with uncostrained hyperboxes", *IEEE Int. Fuzzy Systems Conference*, Seoul, Korea, August 1999, Vol. II, pp. 1075-1080.

Appendix

A.1 Clustering algorithms for rule extraction

Clustering is the basis of the extraction of rules from numerical information. Consequently, it is of paramount importance to be aware of the methods used for carrying out it. Clustering algorithms can be arranged in 3 classes, as pointed out in the following:

- *biologically-motivated*: the algorithm imitates the mechanism underlying the activity of biological neurons belonging to laminar nervous tissues (bubble of activity);
- *physically-motivated*: imitating the mechanisms that originate physical clusters as gravity, molecular attraction, etc.;
- *geometrical*: the clusters take on simple shapes as hyperellissoids, hyperboxes, etc.

We will illustrate briefly the three previous classes by presenting some typical representative algorithm per class. It is important to note preliminarily that the data set to be clustered can possess completely different structures and only some of the available clustering algorithms can discover them. In some case the data set does not present at all any structure, as when its patterns are originated by a random process. We will try to clarify this aspect by examples of bidimensional data sets, which permit a visual inspection of the resulting partitions.

A.2 Biologically-motivated clustering algorithms

The neural net denoted as Self-Organizing Map (SOM), proposed by Kohonen [22], implements the most representative algorithm in this class. The success of the SOM in numerous applications is well documented in [23]. It is constituted by a bidimensional array of neurons. Each neuron represents one cluster and its connection to the inputs is the corresponding centroid. Consequently, the SOM yields an optimal bidimensional visualization of the most characteristic structures of the data set under consideration. The SOM operation is inspired by the biological mechanism present in the laminar nervous system, it is summarized in the flow-chart of Fig. 19. All the samples of the data set to be clustered are presented iteratively to the input several times. The dimension of the neuron neighborhood is reduced in function of the iteration number. The modification of the connections is based on a gradient descent with objective function equal to the distance between the input sample and the connection vector. The learning rate decreases with iteration.

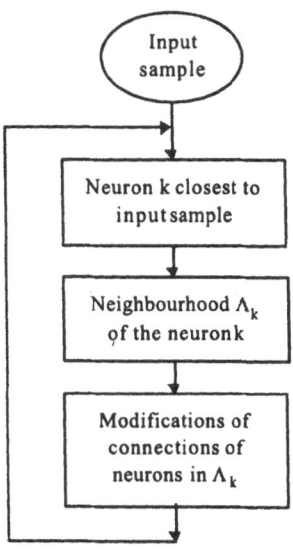

Figure 19.

A.3 Physically-motivated clustering algorithms

The algorithms in this class imitate the mechanisms that originate physical clusters. We limit our attention to two of them regarding respectively gravity and molecular attraction [24]. In the first case (gravitational algorithm) the patterns to be clustered are considered as points of unitary mass subject to a 'pseudo-gravitational force' proportional to their distances. In the second case (molecular algorithm) each pattern attracts the patterns contained in a region coincident with a hypersphere centered on it. It is similar to an atom, which interacts with other atoms by forming molecules. The clusters are these pseudo-molecules.

The flow-chart of Fig. 20 sketches the procedure common to both algorithms. It is clear from the figure that these algorithms are scale-based hierarchical. The optimal partition of the data set is characterized by surviving to the largest scale variation during the iterative hierarchical procedure. The scale coincides with the previous pseudo-force.

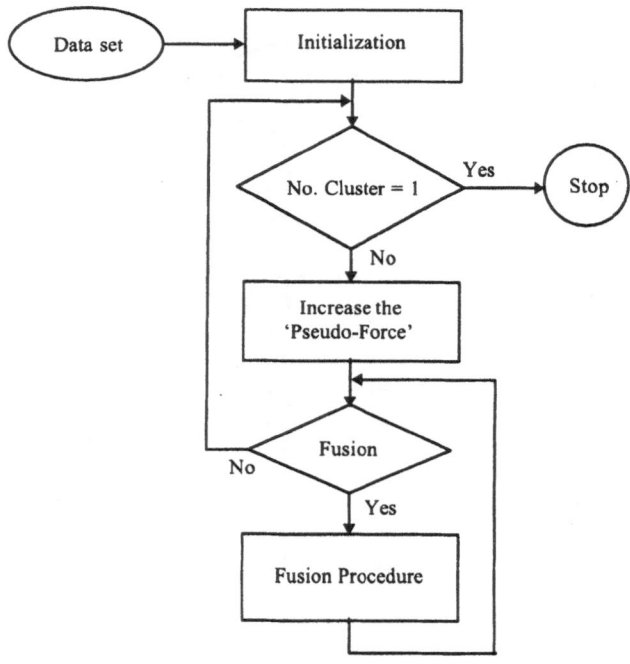

Figure 20.

The two algorithms are suited to discover completely different structures present in the data set. In the gravitational case each cluster is characterized by a representative point and the other points are linked to it. In the molecular case, there is not a representative point; paths constituted by points of the cluster connect all of them. The resulting structures can take on specific shapes as annular, filiform, and so on.

Let us illustrate the previous properties by two characteristic bidimensional examples. In the case of the molecular algorithm, we consider the data set of Fig. 21. By visual inspection, we can deduce that there are possible two partitions having 12 and 4 clusters. They are shown in Fig. 21(a) and 21(b) respectively. The molecular algorithm correctly discovers these clusters. Namely, it yields as the best partition, having the largest stability scale interval, the partition with 12 clusters and, as second best alternative, that with 4 clusters.

In the case of the gravitational algorithm we consider the data set of Fig. 22, which presents fractal structures. By visual inspection we can determine the two partitions of Fig. 22(a) and 22(b) correctly determined by the algorithm. It selects as the best one that with 5 clusters and as the second best alternative that with 25 clusters.

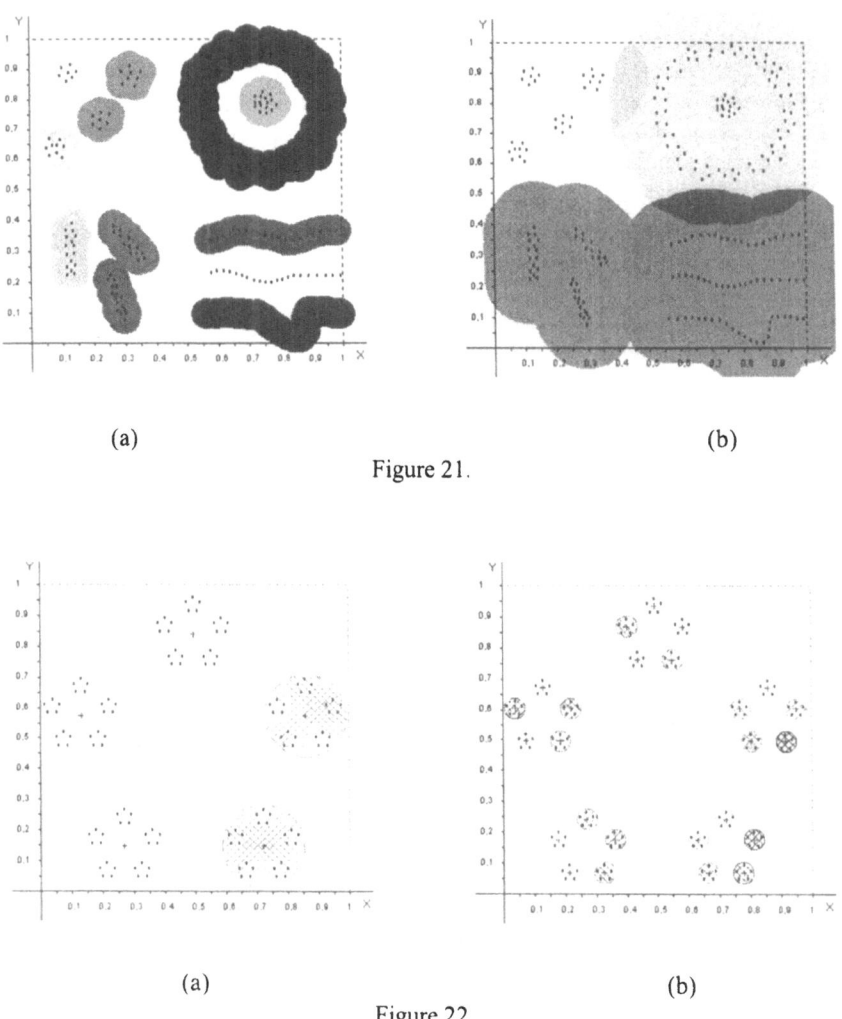

(a)   (b)

Figure 21.

(a)   (b)

Figure 22.

A.4 Geometrical clustering algorithms

The most representative algorithm in this class is the Min-Max algorithm proposed by Simpson [12]. It is characterized by fuzzy clusters having the simple shape of a hyperbox (HB). The original clustering procedure is iterative and driven by the presentation of a pattern at each step. It consists of the following substeps:

- expansion of a HB in order to accommodate the pattern under consideration. The expansion is feasible if the maximum side of the HB to be expanded is less than a threshold θ;
- contraction of the HBs if they overlap;
- addition of a new HB, if the HBs already present in the current partition are not suited to accommodate the pattern under consideration.

The previous procedure has been improved in several ways in order to reduce its main inconvenience of insufficient covering of the structures present in the data set. Some of the remedies proposed at this regard are:

1. variable dimension of the HBs [25]. This result is obtained by controlling the expansion substep on the basis of the MF of each cluster, i.e. the pattern is included in a HB if its MF overcomes a suitable threshold β. This version of the algorithm is denoted as 'β-Min-Max';
2. use of rotated HBs (without the previous constraint) to be oriented along suitable co-ordinate axes [26].

We illustrate the first remedy by considering the use of the Min-Max clustering for solving the classification problem of Fig. 23(a), where two classes are present in the data space. The corresponding training set, obtained from a suitable sampling in this space, is shown in Fig. 23(b). The Min-Max algorithm clusters the patterns separately for each class (i.e. by considering only the patterns belonging to the same class), thus each HB will belong to one of the two classes present in this case. If good partitions were produced, the class regions of Fig. 23(a) should be obtained by merging the HBs belonging to the same class. The partitions operated by the original Min-Max algorithm and by the β-Min-Max are shown in Fig. 23(c) and 23(d), respectively. In the first case there are 64 HBs and in the second case only 14, due to the possibility of using a variable dimension of them. It is important to remark the importance of this result since a simpler partition yields an NFN (neurofuzzy network) having a better generalization capability.

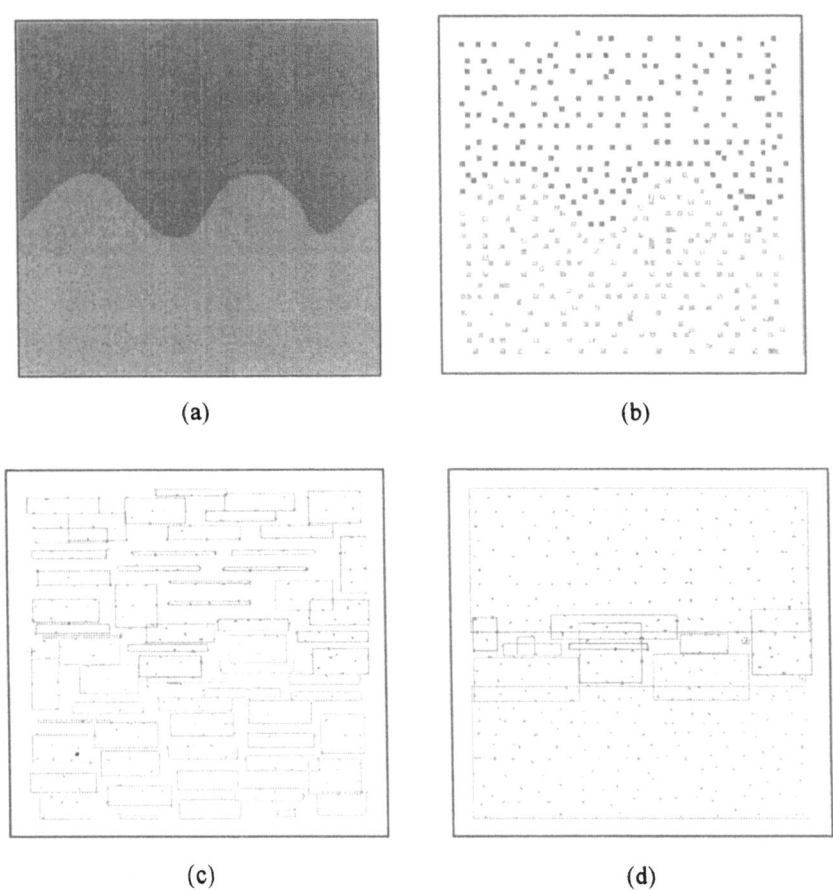

(a)

(b)

(c)

(d)

Figure 23.

Section 3
Eduardo R. Caianiello Lecture

Topics in Blind Signal Processing by Neural Networks
(*Invited Paper*)

Simone Fiori

DIE – University of Perugia, Italy

E-mail: sfr@unipg.it

Abstract

The aim of this paper is to propose a brief summary of the research topics
and results presented in the Author's PhD Thesis, concerning blind signal
processing by artificial neural networks. The results are illustrated by the
citation of the formal instruments involved in the research activity and
by several links to the main published contributions.

1   Introduction

Several signal processing problems are currently tackled by means of linear and
non-linear discrete-time adaptive circuits, which are capable of self-designing
in order to achieve a pre-defined target.

Such structures have raised an ever increasing interest in the international
scientific community as they allow for solving a number of problems which turn
out to be incompatible with the classical solutions; in fact, they allow to easily
manage the uncertainty inherent in any design activity. Furthermore, they
permit to achieve the desired results even in the partial, or sometimes total,
lack of fundamental information about the statistical and temporal features
of the signals under analysis, about the transmission means that the signals
propagate within, and about the receivers and measurement devices used as
sensors and transducers.

Owing to their noticeable flexibility and complexity and their relative novelty, such adaptive structures, linear as well as non-linear, are not endowed
with a complete and consistent theory which would allow their synthesis and
analysis under general conditions: for this reason they appear in the literature
with configurations still not completely satisfactory about their capability of
achieving the desired targets, and rather inefficient about the computational
and structural complexity required in order to achieve these targets. It is thus

of noticeable theoretical and practical interest to develop novel learning models for adaptive neural circuits.

The aim of the present paper is to summarize the scientific results appeared in the Author's PhD Thesis in Electrical Engineering, discussed in March 2000 at the University of Bologna (Italy). The Thesis concerns blind signal processing by artificial neural networks, and the Author was the recipient of the IIASS-SIREN international "E.R. Caianiello Award" for the best PhD thesis of the year about neural networks.

2 Research topics

The research topics considered in the Thesis fall in the following areas of engineering interest:

1. Discrete-time neural circuits applied to optimal compression of multivariate signals and time-series, and speech enhancement, by redundancy discovering and elimination (CMP). The multivariate discrete-time signals are obtained by sampling multiple scalar signals or by collecting successive samples of a single scalar signal;

2. Discrete-time neuromorphic adaptive filtering applied to blind equalization of linear stationary or time-varying channels (ACE), by on-line inversion of distortion and dispersion effects introduced by channels modeled through unknown non-minimum-phase transfer functions or more complicated functions;

3. Discrete-time artificial neural circuits applied to signal separation from linear non-convolutional mixtures ('cocktail party' problem, BSS) for the reduction of unwanted coupling effects between conductors and spatial filtering.

The deep study of the preceding topics has evidenced several ways for better the structures and the adapting algorithms commonly used in the scientific literature. Prior to be solved, the mentioned problems need suitable modeling, which show substantial similarities. Particularly, it is possible to evidence solutions based on common formal principles.

3 Foundations of the research work

3.1 Structures and learning theories

Synthesizing a non-linear discrete-time circuit (neural network) consists in separately designing the architecture of the circuit comprising variable parameters, and in the choice of the learning law of these parameters.

Irrespective of the utilized structure, an adapting procedure (or learning procedure for a neural network) may be defined as supervised or unsupervised. In several applications the supervised mode can be employed, with particular reference to those problems where the circuit is used for approximating or for identifying an unknown dynamical system. In these cases it is known at least the input-output behavior of the analyzed system, and the neural circuit may be adapted by exploiting both input and output data sets, which would be impossible when one of them lacks. In the latter case the learning rule is termed unsupervised in order to stress out the fact that there is no way to teach the system by examples.

Owing to the increasing interest raised in the international scientific community by the class of unsupervised neural circuits, the research activity summarized in the present paper has been conceived to be usefully oriented toward the topics concerning the neural circuits adapted according to the paradigms of the unsupervised learning.

The neural and neuromorphic structures studied here, which proved to be useful for solving the mentioned engineering problems, are:

1. Discrete-time neuromorphic adaptive filters;

2. Symmetric and hierarchical feed-forward neural networks;

3. Adaptive-activation-function neural networks (FANs); these are special structures which adapt the linear parts, as the common weights connecting the units and the biases, as well as the non-linear parts, like the activation functions of the neurons, which appear as tunable non-linearities.

About the unsupervised learning theories, the study and research activity has been oriented toward the following topics:

1. Learning models for neural circuits applied to optimal compression of multivariate signals by the principal component analysis (PCA);

2. Learning models for neural circuits applied to the separation of independent signals from their linear non-convolutional mixtures by the independent component analysis (ICA);

	CMP	ACE	BSS
Adaptive filters	×	×	×
Feedforward Nets	×		×
FAN		×	×

Table 1: Relationships among the research topics and the proposed architectural solutions (× = Existing relationship).

	CMP	ACE	BSS
ICA		×	×
SGM	×		×
PCA	×		×
BDM	×	×	×

Table 2: Relationships among the research topics and the proposed learning theory (× = Existing relationship).

3. Non-conventional neural optimization techniques as unsupervised learning theories and state-space search, and Stiefel-Grassman learning (SGM);

4. Learning models for neuromorphic adaptive digital filters applied to blind deconvolution of non-minimum-phase non-stationary systems (BDM);

5. Unsupervised learning models for adaptive-activation-function neural units.

The relationships existing among the different research problems and the solutions proposed, have been illustrated in the Tables 1 and 2, about the neural architectures and about the learning theories, respectively.

3.2   Scientific background

Conceptually and practically, the unsupervised learning deeply differs from the supervised learning. It answers to the need of designing a neural circuit in absence of fundamental information about the problem to solve; such absence makes it impossible or inadequate to solve the problem by means of classical solutions. An exemplary case is the equalization of one-transmitter/many-receivers transmission channels. In this problem the following hypotheses are made: The source sequences are completely unknown to the receivers and completely arbitrary; the transfer functions of the different branches of the channel are non-stationary. These hypotheses make it impossible to synthesize optimal equalizers able to work rapidly in any circumstance. If we suppose to try to solve this problem by means of a neural network, it is meaningless to think to a supervised learning; in fact, as the source sequences are unknown, a fundamental information lacks, which makes it impossible to define the 'learning error', the basis of the supervised learning.

The lack of fundamental information in the engineering problems which require the use of unsupervised neural circuits is overcome by introducing concepts related to high-order statistics, information theory and optimization.

The three mentioned mathematical theories result to be closely linked and widely employed in the literature in order to cope with blind signal processing problems. By making use of the concept of the information theory, in fact, it is possible to define suitable objective functions which describe in theoretic-informational terms the processing problem under analysis. The mathematical statistics gives then some formal instruments for elaborating theses objective functions, and the optimization theory constitutes the analytical basis for synthesizing global functions containing eventual physical constraints arisen by the problem, and for determining learning algorithms endowed with the necessary requisites about convergence speed, steady-state precision, and sensitivity to external disturbances.

On the basis of the preceding observations, the following general topics form the basic background of the Thesis:

1. Foundations of unsupervised neural circuits, that is linear and non-linear neural circuits without internal dynamics, endowed with static or flexible non-linear functions, with neural units being organized in hierarchical and non-hierarchical layers;

2. Principles of statistics, concerning continuous probabilities, high-order statistical parameters, canonical series expansions, Bayesian estimation, statistical models of systems, interaction between systems and statistics;

3. Principles of information theory, concerning entropy and negentropy, informational divergence, the interaction between systems and information flows;

4. Optimization principles, that is about Lagrange multipliers method as well as penalty and barrier techniques, regularization, non-conventional optimization techniques as genetic algorithms and simulated annealing;

5. Informational statistics oriented to signals processing, like principal/independent component/symbol analysis;

6. Elements of differential geometry, required in order to better understand the geometrical properties of the spaces that the adaptive systems' parameters belong to.

4 Summary of the scientific results

The study and research activity, oriented to the mentioned topics, has produced a number of scientific results which are the subject of the following short summary.

About non-minimum-phase system blind deconvolution, some contributions have appeared [3, 8, 12, 17, 23, 31, 36, 38], which showed that some of the strong and limiting hypotheses usually made about the knowledge a-priori needed for designing an effective equalization system may be relaxed, ultimately suggesting that it is possible to make the blind deconvolution theory 'more blind'. Particularly, in [12, 23, 31] some useful hints coming from the theory of the independent component analysis have been successfully employed for designing an equalization algorithm which requires a very few amount of prior information about the source signals, while in [3, 38] some theoretical contributions to neuromorphic adaptive filtering have been proposed, which take advantage from the learning ability of a non-linear neuron for approximating the optimal non-linearity required by the Bellini's 'Bussgang' algorithm which cannot be computed in a closed form without knowing source stream's probability density function, that is a very strong requirement. A comparison between the two different approaches has been presented in the contribution [36], whose aim is to elucidate their inter-relationships.

The study of the neural circuits for performing principal component analysis has led us to develop new unsupervised learning models for hierarchical (laterally-connected) circuits aiming at compressing real-valued data as well as complex-valued data, and to extract second-order statistical features from data: These models belong to the new class of learning rules termed ψ–APEX [7, 9, 13, 27, 28, 30], which have been developed in order to give a clear and compact form to the class of APEX learning rules by Kung and Diamantaras, to extend their applicability and to better understand their properties. Other contributions have been given in [1, 2], where the new learning rule based on the study of the dynamics of a rigid system of masses under a force field has been proposed and shown to be useful in neural optimal compression too. In [33] the principal component analysis theory is put in a new slant in connection to Moreau-Pesquet's semi-contrast theory which constitute a basis for generalizing PCA-type learning. Also, in [26] a variant of principal component analysis, termed minor component analysis, has been carefully investigated, especially on the important aspect of the stability of existing algorithms; an algorithm, which have been recognized to be unstable, has been endowed with a stabilization theory and the resulting learning paradigm has been used to train a complex-weighted neuron to perform robust beamforming, that is spatial filtering in presence of additive noise and disturbing secondary sources. The contributions [27, 35] are devoted to a wide comparison among PCA neural algorithm performed on both synthetic and real-world data.

About the separation of independent sources from their linear mixtures, some analytical and experimental results have evidenced the possibility of solving some problems about spatial filtering through sensors arrays whose output signals are processed by neural circuits endowed with new learning rules. A close examination of the obtained results shows that these learning paradigms seem to possess interesting features about the working speed, the effectiveness in non-stationary environments and about intrinsic stability. Such results are presented in a theoretical slant in [11, 15, 18, 20, 22, 28, 29, 33] and in a more practical fashion in [1, 16, 21, 37]. Also, a full study has been devoted to adaptive-activation-function networks for blind separation of eterokurtic sources; in this part the ancient problem of separating mixed leptokuric and platikutic sources, which cannot be separated out by the well-known algorithms by Jutten-Hérault, Comon, Laheld-Cardoso, Bell-Sejnowski, has been addressed and a solution has been proposed which relies on low-complexity approximation ability of neural networks formed by neurons endowed with adaptive activation functions. The mentioned contributions may be grouped in algorithms for separating out real-valued source signals [21, 22, 29, 37], and complex-valued source signals [15, 18, 28, 39], mainly dedicated to the separation of signals used in the telecommunication field. The BSS/ICA theory is also currently applied to intelligent electromagnetic data processing [24, 34].

The topic of adaptive activation function networks has been addressed in [4, 10, 19, 29, 32]. It has been possible to define an unsupervised learning model, based on the theory of the transformation of statistics across non-linear systems and on the informational divergence. Applications deal with blind deconvolution and blind source separation. The advantage of using adaptive non-linear functions instead of static ones (classical sigmoids) has been clearly shown by means of applications: in fact, the obtained results have clearly evidenced that the introduction of super-adaptive structures allows for solving blind signal processing problems without the need of explicitly estimating the statistical characteristics of the involved signals.

Some significant results have been obtained in the field on non-classical neural optimization; they are expressed in the theory of learning by weight flow on Stiefel-Grassman manifold, presented in [5, 6, 14, 25, 33]. There a general learning paradigm is developed, which encompasses and explains a large number of known theories about orthonormal learning, that is learning by keeping the connection matrix of a neural layer be orthonormal. After providing general definitions and recalling some definitions from Stiefel-Grassman mathematical work, the contributions present the new learning theory in its general form. Then special sub-cases are studied with details, and finally a large number of algorithms found in the literature are shown to be explainable within the most general one.

As the aim of this paper was to briefly summarize the research activity conducted by the Author on blind signal processing by artificial neural networks, only some contributions have been cited and discussed. A more detailed bibliography may be found in [40].

5   Conclusions

The aim of the summarized Thesis was to present the research work carried out by the Author from November 1996 to November 1999. It concerned unsupervised neural networks devoted to some aspects of blind signal processing, as optimal signal compression by adaptive second-order feature extraction, blind channel/system deconvolution by neuromorphic adaptive filtering, and blind source separation by the independent component analysis. The mentioned topics are currently considered of wide interest in the international scientific community, as proven by the many papers appeared in the recent years on the main journals and related-field conferences.

The researches presented were conceived in the hope to give novel and useful contributions both in the field of theoretical studies and of practical applications. The obtained issues have been introduced to the scientific community in order to validate the achieved results, and valuable and encouraging feedbacks have been obtained.

As in many research fields, any little step toward the solution of a problem opens room for the discussion of new emerged questions, so we guess the pathway to the satisfactory knowledge of unsupervised learning theory, related adaptive structures, and their computational power is still very long. Accordingly, the summarized Thesis has opened the way to new and more challenging studies, which will be carried out in the following years.

6 Acknowledgments

A complex work such the one briefly summarized in this paper would not have been possible without the direct and indirect help of many people. I wish to thank my parents and my friends for their constant availability and support, especially *Paola Baldassarri*, *Paolo Bucciarelli* and *Lorenzo Massaccesi*. I also wish to thank the "E.R. CAIANIELLO AWARD" commettee, formed by Professors *Maria Marinaro*, *Gianni Orlandi* and *Bruno Apolloni*. A special thank also goes to *Roberto Tagliaferri* and *Angelo Ciaramella* for their kindness and encouragement.

References

[1] S. FIORI, A. UNCINI, AND F. PIAZZA, *Application of the MEC Network to Principal Component Analysis and Source Separation*, Proc. of International Conference on Artificial Neural Networks (ICANN), pp. 571 – 576, 1997

[2] S. FIORI, P. CAMPOLUCCI, A. UNCINI, AND F. PIAZZA, *A New Unsupervised Neural Learning Rule for Orthonormal Signal Processing*, Proc. of International Conference on Acoustics, Speech and Signal Processing (ICASSP), pp. 3349 – 3352, 1997

[3] S. FIORI, A. UNCINI, AND F. PIAZZA, *Gradient-Based Blind Deconvolution with Flexible Approximated Bayesian Estimator*, Proc. of International Joint Conference on Neural Networks (IJCNN), pp. 854 – 858, 1998

[4] S. FIORI, P. BUCCIARELLI, AND F. PIAZZA, *Blind Signal Flatting Using Warping Neural Modules*, Proc. of International Joint Conference on Neural Networks, pp. 2312 – 2317 (IJCNN), 1998

[5] S. FIORI AND F. PIAZZA, *Orthonormal Strongly-Constrained Neural Learning*, Proc. of International Joint Conference on Neural Networks (IJCNN), pp. 1332 – 1337, 1998

[6] S. FIORI, A. UNCINI, AND F. PIAZZA, *Neural Learning and Weight Flow on Stiefel Manifold*, Proc. of X Italian Workshop on Neural Networks (WIRN), pp. 325 – 333, 1998

[7] S. FIORI, A. UNCINI, AND F. PIAZZA, *A New Class of APEX-Like PCA Algorithms*, Proc. of International Symposium on Circuits and Systems (ISCAS), Vol. III, pp. 66 – 69, 1998

[8] S. FIORI AND F. PIAZZA, *BLADE: A New On-Line Blind Equalization Method Based on the Burelian Distortion Measure*, Proc. of International Symposium on Circuits and Systems (ISCAS), Vol. IV, pp. 441 – 444, 1998

[9] S. FIORI AND A. UNCINI, *A Unified Approach to Laterally-Connected Neural Nets*, Proc. of IX European Signal Processing Conference (EUSIPCO), Vol. I, pp. 379 – 382, 1998

[10] S. FIORI AND F. PIAZZA, *A Study on Functional-Link Neural Units with Maximum Entropy Response*, Proc. of International Conference on Artificial Neural Networks (ICANN), Vol. 2, pp. 493 – 498, 1998

[11] E. POMPONI, S. FIORI, AND F. PIAZZA, *Complex Independent Component Analysis by Nonlinear Generalized Hebbian Learning with Rayleigh Nonlinearity*, Proc. of International Conference on Acoustics, Speech and Signal Processing (ICASSP), Vol. 2, pp. 1077 – 1080, 1999

[12] S. FIORI AND F. PIAZZA, *Weighted Least-Squares Blind Deconvolution*, Proc. of International Conference on Acoustics, Speech and Signal Processing (ICASSP), Vol. 5, pp. 2507 – 2510, 1999

[13] S. FIORI AND F. PIAZZA, *A Comparison of Three PCA Neural Techniques*, Proc. of European Symposium on Artificial Neural Networks (ESANN), pp. 275 – 280, 1999

[14] S. FIORI AND F. PIAZZA, *A Second-Order Differential System for Orthonormal Optimization*, Proc. of International Symposium on Circuits and Systems (ISCAS), Vol. V, pp. 531 – 534, 1999

[15] S. FIORI AND F. PIAZZA, *Neural Blind Separation of Complex Sources by Extended Hebbian Learning (EGHA)*, Proc. of International Symposium on Circuits and Systems (ISCAS), Vol. V, pp. 339 – 342, 1999

[16] S. FIORI, P. BALDASSARRI, AND F. PIAZZA, *An Efficient Architecture for Independent Component Analysis*, Proc. of International Symposium on Circuits and Systems (ISCAS), Vol. V, pp. 335 – 338, 1999

[17] S. FIORI, A. UNCINI, AND F. PIAZZA, *Blind Deconvolution by Modified Bussgang Algorithm*, Proc. of International Symposium on Circuits and Systems (ISCAS), Vol. III, pp. 1 – 4, 1999

[18] S. FIORI, A. UNCINI, AND F. PIAZZA, *Neural Blind Separation of Complex Sources by Extended APEX Algorithm (EAPEX)*, Proc. of International Symposium on Circuits and Systems (ISCAS), Vol. V, pp. 627 – 630, 1999

[19] S. FIORI AND P. BURRASCANO, *Polynomial Clusterons Exhibit Statistical Estimation Abilities*, Proc. of XI Italian Workshop on Neural Networks (WIRN), pp. 113 – 119, 1999

[20] S. FIORI AND P. BURRASCANO, *'Mechanical' Neural Learning and Info-Max Orthonormal Independent Component Analysis*, Proc. of International Joint Conference on Neural Networks, July 10-16, 1999, Washington D.C. (MD - USA)

[21] S. FIORI, *Blind Source Separation by New M-WARP Algorithm*, Electronics Letters, Vol. 35, No. 4, pp. 269 – 270, Feb. 1999

[22] S. FIORI, *Entropy Optimization by the PFANN Network: Application to Independent Component Analysis*, Journal: "Network: Computation in Neural Systems", Vol. 10, No. 2, pp. 171 – 186, May 1999

[23] S. FIORI, *Blind Deconvolution by Spectral Weighted Least-Squares Technique*, Electronics Letters, Vol. 35, No. 10, pp. 776 – 777, May 1999

[24] P. BURRASCANO, S. FIORI, AND M. MONGIARDO, *A Review of Artificial Neural Networks Applications in Microwave CAD*, Int. Journal of RF and Microwave CAE, Vol. 9, No. 3, pp. 158 – 174, 1999

[25] S. FIORI, *'Mechanical' Neural Learning for Blind Source Separation*, Electronics Letters, Vol. 35, No. 22, Oct. 1999

[26] S. FIORI AND F. PIAZZA, *Neural MCA for Robust Beamforming*, Proc. of International Symposium on Circuits and Systems (ISCAS), Vol. III, pp. 614-617, May 2000

[27] S. FIORI, *An Experimental Comparison of Three PCA Neural Networks*, Neural Processing Letters, Vol. 11, No. 3, pp. 209 – 218, Jun. 2000

[28] S. FIORI, *Blind Separation of Circularly-Distributed Sources by Neural Extended APEX Algorithm*, Neurocomputing, Vol. 34, No. 1-4, pp. 239 – 252, Aug. 2000

[29] S. FIORI, *Blind Signal Processing by the Adaptive Activation Function Neurons*, Neural Networks, Vol. 13, No. 6, pp. 597 – 611, Aug. 2000

[30] S. FIORI AND F. PIAZZA, *A General Class of ψ–APEX PCA Neural Algorithms*, IEEE Trans. on Circuits and Systems - Part I, Vol. 47, No. 9, pp. 1394 – 1398, Sept. 2000

[31] S. FIORI AND G. MAIOLINI, *Weighted Least-Squares Blind Deconvolution of Non-Minimum Phase Systems*, IEE Proceedings – Vision, Image and Signal Processing, Vol. 147, No. 6, pp. 557 – 563, Dec. 2000

[32] S. FIORI AND P. BUCCIARELLI, *Probability Density Estimation Using Adaptive Activation Function Neurons*, Neural Processing Letters, Vol. 13 No. 1, pp. 31 – 42, Feb. 2001

[33] S. FIORI, *A Theory for Learning by Weight Flow on Stiefel-Grassman Manifold*, Neural Computation, Vol. 13, No. 7, July 2001 (In press)

[34] S. FIORI, P. BURRASCANO, E. CARDELLI, AND A. FABA, *A Blind Separation Approach to Electromagnetic Source Localization and Assessment*, Proc. of 7th International Conference on Engineering Applications of Neural Networks (EANN'2001), July 16-18, 2001, Cagliari (Italy)

[35] S. COSTA AND S. FIORI, *Image Compression Using Principal Component Neural Networks*, Image and Vision Computing Journal (special issue on "Artificial Neural Network for Image Analysis and Computer Vision"). Forthcoming, 2001

[36] S. FIORI, *Notes on Cost Functions and Estimators for 'Bussgang' Adaptive Blind Equalization*, European Transactions on Telecommunications (ETT). Accepted for publication

[37] S. FIORI, *Hybrid Independent Component Analysis by Adaptive LUT Activation Function Neurons*, Neural Networks. Accepted for publication

[38] S. FIORI, *A Contribution to (Neuromorphic) Blind Deconvolution by Flexible Approximated Bayesian Estimation*, Signal Processing. Accepted for publication

[39] S. FIORI, *On Blind Separation of Complex-Valued Sources by Extended Hebbian Learning*, IEEE Signal Processing Letters. Accepted for publication

[40] S. FIORI, *Web page at the University of Perugia*, Address: http://www.unipg.it/~sfr/

Section 4
Mark Aizerman Lecture

Fuzzy measure and the Choquet integral for group multicriteria decision making

Silvio Giove
Dept. of Applied Mathematics, University of Venice
Dorsoduro, 3825/E, Venice (ITALY)
E-mail: sgiove@unive.it

1 Introduction

The use of fuzzy measures and the Choquet integral for Multi-Criteria Decision Analysis (MCDA) is briefly rewieved. Subsequently, an extension to group multi-criteria decision problem is suggested, showing how this approach is more suitable than weight averaging aggregation between a set of different decision makers, taking into account both the interaction among the criteria and the interaction among the decision makers.

2 Fuzzy measure and the Choquet integral

Several authors have proposed the use of fuzzy measures for MCDA [4], [5], [9], [10], [11]. To this aim, given a universe set X, a *fuzzy measure* on X is defined as a function $\mu : A \subseteq X \rightarrow [0,1]$ with the following properties

$$\mu(\varnothing) = 0, \ \mu(X) = 1, \ A \subset B \Rightarrow \mu(A) \leq \mu(B) \qquad (2.1)$$

In this context, if X is the set of criteria, the fuzzy measure defined on X represents the relative importance of the coalition of criteria belonging to A. Some other definition about fuzzy measures, $\forall A, B \subseteq X : A \cap B = \varnothing$, are

i)   *additive* $\mu(A \cup B) = \mu(A) + \mu(B)$

ii)   *superadditive* $\mu(A \cup B) \geq \mu(A) + \mu(B)$

iii)   *subadditive* $\mu(A \cup B) \leq \mu(A) + \mu(B)$

We observe that an additive measure implies independency between all the criteria belonging to A, while a superadditive means a renforcing effect for the coalition, the contrary for a subadditive measure. Let X be a finite set, μ a fuzzy measure, $\{x_{(i)}\}$ a permutation of index so that $x_{(i)} \leq \ldots \leq x_{(n)}$, and

This work is partially supported by M.U.R.S.T., research program of national interest "Model for the management of financial, insurance and operations risks".

$X_{(i)} = \{(i),...,(n)\}$, with $X_{(n+1)} = \varnothing$. The discrete Choquet integral $C_\mu(X)$ with respect to μ is defined as

$$C_\mu(X) = \sum_{i=1}^{n} x_{(i)}[\mu(X_{(i)} - \mu(X_{(i+1)})] \qquad (2.2)$$

The Choquet integral is a continuous non decreasing aggregator, satisfying some very useful properties for MCDA. Moreover, it can be verified that

i) weighted arithmetic mean, OWA operator, partial min. and max., can be obtained by the Choquet integral of a suitable fuzzy measure

ii) min. and max. are the lower and the upper bound for the Choquet integral.

Murofushi [11] proposed an example that we briefly resume. A factory is considered, where $X = \{x_1, x_2, .., \dot{x}_n\}$ represents the workers, and $g(x_i)$ is the number of working hours for the $i - th$ worker. Let $g(x_i) \leq ... \leq g(x_n)$. If $i \geq 2$, it is $g(x_i) - g(x_{i-1}) \geq 0$, and so

$$g(x_i) = g(x_1) + [g(x_2) - g(x_1)] + [g(x_3) - g(x_2)] + ... + [g(x_i) - g(x_{i-1})] \qquad (2.3)$$

Clearly, all the n workers in the set X work $g(x_1)$ hours, while $X - \{x_1\}$ workers work $g(x_2) - g(x_1)$ hours, $X - \{x_1, x_2\}$ work $g(x_3) - g(x_2)$ hours and so on, up to the last worker, x_n, that works $g(x_n) - g(x_{n-1})$ hours. If $\mu(A)$ represents the deal produced by the subset $A \subset X$, then the total deal produced is given by

$$J = \sum_{i=1}^{n} [g(x_i) - g(x_{i-1})]\mu(x_1, x_{i+1}.., x_n) \qquad (2.4)$$

After some manipulations, it is easy to recognize in (2.4) the Choquet integral (2.2).

Some indexes are defined in the current literature to compute the interactions among the criteria, we will just recall the *Shapley interaction index*, and the *Banzhaf interaction index* [10]. Let be $M = \{1,2,..,m\} T \subseteq M$, and $\{i,j\} \subseteq M$.

The Möbius transform coefficients is given by the set of the following 2^m coefficients, being $\{\alpha(S)|T \subseteq M\}$

$$\alpha(S) = \sum_{T \subseteq S} (-1)^{s-t} \mu(T), \quad \forall S \subseteq M \qquad (2.5)$$

that need to satisfy the following conditions:

$$\alpha(\varnothing) = 0, \quad \sum_{T \subseteq M} \alpha(T) = 1, \quad \sum_{T: i \in T \subseteq S} \alpha(T) \geq 0, \quad \forall S \subseteq M, \forall i \in S \qquad (2.6)$$

The inverse transform furnishes the Choquet integral, the Shapley index $I_\mu(S)$ (and the Banzhaf index) in function of its Möbius coefficients

$$C_\mu(X) = \sum_{T \subseteq M} \alpha(T) \wedge_{i \in T} x_i, \quad I_\mu(S) = \sum_{T \supseteq S} \frac{1}{t-s+1} \alpha(T), \quad \forall S \subseteq N \qquad (2.7)$$

To reduce the complexity of the model, in the so-called *second order* model we suppose interactions solely among couples of criteria, that is

$\alpha(S) = 0$, $\forall S : |S > 2|$. In this case, the Choquet integral for the i-th alternative can be written as

$$C_\mu(X) = \sum_{j \in M} \alpha(j) x_j + \sum_{\{j,l\} \in N} \alpha(j,l)(x_j \wedge x_l) \qquad (2.8)$$

while the inverse trasform, from (2.5), gives

$$\alpha(i) = \sum_{j \in N} \mu(j), \quad \alpha(i,j) = - \sum_{\{j,k\} \subset N} \mu(i,j) \qquad (2.9)$$

This is a particular case of the k-order model, for $k = 2$, introduced to reduce the numerical complexity [3], to avoid the exponentially growth with n of the number of $\alpha(S)$. Very often, only interactions between couples of criteria can be considered. For a second order model, the sign of $\alpha(i,j)$, if positive (negative), means synergy (redundancy) between the two criteria; if null, it means independence.

3 MCDA: Multi-Criteria Decision Analysis

Given a finite set of alternatives and a finite set of criteria, a multi-criteria decision problem consists in the ranking of the proposed alternatives[1]. Some approaches were proposed in the specialized literature, like the multi-attribute utility theory, outranking algorithms, and more recently, the use of the Choquet integral [3], [4], [9], [10]. To this aim, let $\{A_i\}$ $i = 1,..,n$ be a set of n alternatives, $\{C_i\}$ $i = 1,..,m$ a set of m criteria, and $X_i = \{c_1(i), c_2(i),.., c_m(i)\}$ the *profile* of criteria associated with the $i - th$ alternative. A multi-attribute utility function exists if and only if the mutual preference independence axiom is verified, but in real cases it cannot sometimes be accepted [10]. Then an additive utility function cannot be used, but, among other methods [2], the Choquet integral can be used, obtaining the scoring of the alternatives, $\{\sigma_i\}$, from (2.2) with $X = X_i$ and $C_\mu(X_i) = \sigma_i$. The values of the fuzzy measures can be obtained in a *data driven* approach from:

a) a set of data $\{X_i, \sigma_i\}$

b) three partial preorder (for alternatives, criteria, pairs of criteria)

c) the sign of $\alpha(i,j)$.

Then a linear programming problem can be formulated, for a detailed description the reader can refer to [10]. Let us remark that other alternative methods have been proposed with this aim, see [4], [8].

---

[1] In some cases, only the best alternative need to be selected. For a complete list of multi-criteria problems see [12].

4 GMCDA: Group Multi-Criteria Decision Analysis

Let us consider a *Group* Multi Criteria Decision Analysis, GMCDA, where K decision maker (DM) have to decide about N alternatives using M criteria [1], [6], [7]. In this paper, we suppose that the values of the criteria $c_j(i)$ are the same for every DM (for instance, they can be the results of some test measures). One of the most common approaches consists in assigning a set $\{\omega_{j,k}\} k = 1,.., K$ of positive normalized weighs, each of them taking the relative importance of the k-th DM into account, with respect to the j-th criterion. Thus, the values $c_j(i)$ are averaged with the weights $\omega_{j,k}$. But this simple approach presents the same drawbacks as regards the aggregation of criteria in (single) MCDA, pointed out in the Introduction. Thus, like for MCDA, it seems quite natural to apply the Choquet integral approach even to the set of DMs. For the sake of simplicity, a second order model will be here considered. Let be assigned

i) K fuzzy measures $\mu_C^k, k = 1,.., K$ defined on the set of criteria; let $\alpha_C^k(j), \alpha_C^k(i,j), i = 1,.., m; \ k = 1,.., K$ be the relative Möbius coefficients (2.9)

ii) an other fuzzy measure μ_D defined on the set of DMs, with Möbius coefficients $\alpha_D(k), \alpha_D(h,k), h, k = 1,.., K$

The same remarks discussed in the Chapter 2 can be formulated with regard to the measures μ_C^k, keeping in mind that the index k refers to the k-th DM. The algorithm proceeds in two phases. At first, for each DM, the values $c(i)$ are aggregated using the Choquet integral and the fuzzy measures μ_C^k, obtaining the values σ_i^k formed by the scores of the k-th DM with respect to the i-th alternative. Next the Choquet integral is computed again for each i-th alternative using the fuzzy measure μ_D, thus obtaining the global score of each alternative. In the first phase, the (2.8), can be written as

$$\sigma_i^k = \sum_{j=1}^{m} \alpha_C^k(j) c_j(i) + \sum_{j=1}^{m} \sum_{i=j+1}^{m} \alpha_C^k(j,l)(c_j(i) \wedge c_j(i)) \qquad (4.1)$$

Subsequently , we compute, again from (2.8), the score σ_i using μ

$$\sigma_i = \sum_{k=1}^{K} \alpha_D(k)\sigma_i^k + \sum_{k=1}^{K} \sum_{h=k+1}^{K} \alpha_D(h,k)(\sigma_i^h \wedge \sigma_i^k) \qquad (4.2)$$

It is quite natural to define two DMs as *synergic, redundant* or *independent* with respect to each other, if the sign of $\alpha_D(h,k)$ is positive, negative, or null respectively. Thus such analysis helps to obtain information about the *joint opinion* (and possible *coalitions*) of the members of the group of DMs. To this aim, we can extend the interaction indeces, for istance, the Shapley index in (2.7) becomes the *DM*-Shapley index defined as

$$I_\mu^{DM}(S) = \sum_{T \supseteq \Lambda} \frac{1}{t-\lambda+1}\alpha_D(T), \forall \Lambda \subseteq \{1,2,...,K\} \qquad (4.3)$$

Finally, the alternatives can be ranked on the basis of the scores σ_i. For a better understanding, let us consider the following example, with 3 criteria, 3 alternatives, 3 DMs. Let us suppose the following criteria-alternative table Tab.1 be assigned

	C_1	C_2	C_3
A_1	0.3	0.5	0.9
A_2	0.8	0.5	0.1
A_3	0.9	0.2	0.8

Tab. 1

Moreover, let the following tables Tab.2, Tab.3 contain the coefficients α_C^k (for the 3 DMs, $k = 1,2,3$), and α_D respectively

	$\alpha_C^k(1)$	$\alpha_C^k(2)$	$\alpha_C^k(3)$	$\alpha_C^k(1,2)$	$\alpha_C^k(1,3)$	$\alpha_C^k(2,3)$
$k = 1$	0.3	0.4	0.2	0.6	-0.4	-0.1
$k = 2$	0.1	0.6	0.1	0	0	0.2
$k = 3$	0.2	0.4	0.1	0.5	-0.2	0

Tab. 2

$\alpha_D(1)$	$\alpha_D(2)$	$\alpha_D(3)$	$\alpha_D(1,2)$	$\alpha_D(1,3)$	$\alpha_D(2,3)$
0.2	0.2	0.3	0.4	0	-0.1

Tab. 3

Applying (4.1) and using α_C^k we obtain the following values for $\{\sigma_i\}$

	D_1	D_2	D_3
A_1	0.48	0.52	0.14
A_2	0.71	0.41	0.1
A_3	0.29	0.33	0.08

Tab. 4

Finally, using α_D we obtain the score of the alternatives

A_1	A_2	A_3
0.48	0.53	0.30

Tab. 5

Note that being $\alpha_D(1,2) > 0$, $\alpha_D(1,3) = 0$, the first DM is synergic with the second one, and independent of the third one, while the second and the third DM are redundant with respect to each other, because $\alpha_D(2,3) < 0$. Finally, we remark that after some obvious modification, the same method proposed in [10] can be used to obtain both α_C^k and α_D from numerical data. In this case, not only one, but $(K+1)$ linear programming problems need to be solved, namely K problems for α_C^k, and one for α_D.

5 Conclusion

Fuzzy measure and the Choquet integral can be used to solve a MCDA problem, taking into account the mutual interactions among criteria and coalitions of criteria. In this paper, an extension of this method to GMCDA problem (Group Multi-Criteria Decision problem) has been proposed. In so doing, we can consider both interaction among criteria (for each DM) and interaction among DMs and coalition of DMs. To this aim, if K DMs exist, we need to specify $(K+1)$ fuzzy measure. To semplify the computational effort, a second order model has been considered, that consider iterations between couples of criteria and DMs. Solely one criteria-alternative table was supposed, the same for all the DMs, but the method can be easily extend to the general case, that is, one criteria-alternative table for each DM is assigned. In a further direction of research, the method will be studied into more details, and compared with other multi-criteria decision approaches.

Acknowledgements

The author is grateful to Mirco Scarpa for the development of numerical tests.

References

[1] Chen S.-J., Hwang C.-L., Hwang F.P., *Fuzzy multiple attribute decision making*, Springer-Verlag, Berlin, 1992.

[2] De Bets B., Van de Walle B., Dependency among alternatives and criteria in MCDM, *Proceedings of CIFT'94*, Trento (Italy), 1994, 80-85.

[3] Grabisch M., *k*-order additive discrete fuzzy measures and their representation, *Fuzzy Sets and Systems*, 92, 1997, 167-189.

[4] Grabisch M., The application of fuzzy integrals in multicriteria decision making, *Fuzzy Sets and Systems*, 92, 1997, 167-189.

[5] Greco S., Matarazzo B., Slowinski R., The axiomatic approach to multicriteria sorting, *Proceedings of XXIV A.M.A.S.E.S. Annual Meeting*, Padenghe sul Garda (Italy), 359-366.

[6] Herrera F., Herrera E., Verdegay J.L., A rational consensus model in group decision making using linguistic assessments, *Fuzzy Sets and Systems*, 88, 1997, 31-49.

[7] Kacprzyk J., Fedrizzi M., Nurmi H., Group decision making and consensus under fuzzy preferences and fuzzy majority, *Fuzzy Sets and Systems*, 49, 1992, 21-31.

[8] Klir G., Wang Z., Harmanec D., Constructing fuzzy measures in expert systems, *Fuzzy Sets and Systems*, 92, 1997, 251-264.

[9] Marichal J.L., Behavioral analysis of aggregation in multicriteria decision aid, *Trento'2000 - 3nd international Workshop on Preference and Decision*, Trento (Italy), 2000, 71-80.

[10] Marichal J.L., Roubens M., Dependence between criteria and multiple criteria decision aid, *Trento'98 - 2nd international Workshop on Preference and Decision*, Trento, Italy, 1998, 69-75.

[11] Murofushi T., Sugeno M., An interpretation of fuzzy measures and the Choquet integral as an integral with respect to a fuzzy measure, *Fuzzy Sets and Systems* 29, 1989, 201-227.

[12] Vincke P., *Multicriteria decision-aid*, Wiley & Sons, 1992, Baffins Lane, Chichester, England.

Section 5
Architectures and Algorithms

Solving Min Vertex Cover with Iterated Hopfield Networks*

A. Bertoni, P. Campadelli, G. Grossi

Dipartimento di Scienze dell'Informazione
Università degli Studi di Milano
via Comelico, 39 - 20135 Milano Italy

Abstract A neural approximation algorithm for the Min Vertex Cover
problem is designed and analyzed. This algorithm, having in input a
graphs $G = \langle V, E \rangle$, constructs a sequence of Hopfield networks such that
the attractor of the last one represents a minimal vertex cover of G.
We prove a theoretical upper bound to the sequence length and experimentally compare on random graphs the performances (quality of solutions, computation time) of the algorithm with those of other known
heuristics. The experiments show that the quality of the solutions found
by the neural algorithm is quite satisfactory.

Keywords: Min Vertex Cover, Hopfield networks, approximation algorithms.

1 Introduction

Computing the size of the smallest subset C of vertices in an undirected graph
$G = \langle V, E \rangle$, such that every edge in E is incident to al least one vertex in C
(Min Vertex Cover problem), is one of the first problems shown to be NP-hard [7].
Many problems of practical interest, in the area of traffic control or of electronic
devices design, can be expressed as vertex cover problems.

Many approximation algorithms for vertex cover have been designed and
analyzed; among them we recall here MM (Maximal Matching Algorithm) [3],
Greedy Algorithm, WG (Weighted Greedy Algorithm) [8], BE (Bar-Yehuda Even
Algorithm) [9].

It is known that this problem can be approximated with bounded ratio; in
fact some algorithms (i.e. MM, WG, BE) achieve a ratio of 2. On the other and,
it does not admit a polynomial approximation scheme and the best proved lower
bound for the ratio is at present $\frac{7}{6} - \varepsilon$, for all $\varepsilon > 0$ [4].

In this paper we present an algorithm for approximating Min Vertex Cover
based on the discrete-time Hopfield model [5], following an approach successfully
used for Max Clique problem [6]. Our algorithm constructs a finite sequence of
discrete Hopfield networks by using 2 alternating steps: the first consists in the
stabilization of the current network, the second in the construction of the next

* Supported by MURST project (60%): *Disegno e Analisi di Algoritmi.*

network by updating the weights. In particular, the weights are updated so that the energy function of $(t + 1)$-th network is the energy function of the t-th network augmented by a penalty factor depending on the edges not covered by the current attractor.

We show that this iterative process halts producing a minimal vertex cover and we prove that the length of the sequence of Hopfield networks is $O(|E|)$.

To experimentally evaluate the algorithm performance, we compare on random graphs our algorithm with MM, Greedy, WG and BE. We randomly generate graphs with size (the number of vertices n) ranging from 20 to 600, and density of edges low (10%), medium (50%) and high (90%), corresponding to the probability $p = 0.1, 0.5, 0.9$ of having and edge between a pair of vertices. The results obtained show that the neural algorithm performs better then the other heuristics.

2 Preliminaries

Let $G = \langle V, E \rangle$ be an arbitrary undirected graph, where $V = \{1, \ldots, n\}$ is the set of vertices and $E \subseteq V \oplus V$ (not ordered pairs) is the set of edges $e = \{i, j\}$. A vertex i is *incident* with an edge e if $i \in e$. A set $C \subseteq V$ of vertices is a *cover* of E (or a *vertex cover* of G) if every edge of E is incident with a vertex in C.

The Min Vertex Cover problem is a minimization problem which consist of finding a vertex cover of G of minimum size. Formally

Min Vertex Cover
INSTANCE: Graph $G = \langle V, E \rangle$.
SOLUTION: A vertex cover for G, i.e., a subset $V' \subseteq V$ such that, for each edge
$\{i, j\} \in E$, at least one of i and j belongs to V'.
MEASURE: Cardinality of the vertex cover, i.e., $|V'|$.

The *adjacency matrix* of G is the boolean matrix $A = (a_{ij})$, where $a_{ij} = 1$ if $\{i, j\} \in E$ and $a_{ij} = 0$ otherwise; the degree d_i of the vertex i is the number of edges incident with i.

Since in the next section we present an approximation algorithm for Min Vertex Cover based on the discrete Hopfield model, we briefly recall some notations. A Hopfield network [5] $\mathcal{R}$ of n neurons with states in $\{-1, 1\}$ is described by the pair $\mathcal{R} = \langle W, \lambda \rangle$, where $W = (w_{ij})_{n \times n}$ is a symmetric matrix with $w_{ii} = 0$ $(i = 1, \ldots, n)$, and $\lambda = (\lambda_i)_{1 \times n}$ is a vector. The matrix W is called *weights matrix* and the vector λ is called *thresholds vector*. In this paper we will consider weights matrix and thresholds vector with integer components.

For this model we consider the discrete-time dynamics with *sequential* updating. Let $S_i(t)$ be the state of the neuron i at time t, the dynamics is formally described as follows:

$$S_i(t+1) = \text{HS}\left(\sum_{1\le j<i} w_{ij}S_j(t+1) + \sum_{i<j\le n} w_{ij}S_j(t) - \lambda_i\right) \quad i = 1,\ldots,n, \quad (1)$$

where $\text{HS}(x) = 1$ if $x \ge 0$, 0 otherwise.

Equations (1), given the initial condition $\mathbf{S}(0) = \mathbf{S}_0$, describe a unique trajectory $\{\mathbf{S}(t)\}_{t\ge 0}$.

To every network $\mathcal{R} = \langle W, \lambda \rangle$ can be associated the following Lyapunov function called *energy*:

$$E_{\mathcal{R}}(S_1,\ldots,S_n) = -\frac{1}{2}\sum_{i\ne j} w_{ij}S_iS_j + \sum_i \lambda_iS_i.$$

Known results concerning Hopfield networks can be summarize in the following:

Theorem 1. *The trajectory $\{\mathbf{S}(t)\}_{t\ge 0}$ generated by the Hopfield network $\mathcal{R} = \langle W, \lambda \rangle$ with initial condition $\mathbf{S}_0$ admits an attractor $\tilde{\mathbf{y}}$, and the length $l_{\mathcal{R},\mathbf{S}_0}$ of the transient is bounded by*

$$l_{\mathcal{R},\mathbf{S}_0} \le \frac{1}{2}\left(\max_{\mathbf{S}}\{E_{\mathcal{R}}(\mathbf{S})\} - \min_{\mathbf{S}}\{E_{\mathcal{R}}(\mathbf{S})\}\right).$$

We will say that $\tilde{\mathbf{y}}$ is the attractor *of $\mathcal{R}$ initialized by $\mathbf{S}_0$.*

3 A Neural Algorithm Based on the Hopfield Model

In this Section we introduce a discrete neural algorithm to solve the Min Vertex Cover problem on arbitrary undirected graphs and analyze its computational complexity.

Given a graph $G = \langle\{1,\ldots,n\}, E\rangle$, let us consider the quadratic function $\phi : \{0,1\}^n \to \mathbb{N}$, defined as follows:

$$\phi(x_1,\ldots,x_n) = \sum_{\{i,j\}\in E}(x_i + x_j - x_ix_j) = -\sum_{i<j}a_{ij}x_ix_j + \sum_i d_ix_i, \quad (2)$$

The more interesting property of (2) is stated in the following

Proposition 1. *Let $G = \langle V, E \rangle$ be a graph, $\phi : \{0,1\}^n \to \mathbb{N}$ the function defined in (2), $C \subseteq V$ and $c = (c_1,\ldots,c_n)$ the characteristic vector of C. Then the following statements are equivalent:*

1. *C is a cover for G;*
2. *$\phi(c_1,\ldots,c_n) = \max_{\mathbf{x}\in\{0,1\}^n} \phi(x_1,\ldots,x_n) = |E|$.*

As a consequence, the Min Vertex Cover problem can now be expressed as a problem of maximization of a linear objective function subject to quadratic constraints:

$$\text{maximize} \quad \Psi_G(\mathbf{x}) = -\alpha \sum_{i=1}^{n} x_i$$
$$\text{subject to} \quad \Omega_G(\mathbf{x}) = -\sum_{i<j} a_{ij} x_i x_j + \sum_i d_i x_i = |E| \qquad \mathbf{x} \in \{0,1\}^n, \tag{P}$$

where $\alpha \geq 0$ is an integer constant.

Now, let us show an algorithm that finds approximate solutions for (P), based on a sequence of discrete neural networks. The neurons $\{1, \ldots, n\}$ of each network are the vertices of G and they assume state in $\{0,1\}$.

The sequence $\{\mathcal{R}_k\}_{k \geq 0}$ is inductively defined by

1. $\mathcal{R}_0$ is the network with energy function $\Phi_0(\mathbf{y}) = \Psi_G(\mathbf{y}) + \Omega_G(\mathbf{y})$, and $\tilde{\mathbf{y}}^{(0)}$ is the attractor of $\mathcal{R}_0$ initialized with $(0, \ldots, 0)$;
2. let $\tilde{\mathbf{y}}^{(k)}$ be the attractor of the network $\mathcal{R}_k$ initialized with $\tilde{\mathbf{y}}^{(k-1)}$ $(k > 0)$; $\mathcal{R}_k$ is the network with energy function

$$\Phi_k(\mathbf{y}) = \Phi_{k-1}(\mathbf{y}) + \sum_{\substack{\{i,j\} \in E \\ \tilde{y}_i^{(k)} = \tilde{y}_j^{(k)} = 0}} (y_i + y_j - y_i y_j). \tag{3}$$

For all k, the set $\left\{ \{i,j\} \mid \{i,j\} \in E \text{ and } \tilde{y}_i^{(k)} = \tilde{y}_j^{(k)} = 0 \right\}$ is called the set of *violated constraints* by the attractor $\tilde{\mathbf{y}}^{(k)}$.

We can sketch now the approximation algorithm called COVER-HOPFIELD-NETS (CHN for short):

Algorithm CHN

Input: a graph $G = \langle V, E \rangle$, an integer α;
    $\mathcal{R}_0 \;\; := \;$ Hopfield network with energy $\Phi_0(\mathbf{y}) = \Psi_G(\mathbf{y}) + \Omega_G(\mathbf{y})$;
    $\tilde{\mathbf{y}}^{(0)} := \;$ attractor of $\mathcal{R}_0$ initialized with $(0, \ldots, 0)$;
    $F_0 \;\; := \; \left\{ \{i,j\} \mid \{i,j\} \in E \text{ and } \tilde{y}_i^{(0)} = \tilde{y}_j^{(0)} = 0 \right\}$;
    $k \;\;\;\; := \; 0$;
    while $[\;\; F_k \neq \varnothing \;\;]$ **do**
        $k \;\;\;\; := \; k + 1$;
        $\mathcal{R}_k \;\; := \;$ Hopfield network with energy

$$\Phi_k(\mathbf{y}) = \Phi_{k-1}(\mathbf{y}) + \sum_{\{i,j\} \in F_{k-1}} (y_i + y_j - y_i y_j);$$

        $\tilde{\mathbf{y}}^{(k)} := \;$ attractor of $\mathcal{R}_k$ initialized with $\tilde{\mathbf{y}}^{(k-1)}$;
        $F_k \;\; := \; \left\{ \{i,j\} \mid \{i,j\} \in E \text{ and } \tilde{y}_i^{(k)} = \tilde{y}_j^{(k)} = 0 \right\}$;
        $C \;\;\;\; := \; \left\{ i \mid \tilde{y}_i^{(k)} = 1 \right\}$;
Output: a minimal vertex cover C of G.

The algorithm consists of two alternating phases: one is the evolution of the current network, the other is the weights updating when the current network has reached an attractor.

As far as the analysis of CHN is concerned, the following result proves that the algorithm converges, i.e., the Hopfield networks sequence is finite:

Theorem 2. *For every input graph* $G = \langle V, E \rangle$, *the algorithm* CHN *outputs a minimal cover of* G *after* $\alpha \cdot |E|$ *iterations of the* **while** *cycle at most.*

Proof. Let $A = (a_{ij})$ be the adjacency matrix of G and d_i the degree of the vertex i. Let Φ_k be the energy function of the network $\mathcal{R}_k$ constructed at the k-th step. Then:

$$\Phi_k(y_1, \ldots, y_n) = -\sum_{i<j} w_{ij}^{(k)} y_i y_j + \sum_i \left(\lambda_i^{(k)} - \alpha \right) y_i,$$

for suitable $w_{ij}^{(k)}$ and $\lambda_i^{(k)}$.

By induction it is easy to prove:

1. if $\{i, j\} \in E^c$ then $w_{ij}^{(k)} = 0$ for all $k = 1, \ldots, n$;
2. if $\{i, j\} \in E$ then

$$0 < w_{ij}^{(0)} \le \cdots \le w_{ij}^{(k)} \le \cdots; \tag{4}$$

3.

$$\lambda_i^{(k)} = \sum_{j=1}^{n} w_{ij}^{(k)}, \qquad k = 1, \ldots, n. \tag{5}$$

Since $\bar{\mathbf{y}}^{(k)}$ is the attractor of the network $\mathcal{R}_k$ initialized with $\bar{\mathbf{y}}^{(k-1)}$, then for any $i = 1, \ldots, n$ and by (5):

$$\bar{y}_i^{(k)} = HS \left[-\sum_s w_{is}^{(k)} \bar{y}_s^{(k)} + \lambda_i^{(k)} - \alpha \right]$$

$$= HS \left[\sum_s w_{is}^{(k)} (1 - \bar{y}_s^{(k)}) - \alpha \right]. \tag{6}$$

Under the hypothesis that $\{i, j\} \in E$ and $\bar{y}_i^{(k)} = \bar{y}_j^{(k)} = 0$, it holds:

$$w_{ij}^{(k)} = w_{ij}^{(k-1)} + 1; \tag{7}$$

and

$$w_{ij}^{(k)} \le \alpha. \tag{8}$$

In order to prove (8) observe that, if $\{i, j\} \in E$ and $\bar{y}_i^{(k)} = \bar{y}_j^{(k)} = 0$, by (6) we have:

$$w_{ij}^{(k)} + \sum_{s \neq j} w_{is}^{(k)} (1 - \bar{y}_s^{(k)}) - \alpha < 0. \tag{9}$$

Since $\sum_{s \neq j} w_{is}^{(k)}(1 - \tilde{y}_s^{(k)}) \geq 0$, we conclude $w_{ij}^{(k)} \leq \alpha$.

Now, $\mathcal{R}_k \neq \mathcal{R}_{k-1}$ if and only if there is $\{i, j\} \in E$ such that $\tilde{y}_i^{(k)} = \tilde{y}_j^{(k)} = 0$. Therefore, by (7) and (8), the number of networks constructed by the algorithm is at most $\sum_{\{i,j\} \in E} \alpha = \alpha \cdot |E|$.

Let us show now that the output C is a mimimal cover.

Let $\tilde{y}^{(h)}$ be the attractor of the last network $\mathcal{R}_h$, so that $C = \left\{ i \mid \tilde{y}_i^{(h)} = 1 \right\}$ and $\tilde{y}_i^{(h)} = HS\left[\sum_s w_{is}^{(h)}(1 - \tilde{y}_s^{(h)}) - \alpha \right]$ for all $i = 1, \ldots, n$. Because of the termination condition, we know that

$$\left\{ \{i, j\} \mid \{i, j\} \in E \text{ and } \tilde{y}_i^{(h)} = \tilde{y}_j^{(h)} = 0 \right\} = \varnothing,$$

this implies that C is a cover of G.

Let us suppose that C is not minimal, i.e., there is $v \in C$ such that if $a_{vs} = 1$ implies $s \in C$.

Then:

$$1 = \tilde{y}_v^{(h)} = HS\left[\sum_{s \notin C} w_{is}^{(h)}(1 - \tilde{y}_s^{(h)}) - \alpha \right] = HS[-\alpha] = 0$$

□

4 Experimental Results

In this section the behavior of CHN is experimentally analyzed and compared with that of others heuristics for Min Vertex Cover on p-random graphs. A p-random graphs of size n is a graph $\langle V, E \rangle$ where $V = \{1, \ldots, n\}$ and E is obtained selecting $\{i, j\}$ as edge with probability p $(1 \leq i < j \leq n)$.

First of all, we discuss the dependence of the performances of CHN on parameter α: small values of α (w.r.t. n) give fast execution time, but poor performances in terms of solution quality. On the contrary, according to the theoretic results, large values of α cause large execution time without significantly increase the performances. This behavior has been observed in the following experiment: for various values of n and p $(10 \leq n \leq 500, p =0.1, 0.5, 0.9)$, 30 p-random graphs have been generated and fixed; for all α $(1 \leq \alpha \leq n)$ the average size $C_{\mathsf{CHN}}(\alpha)$ of the vertex cover found by CHN has been computed. In Figure 1 results for $n=100$ and $p = \frac{1}{2}$ are shown.

Experimental results give evidence that:

1. if $\alpha < \frac{n}{10}$ the quality of the solutions is poor;
2. if $\alpha > \frac{n}{10}$ the quality of the solutions dos not significantly increase.

The CHN algorithm (with $\alpha = \frac{n}{10}$) has been experimentally compared on random graphs with other heuristics such as MM (Maximal Matching Algorithm)

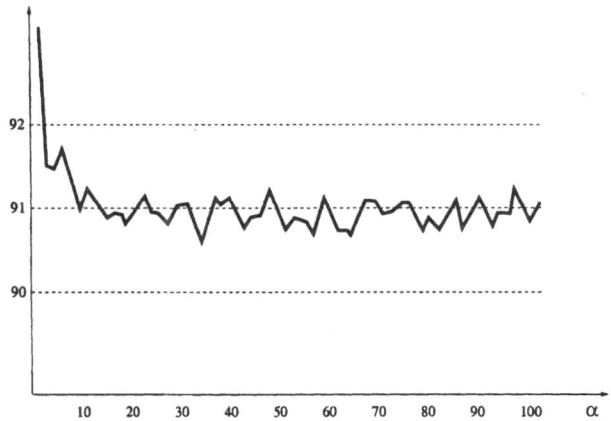

Figure1. Dependence of the performances of CHN on parameter α.

[3], **Greedy** Algorithm, **WG** (Weighted **Greedy** Algorithm) [8], **BE** (Bar-Yehuda Even Algorithm) [9].

The **Greedy** algorithm repeatedly picks and edge that has not yet covered, and places one of its endpoints in the current covering set. This algorithm does not achieve any bounded ratio: on the contrary, the modified **Greedy** algorithm **WG** obtains ratio 2. The basic idea is to assign weights to the vertices: each time a vertex is placed in the cover, each of its neighbors has its weight reduced by an amount equal to the ratio of the selected vertex's current weight and degree. Another heuristic that achieves ratio 2 is **MM** algorithm: pick a maximal matching M in the graph and place both endpoints of edges in M into the cover. Last heuristic we consider is **BE**, obtained starting from a relaxation of an integer programming formulation of min vertex cover; this algorithm achieves a ratio $2 - \frac{\log \log n}{2 \log n}$.

These algorithms have been compared among them both in the quality of solutions and in computation time. They have been implemented in Java and executed on a workstation with Pentium processor 300 MHz.

As regards the solution quality, the **CHN** algorithm performs better than the other, while the worse performances are given by the algorithms **MM** and **BE** (see Figure 2)

As regards the computation time, **CHN**, **Greedy**, **WG** and **BE** have the same order of magnitude (even if **CHN** is slower for dense graphs), while **MM** is faster (see Table 1).

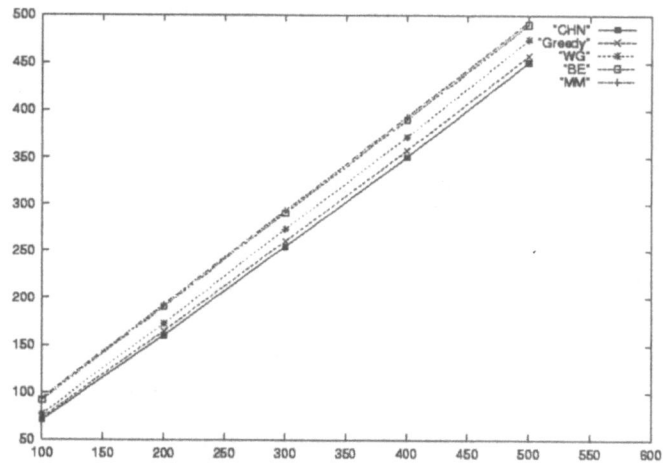

Figure2. Average solution size found by the algorithms CHN, Greedy, WG, BE and MM on 0.1-random graphs, n =100, 200, 300, 400, 500.

Table1. Average execution times on p-random graphs of 600 vertices.

Algorithms	$n = 600$, $p = 0.1$	$n = 600$, $p = 0.5$
CHN	611 sec.	2440 sec.
Greedy	414 sec.	412 sec.
WG	414 sec.	413 sec.
BE	1110 sec.	900 sec.
MM	3 sec.	3 sec.

5   Conclusions

In this paper a neural heuristic for the Min Vertex Cover problem is proposed and experimentally compared with other known heuristics. The results obtained on random graphs show that the neural algorithm find better solutions against a little increment of computation time.

This is quite surprising since it is not an ad-hoc heuristic for Min Vertex Cover (like **BE** or **WG**), but a more general approximation technique that can be applied to other hard constrained problems, such as Max Clique [1].

References

1. A. Bertoni, P. Campadelli, and G. Grossi. A neural algorithm for the maximum clique problem: Analysis, experiments and circuit implementation. *Algoritmica*. (To appear).

2. M. R. Garey and D. S. Johnson. *Computers and Intractability. A Guide to the Theory of NP-Completeness*. W. H. Freeman & Co., San Francisco, CA, 1979.

3. F. Gavril. Quoted in [2], pag. 134.

4. J. Håstad. Some optimal inapproximability results. In M. Sipser, editor, *Proceedings of the 29th ACM Symposium on the Theory of Computation*, pages 1–10, New York, NY, 1997. ACM Press.

5. J. J. Hopfield. Neural networks and physical systems with emergent collective computational abilities. *Proceedings of the National Academy of Sciences of the United States of America*, 79(8):2554–2558, 1982.

6. A. Jagota. Approximating maximum clique with a Hopfield network. Technical Report 92-33, Department of Computer Science, SUNY Buffalo, December 1992.

7. R. M. Karp. *Reducibility among Combinatorial Problems*, pages 85–103. Complexity of Computer Computations. Plenum Press, New York, 1972.

8. Clarkson K. L. A modification of the greedy algorithm for vertex cover. *Information Processing Letters*, (16):23–25, 1983.

9. Bar-Yehuda R. and S. Even. A local-ratio theorem for approximating the weighted vertex cover problem. *Annals of Discrete Mathematics*, (25):27–45, 1985.

Recursive Processing of Directed Acyclic Graphs

M. Bianchini, M. Gori, *IEEE Fellow*, and F. Scarselli
Dipartimento di Ingegneria dell'Informazione, Università di Siena
Via Roma, 56 — 53100 Siena (ITALY)
e–mail: {monica,marco,franco}@dii.unisi.it

Abstract

Recursive neural networks are a new connectionist model particularly tailored to process Directed Positional Acyclic Graphs (DPAGs) [4].
While this assumption is reasonable in some applications, it introduces
unnecessary constraints in others. In this paper, it is shown that the
constraint on the ordering can be relaxed by using an appropriate weight
sharing, that guarantees the independence of the network output with
respect to the permutations of the arcs leaving from each node. Some
theoretical properties of the proposed architecture are given, able to guarantee the approximation capabilities are maintained, despite of the weight
sharing.

1 Introduction

Recursive neural networks [4] are a new connectionist model particularly suited
for processing graphs. They turn out to be interesting in those domains in which
the information involved is organized in entities and relationships among entities. However, according to the model initially proposed in [4], recursive neural
networks can only deal with limited families of graphs, like Directed Positional
Acyclic Graphs (DPAGs) and Directed Ordered Acyclic Graphs (DOAGs). In
the case of DPAGs, each arc coming from a node has an assigned and specific position. In other words, any rearrangement of the children of any node
produces a different graph. While such an assumption is useful in some applications, in others it introduces an unnecessary constraint on the representation.
For example, this hypothesis is not suitable for the representation of a chemical
compound and might not be adequate for several pattern recognition problems.

In this paper we show how the constraint on the ordering can be relaxed by
introducing an appropriate weight sharing in the recursive neural networks, in
order to guarantee the independence of the network output from the permutations of the arcs of each node. Moreover, we discuss the theoretical properties
of the proposed architecture with particular attention to its computational capabilities.

2 Notation

In the following, a graph G is defined as a triple $(V, A, \mathcal{L})$, where V is the set of nodes, $A \subseteq V^2$ is the set of arcs, $\mathcal{L} : V \to L$ is a labeling function, and $L \subset R^m$ is a finite set of labels. Given any node $v \in V$, ch$[v]$ represents the set of *children* of v. The *outdegree* of v, od$[v]$, is the cardinality of ch$[v]$, and $o = \max_{v \in V}\{\text{od}[v]\}$ is the maximal outdegree. The presence of an arc (v, w) in a labeled graph shows the existence of some sort of causal link between the variables contained in v and w.

In this paper, we consider the class of Directed Acyclic Graphs (DAGs), where there is not any path connecting a node to itself and the arcs are directed, i.e. $(v, w) \neq (w, v)$. DPAGs differ from DAGs since an ordering is defined on the children of each node by an injective function $o_v : ch[v] \to \{1, \ldots, o\}$, which assigns a position $o_v(c)$ to each child c of v. The position of the children is a distinctive feature of a DPAG, such that two DPAGs are equal only when a bijective correspondence exists, not only between nodes and arcs, but also between the position of all the children of each node. From a notational point of view, a DPAG is represented by a quadruplet $(V, A, \mathcal{L}, O)$, where $O = \{o_1, \ldots, o_{|V|}\}$ is the set of functions defining the positions of the children. Moreover, in DAGs the children of a node v are correctly denoted by the set $ch[v]$, whereas for DPAGs they can be more properly represented by a fixed dimension vector $[v_1, \ldots, v_o]$, where some components may be null when no child is associated to the corresponding position. Finally, we assume that all the graphs have a supersource. A supersource s is a node from which all the other nodes can be reached.

3 Recursive processing of DPAGs

Recursive neural networks process a DPAG G following the scheme described in Fig. 1. The recursive neural network is unfolded through the graph structure, producing the *encoding* network. At each node v, the *state* $\mathbf{X}_v$ is computed by a *transition* function of the input label $\mathbf{U}_v$ and the state of its children $\mathbf{X}_{v_1}, \ldots, \mathbf{X}_{v_o}$:

$$\mathbf{X}_v = f(\mathbf{X}_{v_1}, \ldots, \mathbf{X}_{v_o}, \mathbf{U}_v, \theta_f).$$

θ_f is a vector of parameters, being θ_f independent of node v [1]. In other words, the computation of the state at each node is carried out according to a bottom-up strategy, i.e. $\mathbf{X}_v$ is calculated only when all the states of the children of v are available. When the i-th child does not exist ($v_i = null$), $\mathbf{X}_{v_i}$ is assigned with a predefined state $\mathbf{X}_{null}$.

At the supersource also an *output* function is evaluated, by a feedforward network called the *output* network:

$$\mathbf{Y}_s = g(\mathbf{X}_s, \theta_g).$$

---

[1]In this case, we say that the recursive neural network is *stationary* [4].

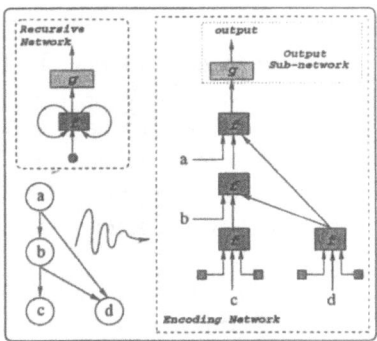

Figure 1: The *encoding* and the *output* networks associated to a DPAG. The *recursive neural network* is unfolded through the structure of the DPAG.

The parametric representations of f and g can be implemented by a variety of neural network models. In the case of a three layered perceptron $\mathcal{N}$, with sigmoidal activation functions in the hidden units and linear activation functions in the output units, f is the network input–output function $f_{\mathcal{N}}$:

$$f_{\mathcal{N}}(\mathbf{X}_{v_1}, \dots, \mathbf{X}_{v_o}, \mathbf{U}_v, \theta_f) = \mathbf{V} \cdot \vec{\sigma} \left(\sum_{k=1}^{o} \mathbf{A}_k \cdot \mathbf{X}_{v_k} + \mathbf{B} \cdot \mathbf{U}_v + \mathbf{C} \right) + \mathbf{D}, \quad (1)$$

where $\vec{\sigma}$ is a vectorial sigmoidal function and the network weights θ_f collect $\mathbf{A}_k \in R^{q,n}$, $k = 1, \dots, o$, $\mathbf{B} \in R^{q,m}$, $\mathbf{C} \in R^q$, $\mathbf{D} \in R^n$, and $\mathbf{V} \in R^{n,q}$. Here, m is the dimension of the label space, n the dimension of the state space, and q represents the number of hidden neurons. A similar equation holds for g:

$$g_{\mathcal{N}}(\mathbf{X}_s, \theta_g) = \mathbf{W} \cdot \vec{\sigma} \left(\mathbf{E} \cdot \mathbf{X}_s + \mathbf{F} \right) + \mathbf{G},$$

θ_g collects $\mathbf{E} \in R^{q',n}$, $\mathbf{F} \in R^{q'}$, $\mathbf{G} \in R^r$, and $\mathbf{W} \in R^{r,q'}$.

Thus, a recursive neural network implements a function $h : \text{DPAGs} \to R^r$, where $h(G) = \mathbf{Y}_s$. Formally, $h = g \circ \tilde{f}$, where $\tilde{f}(G) = \mathbf{X}_s$ denotes the process that takes a graph and returns the state at the supersource. In [5, 1], recursive neural networks are proved to be able to approximate, in probability, any function on trees. More precisely, given a set $T \subset \text{DPAGs}$ of positional trees[2], a function $t : T \to R^r$, a probability measure P on T, and any real ε, there is a function h, realized by a recursive neural network, such that $P(|h(G) - t(G)| \geq \varepsilon) \leq \varepsilon$. The above result also characterizes the approximation capabilities of recursive neural networks w.r.t. the functions on DPAGs [2].

4   Recursive processing of DAGs

Recursive neural networks have been designed to deal directly with DPAGs. Function f naturally considers the position of each child of a node, because the

---

[2]A positional tree is a DPAG where each node has only one parent.

child state has a particular position in the input of f. A simple approach allows us to process also DAGs: each input DAG $(V, A, \mathcal{L})$ is mapped into a DPAG $(V, A, \mathcal{L}, O)$, which is processed instead of the original DAG. The transformation only requires to assign a position to the children of each node. However, such an assignment, which is arbitrary, affects the result of the computation.

In order to avoid this situation, f must produce the same result despite of the position assigned to the children. Formally, f must satisfy the equality

$$f(\mathbf{X}_1, ..., \mathbf{X}_o, \mathbf{U}, \theta_f) = f(\mathbf{X}_{\pi(1)}, ..., \mathbf{X}_{\pi(o)}, \mathbf{U}, \theta_f),$$ (2)

for any permutation π, and any $\mathbf{X}_1, ..., \mathbf{X}_o \in R^n$, $\mathbf{U} \in R^m$, θ_f.

In the following, we show how a three layered neural network, appropriately constrained, can be used for this purpose. The idea we adopt is related to the one proposed by LeCun [6] for convolutional neural networks. Convolutional neural networks are used in image processing for their ability to be insensitive to image translations.

Example 1 Let us consider a three layered network with two input units, $2q$ hidden units, and one output unit. The i–th hidden neuron contributes to the output of the network by a value $v_i \sigma(a_{i,1} x_1 + a_{i,2} x_2 + c_i)$, where x_1, x_2 are the inputs, and $a_{i,1}, a_{i,2}, c_i, v_i$ are the network parameters. Suppose that, for the hidden unit j, the input–to–hidden layer weights are exchanged ($a_{j,1} = a_{i,2}, a_{j,2} = a_{i,1}$), whereas other weights are the same ($c_j = c_i, v_j = v_i$). Therefore, the contribution to the network output due to i and j is:

$$h_i(x_1, x_2) = v_i \sigma(a_{i,1} x_1 + a_{i,2} x_2 + c_i) + v_i \sigma(a_{i,2} x_1 + a_{i,1} x_2 + c_i),$$

where $h_i(x_1, x_2) = h_i(x_2, x_1)$, which is a special case of constraint (2). If such a behavior is shared by q pairs of particularly selected hidden units, the whole output of the network can be calculated as

$$f(x_1, x_2) = \frac{1}{2} \sum_{i=1}^{2q} h_i(x_1, x_2),$$ (3)

where f fulfills the constraint (2).

The arguments of Example 1 can be easily applied to more general architectures, i.e. to networks with many inputs and many outputs. In fact, let $\mathcal{P} = \{\pi_1, ..., \pi_p\}$, $p = o!$, be the set of all the permutation functions on $\{1, ..., o\}$. The network we consider, $\mathcal{SN}$, has the same parameters ($\theta_f = (\mathbf{A}_1, ..., \mathbf{A}_o, \mathbf{B}, \mathbf{C}, \mathbf{D}, \mathbf{V})$) as the network $\mathcal{N}$ in (1), but those parameters are shared among a number of connections. $\mathcal{SN}$ has qp hidden units. The hidden–to–output connection weights are $\overline{\mathbf{V}} \in R^{n,qp}$, the input–to–hidden connection weights are $\overline{\mathbf{A}} \in R^{qp,no+m}$, the hidden thresholds are $\overline{\mathbf{C}} \in R^{qp}$, and the output threshold are $\overline{\mathbf{D}} \in R^n$, where

$$\overline{\mathbf{A}} = \left(\begin{array}{ccc|c} \mathbf{A}_{\pi_1(1)} & \cdots & \mathbf{A}_{\pi_1(o)} & \mathbf{B} \\ \vdots & & \vdots & \vdots \\ \mathbf{A}_{\pi_p(1)} & \cdots & \mathbf{A}_{\pi_p(o)} & \mathbf{B} \end{array} \right)$$ (4)

$$\overline{\mathbf{C}} = (\mathbf{C}, ..., \mathbf{C})' \quad \overline{\mathbf{D}} = p\mathbf{D} \quad \overline{\mathbf{V}} = (\mathbf{V}, ..., \mathbf{V})$$

Moreover, let $\mathbf{I}_v = (\mathbf{X}'_{v_1}, \ldots, \mathbf{X}'_{v_o}, \mathbf{U}'_v)'$ be, where "$'$" is the transpose operator. Intuitively, for each hidden unit in $\mathcal{N}$, there are p units in $\mathcal{SN}$ sharing the same parameters. It is easy to verify that the output of $\mathcal{SN}$ is:

$$
\begin{aligned}
f_{\mathcal{SN}}(\mathbf{X}_{v_1}, \ldots, \mathbf{X}_{v_o}, \mathbf{U}_v, \theta_f) &= \overline{\mathbf{V}} \cdot \overline{\sigma}\left(\overline{\mathbf{A}} \cdot \mathbf{I}_v + \overline{\mathbf{C}}\right) + \overline{\mathbf{D}} \\
&= \sum_{i=1}^{p} f_{\mathcal{N}}(\mathbf{X}_{\pi_i(v_1)}, \ldots, \mathbf{X}_{\pi_i(v_o)}, \mathbf{U}_v, \theta_f). \quad (5)
\end{aligned}
$$

5 Theoretical results

It is a crucial matter to study computational capabilities of the model we have proposed. In order to give to this problem a formal setup, let $\mathcal{CF}(K)$ be the set of continuous functions $f : R^{no+m} \to R^n$ that fulfill (2) on a compact set $K \subseteq R^{no+m}$. Moreover, suppose that $\mathcal{CF}(K)$ is equipped with the supremum norm $L_\infty(K)$. The following theorems assert that the network $\mathcal{SN}$ always fulfills our initial project (see [3] for the proofs).

Theorem 1 Any network $\mathcal{SN}$ satisfies (2), i.e. $f_{\mathcal{SN}} \in \mathcal{CF}(K)$ for any K.

On the other hand, the particular weight sharing schema that constrains $\mathcal{SN}$ does not limit the computational capabilities of the network. In fact, the following theorem shows that our model can approximate any function in $\mathcal{CF}(K)$.

Theorem 2 For any compact set K, any function $l \in \mathcal{CF}(K)$, and any precision $\varepsilon > 0$, there is a network $\mathcal{SN}$, whose input–output function $f_{\mathcal{SN}}$ is such that $\|l - f_{\mathcal{SN}}\|_{L_\infty(K)} \le \varepsilon$.

Theorem 2 allows us to extend the results on approximation capabilities of recursive neural networks from DPAGs to DAGs. In fact, the following theorem proves that the proposed model has the same computational capabilities of recursive neural networks, with the only difference that, of course, the domain consists of DAGs instead of DPAGs.

Theorem 3 Given a set of trees $T \subset \text{DAGs}$, a function $t : T \to R^r$, a probability measure P on T, and a real ε, there is a function $h_{\mathcal{SN}}$, realized by a recursive neural network $\mathcal{SN}$, with shared weights, such that $P(|h_{\mathcal{SN}}(G) - t(G)| \ge \varepsilon) \le \varepsilon$.

Finally, notice that, according to our notation, graphs can have only a finite set of labels. However, Theorem 2 can be easily extended to the case of rational and even real labels. Moreover, the approximation w.r.t. a probability measure can be replaced by the approximation w.r.t. the superior norm, but in this case the height of trees must be bounded and the label set must be finite.

Remark 1 The hidden units of $\mathcal{SN}$ are $qp = qo!$. Thus, this method cannot be applied to DAGs with a large outdegree o, due to the exponential growth of the number of the hidden units. This may be an important limit for some applications, but in many other cases it is possible to build a domain that contains graphs with a small outdegree. On the other hand, the number of hidden units of $S\mathcal{N}$ depends linearly on q, which means that the dimension of the states and the dimension of the labels affect $S\mathcal{N}$ as they affect $\mathcal{N}$. Moreover, the difficulty in processing DAGs with a large number of children is a characteristic of the recursive model and cannot be overcome easily. When $\mathcal{N}$ is used in place of $S\mathcal{N}$, $\mathcal{N}$ has to learn constraint (2) from examples. This necessarily requires a number of examples that grows exponentially with o, such that the computational burden due to the dimension of $S\mathcal{N}$ is transformed into a computational burden due to the number of examples. A solution which may alleviate this problem is discussed in [3].

6 Conclusions

In this paper, we presented a new recursive network model that allows us to process Directed Acyclic Graphs. The feedforward neural network that realizes the transition function has a special architecture with shared weights, which yields the independence with respect to the ordering of the children. Moreover, it was proved that the model can approximate any function on DAGs in probability up to any degree of precision.

References

[1] M. Bianchini, M. Gori, and F. Scarselli. Recursive networks: An overview of theoretical results. In M. Marinaro and R. Tagliaferri, editors, *Neural Nets — WIRN '99*, pages 237–242. Springer, Vietri (Salerno, Italy), 1999.

[2] M. Bianchini, M. Gori, and F. Scarselli. Theoretical properties of recursive networks with linear neurons. Technical Report DII–31/99, Dip. di Ingegneria dell'Informazione, Università di Siena, Siena, Italy, 1999. submitted to *IEEE Trans. on Neural Networks*.

[3] M. Bianchini, M. Gori, and F. Scarselli. Processing directed acyclic graphs with recursive neural networks. Submitted to *"IEEE Transactions on Neural Networks"*, 2000.

[4] P. Frasconi, M. Gori, and A. Sperduti. A general framework for adaptive processing of data structures. *IEEE Transactions on Neural Networks*, 9(5):768–786, September 1998.

[5] B. Hammer. Approximation capabilities of folding networks. In *ESANN '99*, pages 33–38, Bruges, (Belgium), April 1999.

[6] Y. leCun, L. Bottou, Y. Bengio, and P. Haffner. Gradient-based learning applied to document recognition. *Proceedings of the IEEE*, 86(11):2278–2324, 1998.

Detecting uncertainty regions for characterizing classification problems

Gian Paolo Drago, Marco Muselli

Istituto per i Circuiti Elettronici - CNR

via De Marini, 6 - 16149 Genova, Italy

Abstract

A mathematical framework for the analysis of critical zones of the input space in a classification problem is introduced. It is based on the definition of uncertainty region, which is the collection of the input patterns whose classification is not certain. Through this definition a characterization of optimal decision functions can be derived.

A general method for detecting the uncertainty region in real-world problems is then proposed, whose implementation can vary according to the connectionist model employed. Its application allows to improve the performance of the resulting neural network.

1 Introduction

Generalization ability is the quantity usually employed to measure the quality of a connectionist model, which has been trained to solve a real-world classification problem. The value of this quantity is normally obtained by observing the performance of the neural network on a validation set, containing some samples pertaining to the given classification problem and not used in the training process.

However, generalization ability gives only an overall evaluation of the effectiveness of our artificial device and does not shed much light on its local properties or on the characteristics of the real-world problem at hand. In particular, no information is provided about the quality of the classification for a specific input pattern; consequently, we cannot know if the point lies in a critical region of the input space or if its class can be assigned with a high confidence.

This knowledge is not only important when the trained connectionist model is used; the learning process can indeed search more carefully critical zones of the input space so as to achieve a better final performance. Unfortunately, no way of formally characterizing these critical zones is available in the literature; only some heuristic methods is given [4, 5, 2], whose validity is not generally ensured.

In the following sections a mathematical framework for two-class problems is introduced, which allows to define the concept of *uncertainty region U* as the collection of the input patterns whose classification is not certain. A characterization of optimal decision functions based on the uncertainty region U is then introduced. However, the practical application of this framework requires the ability of computing U in a real-world pattern recognition problem. To this aim a general algorithm is presented, whose implementation may differ according to the connectionist model considered. A version based on Support Vector Machines is presented in a companion paper [3].

2 The mathematical framework

Consider a general pattern recognition problem, where vectors $x \in \mathcal{R}^d$ have to be assigned to one of two possible classes, associated with the values of a binary output y, coded by the integers -1 and $+1$. Following the mathematical model of [1], this problem can be thoroughly described by a pair of probability measures (μ, η), where μ is defined on the Borel sets of $\mathcal{R}^d$ and η is the so-called *a posteriori probability* given by $\eta(x) = \mathbf{P}\{Y = +1 \mid X = x\}$. X and Y are random variables assuming values in $\mathcal{R}^d$ and $\{-1, +1\}$, respectively.

It can be easily seen that the conditional probability $\eta(x)$ contains all the necessary information about the pattern recognition problem at hand. The goal is to find a *decision function* (also called *classifier*) $g : \mathcal{R}^d \to \{-1, +1\}$ that minimizes the error probability $L(g) = \mathbf{P}\{g(X) \neq Y\}$. A one-one correspondence between the class of decision functions and the collection of Borel subsets of $\mathcal{R}^d$ is directly obtained; for example, we can associate with any classifier g the set $D^+(g)$ containing all the points x of the input space $\mathcal{R}^d$ for which $g(x) = +1$. A corresponding subset $D^-(g)$ including the portion of $\mathcal{R}^d$ where $g(x) = -1$ can also be introduced.

$$D^+(g) = \{x \in \mathcal{R}^d : g(x) = +1\}, \quad D^-(g) = \{x \in \mathcal{R}^d : g(x) = -1\}$$

The boundary between $D^-(g)$ and $D^+(g)$, defined as $B(g) = \text{cl}\, D^-(g) \cap \text{cl}\, D^+(g)$, being $\text{cl}\, A$ the closure of A, will be called *separating set* of the classifier g.

Two decision functions g and g' can be considered equivalent if $g = g'$ a.s., that is $\mu\{g(X) \neq g'(X)\} = 0$; in this case we write $g \sim g'$. Thus, equivalence classes in the set of classifiers can be determined, according to the given measure probability μ acting on the input space $\mathcal{R}^d$. It is straightforward to see that $L(g) = L(g')$ when $g \sim g'$.

Let $\mathcal{G}$ be the set containing one measurable decision function g for each of the equivalence classes just introduced. If $\eta(x)$ were known, the optimal classifier for our pattern recognition problem is the *Bayes decision function* $g^* \in \mathcal{G}$, defined as $g^*(x) = +1$, if $\eta(x) > 1/2$, and $g^*(x) = -1$ otherwise. The error probability $L^* = L(g^*)$ has been shown to be minimal [1], that is $L^* \leq L(g)$ for any decision function $g \in \mathcal{G}$.

Two subsets C^- and C^+ in the input space $\mathcal{R}^d$ may be determined, according to the value assumed by the a posteriori probability $\eta(x)$

$$C^- = \{x \in \mathcal{R}^d : \eta(x) = 0\}, \quad C^+ = \{x \in \mathcal{R}^d : \eta(x) = 1\}$$

they will be called *certainty regions*, since the points belonging to C^- and C^+ are univocally associated with a specific output. For a similar reason, the remaining portion of the input space $U = \mathcal{R}^d \setminus (C^- \cup C^+)$ will be named *uncertainty region*.

The knowledge of the subsets C^-, C^+, and U gives important insights into the classification problem at hand. In fact, it will be shown that every valid classifier g must assume value -1 in C^- and value $+1$ in C^+. To see this, let us introduce the class of functions $\bar{\mathcal{G}} \subset \mathcal{G}$ containing this kind of classifiers

$$\bar{\mathcal{G}} = \{ g \in \mathcal{G} : C^+ \subset D^+(g), C^- \subset D^-(g) \}$$

Then, a proper transformation $T : \mathcal{G} \to \bar{\mathcal{G}}$ can be defined

$$T(g)(x) = \begin{cases} -1 & \text{if } x \in C^- \\ +1 & \text{if } x \in C^+ \\ g(x) & \text{if } x \in U \end{cases}$$

Note that $\bar{\mathcal{G}}$ is invariant under this transformation, since $T(g) = g$ for every $g \in \bar{\mathcal{G}}$. With these definitions it will be shown that best classifiers are included in $\bar{\mathcal{G}}$.

Theorem 1 *For every decision function $g \in \mathcal{G} \setminus \bar{\mathcal{G}}$ we have $L(T(g)) < L(g)$.*

Proof. The conditional error probability of any classifier $g \in \mathcal{G}$, given $X = x$, can be written as [1]

$$\begin{aligned}
\mathbf{P}\{g(X) \neq Y \mid X = x\} &= 1 - \mathbf{P}\{g(X) = Y \mid X = x\} \\
&= 1 - \left(I_{D^+(g)} \mathbf{P}\{Y = +1 \mid X = x\} + I_{D^-(g)} \mathbf{P}\{Y = -1 \mid X = x\} \right) \\
&= 1 - \left(I_{D^+(g)} \eta(x) + I_{D^-(g)}(1 - \eta(x)) \right)
\end{aligned}$$

being I_A the indicator function of the set A. Thus, for every $x \in \mathcal{R}^d$, we have

$$\begin{aligned}
&\mathbf{P}\{g(X) \neq Y \mid X = x\} - \mathbf{P}\{T(g)(X) \neq Y \mid X = x\} \\
&= \eta(x) \left(I_{D^+(T(g))} - I_{D^+(g)} \right) + (1 - \eta(x)) \left(I_{D^-(T(g))} - I_{D^-(g)} \right) \\
&= I_{D^-(g)} I_{C^+} + I_{D^+(g)} I_{C^-}
\end{aligned}$$

since $T(g)(x) = g(x)$ when $x \in U$. By definition of $\mathcal{G}$, this allows to conclude that $L(g) - L(T(g)) = \mu(C^+ \cap D^-(g)) + \mu(C^- \cap D^+(g)) > 0$ if $g \in \mathcal{G} \setminus \bar{\mathcal{G}}$. $\qquad \square$

As a consequence of Theorem 1 we obtain that the Bayes classifier g^* lies in the class $\bar{\mathcal{G}}$; otherwise, the decision function $T(g^*)$ would achieve a lower error probability. Furthermore, it is possible to determine two classifiers $g^-, g^+ \in \bar{\mathcal{G}}$ such that $D^-(g^-) = C^-$ and $D^+(g^+) = C^+$ a.s. Due to the above defined one-one correspondence between the class of decision functions and the collection of subsets of $\mathcal{R}^d$, the introduction of g^- and g^+ can be viewed as an alternative definition of the sets C^- and C^+, which leads to $U = D^+(g^-) \cap D^-(g^+)$.

3   A general algorithm for detecting U

When solving real world pattern recognition problems, usually we do not know the probability measures μ and η, but have only access to a training set S_n containing n samples (X_j, Y_j), $j = 1, \ldots, n$, supposed to be obtained through n i.i.d. applications of μ and η. Consequently, the problem of determining the regions C^-, C^+, and U cannot be solved unless some kind of regularity is imposed on the choice of the decision functions g^- and g^+ [6].

To this aim, let us introduce a hypothesis set $\mathcal{H}$, containing all the classifiers g among which the desired behaviors for g^- and g^+ are searched for. Since the decision functions g^- and g^+ may not belong to the class $\mathcal{H}$, our target is therefore to determine two classifiers $\hat{g}^-, \hat{g}^+ \in \mathcal{H}$, such that $D^-(\hat{g}^-) \subset C^-$ and $D^+(\hat{g}^+) \subset C^+$, while the portion of C^- and C^+ contained in $D^+(\hat{g}^-)$ and $D^-(\hat{g}^+)$, respectively, is minimal, according to the unknown probability measure μ. Formally, we have

$$\hat{g}^- = \arg\min_{g \in \mathcal{H}} \{\mu(D^+(g) \cap C^-) \ : \ D^-(g) \subset C^-\}$$

$$\hat{g}^+ = \arg\min_{g \in \mathcal{H}} \{\mu(D^-(g) \cap C^+) \ : \ D^+(g) \subset C^+\}$$

A possible way to determine through the training set S_n the behavior of the decision functions $\hat{g}^-$ and $\hat{g}^+$ is to perform the following couple of maximizations

$$\max_{g \in \mathcal{H}_n^-} \left| S_n^- \cap D^-(g) \right| \ , \quad \max_{g \in \mathcal{H}_n^+} \left| S_n^+ \cap D^+(g) \right| \tag{1}$$

where $|A|$ is the *cardinality* of the set A (i.e. the number of elements in A when it is finite), whereas the sets $\mathcal{H}_n^-$, $\mathcal{H}_n^+$, S_n^-, and S_n^+ are defined as follows:

$$\mathcal{H}_n^- = \{g \in \mathcal{H} \ : \ D^-(g) \cap S_n^+ = \emptyset\}$$
$$\mathcal{H}_n^+ = \{g \in \mathcal{H} \ : \ D^+(g) \cap S_n^- = \emptyset\}$$
$$S_n^- = \{X \in \mathcal{R}^d \ : \ (X, Y) \in S_n, \ Y = -1\}$$
$$S_n^+ = \{X \in \mathcal{R}^d \ : \ (X, Y) \in S_n, \ Y = +1\}$$

The goal of the first term in (1) is to determine the decision functions $g \in \mathcal{H}$ that maximize the number of correctly classified patterns X in the training set S_n, having corresponding output $Y = -1$, while satisfying all the samples $(X, Y) \in S_n$ with $Y = +1$. For notational purposes we have therefore introduced the class $\mathcal{H}_n^-$ containing all the decision functions $g \in \mathcal{H}$ that give output $g(X) = +1$ in correspondence of the elements of the set S_n^+; this is formed by the input patterns X belonging to the training set S_n with an associated $Y = +1$.

Similar definitions for $\mathcal{H}_n^+$ and S_n^- have also been employed in the determination of the classifier $\hat{g}^+$. Actually, maximizations (1) may not lead to a unique solution, but several decision functions of $\mathcal{H}$ may achieve the same maximum number of correctly classified patterns. Let $\bar{\mathcal{H}}_n^-$ and $\bar{\mathcal{H}}_n^+$ be the two subsets of $\mathcal{H}$ containing the possible arguments of maxima in (1).

A further choice among the elements of $\bar{\mathcal{H}}_n^-$ and $\bar{\mathcal{H}}_n^+$ is therefore necessary to obtain good approximations $\hat{g}_n^-$, $\hat{g}_n^+$ for the desired decision functions $\hat{g}^-$ and $\hat{g}^+$. This choice can be made in the following way, although several valid alternatives exist:

$$\hat{g}_n^- = \arg \max_{g \in \bar{\mathcal{H}}_n^-} \lambda(D^-(g)), \qquad \hat{g}_n^+ = \arg \max_{g \in \bar{\mathcal{H}}_n^+} \lambda(D^+(g))$$

being $\lambda(A)$ the Lebesgue measure of the set $A \subset \mathcal{R}^d$. In this way the classifiers $\hat{g}_n^-$ and $\hat{g}_n^+$ are selected, which maximize the extension (in the sense of Lebesgue measure) of the sets $D^-(g)$ and $D^+(g)$, respectively.

Now, the approximations C_n^-, C_n^+, and U_n for the desired sets C^-, C^+, and U can be obtained through the equations

$$
\begin{aligned}
C_n^- &= D^-(\hat{g}_n^-) \cap D^-(\hat{g}_n^+), \qquad C_n^+ = D^+(\hat{g}_n^+) \cap D^+(\hat{g}_n^-) \\
U_n &= \mathcal{R}^d \setminus (C_n^- \cup C_n^+)
\end{aligned}
$$

Summing up, the procedure to be employed for obtaining from the given training set S_n the estimates C_n^-, C_n^+, and U_n can be outlined as in Fig. 1.

PROCEDURE FOR APPROXIMATING C^-, C^+, AND U

1. Determine the sets of decision functions $\bar{\mathcal{H}}_n^-$ and $\bar{\mathcal{H}}_n^+$, whose elements achieve the maxima in (1).

2. Choose in $\bar{\mathcal{H}}_n^-$ and in $\bar{\mathcal{H}}_n^+$ the classifiers $\hat{g}_n^-$ and $\hat{g}_n^+$, which maximize the Lebesgue measure of $D^-(g)$ and $D^+(g)$, respectively.

3. Set $C_n^- = D^-(\hat{g}_n^-) \cap D^-(\hat{g}_n^+)$, $C_n^+ = D^+(\hat{g}_n^+) \cap D^+(\hat{g}_n^-)$, and $U_n = \mathcal{R}^d \setminus (C_n^- \cup C_n^+)$.

Figure 1: General procedure followed to obtain reasonable approximations for the sets C^-, C^+, and U from a finite training set S_n.

4 Discussions

It is interesting to note that if the training set S_n is perfectly separable by a decision function $g \in \mathcal{H}$, i.e. $S_n^- \subset D^-(g)$ and $S_n^+ \subset D^+(g)$, the estimated uncertainty region U_n includes the largest region of the input space, realizable through the classifiers in $\mathcal{H}$, which does not contain patterns of S_n. In this case, the separating set $B(g)$ of every decision function $g \in \mathcal{H}$ that correctly classifies all the patterns in the given training set S_n is contained in cl U_n.

However, in a general case Theorem 1 ensures that the separating set of any good classifier lies into cl U. Thus, if we are confident with our approximations C_n^- and C_n^+, obtained through S_n by employing the procedure in Fig. 1, the solution of the classification problem at hand can be pursued by examining only the behavior inside the uncertainty region U_n. Consequently, the samples of S_n included in C_n^- and C_n^+ may be removed from the training set, without compromising the search for the target decision function. This leads to a reduction of the computational burden needed for the application of any pattern recognition algorithm.

Furthermore, if new samples are to be added to the actual training set, we should discard all the input patterns belonging to C_n^- and C_n^+, since their presence does not bring essential information for the problem at hand. In particular, if an oracle is available, which gives the corresponding output y for any selected pattern x, we can consider for a possible inclusion in the training set only the points of the uncertainty region U_n.

If rejections are admissible in the application we are dealing with, one can adopt the following decision function with reject option

$$g(x) = \begin{cases} -1 & \text{if } x \in C_n^- \\ +1 & \text{if } x \in C_n^+ \\ \text{"reject"} & \text{if } x \in U_n \end{cases}$$

as the solution of the classification problem at hand. In this case, no further computation is required to achieve a final two-valued decision function. Naturally, the size of the uncertainty region U_n must be small enough to keep low the rejection rate.

References

[1] L. DEVROYE, L. GYÖRFI, AND G. LUGOSI, *A Probabilistic Theory of Pattern Recognition.* New York: Springer-Verlag (1997).

[2] G. P. DRAGO AND S. RIDELLA, Possibility and necessity pattern classification using an interval arithmetic perceptron. *Neural Computing & Applications*, **8** (1999), 40–52.

[3] G. P. DRAGO AND M. MUSELLI, Support Vector Machines for uncertainty region detection. Submitted to the *12-th Italian Workshop on Neural Nets* (2001).

[4] H. ISHIBUCHI, R. FUJIOKA, AND H. TANAKA, Possibility and necessity pattern classification using neural networks. *Fuzzy Sets and Systems*, **48** (1992), 331–340.

[5] H. ISHIBUCHI, H. TANAKA, AND H. OKADA, An architecture of neural networks with interval weights and its application to fuzzy regression analysis. *Fuzzy Sets and Systems*, **57** (1993), 27–39.

[6] V. N. VAPNIK, *Statistical Learning Theory.* New York: John Wiley & Sons (1998).

Support Vector Machines for uncertainty region detection

Gian Paolo Drago, Marco Muselli

Istituto per i Circuiti Elettronici - CNR

via De Marini, 6 - 16149 Genova, Italy

Abstract

A new technique for the detection of the uncertainty region in classification problems is presented. The core of the method is the determination of the best supporting hyperplane for convex hulls of sets of points in a multidimensional input space. To this aim a modified version of the algorithm for the Generalized Optimal Hyperplane is shown to be effective.

As in the Support Vector Machine approach, kernel functions can be used to generalize the proposed technique, so as to detect uncertainty regions with nonlinear boundaries. Simulations concerning artificial benchmarks show the quality of the resulting method.

1 Introduction

Support Vector Machines (SVM) [6] show the interesting property of detecting, as a byproduct of the learning process, a group of input patterns in the training set, which represent borderline samples between different classes. These patterns, called *support vectors*, contain the essential information about the classification problem at hand, since the knowledge of their only position makes possible to reconstruct the decision function in the whole input space.

Due to their boundary location, support vectors can also give information about the region where the class assignment is more critical. However, no method based on SVM is currently available to determine the effective extension of this borderline zone, called *uncertainty region*. Some heuristic algorithms for multilayer feedforward neural networks have been proposed in the literature [5, 4], but their computational burden is very high, since they have to solve a nonlinear constrained optimization in the weight space.

A formal definition of the uncertainty region, together with a general method for its identification is contained in a companion paper [3]. In this contribution a specific implementation of that general method is proposed, which uses a modified version of the classical technique for training SVMs. The resulting algorithm presents a reduced computational burden and achieves good approximations in all the situations examined.

Some tests have been performed to access the quality of the solution obtained through the new connectionist models, called *Asymmetric Support Vector Machines (ASVM)*. Even in the case of linearly separable training sets they give a better correspondence with the effective uncertainty region than conventional SVMs.

2 Asymmetric Support Vector Machines

In a general pattern recognition problem input patterns $x \in \mathcal{R}^d$ have to be assigned to one of two possible classes, associated with the values of a binary output y, coded by the integers -1 and $+1$. The a posteriori probability $\eta(x) = \mathbf{P}\{Y = +1 | X = x\}$ plays a fundamental role in this kind of problem and allows to define the zone $U \subset \mathcal{R}^d$, called *uncertainty region*, where the classification is critical [3]:

$$U = \{x \in \mathcal{R}^d \; : \; 0 < \eta(x) < 1\}$$

By contrast, the sets

$$C^- = \{x \in \mathcal{R}^d \; : \; \eta(x) = 0\}, \qquad C^+ = \{x \in \mathcal{R}^d \; : \; \eta(x) = 1\}$$

will be called *certainty regions* for the problem at hand.

In a practical situation usually we do not know the probability η, but have only access to a training set S_n containing n samples (x_j, y_j), $j = 1, \ldots, n$. Consequently, the problem of determining the regions C^-, C^+, and U cannot be solved exactly, but some good approximations C_n^-, C_n^+, and U_n must be searched for. A general algorithm that pursues this aim is described in [3]; however, its implementation depends on the connectionist model to be used.

A version of this algorithm which resembles the original method for SVMs can be obtained by considering the classical definition of supporting hyperplane [1] for convex hulls. Denote with S_n^+ and S_n^- the sets of input patterns x_j contained in the training set S_n, having a corresponding output $y_j = +1$ or $y_j = -1$, respectively. Suppose, without loss of generality, that the set S_n^+ contains the first n^+ input patterns of the training set S_n, whereas S_n^- is formed by the remaining $n^- = n - n^+$ points.

A halfspace C_n^+ approximating C^+ is then delimited by the supporting hyperplane for S_n^- that scores the minimum number of errors on the patterns of S_n^+. The directional vector w^+ of this hyperplane can be found by solving the following quadratic programming problem: minimize the functional

$$\Phi(w^+, \xi) = \frac{1}{2}(w^+ \cdot w^+) + \lambda \sum_{j=1}^{n^+} \xi_j \tag{1}$$

subject to the constraints

$$w_0^+ + w^+ \cdot x_j \geq 1 - \xi_j \quad \text{for } j = 1, \ldots, n^+ \tag{2}$$

$$w_0^+ + w^+ \cdot x_j \leq -1 \quad \text{for } j = n^+ + 1, \ldots, n \tag{3}$$

$$\xi_j \geq 0 \quad \text{for } j = 1, \ldots, n^+ \tag{4}$$

being $\cdot$ the usual inner product in $\mathcal{R}^d$. As one can note, this problem resembles that used to find the Generalized Optimal Hyperplane [6]; the only difference lies in the errors ξ_j, since they are allowed only on the patterns with positive output.

To reduce computational burden, dual programming problems can be considered, as in [6]; the following theorem gives the procedure to be followed. For the sake of brevity, the proof will be omitted, but can be found in [2].

Theorem 1 *The solution w^+ of the quadratic programming problem (1) with constraints (2)–(4) is given by*

$$w^+ = \sum_{j=1}^{n} \alpha_j y_j x_j \tag{5}$$

where the scalar α_j can be obtained by minimizing the functional

$$W(\alpha) = \frac{1}{2} \sum_{j=1}^{n} \sum_{k=1}^{n} \alpha_j \alpha_k y_j y_k (x_j \cdot x_k) - \sum_{j=1}^{n} \alpha_j$$

subject to

$$\sum_{j=1}^{n} \alpha_j y_j = 0 \tag{6}$$

$$0 \leq \alpha_j \leq \lambda \quad \text{for } j = 1, \ldots, n^+ \tag{7}$$

$$\alpha_j \geq 0 \quad \text{for } j = n^+ + 1, \ldots, n \tag{8}$$

The directional vector w^- of the hyperplane bounding C_n^- can be obtained by using the same dual quadratic programming problem; it is sufficient to employ constraint (7) when $j = n^+ + 1, \ldots, n$ and (8) for $j = 1, \ldots, n^+$. As in the algorithm for the Generalized Optimal Hyperplane, the input patterns x_j with $\alpha_j > 0$ are called *support vectors*.

More general forms for the regions C_n^-, C_n^+, and U_n can be obtained by employing boundary functions g^+ and g^- with the following expression:

$$g^+(x) = w_0^+ + \sum_{j=1}^{n} \alpha_j^+ y_j K(x_j, x), \quad g^-(x) = w_0^- + \sum_{j=1}^{n} \alpha_j^- y_j K(x_j, x)$$

where $K(\cdot, \cdot)$ is the *kernel* of a Reproducing Kernel Hilbert Space (RKHS) [6]. The coefficients α_j^+ and α_j^- can then be derived by solving two quadratic programming problems sharing the same cost function

$$W(\alpha) = \frac{1}{2} \sum_{j=1}^{n} \sum_{k=1}^{n} \alpha_j \alpha_k y_j y_k K(x_j, x_k) - \sum_{j=1}^{n} \alpha_j$$

and the constraints

$$\sum_{j=1}^{n} \alpha_j y_j = 0, \quad \alpha_j \geq 0 \quad \text{for } j = 1, \ldots, n$$

The only difference between these two problems lies in the upper bound for the unknown quantities α_j: when searching for the decision function g^+, delimiting C_n^+, only the α_j associated with patterns in S_n^+ must be upper bounded

$$\alpha_j \leq \lambda \quad \text{for } j = 1, \ldots, n^+$$

The same inequality constraint must be used in the determination of g^- (delimiting C_n^-) for α_j with $j = n^+ + 1, \ldots, n$.

Since this kind of devices treats differently patterns belonging to the two classes, they will be called *Asymmetric Support Vector Machines (ASVM)*. Biases w_0^+ and w_0^- for g^+ and g^-, respectively, can be computed through the following expressions:

$$w_0^+ = -\max_{x \in S_n^-} g^+(x), \quad w_0^- = -\min_{x \in S_n^+} g^-(x)$$

Then, the regions C_n^+, C_n^-, and U_n can be written as

$$
\begin{aligned}
C_n^+ &= \{x \in \mathcal{R}^d : g^+(x) \geq 0, g^-(x) \geq 0\} \\
C_n^- &= \{x \in \mathcal{R}^d : g^+(x) < 0, g^-(x) < 0\} \\
U_n &= \mathcal{R}^d \setminus (C_n^- \cup C_n^+)
\end{aligned}
$$

Several different kernels $K(\cdot, \cdot)$ have been proposed in the literature for the construction of SVM [6]; simulation results reported in the next section refer to classifiers constructed by employing the following symmetric functions:

1. Simple inner product: $K(u, v) = u \cdot v$

2. Polynomial of degree m: $K(u, v) = (1 + (u \cdot v))^m$

3. Gaussian Radial Basis Function: $K(u, v) = e^{-\gamma \|u - v\|^2}$

The values employed for the parameters are $m = 3$ and $\gamma = 1$.

3   Simulation results

Two experiments on artificial classification problems have been performed to analyze the properties of the proposed algorithm for the detection of the uncertainty region U. The target of these benchmarks is to examine the ability of these methods in reconstructing a predefined set U by knowing only a finite collection of samples S_n. Both linear and nonlinear separating sets will be considered.

Asymmetric Support Vector Machines (ASVM) will be employed to solve each of the considered benchmarks; comparisons with classical SVM will also be reported. The value of λ has been always set to 10.

The first test deals with the detection of the uncertainty region U depicted in Fig. 1a. A training set S_n with $n = 300$ has been generated through a random sampling with uniform probability into the certainty regions C^+ and C^-. The resulting classification problem is shown in Figs. 1b–1c, where input patterns with positive (negative) output are represented by crosses (triangles);

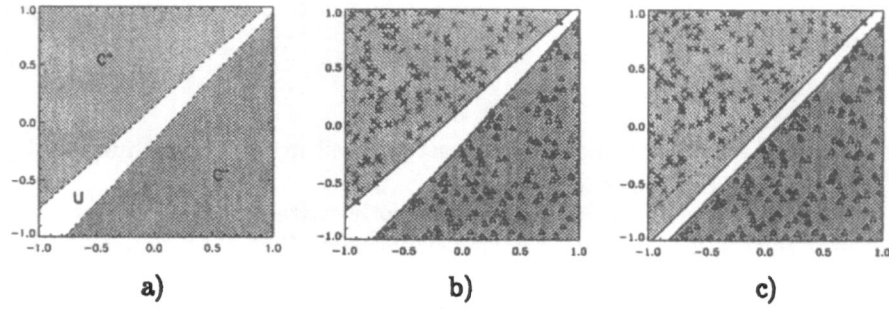

Figure 1: Uncertainty regions U_n for a linearly separable training set S_n: a) real, b) found by ASVM, and c) obtained by SVM.

in all the figures dashed lines delimit the uncertainty region U, which has to be found.

The application of ASVM, adopting the inner product as kernel leads to the (white) uncertainty regions U_n depicted in Fig. 1b. As one can see, the agreement with the desired region U is almost perfect. As a comparison, Fig. 1c shows the boundaries for U_n, obtained through the application of the method for generating the optimal hyperplane (SVM). The width of the uncertainty region is given by (twice) the value of the margin. The requirement of having two parallel straight lines as the boundaries of U_n prevents this method from determining the correct extension of the uncertainty region U.

In all the figures highlighted input patterns denote the support vectors produced by each method. It should be observed that ASVM reduces the number of support vectors to the minimum (four), while allowing the determination of the separating straight lines. According to a theorem on SVM [6], this leads to an improvement of the generalization ability of resulting devices.

In order to analyze the ability of ASVM in reconstructing uncertainty regions U with nonlinear boundaries, a second artificial experiment has been devised. It aims at determining the square frame in Fig. 2a by acting on the training set shown there, which includes 250 input patterns (150 with positive output and 100 with negative output) obtained through a random sampling with uniform probability over the domain $[-1, 1] \times [-1, 1]$.

The application of ASVM with polynomial and Gaussian kernels has produced the uncertainty regions U_n depicted in Figs. 2b and 2c, respectively. As one can note, the two results are very similar: the target region U is determined with sufficient precision, given the (relatively) small size of the training set. Dotted lines refer to the separating sets produced by classical SVM with the same kernels; it can be observed that they are essentially contained into the region U_n generated by ASVM.

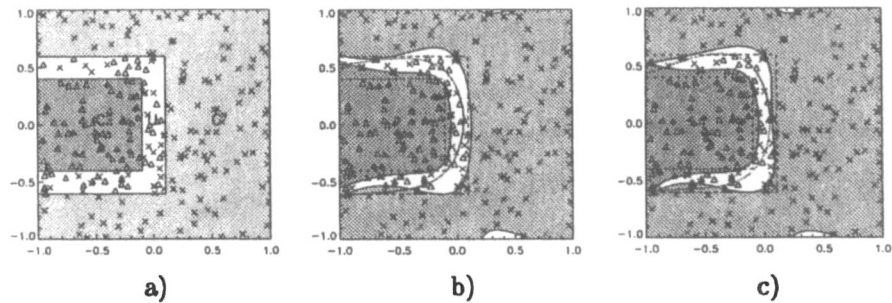

Figure 2: Uncertainty regions U_n with a nonlinear boundary: a) real, b) found by ASVM, and c) obtained by SVM.

References

[1] M. S. BAZARAA AND C. M. SHETTY, *Nonlinear Programming*. New York: John Wiley and Sons, (1979).

[2] G. P. DRAGO AND M. MUSELLI, Asymmetric Support Vector Machines. Rapporto interno ICE 1/01 (2001), Istituto per i Circuiti Elettronici, Consiglio Nazionale delle Ricerche.

[3] G. P. DRAGO AND M. MUSELLI, Detecting uncertainty regions for characterizing classification problems. Submitted to the *12-th Italian Workshop on Neural Nets* (2001).

[4] G. P. DRAGO AND S. RIDELLA, Possibility and necessity pattern classification using an interval arithmetic perceptron. *Neural Computing & Applications*, 8 (1999), pp. 40–52.

[5] H. ISHIBUCHI, R. FUJIOKA, AND H. TANAKA, Possibility and necessity pattern classification using neural networks. *Fuzzy Sets and Systems*, 48 (1992), 331–340.

[6] V. N. VAPNIK, *Statistical Learning Theory*. New York: John Wiley & Sons (1998).

A Learning Algorithm for Piecewise Linear Regression

Giancarlo Ferrari-Trecate [1], Marco Muselli [2],
Diego Liberati [3], Manfred Morari [1]

[1]Institute für Automatik, ETHZ - ETL
CH 8092 Zürich, Switzerland

[2]Istituto per i Circuiti Elettronici - CNR
via De Marini, 6 - 16149 Genova, Italy

[3]Ce.S.T.I.A. - CNR c/o Politecnico di Milano
Piazza Leonardo da Vinci, 32 - 20133 Milano, Italy

Abstract

A new learning algorithm for solving piecewise linear regression problems is proposed. It is able to train a proper multilayer feedforward neural network so as to reconstruct a target function assuming a different linear behavior on each set of a polyhedral partition of the input domain.

The proposed method combine local estimation, clustering in weight space, classification and regression in order to achieve the desired result. A simulation on a benchmark problem shows the good properties of this new learning algorithm.

1 Introduction

Real-world problems to be solved by artificial neural networks are normally subdivided in two groups according to the range of values assumed by the output. If it is Boolean or nominal, we speak of classification problems; otherwise, when the output is coded by a continuous variable, we are facing with a regression problem. In most cases, the techniques employed to train a connectionist model depend on the kind of problem we are dealing with.

However, applications can be found, which lie on the borderline between classification and regression; these occur when the input space can be subdivided into disjoint regions X_i characterized by different behaviors of the function f to be reconstructed. The target of the learning problem is consequently twofold: by analyzing a set of samples of f, possibly affected by noise, it has to generate both the collection of regions X_i and the behavior of the unknown function f in each of them.

If the region X_i corresponding to each sample in the training set were known, we could add the index i of the region as an output, thus obtaining a classification problem which has the target of finding the effective form of each X_i. On the other side, if the actual partition X_i were known, we could solve several regression problems to find the behavior of the function f within each X_i.

Because of this mixed nature, classical techniques for neural network training cannot be directly applied, but specific methods are necessary to deal with this kind of problems.

Perhaps, the simplest situation one can think of is piecewise linear regression: in this case the regions X_i are polyhedra and the behavior of the function f in each X_i can be modeled by a linear expression. Several authors have treated this kind of problem [2, 3, 4, 8], providing algorithms for reaching the desired result. Unfortunately, most of them are difficult to extend beyond two dimensions [2], whereas others consider only local approximations [3, 4], thus missing the effective extension of regions X_i.

In this contribution a new training algorithm for neural networks solving piecewise linear regression problems is proposed. It combines clustering and supervised learning to obtain the correct values for the weights of a proper multilayer feedforward architecture.

2 The piecewise linear regression problem

Let X be a polyhedron in the n-dimensional space $\mathcal{R}^n$ and X_i, $i = 1, \ldots, s$, a polyhedral partition of X, i.e. $X_i \cap X_j = \emptyset$ for every $i, j = 1, \ldots, s$ and $\bigcup_{i=1}^{s} X_i = X$. The target of a Piecewise Linear Regression (PLR) problem is to reconstruct an unknown function $f : X \to \mathcal{R}$ having a linear behavior in each region X_i

$$f(\mathbf{x}) = z_i = w_{i0} + \sum_{j=1}^{n} w_{ij} x_j$$

when only a training set S containing m samples $(\mathbf{x}_k, y_k)$, $k = 1, \ldots, m$, is available. The output y_k gives an evaluation of $f(\mathbf{x}_k)$ subject to noise, being $\mathbf{x}_k \in X$; the region X_i to which $\mathbf{x}_k$ belongs is not known in advance. Scalars $w_{i0}, w_{i1}, \ldots, w_{in}$, for $i = 1, \ldots, s$, characterize univocally the function f and their estimate is a target of the PLR problem; for notational purposes they will be included in a vector $\mathbf{w}_i$.

Since regions X_i are polyhedral, they can be defined by a set of l_i linear inequalities of the following kind:

$$a_{ij0} + \sum_{k=1}^{n} a_{ijk} x_k \leq 0 \tag{1}$$

Scalar a_{ijk}, for $j = 1, \ldots, l_i$ and $k = 0, 1, \ldots, n$, can be included in a matrix A_i, whose estimate is still a target of the reconstruction process for every $i = 1, \ldots, s$. Discontinuities may be present in the function f at the boundaries between two regions X_i.

Following the general idea presented in [8], a neural network realizing a piecewise linear function f of this kind can be modeled as in Fig. 1. It contains a gate layer that verifies inequalities (1) and decides which of the terms z_i must be used as the output y of the whole network. Thus, the i-th unit in the gate

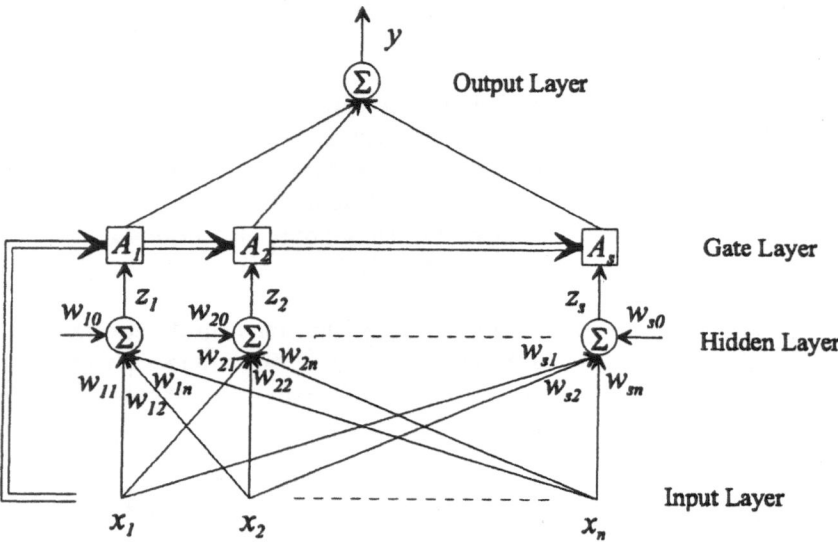

Figure 1: General neural network realizing a piecewise linear function.

layer has output equal to its input z_i, if all the constraints (1) are satisfied for $j = 1, \ldots, l_i$, and equal to 0 in the opposite case. All the other units perform a weighted sum of their inputs; the weights of the output neuron, having no bias, are always set to 1.

3 The proposed learning algorithm

As previously noted, the solution of a PLR problem requires a technique that combine classification and regression: the first has the aim of finding matrices A_i to be inserted in the gate layer of the neural network (Fig. 1), whereas the latter provides weight vectors $\mathbf{w}_i$ for the input to hidden layer connections. A method of this kind is reported in Fig. 2; it is composed of four steps, each of which is devoted to a specific task.

The first of them (Step 1) has the aim of obtaining a first estimate of the weight vectors $\mathbf{w}_i$ by performing local linear regressions based on small subsets of the whole training set S. In fact, points $\mathbf{x}_k$ that are close to each other are likely to belong to the same region X_i. Then, for each sample $(\mathbf{x}_k, y_k)$, with $k = 1, \ldots, m$, we build a set C_k containing $(\mathbf{x}_k, y_k)$ and the $c - 1$ distinct pairs $(\mathbf{x}, y) \in S$ that score the lowest values of the distance $\|\mathbf{x}_k - \mathbf{x}\|$.

The parameter c can be freely chosen, though the inequality $c \geq n$ must be respected to perform the linear regression. It can be easily seen that some sets C_k, called *mixed*, will contain input patterns belonging to different regions X_i. They lead to wrong estimates for $\mathbf{w}_i$ and consequently their number must be kept minimum; this can be obtained by lowering the value of c. However,

---

ALGORITHM FOR PIECEWISE LINEAR REGRESSION

1. *(Local regression)* For every $k = 1, \ldots, m$ do

    1a. Form the set C_k containing the pair $(\mathbf{x}_k, y_k)$ and the samples $(\mathbf{x}, y) \in S$ associated with the $c - 1$ nearest neighbors $\mathbf{x}$ to $\mathbf{x}_k$.

    1b. Perform a linear regression to obtain the weight vector $\mathbf{v}_k$ of a linear unit fitting the samples in C_k.

2. *(Clustering)* Perform a clustering process in the space $\mathcal{R}^{n+1}$ to subdivide the set of weight vectors $\mathbf{v}_k$ into s groups V_i.

3. *(Classification)* Build a new training set S' containing the m pairs $(\mathbf{x}_k, i_k)$, being V_{i_k} the cluster including $\mathbf{v}_k$. Train a multicategory classification method to produce the matrices A_i for the regions X_i.

4. *(Regression)* For every $i = 1, \ldots, s$ perform a linear regression on the samples $(\mathbf{x}, y) \in S$ with $\mathbf{x} \in X_i$ to obtain the weight vector $\mathbf{w}_i$ for the i-th unit in the hidden layer.

Figure 2: Proposed learning method for piecewise linear regression.

the quality of the estimate improves when the size c of the sets C_k increases; a tradeoff must therefore be attained in selecting a reasonable value for c.

Denote with $\mathbf{v}_k$ the weight vector of the linear unit produced through the linear regression on the samples in C_k. If the generation of the samples in the training set is not affected by noise, most of the $\mathbf{v}_k$ coincide with the desired weight vectors $\mathbf{w}_i$. Only mixed sets C_k yield spurious vectors $\mathbf{v}_k$, which can be considered as outliers. Nevertheless, even in presence of noise, a clustering algorithm (Step 2) can be used to determine the sets V_i of vectors $\mathbf{v}_k$ associated with the same $\mathbf{w}_i$. A proper version of the K-means algorithm [6] can be adopted to this aim if the number s of regions is fixed beforehand; otherwise, adaptive techniques, such as the Growing Neural Gas [7], can be employed to find at the same time the value of s.

The sets V_i generated by the clustering process induce a classification on the input patterns $\mathbf{x}_k$ belonging to the training set S. As a matter of fact, if $\mathbf{v}_k \in V_i$ for a given i, the set C_k is fitted by the linear neuron with weight vector $\mathbf{w}_i$ and consequently $\mathbf{x}_k$ is located into the region X_i. The effective extension of this region can be determined by solving a linear multicategory classification problem (Step 3), whose training set S' is built by adding as output to each input pattern $\mathbf{x}_k$ the index i_k of the set V_{i_k} to which the corresponding vector $\mathbf{v}_k$ belongs.

To avoid the presence of multiply classified points or of unclassified patterns in the input space, proper techniques [1] based on linear and quadratic programming can be employed. In this way the s matrices A_i for the gate layer are generated; they can include redundant rows that are not necessary in the determination of the polyhedral regions X_i. These rows can be removed by applying standard linear programming techniques.

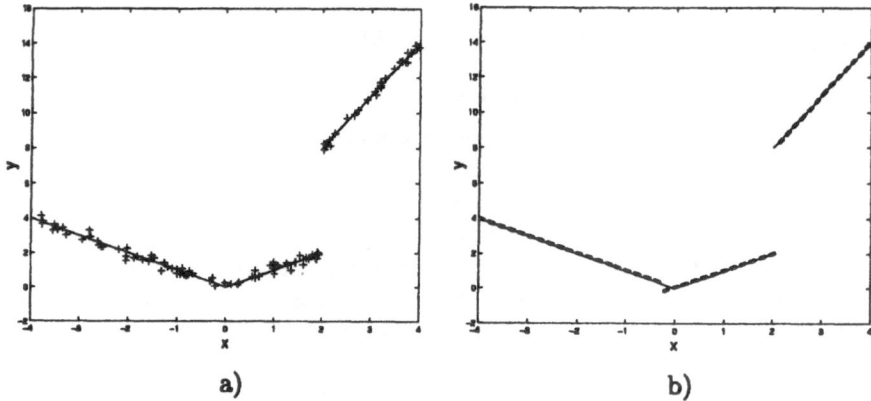

Figure 3: Simulation results for a benchmark problem: a) unknown piecewise linear function f and training set S, b) function realized by the trained neural network (dashed line).

Finally, weight vectors $\mathbf{w}_i$ for the neural network in Fig. 1 can be directly obtained by solve s linear regression problems (Step 4) having as training sets the samples $(\mathbf{x}, y) \in S$ with $\mathbf{x} \in X_i$, where $X_1, \ldots X_s$ are the regions built by the classification process.

4 Simulation results

The proposed algorithm for piecewise linear regression has been tested on a one-dimensional benchmark problem, in order to analyze the quality of the resulting neural network. The unknown function to be reconstructed is the following

$$f(x) = \begin{cases} -x & \text{if } -4 \le x \le 0 \\ x & \text{if } 0 < x < 2 \\ 2 + 3x & \text{if } 2 \le x \le 4 \end{cases} \tag{2}$$

with $X = [-4, 4]$ and $s = 3$. A training set S containing $m = 100$ samples (x, y) has been generated, where $y = f(x) + \varepsilon$ and ε is a normal random variable with zero mean and variance $\sigma^2 = 0.05$. The behavior of $f(x)$ together with the elements of S are depicted in Fig. 3a.

The method described in Fig. 2 has been applied by choosing at Step 1 the value $c = 6$. At Step 2 the number s of regions has been supposed to be known, thus allowing the application of the K-means clustering algorithm [5]; a proper definition of norm has been employed to improve the convergence of the clustering process [6]. Multicategory classification (Step 3) has then been performed by using the method described in [1], which can be easily extended to realize nonlinear boundaries among the X_i when treating a multidimensional problem. Finally, least square estimation is adopted to generate vectors $\mathbf{w}_i$ for piecewise linear regression. The resulting neural network realizes the following function, represented as a dashed line in Fig. 3b:

$$f(x) = \begin{cases} -0.0043 - 0.9787x & \text{if } -4 \leq x \leq -0.24 \\ 0.0899 + 0.9597x & \text{if } -0.24 < x < 2.12 \\ 1.8208 + 3.0608x & \text{if } 2.12 \leq x \leq 4 \end{cases}$$

As one can note, this is a good approximation to the unknown function (2). Errors can only be detected at the boundaries between two adjacent regions X_i; they are mainly due to the effect of mixed sets C_k on the classification process.

References

[1] E. J. BREDENSTEINER AND K. P. BENNETT, Multicategory classification by support vector machines. *Computational Optimizations and Applications*, **12** (1999) 53–79.

[2] V. CHERKASSKY AND H. LARI-NAJAFI, Constrained topological mapping for nonparametric regression analysis. *Neural Networks*, **4** (1991) 27–40.

[3] C.-H. CHOI AND J. Y. CHOI, Constructive neural networks with piecewise interpolation capabilities for function approximation. *IEEE Transactions on Neural Networks*, **5** (1994) 936–944.

[4] J. Y. CHOI AND J. A. FARRELL, Nonlinear adaptive control using networks of piecewise linear approximators. *IEEE Transactions on Neural Networks*, **11** (2000) 390–401.

[5] R. O. DUDA AND P. E. HART, *Pattern Classification and Scene Analysis.* (1973) New York: John Wiley and Sons.

[6] G. FERRARI-TRECATE, M. MUSELLI, D. LIBERATI, AND M. MORARI, A Clustering Technique for the Identification of Piecewise Affine Systems. Accepted at the *Fourth International Workshop on Hybrid Systems: Computation and Control*, Roma, Italy, March 28-30, 2001.

[7] B. FRITZKE, A growing neural gas network learns topologies. In *Advances in Neural Information Processing Systems 7* (1995) Cambridge, MA: MIT Press, 625–632.

[8] K. NAKAYAMA, A. HIRANO, AND A. KANBE, A structure trainable neural network with embedded gating units and its learning algorithm. In *Proceedings of the International Joint Conference on Neural Networks* (2000) Como, Italy, III–253–258.

Specific Sequence Learning by an Adaptable Boolean Neural Network

F.E.Lauria, R.Prevete

INFM & Dipartimento di Scienze Fisiche, Università di Napoli Federico II
Complesso Universitario di Monte Sant' Angelo, Via Vicinale Cupa Cintia 16
I-80126 Napoli, Italy (EU)
lauria@na.infn.it, lauria@unina.it
http://www.na.infn.it/Gener/cyber/nnet.htm

Abstract

In sequence learning studies we can distinguish two fundamental approaches: general-regularity learning and specific sequence learning. Because it is possible to focus on only one of the two aspects we consider a Boolean neural network achieving specific sequence learning. An adaptable Boolean neural network is described in which time representation is implicit. This means giving the neural network dynamic properties which are responsive to temporal sequences.

1   Introduction

The ability to learn and to use sequences is fundamental to human performance: we use sequences of information and/or sequences of actions in a variety of everyday tasks. The human brain is a highly parallel "machine" then a question arises: how can a highly parallel machine learn and control information sequences and/or sequences of tasks?. We can distinguish two aspects [8] of the sequence learning:

1) *general-regularity learning*, in this case the focus is on the ability to learn the environment general-regularity. For example, in artificial-grammar learning (e.g, see [8], participants first view letter strings composed of an unstated finite-state rule system (the rule defines which letters follow others within a string), then they write down each string. After a period of training, participants continue to write down new letter strings, some of which following the old rule but others following either a new rule or randomly composed. The main implication we can deduce form this experiment is that participants process the strings constructed by the old rule more accurately than the other strings. Therefore the participants exhibit general-regularity learning.

2) *specific-sequence learning*, in this case the focus is on measuring acquisition of specific sequences, that is the ability to learn new associations sensorial input – suitable specific sequence of motor activities. For example, in serial reaction-time studies (e.g., see [8]) participants press one of four keys in response to an stimulus (an asterisk) presented in one out of four spatial locations. Performance is faster when the stimuli are presented as a single specific sequence of 10 locations, repeated cyclically during training session than when the stimuli appear randomly. This experiments allows to deduce that the participants exhibit specific-sequence learning.

Because it is possible to focus on only one aspect of the sequence learning (e.g., see [8][9]), in this paper we investigate how to configure a Boolean neural network such that it is able to achieve specific-sequence learning.

One way of dealing with sequential inputs is to represent time explicitly by giving it a spatial representation in a input vector: each temporal event is represented by one element in the input vector and the entire input vector is processed in parallel by the system (e.g., see [2]). There are several drawbacks to this approach [3], for example: 1) it requires that there be some interface with the environment which buffers the input so that it can be presented all at once , however the question arises, when a buffer's contents should be examined? 2) the presence of a buffer suggests that all input vectors have the same length, but this is an unwanted restriction. Hence, a richer representation of time which does not have these problems is required.

On the other hand, it is possible to represent the time by the effect it has on processing. This means giving the processing system dynamic properties which are responsive to temporal sequences. There are several ways in which this approach can be accomplished (e.g., see [5][13][12]). Typically these approaches define a network with memory: the networks are augmented at the input level by additional units which compose the *context layer* representing a *memory*. The context layer remembers the previous output state or the previous internal state. Hence, the effect of the time is implicit in the context layer representing an explicit memory. However this approach, i.e. the presence of an explicit memory, is not a sufficient condition to capture as complex behaviors as the learning of specific sequences because to set the network connection weights is a non trivial job.

Consequently, on one side it seems that an implicit representation of time is richer than an explicit representation, on the other side an implicit representation of time by an explicit memory (the context layer) is not sufficient.

Hence we propose a different approach: the network memory is represented by suitable variations of the network weights, that is we propose an implicit representation of the time by means of an *implicit memory*.

For this aim, we consider a Boolean neural network with a low-level learning rule (Hebb's rule). We arrange it in order to obtain a neural network with a high-level learning rule able to associate specific inputs to specific output sequences. Moreover, the high-level learning rule allows *continual learning* [11]. For continual learning we mean the constant development of complex behaviors with no final end in mind. Continual learning is characterized by the following features: 1) the network is able to receive input information, to produce outputs that can potentially affect the information it receives, and to change autonomously the network weights; 2) the network presents *incremental learning*, that is a continuing process whereby learning occurs with each experience rather that from fixed and complete set of data; 3) the network presents *hierarchical development*, that is the subsumption of an extant mechanism or behaviors by newer, more sophisticated ones. This bottom-up process uses the system's old behaviors as constituents of newly created behaviors. We are going to introduce our Boolean neural network

2 The Boolean Neural Network

We consider a classical network paradigm arising from the McCulloch & Pitts Network [10] as formalized by Caianiello [1].

The net is composed of N ordered elementary elements n_i, called *neurons* or *nodes*. Let us call *input nodes* the first m elementary elements and *inner nodes* the last N elementary elements. We suppose that the time t is a discrete quantity: $t = l \cdot \tau$, with τ constant and $l \in \aleph$ belonging to positive integer number. Each n_i can be only in one of two states, i.e. at each time t the n_i state is either 1 or 0. For each triplet i, j and d, with i=m+1, m+2, ...,N, j=1,2, ...,N and d=1,2,...,D$\in \aleph$, one monodirectional d-delayed connection, going from n_j to n_i, exists. At each time t every n_i state is formally represented by the variable $f_i(t) \in \{0,1\}$, with $i=1$, ..., $m+N$. The last N variables $f_i(t)$, the inner node states , are defined in *def.1*, instead the function defining the first m variables $f_i(t)$, the input node states, depends on the environment interacting with the net. Therefore, the inner node state is:

[def.1.] $f_i(t) = \theta(\sum_j \sum_d C_{ijd} f_j(t-d\tau) - T)$

with: 1) $\theta(x)=1$ if $x \geq 0$, otherwise $\theta(x)=0$ (the Heaveside function). 2) $C_{ijd} \in \_$ is the *weight*, or the *coupling coefficient*, associated to the monodirectional d-delayed connection going from n_j to n_i. 3) D is the *maximum delay*. 4) $T > 0$ is the *activation threshold*.

We will say that:

- n_i is *active* (or *on*) if $f_i(t)=1$, otherwise n_i is *not active* (or *off*).
- A monodirectional d-delayed connection is *excitatory* if the associated *coupling coefficient* C_{ijd} is greater than zero. A monodirectional d-delayed connection is *absolutely inhibitory* if the associated *coupling coefficient* C_{ijd} is : $C_{ijd}<0$ such that

$$|C_{ijd}| > \sum_{j'} \sum_{d=1}^{D} C_{ij'd} ,$$

with j':$C_{ij'd}>0$. If there is an absolutely inhibitory connection going from n_j to n_i with delay d then $f_i(t)=0$ whenever $f_j(t-d \cdot \tau)=1$.

- We denominate *input layer* the first m nodes, *inner layer* the following N-p nodes and *output layer* the last p nodes. Connections go only from the input layer to the inner layer and from the inner layer to both the inner layer and the output layer. We will call *net input state* and *net output state* at the time t the following two vectors $[f_1(t); f_2(t);...; f_m(t)] \in \{0,1\}^m$ and $[f_{N-1}(t); f_{N-2}(t);...;f_{N-p}(t)] \in \{0,1\}^p$, respectively.

2.1 The learning rule

Some network weights are time dependent values regulated by a local learning rule arising from the Hebb's rule [4].

Let *Hebb_in* and *Hebb_out* be two node *tags* (or *properties*). We assume that each node can be marked with:

- no tags
- either the tag *Hebb_in* or the tag *Hebb_out*

- both the tags.

If a node n_i is marked with the tag *Hebb_in* we will call it *Hebb_in* node n_i and if a node n_i is marked with the tag *Hebb_out* we will call it *Hebb_out* node n_i. We associate a real value $H(i)$ to each *Hebb_in* node n_i and we call $H(i)$ the *Hebbian Threshold associated to the Hebb_in node n_i*.

Moreover, let H_{in} and H_{out} be the finite sets containing the indices of all *Hebb_in* and *Hebb_out* nodes, respectively.

From now on, for simplicity sake, if the delay d is equal to 1 then we omit it (e.g., we write C_{ij} instead of C_{ij1}).

We introduce the notion of *time dependent coupling coefficient (tdcc)* and *Hebbian connection*: At each time t for each i and j, with $i \in H_{in}$ and $j \in H_{out}$, we consider the associated coupling coefficient C_{ij} as time dependent and we indicate it with $C_{ij}(t)$.Moreover, we call *Hebbian connection* the monodirectional delayed connection going from n_j to n_i.

We define the following learning rule:

[def.2.]

Let α, β and δ belong to the interval (0,1), at each time t for each i and j, with $i \in H_{in}$ and $j \in H_{out}$, is:

- $C_{ij}(t) = min\{C_{ij}(t-\tau) + \alpha2\,H(i)\,,\,H(i)\,\}$

  if $f_i(t) = f_j(t-\tau) = 1$ AND $C_{ij}(t-\tau) < H(i)$

- $C_{ij}(t) = max\{C_{ij}(t-\tau) - \beta2\,H(i)\,,\,0\}$

  if $f_i(t) = 0$ AND $f_j(t-\tau) = 1$ AND $C_{ij}(t-\tau) < H(i)$

- $C_{ij}(t) = max\{C_{ij}(t-\tau) - \delta2\,H(i)\,,\,0\}$

  if $f_j(t-\tau) = 0$ AND $C_{ij}(t-\tau) < H(i)$

- $C_{ij}(t) = C_{ij}(t-\tau) = H(i)$ *otherwise*

If $C_{ij}(t) = H(i)$ we call *frozen* the monodirectional Hebbian connection, with delay equal to one, going from n_j to n_i. In this case, the $C_{ij}(t)$ value becomes constant.

3   An adaptable Boolean neural network as a rule system

In this section we describe the wanted network behaviour. Lets $I = \{I_1, I_2, ..., I_Q\}$ be a partition of the set composed of all the input vector values and $O = \{O_1, O_2, ..., O_{N_P}\}$ the set composed of all the output vector values, with $N_P < Q$. We propose to arrange the inner layer in $N_P + N_A$ disjointed subsets of nodes [7][6], see Figure 1. The first N_P subsets, $B_1, B_2, ..., B_{N_P}$, are said primitives. The last N_A subsets, $B_{N_P+1}, B_{N_P+2}, ..., B_{N_P+N_A}$, are said assemblies. Each Input[t]$\in I_i$, with i=1,2, ...,Q, can activate exclusively nodes belonging to B_i. In this sense, I_i is the identifier of the primitive or assembly B_i. The output layer receives connections from the primitives exclusively. The network behaviour should be as the following rule-system [7]:

Initially the rule-system should be able to control a finite set of rules (primitive rules) and, then, the system should be able to learn new rules when it receives suitable input sub-sequences (the examples).

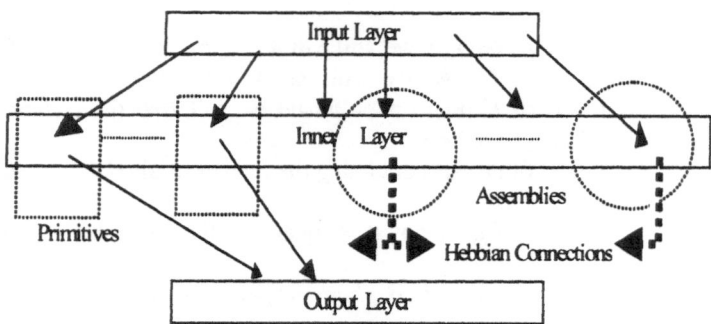

Figure 1: *Network Organisation.* Our network is arranged in three layers: 1) the input layer, receiving the network input; 2) the inner layer composed of nodes interacting exclusively with both the nodes of the input layers and other hidden nodes; 3) the *output layer* composed of nodes receiving exclusively connections from the hidden layer. Moreover, we arrange the hidden layer in N_P+N_A disjointed subsets of nodes. The first N_P subsets, B_1, B_2, ..., B_{N_P}, are said *primitives*. The last N_A subsets, B_{N_P+1}, B_{N_P+2}, ..., $B_{N_P+N_A}$, are said *assemblies*.

The task of each primitive B_j is to execute a primitive rule. The task of each assembly B_i is of learning to execute new rules.

Initially, hence, each primitive B_j is able to control the execution of the following rule (*primitive rule*):

r_j= IF Input[t]$\in I_j$ THEN O_j, with $j=1,2, ..., N_P$

In order to explain their meaning we give the definition [def.3.] . Then, the meaning of each rule r_j, with $j=1,2, ..., N_P$, is defined in [def.4.] .

[def.3.] *The r_j execution, with $j=1,2, ..., N_P$, causes the O_j occurrence. As O_j occurs then the rule r_j has been executed.*

[def.4.] *If at the time t is Input[t]$\in I_j$ and no other rules is in execution then the rule r_j is executed, that is the output O_j occurs at the time $t_2>t$. At the time t_1, $t< t_1< t_2$ we say the rule r_j is in execution.*

Moreover, let us give the following definitions:

[def.5.] *O_j is a primitive output and the index of the rule r_j is j.*

[def.6.] *$R(t)=\{j: j$ is the index of a rule that the system is able to execute$\}$.*

At the time t, each assembly B_i is able to learn a rule of the form:

r_i= IF Input[t]$\in I_i$ THEN $(r_{j_1}, r_{j_2}, ...,r_{j_k})$ with $j_1, j_2, ...j_k \in R(t)$, $k<r_{max}$, $i\notin R(t)$

where r_{max} is a given value.

As first step we give the r_i meaning, and in the section 3.1 we define how these rules are learned.

In order to understand the r_i meaning we give the definitions [def.7.] , [def.8.] and [def.9.] . The meaning of the rules r_i , with $i=N_P+1, N_P+2, ..., S$, is given in [def.10.]

[def.7.] *Given the rule r_i= IF Input[t]$\in I_i$ THEN $(r_{j_1}, r_{j_2} ...,r_{j_k})$ then the rule r_{j_h} is the h-th son of r_i, with $h=1,2, ...,k$.*

[def.8.] *Given the rule r_i= IF Input[t]∈I_i THEN $(r_{j_1}, r_{j_2}, ...,r_{j_k})$ then j_h represents the index of the h-th son and i represents the index of the rule r_i. The index k is the number of r_i sons.*

[def.9.] *The execution of the rule with index i, where i∉R(0), causes the execution of the sons of r_i according to the following algorithm RuleActivation(Input i).*

RuleActivation(Input i)

1) Let it be h=1 and k the number of sons of the rule with index i.
2) Let j_h be the index of the h-th son of the rule with index i
3) If h>k then go to the step 6) else go to the following step.
4) If j_h∈R(0) then the primitive rule with index j_h is executed and the primitive output O_{j_h} occurs, otherwise **RuleActivation**(j_h).
5) Set h=h+1 and go back to the step 2);
6) The rule with index i has been executed

[def.10.] *If at the time t Input[t]∈I_i and no other rule is in execution then the rule r_i is executed (see [def.9.])*

Moreover, as soon as a rule r_i is learned at the time t (see section 3.1) then the index i is added into the set R(t). So, at each time t the set R(t) contains only the indices of the rules that the system is able to execute.

We remark that each rule links a subset of input values, eventually just one value, to one specific sequence of primitive outputs.

For example, supposed P=3, r_{max}=3 and at the time t the system is already able to execute the following rules:

- r_1= IF Input[t]∈I_1 THEN O_1
- r_2= IF Input[t]∈I_2 THEN O_2
- r_3= IF Input[t]∈I_3 THEN O_3
- r_4= IF Input[t]∈I_4 THEN (r_1, r_2)

with R(t)={1, 2, 3, 4}, then some rules the system could learn are:

- r_5= IF Input[t]∈I_5 THEN (r_1, r_3)
- r_6= IF Input[t]∈I_6 THEN (r_4, r_3)
- r_7= IF Input[t]∈I_7 THEN (r_4, r_4)

If those rules are learned then as they are executed the following output occurs O_1O_3, $O_1O_2O_3$ e $O_1O_2O_1O_2$, respectively. For example, if the rule r_6 has been learned and at the time t is Input[t]∈I_6 the following steps occur:

1. the rule r_4 executed:
   1.1. the rule r_1 is executed: the output vector is O_1
   1.2. the rule r_2 is executed: the output vector is O_2
2. the rule r_3 is executed: the output vector is O_3

So the input vector Input[t] belonging to I_6 causes the sequence of outputs $O_1O_2O_3$ by the rule r_6. Consequently, the inputs belonging to I_6 are associated to the specific sequence $O_1O_2O_3$.

3.1 Learning of rules by examples

The neural network interacts with an environment continuously in evolution and, so, the neural network receives input sequences. The neural network is able to select information recognising suitable input sub-sequences. For this reason, we call *example sub-sequence* or *example* the suitable input sub-sequence that allows the rule learning. In [def.13.] we define the examples.

[def.11.] *At the time $t=n\cdot\tau$ the input sequence, $I(n)$, is the sequence composed of $n+1$ elements so that the $(i+1)$-th element of $I(n)$ is equal to Input$[i\cdot\tau]$, with $i=0,1$, ...,n. Hence $I(n)$ represents the sequence of the first $n+1$ input vectors.*

[def.12.] *$I_q(r)$ is the sub-sequence of $I(n)$ with base q and length equal to r composed of r elements with i-th element equal to the $(q+i)$-th element of $I(n)$, with $q\geq0$, $r\geq1$, $1<q+r\leq(n+1)$ and $i=1,2,...,r$.*

[def.13.] *The example sub-sequence or example $E(I_{i_1}, I_{i_2}, ..., I_{i_k})$ at the time t, with $3\leq k\leq r_{max}$ and $i_1\notin S(t)$, $i_2, i_3, ...,i_k\in S(t)$, is a sub-sequence $I_{q_1}(D_E)$ fulfils the following conditions:*

- *There are k sub-sequence $I_{q_j}(D_j)$, with $\Sigma_j D_j = D_E$, $D_{min}\leq D_j\leq D_{min}+b_{max}$ and $q_j= q_{j-1} + D_{j-1}$ $+1$ for $j=1,3,...,k$ and $q_0+D_0+1=t$, such that only the first element of each sub-sequence $I_{q_j}(D_j)$ belongs to I_{i_j}. Where D_{min} and b_{max} are constant values.*

- *An example $E(I_{i_1}, I_{i_2}, ..., I_{i_k})$ is occurred at the time $t=n\cdot\tau$ if and only if at the time t the last element of the example is occurred.*

In other words, defined $d_j=(q_j-q_1+1)$ with $j=2, 3, ..., k$, an example $E(I_{i_1}, I_{i_2}, ..., I_{i_k})$ at the time t is the sub-sequence of $I(n)$ containing as first element an input vector belonging to I_{i_1}, as d_2-th element an input vector belonging to I_{i_2}, as d_3-th element an input vector belonging to I_{i_3} and so on. The other elements are input vectors belonging to a I_s with $s\notin S(t)$.

Now we can define a high-level learning rule [def.14.] .

[def.14.] *If at the time $t=n\cdot\tau$ is occurred an example $E(I_{i_1}, I_{i_2}, ..., I_{i_k})$ with length D_E and there is an interval $[n_i\cdot\tau, n\cdot\tau]$ in which the example has been present ν_E times and it is both $(\nu_E-1)\cdot D_E/\Delta n>\nu_0$ and $\nu_E\geq\nu_{min}$ (where $\nu_0>0$ and $\nu_{min}>0$ are given integer number and $\Delta n=n-n_i$) then the following rule is learned: $r_{i_1}=$ IF Input$[t]\in I_{i_1}$ THEN $(r_{j_2}, ...,r_{j_k})$*

4 Conclusion

Starting from a low-level learning rule ([def.2.]) we have set the weights of a Boolean Neural Network ([def.1.]) so that the network performs a high-level learning ([def.14.]). The network is able to learn autonomously new cause-effect relations between specific inputs and specific output sequences by means of continual learning.

We have remarked that although it is possible for a single subsystem underlie both general-regularity and specific-sequence learning, relatively independent subsystems can execute the two types of learning more efficiently than a single subsystem can do. In this paper, we have focus our attention on one aspect of sequence learning. We propose dealing specific sequence learning with a neural network having an implicit representation of time and no explicit memory.

The time is represented by its effects on the data processing. The memory instead is represented by means of an subdivision of the network into suitable subnets, the assemblies and the primitives, which regulate the weight modifications dependent on a low level learning rule as the Hebbian learning algorithm .

5 REFERENCES

[1]   Caianiello E.R., *Outline of a theory of thought processes and thinking machines*, J. of Theor. Biol., 2, pp.204-235, 1961.

[2]   Elman J.L and Zipper D., *Discovering the hidden structure of speech, Journal of the Acoustical Society of America*, 83, pp.1615-1626, 1988.

[3]   Elman J.L., *Finding Structure in Time*, Cognitive Science, 14, 179-211, 1990.

[4]   Hebb D.O., *The organitation of behavior* (John Wiley and Songs, New York), 1949.

[5]   Jordan M.I., *Serial order: A parallel distributed processing approach*, Institute for Cognitive Science Report 8604, University of California, San Diego, 1986.

[6]   Lauria F. E., Prevete R, *An Algebraic approach to an autonomously self-adaptable Boolean neural network*, Memorie dell'Accademia di Scienze Fisiche e Matematiche, 299+xi, ISBN 88-207-3266-1, 2001

[7]   Lauria F. E., Prevete R., Milo M., Visco S., *A Boolean neural network as a ruled based system learning new rules by examples*, in ICONIP. '98 (Shiro Usui & Takashi Omori eds IOS Press, Kitakyushu, Japan),1637-1641, 1998.

[8]   Marsolek C.J. and Field J.E., *Perceptual-Motor Sequence Learning of General Regularities and Specific Sequences*, JEP: Human Perception and Performance, vol.25, no.3, 1999.

[9]   Marsolek C.J., Schacter D.L & Nicholas C.D, *Form-specific visual priming for new associations in the right cerebral hemisphere*, in Memory & Cognition, 24, pp.539-556, 1996.

[10] Mc Culloch W.S. & Pitts W., *A logical calculus of the ideas immanent in the nervous activity*, Bull. Math. Bioph., 5:115-143, 1943.

[11] Ring M.B., *Continual Learning in Reinforcement Environments*, Oldenbourg Verlag (Publishers), ISBN 3-486-23603-2, 1994.

[12] Stornetta W.S., Hogg T. and Huberman B.A., *A dynamical approach to temporal pattern processing*, in proceedings of the IEEE Conference on Neural Information Processing Systems, Denver, conota 14, 1987

[13] Tank D.W. and Hopfield J.J., *Neural computation by concentrating information in time*, in proceedings of the IEEE International Conference on Neural Networks, San Diego, 1987.

Node Relevance Determination

Neil D. Lawrence

Microsoft Research, Cambridge, U.K.*

neil@thelawrences.net

Abstract

Hierarchical Bayesian inference in parameterised models offers an approach for controlling complexity. In this paper we utilise a novel prior for the leaning of a model's structure. We call the prior *node relevance determination*. It is applicable in a range of models including sigmoid belief networks and Boltzmann machines. We demonstrate how the approach may be applied to determine structure in a multi-layer perceptron.

1 Introduction

Bayesian inference provides one approach to optimising model complexity. In *maximum likelihood learning* we find a particular parameterisation, $\hat{\boldsymbol{\theta}}$, for our model, $\mathcal{M}$, from the set of all possible parameterisations, $\boldsymbol{\theta}$, through maximising the log likelihood of the data:

$$\ln p(D|\boldsymbol{\theta}, \mathcal{M}) = \sum_{n=1}^{N} \ln p(\mathbf{x}_n|\boldsymbol{\theta}, \mathcal{M}). \tag{1}$$

Here the data-set, D, has been assumed to be composed of N independent observations $\mathbf{x}_n$. In *Bayesian learning* an inference process replaces this optimisation. Rather than considering point estimates, $\hat{\boldsymbol{\theta}}$, of the parameters we treat them as stochastic variables. We then infer the posterior distribution of the parameters given the data. To determine this posterior we are also required to define a *prior* distribution over the parameters, $p(\boldsymbol{\theta})$. Once we have selected a prior we marginalise the parameters and obtain the model likelihood

$$p(D|\mathcal{M}) = \int p(D|\boldsymbol{\theta}, \mathcal{M})p(\boldsymbol{\theta})d\boldsymbol{\theta}. \tag{2}$$

This model likelihood can then be made use of in model selection.

When the parameters are continuous, a common choice for the prior is a spherical, zero mean, Gaussian distribution. More complex priors are also possible, the parameters may be placed into G vectors, $\boldsymbol{\theta}_g$, each of which is associated with a separate hyper-parameter α_g: $p(\boldsymbol{\theta}|\boldsymbol{\alpha}) = \prod_{g=1}^{G} \left(\frac{\alpha_g^{K_g}}{2\pi} \right)^{\frac{1}{2}} \exp\left(-\frac{\alpha_g}{2}\boldsymbol{\theta}_g^{\mathsf{T}}\boldsymbol{\theta}_g \right)$. Here K_g is the number of parameters in group g. In its most flexible form such a

---

*This work was completed while the author was at The Computer Laboratory, Cambridge University, Cambridge, U.K.

prior might contain a hyper-parameter for every parameter [7]. Normally, however, the groups will be larger. In the context of neural networks, for example, the weights may be grouped according to the role they play in the network, e.g. ARD priors [5, 4].

2 Node Relevance Determination

In this paper we present a novel prior which takes the grouping of weights a stage further. We consider a prior which places each parameter in two groups and utilise this prior to optimise model structure.

We will apply our prior to a two-layer feed-forward neural network with I input nodes, H hidden nodes and a single output node. The network function may therefore be written as $f(\mathbf{x}, \mathbf{w}) = \sum_{h=1}^{H} v_h g(\mathbf{u}_h^T \mathbf{x})$, where $\mathbf{w} = \{\mathbf{u}_1 \dots \mathbf{u}_H, \mathbf{v}\}$ is a vector representing the parameters or 'weights' of the network. The input to hidden weights are represented by a matrix, $\mathbf{U}$, of H vectors $\mathbf{u}_h$, each vector being the weights that 'fan-in' to hidden unit h. $\mathbf{v}$ is the vector of the hidden to output weights, consisting of H elements v_h. We account for 'biases' by considering additional input and hidden nodes whose values are taken to be one at all times. The activation function $g(\cdot)$ is often taken to be a hyperbolic tangent, for reasons of tractability though we use an alternative, the cumulative Gaussian distribution function[1].

We model the data-set, $D = \{\mathbf{x}_n, t_n\}_{n=1}^{N}$, as being derived from a underlying true function $y(\mathbf{x})$ with Gaussian noise added. This leads us to consider a likelihood function of the form:

$$p(D|\mathbf{w}, \beta) = \left(\frac{\beta}{2\pi}\right)^{N/2} \exp\left(-\frac{\beta}{2}\sum_{n=1}^{N}(t_n - f(\mathbf{x}_n, \mathbf{w}))^2\right), \qquad (3)$$

where β is a parameter governing the inverse noise variance. We implement the node relevance determination prior by associating a hyper-parameter with each node in the network. We split the hyper-parameters into three sub-groups: $\boldsymbol{\alpha}^{(I)}$, $\boldsymbol{\alpha}^{(H)}$ and $\alpha^{(O)}$, the sub-groups contain the hyper parameters associated with the input nodes, hidden nodes and output node respectively.

Our prior then takes the form

$$p(\mathbf{w}|\boldsymbol{\alpha}^{(I)}, \boldsymbol{\alpha}^{(H)}, \alpha^{(O)}) = \prod_{i=1}^{I}\prod_{h=1}^{H}\left(\frac{\alpha_i^{(I)}\alpha_h^{(H)}}{2\pi}\right)^{\frac{1}{2}} \exp\left\{-\frac{1}{2}\alpha_i^{(I)}\alpha_h^{(H)}u_{ih}^2\right\}$$

$$\times \prod_{i=1}^{H}\left(\frac{\alpha_i^{(H)}\alpha^{(O)}}{2\pi}\right)^{\frac{1}{2}} \exp\left\{-\frac{1}{2}\alpha_i^{(H)}\alpha^{(O)}v_i^2\right\}, (4)$$

where u_{ih} and v_i are elements of the matrix $\mathbf{U}$ and the vector $\mathbf{v}$. We term this prior node relevance determination (NRD) because its objective is to determine the relevance of each node in the model.

---

[1] $g(x) = \sqrt{\frac{2}{\pi}} \int_0^x \exp(-t^2)\, dt$

We may treat the hyper-parameters with a second level of Bayesian inference for which we utilise the following hyper-prior: $p(\boldsymbol{\alpha}) = \prod_{i=1}^{I+H+1} \text{gam}(\alpha_i | a, b)$. where $\text{gam}(\cdot)$ is the gamma distribution[2]. Note that exact Bayesian inference in this model is intractable. We therefore turn to variational methods to make progress.

2.1 The Variational Approach

Consider the bound on the likelihood obtained through the introduction of a variational distribution $q(\mathbf{w}, \boldsymbol{\alpha}, \beta)$,

$$\ln p(D) \geq \int q(\mathbf{w}, \boldsymbol{\alpha}, \beta) \ln \frac{p(D, \mathbf{w}, \boldsymbol{\alpha}, \beta)}{q(\mathbf{w}, \boldsymbol{\alpha}, \beta)} \, d\mathbf{w} \, d\boldsymbol{\alpha} \, d\beta. \tag{5}$$

We now assume that the variational distribution factorises, $q_w(\mathbf{w}, \boldsymbol{\alpha}, \beta) = q_w(\mathbf{w}) q_\beta(\beta) q_{\alpha^{(I)}}(\boldsymbol{\alpha}^{(I)}) q_{\alpha^{(H)}}(\boldsymbol{\alpha}^{(H)}) q_{\alpha^{(O)}}(\boldsymbol{\alpha}^{(O)})$. As we are constraining our investigations to the treatment of the distribution, q_α, we only consider the *free-form optimisation* of that distribution [3, 1] leading to $q_\alpha(\boldsymbol{\alpha}) \propto \exp \langle \ln p(\mathbf{w}|\boldsymbol{\alpha}) p(\boldsymbol{\alpha}) \rangle_{q_w}$, where we have utilised $\langle \cdot \rangle_q$ to represent an expectation with respect to the distribution q. The free-form optimisation gives

$$q_{\alpha^{(H)}}(\boldsymbol{\alpha}^{(H)}) = \prod_{i=1}^{H} \Gamma(\alpha_i^{(H)} | \tilde{a}_\alpha^{(H)}, \tilde{b}_{\alpha^{(H)}i}). \tag{6}$$

Similar forms for the input and output hyper-parameters may also be obtained. The parameters of these q-distributions are found as

$$\tilde{a}_\alpha^{(I)} = a_\alpha^{(I)} + \frac{H}{2}, \qquad \tilde{b}_{\alpha^{(I)}i} = b_\alpha^{(I)} + \sum_{h=1}^{H} \frac{\left\langle \alpha_h^{(H)} \right\rangle \left\langle u_{ih}^2 \right\rangle}{2}$$

$$\tilde{a}_\alpha^{(H)} = a_\alpha^{(H)} + \frac{I+2}{2}, \qquad \tilde{b}_{\alpha^{(H)}h} = b_\alpha^{(H)} + \sum_{i=0}^{I} \frac{\left\langle \alpha_i^{(I)} \right\rangle \left\langle u_{ih}^2 \right\rangle}{2} + \frac{\left\langle \alpha^{(O)} \right\rangle \left\langle v_h^2 \right\rangle}{2}$$

$$\tilde{a}_\alpha^{(O)} = a_\alpha^{(O)} + \frac{H+1}{2}, \qquad \tilde{b}_{\alpha^{(O)}} = b_\alpha^{(O)} + \sum_{h=0}^{H} \frac{\left\langle \alpha_h^{(H)} \right\rangle \left\langle v_h^2 \right\rangle}{2}.$$

In the above equation the variable averages, $\langle \cdot \rangle$, are over their respective distributions. In the case of the likelihood function we defined for the regression neural network we may also calculate bound (5) (see [2]). This enables us to monitor convergence of the optimisation and additionally to perform model comparison.

---

[2] $\text{gam}(\tau|a, b) = \frac{b^a}{\Gamma(a)} \tau^{a-1} \exp(-b\tau)$.

2.2 Expectation-Maximisation Structure Optimisation

Optimisation of the lower bound on $p(D|\mathcal{M})$ with respect to the q-distributions can be viewed, in the context of the EM-algorithm, as an approximate expectation step. This expectation step can then be followed by a maximisation step which maximises the lower bound on $p(D|\mathcal{M})$ with respect to the structure of the model $\mathcal{N}$. This could involve the removal of individual weights, but here we consider only node removal. We use the following heuristic to select a node to remove. If we wish to remove a node in the hidden layer we first compute bound (5). We then compute the *effective number of parameters*[3] for each hidden node, $\gamma_h = \sum_i \frac{\left\langle \alpha_h^{(H)} \right\rangle \left\langle \alpha_i^{(I)} \right\rangle}{\left\langle u_{ih}^2 \right\rangle - \left\langle u_{ih} \right\rangle^2} + \frac{\left\langle \alpha_h^{(H)} \right\rangle \left\langle \alpha^{(O)} \right\rangle}{\left\langle v_h^2 \right\rangle - \left\langle v_h \right\rangle^2}$ (see [4]). We remove the node with the lowest effective number of parameters and re-evaluate the bound. If it has increased we continue training with the new structure; otherwise we replace the node. The same process can be undertaken for the input nodes.

3 Results

In all the experiments the variational distribution governing the parameters **w** was chosen to be a diagonal covariance Gaussian for its ease of implementation. Gamma priors were placed over the parameter governing noise variance, β. The posterior distribution of which was then determined by a variational free-form optimisation.

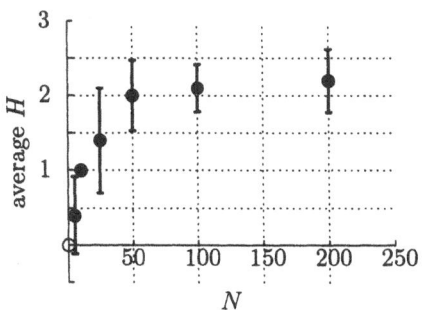

Figure 1: The average determined number of hidden nodes vs. number of data for the toy problem. The error bars show the standard deviation of the number of hidden nodes.

3.1 Toy Problem

To determine the effectiveness of the node-removal prior, we first studied a simple problem involving samples from a sine wave. We took N values from the function $0.4\sin(2\pi x)$. The x value was sampled from a uniform distribution over the interval[4] $(0, 1)$. We added Gaussian noise of variance 0.0025 to the funciton output. Using this data a regression neural network with five hidden nodes was trained using the node relevance prior. We chose very broad hyper-priors by setting $a_\alpha^{(I)} = a_\alpha^{(H)} = a_\alpha^{(O)} = \sqrt{3 \times 10^{-4}}$ and $b_\alpha^{(I)} = b_\alpha^{(H)} = b_\alpha^{(O)} = 1 \times 10^{-3}$. A quasi-newton optimiser was used to optimise q_w. Optimisation was followed by an update of the posterior of β and $\boldsymbol{\alpha}$. We then attempted to optimise structure, in the manner described in the previous

---

[3] Also known as the *number of well determined parameters*.
[4] This is one period of oscillation.

Table 1: Performance of different priors on the data-sets.

Prior type	Sunspot	Tecator
Single	0.190 ($12 \times 8 \times 1$)	0.549 ($10 \times 8 \times 1$)
Grouped	0.194 ($12 \times 8 \times 1$)	0.540 ($10 \times 8 \times 1$)
ARD	0.153 ($3 \times 8 \times 1$)	0.539 ($10 \times 8 \times 1$)
NRD	0.163 ($5 \times 5 \times 1$)	0.532 ($10 \times 2 \times 1$)

section, by cycling through these operations ten times. The experiment was repeated for $N = 5, 10, 25, 50, 100, 200$. Ten networks were trained for N using a different set of samples from the function. The results are summarised in Figure 1, where the average number of determined hidden nodes is plotted against the number of data-points.

3.2 Real Data

Our first real world data-set involves the annual average[5] of sunspots from 1700 to 1920. This time series has served as a benchmark in the statistical literature [8]. The number of hidden nodes was initially taken to be eight and the input window was chosen arbitrarily to be 12, i. e. we modelled $x_n = f(x_{n-1}, \ldots x_{n-12})$. Training and test set selection was as in [9]. We also assessed the performance of our approach on the Tecator data-set[6]. This benchmark was first used by Thodberg [6] to demonstrate the benefits of an evidence approximation based Bayesian approach compared to the early stopping technique[7].

The optimisations, for both data-sets, were undertaken in a similar manner to those of the toy-problem. The NRD network with the highest model likelihood on the Tecator data used two hidden nodes and all the input nodes. For the sunspot data, the NRD network with the highest model likelihood used three hidden nodes and five input nodes. The input nodes used to predict[8] x_n were $x_{n-1}, x_{n-2}, x_{n-5}, x_{n-7}$ and x_{n-8}. For the sunspot data networks were initialised with $I = 12$ and $H = 8$, for the Tecator data $I = 10$ and $H = 8$. Table 1 summarises the results obtained. Alongside each result is the structure of the networks obtained in the form $I \times H \times 1$. The sunspot results quote the normalised mean squared error, however for the Tecator results we follow Thodberg [6] in our use of the standard error of prediction to enable comparisons. The priors we tried are named 'single' which considers only one hyper-parameter, 'grouped' which groups the weights according as input-hidden layer, hidden biases, hidden-output layer and output biases; ARD which further groups the

---

[5]The data are daily, monthly and annually reported by the Royal Observatory of Belgium and can be found at http://www.oma.be/KSB-ORB/SIDC/sidc_txt.html.

[6]The data are recorded on a Tecator Infratec Food and Feed Analyser working in the wavelength range 850 - 1050 nm by the Near Infrared Transmission (NIT) principle.

[7]The data-set is available from http://temper.stat.cmu.edu/datasets/Tecator

[8]Note that in time series prediction it is normal to try and select optimal windows of inputs. Normally a window of size W would include the inputs from $n - 1$ to $n - W$.

input-hidden layer weights according to the input node with which they are associated and the NRD prior described above.

4 Discussion

We have introduced a novel form of prior for determining the relevance of individual nodes or variables in the network and showed how it may be used to determine structure automatically.

When implemented with the noisy sine data, higher complexity (in the form of more hidden nodes) was utilised by the algorithm as more data-points were presented to the model. This behaviour is in line with our expectations. Model complexity is able to increase as more information is provided.

In the benchmark data-sets we studied, the performance of the NRD prior was comparable with that of other widely used approaches. However, the NRD prior was able to discover more compact representations of the data.

References

[1] N. D. Lawrence. *Variational Inference in Probabilistic Models.* PhD thesis, Computer Laboratory, University of Cambridge, New Museums Site, Pembroke Street, Cambridge, CB2 3QG, U.K., 2000. Available from http://www.thelawrences.net/neil.

[2] N. D. Lawrence and M. Azzouzi. A variational Bayesian committee of neural networks. Available from http://www.thelawrences.net/neil, 1999.

[3] D. J. C. MacKay. Developments in probabilistic modelling with neural networks—ensemble learning. In *Neural Networks: Artificial Intelligence and Industrial Applications. Proceedings of the 3rd Annual Symposium on Neural Networks, Nijmegen, Netherlands, 14-15 September 1995*, pages 191–198, Berlin, 1995. Springer.

[4] D. J. C. MacKay. Probable networks and plausible predictions – a review of practical Bayesian methods for supervised neural networks. *Network: Computation in Neural Systems*, 6(3):469–505, 1995.

[5] R. M. Neal. *Bayesian Learning for Neural Networks.* Springer, 1996. Lecture Notes in Statistics 118.

[6] H. H. Thodberg. A review of Bayesian neural networks with an application to near infrared spectroscopy. *IEEE Transactions on Neural Networks*, 7(1):56–72, 1996.

[7] M. E. Tipping. The relevance vector machine. In S. A. Solla, T. K. Leen, and K.-R. Müller, editors, *Advances in Neural Information Processing Systems*, volume 12, pages 652–658, Cambridge, MA, 2000. MIT Press.

[8] H. Tong. *Non-linear Time Series: a Dynamical System Approach*, volume 6 of *Oxford Statistical Science Series*. Clarendon Press, Oxford, 1995.

[9] A. S. Weigend, B. A. Huberman, and D. E. Rumelhart. Predicting sunspots and exchange rates with connectionist networks. In S. Eubank and M. Casdagli, editors, *Proceedings of the 1990 NATO Workshop on Nonlinear Modeling and Forcasting, Santa Fe, New Mexico.* Addison-Wesley, 1990.

Learning Distributed Representations of Relational Data using Linear Relational Embedding

Alberto Paccanaro
Geoffrey E. Hinton
Gatsby Computational Neuroscience Unit
University College London, London, UK
{alberto,hinton}@gatsby.ucl.ac.uk

Abstract

Linear Relational Embedding (LRE) is a new method of learning a distributed representation of concepts from data consisting of binary relations between concepts. The final goal of LRE is to be able to generalize, i.e. to infer new relations among the concepts. The version presented here is capable of handling incomplete information and multiple correct answers. We present results on two simple domains, that show an excellent generalization performance.

1 Introduction

Let us consider a world in which we have objects related to each other through some relations. Let us look for now only at *binary* relations, i.e. relations involving two objects. The way in which these objects relate by means of these relations can be written out as triplets, of the kind {*object1, Relation, object2*}. We are interested in the following problem: *given a few of these triplets, is it possible to infer the other ones?*

Clearly this problem is hopeless if the relations associate objects in a random fashion. Fortunately this is unlikely to happen if the data is taken from the real world where, in general, a lot of structure is present since real objects relate to each other depending on "what" they are, i.e. according to their features. Think for example, of the relations that relate the members of a family. The relation *"has mother"* relates any person to another which must have the features of being *older* than that person (by exactly one generation) and *female.*

This gives us a starting point to try to solve our problem: if objects relate to each other according to their features, then if we could obtain the features of each object which are relevant for the set of relations at hand and the correct rules for how these features interact, it should possible to infer how objects relate. Our approach to solving this problem is therefore to assume structure in the world, to learn a set of features for each object and the rules on how they interact, and then to use these features to infer new triplets. We want to find a mapping from the objects into a feature-space and our idea is to do this by imposing the constraint that relations in this feature-space can be modeled by linear operations. We represent each object as a learned vector in a Euclidean space and each relationship between objects as a learned matrix that maps an object into an approximation of another object. We call this technique *Linear Relational Embedding* (LRE).

Several methods already exist for learning sensible distributed representations from relational data. Multidimensional Scaling [2, 9] finds a representation of concepts as vectors in a multi-dimensional space, in such a way that the dissimilarity of two concepts is modeled by the Euclidean distance between their vectors. Unfortunately, dissimilarity is the only relationship used by multidimensional scaling so it cannot make use of the far more specific information about concepts contained in a triplet like (Mary, has_father, John).

Latent Semantic Analysis (LSA) [3, 4] assumes that the meaning of a word is reflected in the way in which it co-occurs with other words. LSA finds features by performing singular value decomposition on a large matrix and taking the eigenvectors with the largest eigenvalues. Each row of the matrix corresponds to a paragraph of text and the entry in each column is the number of times a particular word occurs in the paragraph or a suitably transformed representation of this count. Each word can then be represented by its projection onto each of the learned features and words with similar meanings will have similar projections. Again, LSA is unable to make use of the specific relational information in a triplet.

Hinton (1986) showed that a multilayer neural network trained using backpropagation could make explicit the semantic features of concepts and relations present in the data. This was done on a simple task called the *family tree problem*. In this problem, the data consists of people and relations among people belonging to two families, one Italian and one English, shown in figure 1 [1]. All the information in these trees can be represented in simple propositions of the form *(person1, relation, person2)*. Using the relations *father, mother, husband, wife, son, daughter, uncle, aunt, brother, sister, nephew, niece* there are 112 such triplets in the two trees. Unfortunately, the system had problems in generalizing when many triplets were missing from the training set.

Finally, it should be mentioned that there has been also a different, more logic-based, approach to the problem of learning relational data. FOIL [8] assumes that relational information can be represented as a set of predicates, i.e. mappings from k-tuples of objects onto truth values. Given data consisting of these mappings for a particular set of concepts (and under the closed-world assumption) FOIL learns a definition of each predicate in terms of the other ones and itself. This is particularly interesting when the data contains a set of basic predicates: FOIL is then able to learn other predicates that can be expressed as a combination of the basic ones. The definitions which are learned are very similar to Horn clauses and will then hold for any other set of data. A limitation of FOIL is that it can learn the definition of a predicate only when

---

[1]The names of the Italian family have been altered from those originally used in Hinton (1986) to match those of one of the author's family.

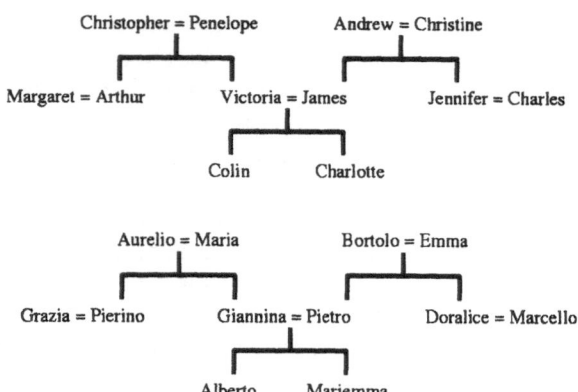

Figure 1: Two isomorphic family trees. The symbol "=" means "married to".

it is possible to define it in terms of the predicates available.

The next section presents the details of Linear Relational Embedding, showing how it overcomes the limitations of the systems which we have presented here.

2   Linear Relational Embedding

Let us assume that our data consists of C triplets (*concept1, relation, concept2*) containing N distinct objects and M binary relations. We shall call this set of triplets $\mathcal{C}$. As anticipated in section 1, the main idea of Linear Relational Embedding is to represent each concept with an n-dimensional vector, and each relation with an $(n \times n)$ matrix. We shall call: $\mathcal{V} = \{\mathbf{v}_\infty, ..., \mathbf{v}_N\}$ the set of vectors corresponding to the N objects, and $\mathcal{R} = \{\mathcal{R}_\infty, ..., \mathcal{R}_M\}$ the set of matrices corresponding to the M relations. Often we shall need to indicate the vectors and the matrix which correspond to the concepts and the relation in a certain triplet c. In this case we shall denote the vector corresponding to the first concept with $\mathbf{a}$, the vector corresponding to the second concept with $\mathbf{b}$ and the matrix corresponding to the relation with R. We shall therefore write the triplet c as $(\mathbf{a}^c, R^c, \mathbf{b}^c)$ where $\mathbf{a}^c, \mathbf{b}^c \in \mathcal{V}$ and $R^c \in \mathcal{R}$. The operation that relates a pair $(\mathbf{a}^c, R^c)$ to a vector $\mathbf{b}^c$ is the matrix-vector multiplication, $R^c \cdot \mathbf{a}^c$, which produces an approximation to $\mathbf{b}^c$.

Here we discuss how to learn an embedding given a set of data, that is how to find suitable vectors and matrices such that for each triplet $(\mathbf{a}^c, R^c, \mathbf{b}^c)$, $\mathbf{b}^c$ is as close as possible to $R^c \cdot \mathbf{a}^c$. The obvious approach is to minimize the sum of squared distances between $R^c \cdot \mathbf{a}^c$ and $\mathbf{b}^c$ over all the triplets

$$S = \sum_{c=1}^{C} \|R^c \cdot \mathbf{a}^c - \mathbf{b}^c\|^2 \tag{1}$$

with respect to all the vector and matrix components. Unfortunately minimizing S (almost) always causes all of the vectors and matrices to collapse to

0. In order to be able to learn a linear embedding, we need a way to minimize S, while at the same time keeping away from the trivial **0** solution. To achieve this we used a discriminative function: for each triplet, c in addition to minimizing the squared distance between $R^c \cdot \mathbf{a}^c$ and $\mathbf{b}^c$ we also maximize the squared distances to other concept vectors that are nearby. This keeps the vectors different from each other, and thus away from the **0** solution. One way of writing such a discriminative function is to think of $R^c \cdot \mathbf{a}^c$ as a noisy version of one of the concept vectors, and to maximize the probability that it is a noisy version of the correct answer, $\mathbf{b}^c$, rather than any of the other possibilities. We imagine that a concept has an average location in the space but that each "observation" of the concept is a noisy realization of this average location. Assuming spherical Gaussian noise with a variance of $1/2$ on each dimension, the probability that a realization of concept i would occur at $R^c \cdot \mathbf{a}^c$ is proportional to $\exp(-\|R^c \cdot \mathbf{a}^c - \mathbf{v}_i\|^2)$. So the posterior probability that $R^c \cdot \mathbf{a}^c$ matches concept $\mathbf{b}^c$ given that it must match one of the known concepts is:

$$P(\mathbf{b}^c | R^c \cdot \mathbf{a}^c) = \frac{e^{-\|R^c \cdot \mathbf{a}^c - \mathbf{b}^c\|^2}}{\sum_{\mathbf{v}_i \in \mathcal{V}} e^{-\|R^c \cdot \mathbf{a}^c - \mathbf{v}_i\|^2}} \tag{2}$$

A discriminative goodness function D, that corresponds to the log probability of getting the right answer, summed over all training triplets is therefore:

$$D = \sum_{c=1}^{C} \frac{1}{k_c} \log \frac{e^{-\|R^c \cdot \mathbf{a}^c - \mathbf{b}^c\|^2}}{\sum_{\mathbf{v}_i \in \mathcal{V}} e^{-\|R^c \cdot \mathbf{a}^c - \mathbf{v}_i\|^2}} \tag{3}$$

where k_c is the number of triplets in $\mathcal{C}$ having the first two terms equal to the ones of c, but differing in the third term. Learning based on maximizing D has given good results, and has proved successful in generalization as well. Examples of this learning can be found in Paccanaro and Hinton (2000a, 2000b, 2001). However, when we learn an embedding by maximizing D, we are not making use of exactly the information that we have in the triplets. For each triplet c, we are making the vector representing the correct completion $\mathbf{b}^c$ more likely than any other concept vector given $R^c \cdot \mathbf{a}^c$ assuming Gaussian noise, while the triplet states that $R^c \cdot \mathbf{a}^c$ must be *equal* to $\mathbf{b}^c$. The numerator of D does exactly that, but then there is the denominator, that is necessary in order to stay away from the **0** solution. We noticed that the denominator is critical at the beginning of the learning, when the vector and matrices could easily shrink to **0**. But as they differentiate, we could gradually lift this burden, allowing $R^c \cdot \mathbf{a}^c = \mathbf{b}^c$ to become the real goal of the learning. To do this we propose here a modified discriminative function that includes a parameter α, which is annealed from 1 to 0 during learning:

$$G = \sum_{c=1}^{C} \frac{1}{k_c} \log \frac{e^{-\|R^c \cdot \mathbf{a}^c - \mathbf{b}^c\|^2}}{[\sum_{\mathbf{v}_i \in \mathcal{V}} e^{-\|R^c \cdot \mathbf{a}^c - \mathbf{v}_i\|^2}]^\alpha} \tag{4}$$

This function G (for Goodness) is maximized during learning. At the beginning, when $\alpha = 1$, maximizing G is equivalent to maximizing D. Then annealing α amounts to gradually changing the error function, until we end up minimizing S. This gives a much better generalization performance than the one obtained by just maximizing D [2].

The results presented in the next sections were obtained by maximizing G using gradient ascent. All the vector and matrix components were updated simultaneously at each iteration. One effective method of performing the optimization is conjugate gradient. Learning was fast, usually requiring only a few hundred updates. In general, different initial configurations and optimization algorithms caused the system to arrive at different solutions, but these solutions were almost always equivalent in terms of generalization performance.

3   Results

Here we shall present the results we obtained using LRE on the *family tree problem* [1] presented earlier, as well as on a simpler task, which we called the *number problem*. In the number problem, the objects are the integers in the set $\mathfrak{D} = [0 \ldots m - 1]$ and the relations are the operations $\mathfrak{L} = \{+1, -1, +2, -2, +3, -3, +4, -4, +0\}$. The data then consists of all or some of the triplets (num_1, op, num_2) where $num_1, num_2 \in \mathfrak{D}$, $op \in \mathfrak{L}$, and num_2 is the result of applying operation op to number num_1 — when the result of the operation is outside $[0 \ldots m - 1]$ we omit the corresponding triplet from the data set.

Fig. 2 show the layout of the vectors obtained for a run of the algorithm for the two problems. In the solution for the family tree problem, notice how the Italians are linearly separable from the English people. From the Hinton diagram, we can see that each member of a family is symmetric to the corresponding member in the other family. The third component of the vectors is almost a feature for the nationality.

The interesting question is whether the system can correctly complete triplets on which it has not been trained. The obvious method for completing triplet $(\mathbf{a}, R, ?)$ is to choose as completion the concept which is closest to $R \cdot \mathbf{a}$. After a concept, say $\mathbf{k}$, has been chosen, we can check whether the triplet $(\mathbf{a}, R, \mathbf{k})$ belongs to the data set. If we use this method for evaluating the system, results are very good. For example, the solution to the number problem shown in figure 2 was trained using only 1/3 of the total number of triplets (143) and still the system was able to complete correctly all of them (430). For the family tree problem the system was generally able to complete correctly all 112 triplets even if 28 of them had been left out during training. These results on the Family Tree problem are much better than the ones obtained by Quinlan (1990) and Hinton (1986) on the same problem.

---

[2] For one-to-many relations we must not decrease the value of α all the way to 0, because this would cause some concept vectors to become coincident. This is because the only way to make $R^c \cdot \mathbf{a}^c$ equal to k_c different vectors, is by collapsing them onto a unique vector.

This method for completing the triplets works well if all the relations are one-to-one. It clearly cannot deal properly with one-to-many relations, in which we may have multiple correct answers. In the Family Tree problem, `Colin` has 2 aunts, namely `Jennifer` and `Margaret`. But if we complete the triplets as described above, the system will always output only one of them, the one which is closest to the dot product of matrix ``aunt'' and vector ``Colin''. Although the answer given is correct, we would like to obtain *all* the correct answers.

Moreover, here we argue that for this kind of problem it is not sufficient to test generalization by merely testing the completion of those valid triplets which have not been used for training. The proper test for generalization is to see how the system completes any triplet of the kind $(\mathbf{a}, R, ?)$ where $\mathbf{a}$ ranges over the concepts and R over the relations. This is because in real world applications we cannot expect to know in advance that triplets like (`Christopher, father, ?`) cannot be completed, because our tree is incomplete (and `Christopher` belongs to the first generation). More generally, we should not suppose to have knowledge of which completions can be asked, and which ones cannot. To our knowledge this issue has never been analyzed before (even though FOIL should be able to correctly handle this problem).

The system needs a way to indicate for those triplets that do not admit a completion that the correct answer is "don't know". To accomplish this, although at the end of the learning we were optimizing S, once the learning has finished we switch back to a probabilistic model. This model is constituted, for each relation, of a mixture of N identical spherical Gaussians, each centered on a vector, and a Uniform distribution. The Uniform distribution will take care of the "don't know" answers, and will be competing with all the other Gaussians, each representing a vector constituting an answer in our dataset. For each relation the Gaussians have different variances and the Uniform a different height. The parameters of this probabilistic model are, for each relation R, the variances of the Gaussians σ_R and the relative density under the Uniform distribution, which we shall write as $\exp(-\frac{r_R^2}{2\sigma_R^2})$. These parameters are learned using a validation set, which will be the union of a set of completable triplets $\mathcal{P}$ and a set of pairs which cannot be completed $\mathcal{N}$; that is $\mathcal{P} = \{\mathbf{a}, \mathcal{R}, \mathbf{b}\}_-^{\mathcal{P}}$ and $\mathcal{N} = \{\mathbf{a}, \mathcal{R}, \perp\}_-^{\mathcal{Q}}$ where $\perp$ indicates the fact that the result of applying relation R^q to $\mathbf{a}^q$ does not belong to $\mathcal{V}$. This is done by maximizing the following discriminative goodness function F over the validation set :

$$
\begin{aligned}
F \;=\; & \sum_{q=1}^{Q} \log \frac{\exp(-\frac{r_R^2}{2\sigma_R^2})}{\exp(-\frac{r_R^2}{2\sigma_R^2}) + \sum_{v_i \in \mathcal{V}} \exp(-\frac{\|R^q \cdot \mathbf{a}^q - \mathbf{v}_i\|^2}{2\sigma_R^2})} \\
& + \sum_{p=1}^{P} \frac{1}{k_p} \cdot \log \frac{\exp(-\frac{\|R^p \cdot \mathbf{a}^p - \mathbf{b}^p\|^2}{2\sigma_R^2})}{\exp(-\frac{r_R^2}{2\sigma_R^2}) + \sum_{v_i \in \mathcal{V}} \exp(-\frac{\|R^p \cdot \mathbf{a}^p - \mathbf{v}_i\|^2}{2\sigma_R^2})}
\end{aligned}
\tag{5}
$$

with respect to the σ_R and r_R parameters, while everything else is kept fixed. As before, k_p is the number of triplets in $\mathcal{P}$ having the first two elements equal to the ones of p, but differing in the third one. Thus for each triplet in $\mathcal{P}$, we maximize the probability that the vector $R^p \cdot \mathbf{a}^p$ is generated from the Gaussian centered on $\mathbf{b}^p$ while minimizing the probability that it comes from any other Gaussian or the Uniform distribution. At the same time, for each triplet in $\mathcal{N}$, we maximize the probability that the vector $R^q \cdot \mathbf{a}^q$ is generated from the Uniform distribution while minimizing the probability that it comes from any of the Gaussians.

Having learned these parameters, in order to complete any triplet $(R, \mathbf{a}, ?)$ we compute the probability distribution over each of the Gaussians and the Uniform distribution given $R \cdot \mathbf{a}$. The system then chooses a vector $\mathbf{v}_i$ or the "don't know" answer according to those probabilities, as the completion to the triplet.

When we tried this method on the number problems, the system always assigned a probability of 1 to the correct answers and 0 to the wrong answers for each of the completable triplets. It also assigned a probability of 1 to the "don't know" symbol for every triplet for which a completion did not exist. In other words, it answered correctly to all 450 possible completions.

For the family tree problem we first picked 12 triplets for the test set, out of the 112 total set of triplets. These were chosen at random, but such that the test set had a triplet for each relation. The same operation was done to obtain another 12 completable triplets for the validation set. Then another 12 uncompletable triplets, 1 per relation, were added to the validation set. So the training set was constituted by 88 triplets, the validation set by 24 triplets and the test set by 12. Once the embedding was learned using the training set, we learned the values of σ_R and r_R for each relation by maximizing F, using the validation set, as described above. We then tested the system by attempting to complete all the 288 possible triplets $(R, \mathbf{a}, ?)$. Figure 3 shows the distribution of the probabilities assigned to each of the 24 concept vectors representing a person, together with the probability assigned to the "don't know" answer when completing the 12 completable triplets in the test set. We can see that the system gives the correct answer, but sometimes it also communicates that "it is not very sure about it" by assigning some probability to the "don't know" answer as well. When tested on uncompletable triplets the system almost always assigned a probability of 1 to the "don't know" symbol, and only very seldom it assigned a small probability to one of the people in the dataset.

4   Conclusions

Linear Relational Embedding is a new method for discovering distributed representations of concepts and relations from data consisting of binary relations between concepts. On the task on which we tried it, it was able to learn sensible representations of the data, and this allowed it to generalize better than any other published method on the datasets used. The main open question is how well it will scale up to problems of bigger size, even if preliminary results on larger data sets seem to be encouraging. LRE can handle any kind of binary relations, learning is fast, generalization is very good. A major limitation at present is that relations need to be binary. We are working on a version that uses higher order tensors to be able to handle higher arity relations.

References

[1] Geoffrey E. Hinton. Learning distributed representations of concepts. In *Proceedings of the Eighth Annual Conference of the Cognitive Science Society*, pages 1–12. Erlbaum, NJ, 1986.

[2] J. B. Kruskal. Multidimensional scaling by optimizing goodness of fit to a nonmetric hypothesis. *Psychometrika*, 29, 1:1–27, 1964.

[3] Thomas K. Landauer and Susan T. Dumais. A solution to Plato's problem: The latent semantic analysis theory of acquisition, induction and representation of knowledge. *Psychological Review*, 104, 2:211–240, 1997.

[4] Thomas K. Landauer, Darrel Laham, and Peter Foltz. Learning human-like knowledge by singular value decomposition: A progress report. In Michael I. Jordan, Michael J. Kearns, and sara A. Solla, editors, *Advances in Neural Processing Information Systems 10*, pages 45–51. The MIT Press, Cambridge Massachusetts, 1998.

[5] Alberto Paccanaro and Geoffrey E. Hinton. Extracting distributed representations of concepts and relations from positive and negative propositions. In *Proceedings of the International Joint Conference on Neural Networks, IJCNN 2000*. 2000.

[6] Alberto Paccanaro and Geoffrey E. Hinton. Learning distributed representations by mapping concepts and relations into a linear space. In Pat Langley, editor, *Proceedings of the Seventeenth International Conference on Machine Learning, ICML2000*, pages 711–718. Morgan Kaufmann Publishers, Stanford University, San Francisco, 2000.

[7] Alberto Paccanaro and Geoffrey E. Hinton. Learning distributed representation of concepts using linear relational embedding. *to appear in IEEE Trans. on Knowledge and Data Engineering - special issue on 'Connectionists Models for Learning in Structured Domains*, 2001.

[8] J. R. Quinlan. Learning logical definitions from relations. *Machine Learning*, 5:239–266, 1990.

[9] F. W. Young and R. M. Hamer. *Multidimensional Scaling: History, Theory and Applications*. Hillsdale, NJ: Lawrence Erlbaum Associates, Publishers,, 1987.

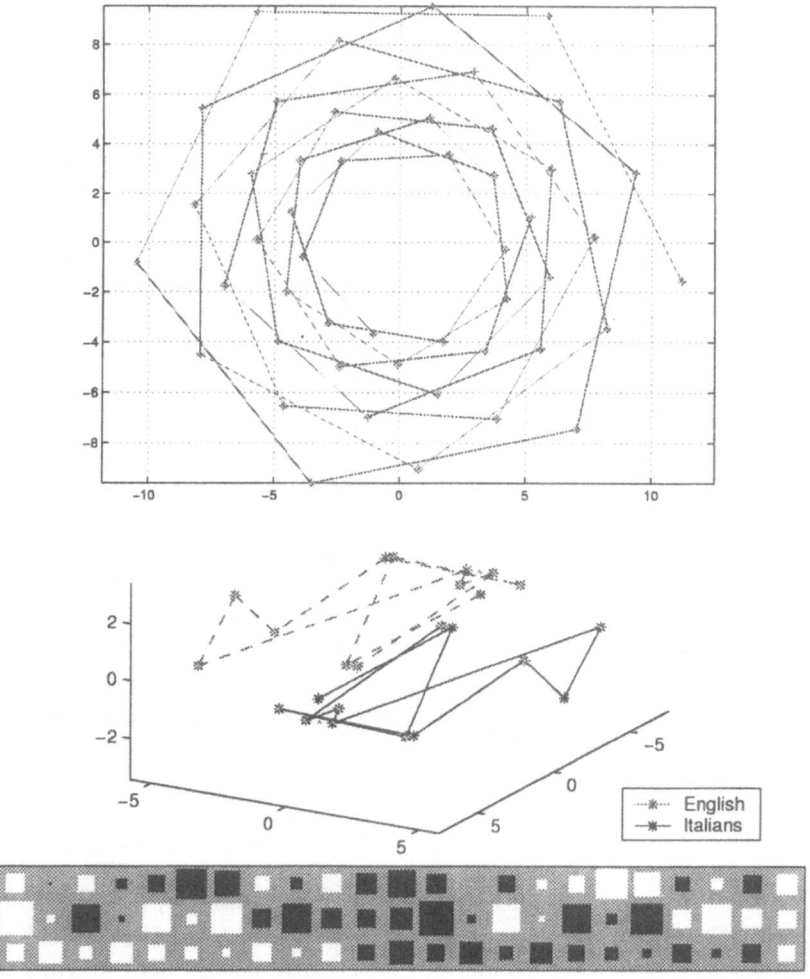

Figure 2: (a)Vectors obtained after learning the number problem with numbers ∈ [1...50] in two dimensions. Vector endpoints are marked with stars and a solid line connects the ones representing consecutive numbers. Vectors corresponding to smaller numbers are closer to the center of the spiral. The training set was constituted by 143 triplets randomly chosen from the total 430 correct triplets. (b)Top: layout of the vectors in 3D space obtained for the family tree problem. Vectors endpoints are indicated by *, the ones in the same family tree are connected to each other. All 112 triplets were used for training. Bottom: Hinton diagrams of the vectors in 3D space obtained for the family tree problem. The vector of each person is a column, in the following order from left to right: 1=Christopher; 2=Andrew; 3=Arthur; 4=James; 5=Charles; 6=Colin; 7=Penelope; 8=Christine; 9=Margaret; 10=Victoria; 11=Jennifer; 12=Charlotte; 13=Aurelio; 14=Bortolo; 15=Pierino; 16=Pietro; 17=Marcello; 18=Alberto; 19=Maria; 20=Emma; 21=Grazia; 22=Giannina; 23=Doralice; 24=Mariemma.

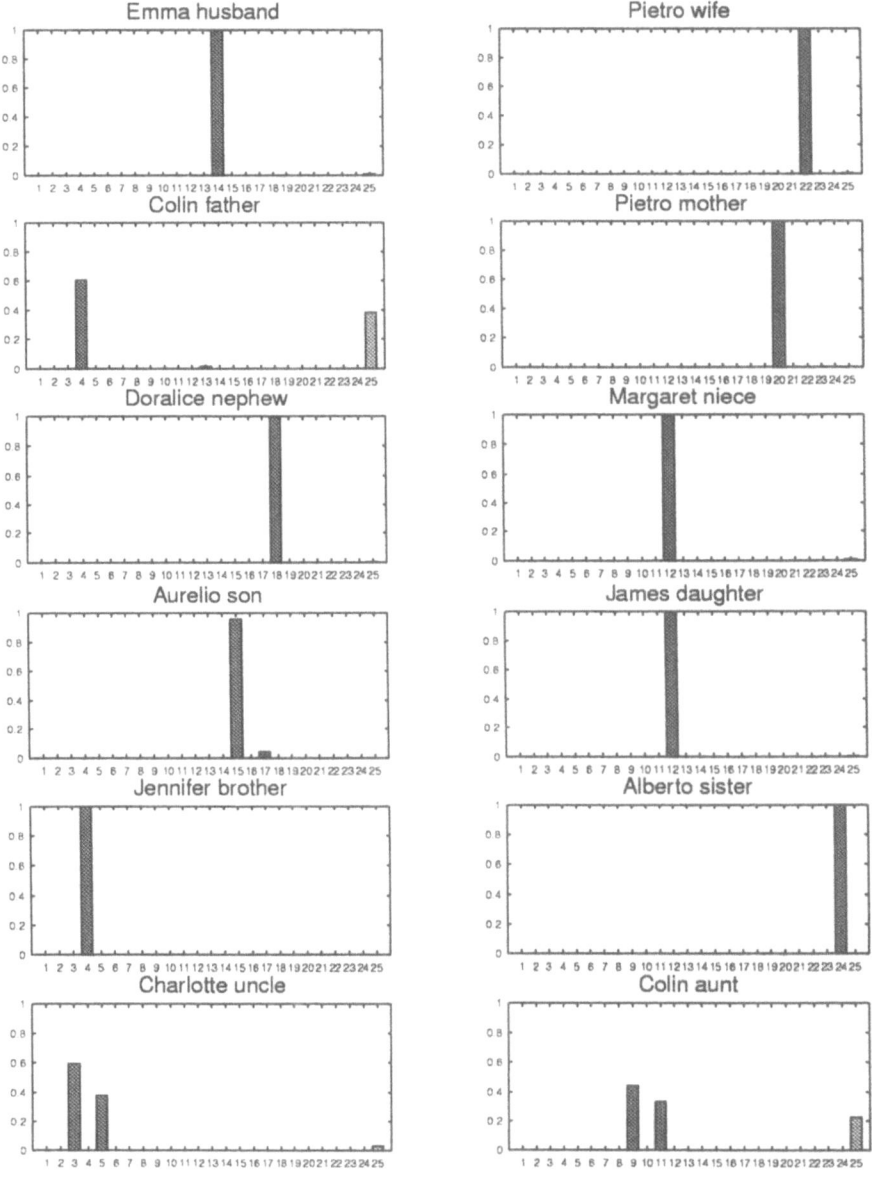

Figure 3: Distribution of the probabilities assigned to each concept for each of the triplet in the test set, written above each diagram. Black bars from 1 to 24 are the probabilities of the people in the order specified in fig. 2. The last grey bar on the right, is the probability of the "don't know" answer.

Payoff-monotonic Game Dynamics for the Maximum Clique Problem

Marcello Pelillo and Claudio Rossi

Dipartimento di Informatica, Università Ca' Foscari di Venezia
Via Torino 155, 30173 Mestre (Venezia), Italy

Abstract

Replicator equations, which arise in evolutionary game theory to model the evolution of animal behavior, have recently been applied with significant success to combinatorial optimization problems such as the maximum clique problem. This paper substantially expands on previous work along these lines, by proposing *payoff-monotonic* dynamics, a wide family of game dynamics of which replicator equations are just a special instance. Experiments show that this class contains dynamics which are considerably faster than and as accurate as replicator equations.

1 Introduction

The maximum clique problem is a well-known graph-theoretic problem which finds important applications in many different domains. Since it is known to be NP-hard, however, exact algorithms are guaranteed to return a solution only in a time which increases exponentially with the number of vertices in the graph. This makes them inapplicable even to moderately large problem instances. Moreover, a series of recent theoretical results show that the problem is in fact difficult to solve even in terms of approximation. In light of these negative results, much effort has recently been directed towards devising efficient clique-finding heuristics, for which no formal guarantee of performance may be provided, but are anyway of interest in practical applications. In the neural network community, there has also been much recent interest around this important problem (see, e.g., [1, 4, 8, 10] and references therein). We refer to [3] for an up-to-date review concerning algorithms, applications, and complexity issues related to the maximum clique problem.

In the mid-1960s, Motzkin and Straus [9] established a remarkable connection between the maximum clique problem and a quadratic programming problem on the standard simplex. The Motzkin-Straus formulation, and variations thereof, has motivated the development of various neural network heuristics for maximum clique. In particular, *replicator equations* from evolutionary game theory have proven to be quite effective in solving this and related combinatorial optimization problems [2, 5, 4, 10, 11, 14].

This paper substantially expands on previous works along these lines. We introduce a wide family of *payoff-monotonic* dynamical systems of which replicator equations are just a special instance. The models in this family enjoy precisely the same dynamical properties as replicator equations, and hence they naturally suggest themselves as heuristics for the maximum clique problem.

Preliminary experiments conducted on random graphs of various order and density show that this class contains dynamics which are considerably faster and as accurate as replicator equations.

2 Payoff-monotonic dynamics and their properties

Consider a large, ideally infinite population of individuals of the same species which compete for a particular limited resource, such as food, territory, etc. In evolutionary game theory, this kind of conflict is modeled as a symmetric two-players game, the players being pairs of randomly selected population members. In contrast to traditional application fields of game theory, such as economics or sociology, players here do not behave "rationally", but act instead according to a pre-programmed behavior pattern, or *pure strategy*. Reproduction is assumed to be asexual, which means that, apart from mutation, offspring will inherit the same genetic material, and hence behavioral phenotype, as its parent.

Let $J = \{1, \cdots, n\}$ be the set of available pure strategies and, for all $i \in J$, let $x_i(t)$ be the proportion of population members playing strategy i, at time t. The state of the population at a given instant is the vector $\mathbf{x} = (x_1, \cdots, x_n)'$. Clearly, population states are constrained to lie in the standard simplex of the n–dimensional Euclidean space $\mathbb{R}^n$:

$$\Delta = \left\{ \mathbf{x} \in \mathbb{R}^n \ : \ x_i \geq 0 \text{ for all } i \in J, \ \sum_i x_i = 1 \right\}$$

Let $A = (a_{ij})$ be the $n \times n$ payoff (or utility) matrix. Specifically, for each pair of strategies $i, j \in J$, a_{ij} represents the payoff of an individual playing strategy i against an opponent playing strategy j. In biological contexts a player's utility can simply be measured in terms of Darwinian fitness or reproductive success, i.e., the player's expected number of offspring. If the population is in state $\mathbf{x}$, the expected payoff earnt by an i-strategist is:

$$\pi_i(\mathbf{x}) = \sum_{j=1}^{n} a_{ij} x_j = (A\mathbf{x})_i \tag{1}$$

while the mean payoff over the entire population is

$$\pi(\mathbf{x}) = \sum_{i=1}^{n} x_i \pi_i(\mathbf{x}) = \mathbf{x}' A \mathbf{x} . \tag{2}$$

In evolutionary game theory the assumption is made that the game is played over and over, generation after generation, and that the action of natural selection will result in the evolution of the fittest strategies. If successive generations blend into each other, the evolution of behavioral phenotypes can be described by a set of ordinary differential equations. A general class of evolution equations are given by:

$$\dot{x}_i = x_i g_i(\mathbf{x}) \tag{3}$$

where a dot signifies derivative with respect to time, and $g = (g_1, \ldots, g_n)$ is a function with open domain containing Δ. Here, the function g_i ($i \in J$) specifies the rate at which pure strategy i replicates. It is usually required that the growth functions g be *regular* [15], which means that it is Lipschitz continuous and that $g(\mathbf{x}) \cdot \mathbf{x} = 0$. The former condition guarantees us that the system of differential equations (3) has a unique solution through any initial population state. The condition $g(\mathbf{x}) \cdot \mathbf{x} = 0$, instead, ensures that the simplex Δ is invariant under (3), namely any trajectory starting in Δ will remain in Δ.

Payoff-monotonic game dynamics represent a wide class of regular selection dynamics for which useful properties hold. Intuitively, for a payoff-monotonic dynamics the strategies associated to higher payoffs will increase at higher rate. Formally, a regular selection dynamics (3) is said to be payoff-monotonic if:

$$g_i(\mathbf{x}) > g_j(\mathbf{x}) \Leftrightarrow \pi_i(\mathbf{x}) > \pi_j(\mathbf{x}), \qquad \mathbf{x} \in \Delta. \tag{4}$$

The following result, proved in [6], generalizes the celebrated fundamental theorem of natural selection [7, 15].

Theorem 1 *If the payoff matrix A is symmetric, then $\pi(\mathbf{x}) = \mathbf{x}'A\mathbf{x}$ is strictly increasing along any non-constant trajectory of any payoff-monotonic dynamics. In other words, $\dot{\pi}(\mathbf{x}(t)) \geq 0$ for all t, with equality if and only if $\mathbf{x} = \mathbf{x}(t)$ is a stationary point. Furthermore, a vector $\mathbf{x}$ is an asymptotically stable point if and only if it is a strict local maximizer of $\pi(\mathbf{x})$ in Δ.*

A well-known subclass of payoff-monotonic game dynamics is given by:

$$\dot{x}_i = x_i \left(f(\pi_i(\mathbf{x})) - \sum_{j=1}^{n} x_j f(\pi_j(\mathbf{x})) \right) \tag{5}$$

where $f(u)$ is an increasing function of u. These models arise in modeling the evolution of behavior by way of imitation processes, where players are occasionally given the opportunity to change their own strategies [6, 15].

When f is the identity function, i.e., $f(u) = u$, we obtain the standard replicator equations:

$$\dot{x}_i = x_i \left(\pi_i(\mathbf{x}) - \sum_{j=1}^{n} x_j \pi_j(\mathbf{x}) \right) \tag{6}$$

whose basic idea is that the average rate of increase $\dot{x}_i/x_i$ equals the difference between the average fitness of strategy i and the mean fitness over the entire population.

Another popular model arises when $f(u) = e^{\kappa u}$ which yields:

$$\dot{x}_i = x_i \left(e^{\kappa \pi_i(\mathbf{x})} - \sum_{j=1}^{n} x_j e^{\kappa \pi_j(\mathbf{x})} \right) \tag{7}$$

where κ is a positive constant. As κ tends to 0, the orbits of this dynamics approach those of the standard, first-order replicator model (6), slowed down by the factor κ; moreover, for large values of κ the model approximates the so-called "best-reply" dynamics [6, 7].

3 Clique finding payoff-monotonic dynamics

Let $G = (V, E)$ be an undirected graph, where $V = \{1, \cdots n\}$ is the set of vertices and $E \subseteq V \times V$ is the set of edges. A subset of vertices C is called a *clique* if all its vertices are mutually adjacent, i.e., for all $i, j \in C$ $(i \neq j)$ we have $(i, j) \in E$. A clique is said to be *maximal* if it is not contained in any larger clique, and *maximum* if it is the largest clique in the graph. The maximum clique problem asks for a clique of maximum cardinality.

Given a subset of vertices C of G, we will denote by $\mathbf{x}^c$ its *characteristic vector*, which is the point in Δ defined as $x_i^c = 1/|C|$ if $i \in C$, $x_i^c = 0$ otherwise, where $|C|$ denotes the cardinality of C. Now, consider the following quadratic function

$$f_G(\mathbf{x}) = \mathbf{x}' A_G \mathbf{x} + \frac{1}{2}\mathbf{x}'\mathbf{x} \qquad (8)$$

where $A_G = (a_{ij})$ is the adjacency matrix of G, i.e., the $n \times n$ symmetric matrix defined as $a_{ij} = 1$ if $(i, j) \in E$ and $a_{ij} = 0$ otherwise.

The following theorem, proved by Bomze [2], expands on the Motzkin-Straus theorem [9], a remarkable result which establishes a connection between the maximum clique problem and a certain quadratic program. This has an intriguing computational significance in that it allows us to shift from the discrete to the continuous domain in an elegant manner.

Theorem 2 *Let C be a subset of vertices of a graph G, and let $\mathbf{x}^c$ be its characteristic vector. Then, C is a maximum (maximal) clique of G if and only if $\mathbf{x}^c$ is a global (local) maximizer of f_G in Δ. Moreover, all local (and hence global) maximizers of f_G in Δ are strict.*

Unlike the original Motzkin-Straus formulation, which is plagued by the presence of "spurious" solutions [12], this result guarantees us that *all* maximizers of f_G on Δ are strict, and are characteristic vectors of maximal/maximum cliques in the graph. In a formal sense, therefore, a one-to-one correspondence exists between maximal cliques and local maximizers of f_G in Δ on the one hand, and maximum cliques and global maximizers on the other hand.

The previous result naturally suggests using payoff-monotonic dynamics as a useful heuristic for the maximum clique problem. Indeed, let $G = (V, E)$ be a graph and let A_G denote its adjacency matrix. By putting

$$A = A_G + \frac{1}{2}I \qquad (9)$$

where I is the identity matrix, we know from Theorem 1 that any payoff-monotonic dynamics, starting from an arbitrary initial state, will iteratively maximize the function f_G in Δ and will eventually converge to a strict local maximizer which, by virtue of Theorem 2, will then correspond to the characteristic vector of a maximal clique of G. Clearly, in theory there is no guarantee that the converged solution will be a *global* maximizer of f_G, and therefore that it will yield a *maximum* clique in G. However, previous experimental work [5, 4, 10, 11, 14], and also the results presented in this paper, suggest that the basins of attraction of global maximizers are quite large and local, gradient-based procedures frequently converge to one of them. Without any heuristic information about the optimal solution, it is customary to start out the evolution process from the simplex barycenter. This choice ensures that no particular solution is favored.

4 Experimental results

In this section we present some preliminary experiments of applying payoff-monotonic dynamics to the maximum clique problem. In our simulations, we used the following discrete-time models:

$$x_i(t+1) = \frac{x_i(t)\pi_i(t)}{\sum_{j=1}^{n} x_j(t)\pi_j(t)} \quad \text{and} \quad x_i(t+1) = \frac{x_i(t)e^{\kappa\pi_i(t)}}{\sum_{j=1}^{n} x_j(t)e^{\kappa\pi_j(t)}} \quad (10)$$

which correspond to well-known discretizations of equations (6) and (7), respectively. Note that the model (10)-left is the standard discrete-time replicator dynamics, which have already proven to be remarkably effective in tackling maximum clique and related problems, and to be competitive to other more elaborated neural network heuristics (we do not report here these results due to lack of space, see, e.g. [2, 5, 4, 10, 11, 14]). Equation (10)-right has been used in [11] to approximate the graph isomorphism problem. For the latter dynamics the following values of κ were used: 1, 3, 5, 7 and 10. Both the first-order and the exponential processes were started from the simplex baycenter and stopped when a maximal clique (i.e. a strict local maximizer of f_G) was found. Occasionally, it may happen that the algorithms converge to a non-maximizer stationary point (a saddle of the objective function). In these cases we adopted a simple greedy heuristic which allows us to obtain a new, better point from the current one (see [13] for details).

In the experiments reported here, we ran the algorithms over 100-, 200- and 500-vertex random graphs with densities ranging from 0.1 to 0.99. For each order and density value 10 different graphs were generated. Figures 1–3 show the results obtained, in terms of clique size obtained and CPU time.[1] Each point on the curves represents an average over ten trials. From the results obtained a remarkable regularity does emerge. All the dynamics yielded similar results in terms of quality of solution (i.e. size of maximal clique found). As far as the computational time is concerned, instead, note how for dense graphs the exponential dynamics is dramatically faster than the first-order model. Note

---

[1] All experiments were performed on a 200 MHz Pentium II machine.

also how, as expected, the parameter κ in the exponential dynamics play a major role on the speed of convergence: the higher κ the faster the convergence. When κ becomes too high, however, we noted that numerical stability problems can arise, and oscillatory behaviors can emerge (cfr [11]). Other experiments, not reported here due to lack of space, on other types of random graphs as well as on DIMACS benchmark graphs also confirm this kind of behavior (see [13]).

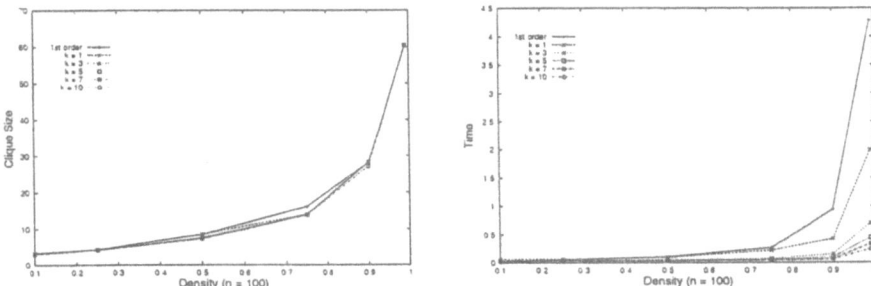

Figure 1: Results on 100-vertex random graphs. Left: clique size. Right: CPU time (sec).

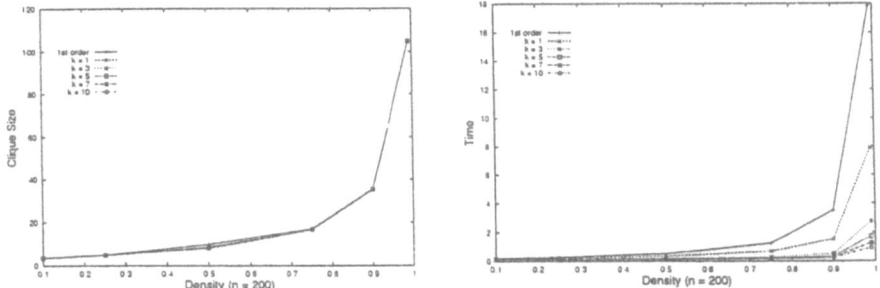

Figure 2: Results on 200-vertex random graphs. Left: clique size. Right: CPU time (sec).

5 Conclusions

We have presented a class of evolutionary game dynamics which, thanks to their properties, naturally lend themselves to solve quadratic optimization problems. We have applied them to the maximum clique problem, using the Motzkin-Straus continuous formulation, and have experimentally shown that there are dynamics in this class which are fast and accurate. The class is large enough to contain other interesting dynamics and we are currently investigating their uselfulness in combinatorial optimization.

References

[1] A. Bertoni, P. Campadelli, and G. Grossi. A discrete neural algorithm for the maximum clique problem: Analysis and circuit implementation. In *Proc.*

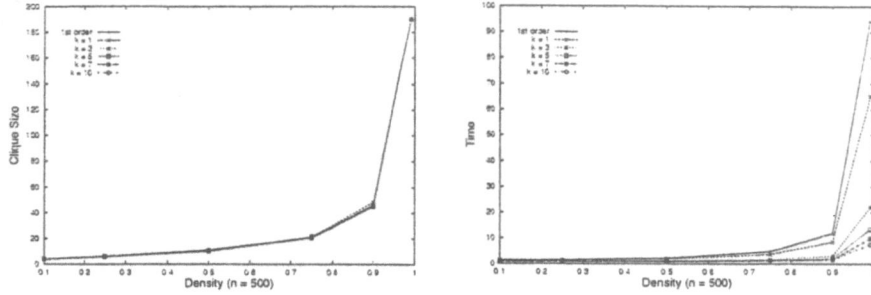

Figure 3: Results on 500-vertex random graphs. Left: clique size. Right: CPU time (sec).

WAE'97: Int. Workshop on Algorithm Engineering, Venice, Italy, 1997.

[2] I. M. Bomze. Evolution towards the maximum clique. J. Global Optim., 10:143–164, 1997.

[3] I. M. Bomze, M. Budinich, P. M. Pardalos, and M. Pelillo. The maximum clique problem. In D.-Z. Du and P. M. Pardalos, editors, Handbook of Combinatorial Optimization (Suppl. Vol. A), pages 1–74. Kluwer, Boston, MA, 1999.

[4] I. M. Bomze, M. Pelillo, and V. Stix. Approximating the maximum weight clique using replicator dynamics. IEEE Trans. Neural Networks, 11(6):1228–1241, 2000.

[5] I. M. Bomze et.al. Evolutionary approach to the maximum clique problem: Empirical evidence on a larger scale. In I. M. Bomze et.al., editor, Developments in Global Optimization, pages 95–108. Kluwer, Dordrecht, The Netherlands, 1997.

[6] J. Hofbauer. Imitation dynamics for games. Collegium Budapest, preprint, 1995.

[7] J. Hofbauer and K. Sigmund. Evolutionary Games and Population Dynamics. Cambridge University Press, Cambridge, UK, 1998.

[8] A. Jagota, L. Sanchis, and R. Ganesan. Approximately solving maximum clique using neural networks and related heuristics. In D. Johnson and M. Trick, editors, Cliques, Coloring, and Satisfiability, DIMACS, 26:169–204. AMS, 1996.

[9] T. S. Motzkin and E. G. Straus. Maxima for graphs and a new proof of a theorem of Turán. Canad. J. Math., 17:533–540, 1965.

[10] M. Pelillo. Relaxation labeling networks for the maximum clique problem. J. Artif. Neural Networks, 2:313–328, 1995.

[11] M. Pelillo. Replicator equations, maximal cliques, and graph isomorphism. Neural Computation, 11(8):2023–2045, 1999.

[12] M. Pelillo and A. Jagota. Feasible and infeasible maxima in a quadratic program for maximum clique. J. Artif. Neural Networks, 2:411–420, 1995.

[13] M. Pelillo and C. Rossi. Payoff-monotonic game dynamics and the maximum clique problem. In preparation.

[14] M. Pelillo, K. Siddiqi, and S. W. Zucker. Matching hierarchical structures using association graphs. IEEE Trans. PAMI, 21(11):1105–1120, 1999.

[15] J. W. Weibull. Evolutionary Game Theory. MIT Press, Cambridge, MA, 1995.

PHASE TRANSITIONS IN A NEURAL MODEL OF PROBLEM SOLVING

Maria Pietronilla Penna   Eliano Pessa

Dipartimento di Filosofia – Sezione Psicologia
Università degli Studi di Pavia
Piazza Botta, 6 (Palazzo S.Felice), 27100 Pavia, Italy
e-mail: npenna@ hotmail.com, eliano.pessa@unipv.it

Abstract
In order to model the process of acquisition of competence by children in solving problems of addition between integer numbers, we introduced a generalization of a celebrated neural network model, the Harmony Theory proposed by Smolensky. The generalization consists in allowing a variable number of atoms of knowledge, as well as variable strengths associated to them. The variation of these quantities depends on the rightness of the answer given by the network to a particular addition problem. We monitored the average values of correctly solved problems and the maximum values of $\Delta C/\Delta T$, C being the specific heat and T the temperature, as defined by Smolensky, in order to find evidence for phase transitions in a simulated learning process. We found only partial evidence of such phase transitions. Besides, the network performance was strongly dependent on the structuration of initial dotation of knowledge atoms.

1. Introduction

Connectionist approach introduces two different levels of description of cognitive processes: the *microscopic* one, in which we monitor the activity patterns of a number of microcognitive units, each one devoted to detect a particular feature of input pattern, and the *macroscopic* one, in which observable effects of cognitive processing emerge as a collective effect of the interaction between microcognitive units. The metaphor most used to picture such a form of emergence is the one of *symmetry breaking phase transitions*, as occurring, e.g., in correspondence to transition from paramagnetic to ferromagnetic state [1]. A concrete application of this idea to neural networks, however, is still lacking, except for a particular model, built at the very beginning of connectionist era: Smolensky's *Harmony Theory* [4]. Model's main assumptions can be listed as follows:

a) knowledge is represented, at a microscopic level, by a suitable set of *knowledge atoms*, whereas input and output relationships are described through a suitable set of *microfeature units*;

b) the activations, both of knowledge atoms and of microfeature units, change with time, as a result of the mutual interactions between these units; such interactions, mediated by suitable interconnections, are ruled by an evolutionary dynamics maximizing a suitable global Ljapunov function, usually called *Harmony* function;

c) the outcome of a cognitive process is to be identified with the final equilibrium activation pattern of microfeature units corresponding to a maximum of Harmony function; the evolution from an initial activation pattern of these units (the initial state of cognitive process) to a final equilibrium activation pattern is equivalent to a symmetry breaking phase transition.

Such a model leaves unanswered a number of questions:

1) what happens when cognitive system is an open system, in which the number of knowledge atoms can vary as a function of information coming from external environment through, e.g., the action of a teacher?

2) what kinds of knowledge atoms could grant for a cognitive performance similar to the one observed in human subjects?

3) what proof we have that every cognitive process is always associated to a symmetry breaking phase transition?

In order to answer these questions in this paper we introduced a suitable generalization of Smolensky's Harmony Theory, and we applied it to the modelling of a particular cognitive process: the acquisition, by a child, of the ability to solve a simple arithmetical problem, consisting in adding two integer numbers. The results we obtained from cognitive simulations of model behavior can be thus synthetized:

I)   a good model's performance in solving addition problems can be obtained if and only if two conditions are simultaneously satisfied: α) the set of knowledge atoms includes, besides examples of particular additions, *general rules* for performing an addition whatsoever, β) the initial dotation of knowledge atoms includes examples of the simplest possible additions;

II) symmetry breaking phase transitions really occur in correspondence to the solution of particular addition problems; there is no indication, however, of their occurring in correspondence to the solution of *every* addition problem; besides, we didn't find any connection between the occurring of a symmetry breaking phase transition and the features of solution process.

These results evidence, on one hand, that emergence of cognitive processes can take place only in presence of a suitable pre-structuring of initial knowledge base, and, on the other hand, cast some doubt on usefulness and feasibility of an approach to cognitive modelling, such as the one proposed by Smolensky, based only on a single global Ljapunov function.

2. The generalization of Harmony Theory

The original formulation of Harmony Theory is based on a neural network architecture designed to do *completion tasks*, containing a layer of microfeature units, or *feature layer*, in which each unit has two possible levels of activation (+1 or −1), and a *knowledge layer*, in which each unit, or knowledge atom, is still associated to two different activation levels, this time corresponding to 1 or 0. Each knowledge atom is characterized by a static vector of feature values, each one of which can be represented by +1, 0 or −1. Knowledge atoms whose feature vectors contain only +1 or −1 values can be considered as describing *particular examples of successful completions*, whereas knowledge atoms whose feature vectors contain also zero values can be associated to descriptions of (more or less general) *rules*.

Each microfeature unit is connected to each knowledge atom by a bidirectional connection with weights fixed and equal in both directions. The weight w_{ij} of the interconnection linking the i-th knowledge atom to the j-th microfeature unit is given by:

$$w_{ij} = k_{ij} / \sum_j | k_{ij} | \tag{1}$$

where k_{ij} is the j-th element of the feature vector associated to the i-th knowledge atom. The dynamics of such a network is such as to maximize a global Harmony function given by:

$$H = \Sigma_i \; \sigma_i \; a_i \; [\; (\Sigma_j \; r_j w_{ij}) - \kappa \;] \qquad\qquad (2)$$

where σ_i is the *strength* of the i-th knowledge atom, a_i denotes its activation level, whereas r_j is the activation level of the j-th microfeature unit. The parameter κ (lying between 0 and 1) represents a sort of *threshold*, introduced to avoid local maxima of H during network activation dynamics. The latter consists in a relaxation process, based on an asynchronous dynamics of network units based on a suitable 'simulated annealing' schedule [2].

In order to generalize such a model we introduced the following assumptions:

$a.1$) when the equilibrium activation pattern of microfeature units corresponds to a *right* answer of the network to the problem to be solved , then all strengths of knowledge atoms with nonzero activations in the final equilibrium state are *increased* according to the following law:

$$\sigma_i \rightarrow \sigma_i + \eta_p \quad , \qquad\qquad (3)$$

where η_p is a suitable parameter;

$a.2$) when, on the contrary, the previous equilibrium pattern corresponds to a *wrong* answer, then all strengths of knowledge atoms with nonzero activations are *decreased* according to the law:

$$\sigma_i \rightarrow \sigma_i \, (1 - \eta_m) \quad , \qquad\qquad (4)$$

where η_m is another parameter; besides, the right answer is added to the network as a new knowledge atom, whose feature vector coincides with the right example itself.

These generalizations let us take into account the feedback exerted on the network by an external teacher.

3. Numerical Experiments

In our simulations we studied how our network was able to solve the problem of adding two positive integer numbers, whose sum was not greater than 31. Each number was represented through a sequence of 5 binary digits (with 0 values recoded as -1), so that the total number of microfeature units was 15; the activation levels of 10 of them (representing the two addends) were kept fixed during the whole simulation, whereas the completion task was consisting in finding the right microfeature activations of the remaining 5 microfeature units, representing the sum. The simulations described in this paper were designed to address the following issues:

$p.1$) can an initial activation of knowledge atoms, constituted only by particular examples of rightly performed sums, grant for a good performance in solving new addition problems, never encountered before?

p.2) do we need the inclusion, within the set of initial knowledge atoms, of the simplest examples of additions (like happens when teaching to children in schools)?

p.3) do we need a value of κ very close to 1, as claimed by Smolensky, in order to obtain a good network performance?

p.4) is every solution process associated to a symmetry breaking phase transition?

To this regard, for each simulation we monitored the following quantities:

q.1) the percentage *p* of correctly solved addition problems;

q.2) the average number *A* , on the set of correctly solved problems, of knowledge atoms activated in the final state;

q.3) the average value Γ , on the set of correctly solved problems, of the maximum value of $\Delta C/\Delta T$ found in each solution process; here the 'specific heat' *C* is defined, according to Smolensky's proposal, by:

$$C = [<H^2> - <H>^2]/T^2 \quad , \tag{5}$$

where the symbol <...> denotes averages taken with respect to epochs, during relaxation process, in which annealing temperature *T* stays constant; the rationale for such a choice is dictated by the fact that a symmetry breaking phase transition is associated (theoretically) to a divergence (or a discontinuity) of the curve giving *C* as a function of *T*; therefore a high value of $\Delta C/\Delta T$ should evidence the presence of such a circumstance and, consequently, of a symmetry breaking phase transition.

All simulations we performed were based on a set of 16 addition problems, 6 of which were chosen to enter into the initial dotation of knowledge atoms, whereas the remaining 10 had to be solved by the network. All problems were different one from another. Our experiments can be subdivided into three groups:

g.1) simulations in which the initial dotation of knowledge atoms was consisting only of 6 examples of rightly performed sums; κ was kept constant in each simulation;

g.2) simulations in which the initial dotation of knowledge atoms was consisting both of 6 examples of rightly performed sums and of 14 different rules of additions between single binary digits; κ was again kept constant;

g.3) simulations in which the initial dotation of knowledge atoms was as in *g*.2), but κ varied within each simulation as a function of *T*, according to the law:

$$\kappa = \kappa_0 /[\kappa_0 + T(t)] \quad , \tag{6}$$

where κ_0 is a suitable parameter.

Each group was further composed by two sub-cases: the *unstructured* one, in which the 6 initial examples of rightly performed sums were chosen at random, and the *structured* one, in which the 6 initial examples were corresponding to the simplest additions: 1 + 1, 2 + 1, 1 + 2, 3 + 1, 2 + 2, 1 + 3. In correspondence to each sub-case we experimented the effect of 9 different values of κ (0.1, 0.2, 0.3, 0.4, 0.5, 0.6, 0.7, 0.8, 0.9) or of κ_0 . Besides, for each choice of κ we performed three different simulations, by averaging the obtained results, for a total of 3x9x2x3 = 162 different simulations. In all simulations we adopted the values $\eta_p = \eta_m = 0.1$, and a total duration of relaxation process of 500 epochs, with a simulated annealing schedule as described in Figure 1.

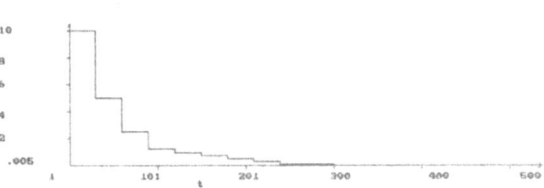

Figure 1

As regards the simulations of the group g.1), none of the proposed problems was solved in the structured case, for whatever choice of κ, whereas, in the unstructured case, the only nonzero percentages of solved problems were corresponding to κ = 0.1 (10%), κ = 0.5 (20%), κ = 0.6 (10%), κ = 0.7 (10%), κ = 0.8 (10%).
The simulations of group g.2) evidenced a consistent improvement of performance with respect to the group g.1). In the Figures 2a and 2b we show, respectively, the percentages of correctly solved problems as a function of κ in the unstructured and in the structured case.

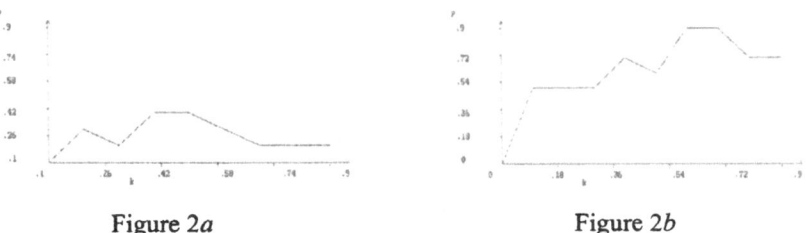

Figure 2a   Figure 2b

It can be seen from these graphs that the performance in the structured case is far better than in the unstructured one. As regards the average numbers of activated knowledge atoms, in both cases we observed a regular diminution of A with increasing κ (the Bravais-Pearson correlation coefficient between A and κ is − 0.912 in the unstructured case and − 0.892 in the structured one). On the contrary, the value of Γ evidences strong fluctuations, without being correlated in a significant way with the corresponding values of κ , p or A . In the unstructured case we go from a minimum corresponding to Γ = 22.46727 for κ = 0.8 to a maximum corresponding to Γ = 2111.229 for κ = 0.7. In the structured case the maximum Γ = 1090.083 corresponds to κ = 0.2, whereas the minimum Γ = 8.840702 corresponds to κ = 0.7. A trend similar to the one of group g.2) is evidenced also by the simulations belonging to the group g.3), even if the performance is, on the average, slightly worse and, in the structured case, its highest values are associated to low initial values of κ . In Figures 3a and 3b we show the percentage of solved problems as a function of the initial value of κ , respectively in the unstructured and in the structured case.

156

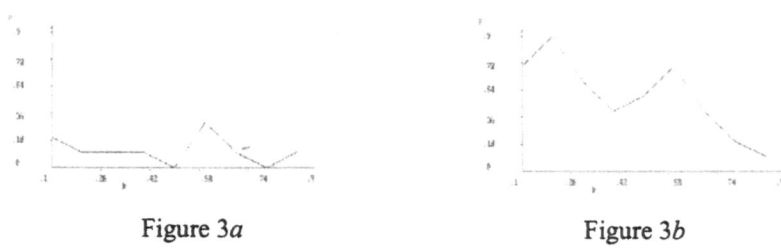

Figure 3*a*   Figure 3*b*

The trend of *A* as a function of the initial value of κ is, more or less, similar to the one of the group *g*.2). Equally puzzling is the strongly fluctuating behavior of Γ as a function of κ.

4. Discussion and conclusions

The data so far obtained evidence that an initial dotation of knowledge atoms containing only single examples of rightly performed sums cannot give rise to acceptable network performance. Besides, even if we include rules within the initial set of knowledge atoms, the network performance is notably improved when we add to this set particular examples relative to the simplest possible additions. As regards the values of κ, our results show that maximum performance doesn't correspond to highest κ values. Such a circumstance is supported by the fact that the increase of κ value during relaxation process, as done in the simulations of the group *g*.3), produces a worsening, instead of an improvement, of performance. Finally, we found evidence of a number of cases in which the value of Γ was so high as to suggest the presence of a symmetry breaking phase transition.

We can thus conclude that our generalization of Harmony Theory can work very well only in presence of a suitable structuration of the initial dotation of knowledge atoms. Besides it can, in some cases, give rise to symmetry breaking phase transitions associated to problem solving process. We remark that our neural network model can be used as a psychological theory of acquisition of arithmetic skills, to be compared both with data obtained from real behavior of children solving problems, and with the forecastings of traditional symbolic theories · about arithmetic competence (cfr. [3]).

References

[1] D.R. Hofstadter, *Fluid concepts and creative analogies*, Basic Books, New York 1995.
[2] S.Kirpatrick, C.D.Gelatt, M.P.Vecchi. Optimization by simulated annealing. *Science,*220:671-680,1983.
[3] R.S.Siegler, *Children's Thinking*, Third Edition, Prentice-Hall, Englewood Cliffs, NJ, 1998.
[4] P.Smolensky. Information Processing in Dynamical Systems: Foundations of Harmony Theory. In J.L.McClelland, D.E.Rumelhart, editors, *Parallel Distributed Processing: Explorations in the Microstructure of Cognition*, vol. I, pages 154-281, MIT Press, Cambridge MA, 1986.

A Cortical Architecture for the Binocular Perception of Motion-in-depth

Silvio P. Sabatini, Fabio Solari and Giacomo M. Bisio

DIBE, PSPC-Group - University of Genoa [pspc@dibe.unige.it]

Abstract

A model for the generation of cortical cells selective to motion-in-depth is presented. The model relies upon the computation of the total rate of change of the disparity through the combination of the outputs of monocular cortical units characterized by spatiotemporal receptive fields extracting temporal variations of phase information on the left and right retinal images. Each monocular unit of the cortical architecture can be directly compared to the Adelson and Bergen's motion detector, thus establishing a link between the information contained in the total derivative of the binocular disparity and those hold in the interocular velocity differences. Experimental simulations on stereo sequences evidenced that the model can quantitatively predict motion-in-depth information.

1 Introduction

The analysis of a dynamic scene implies the estimates of motion parameters to infer spatio-temporal information about the visual world. Among them, the perception of motion-in-depth (MID), i.e. the capability of discriminating between forward and backward movements of objects from an observer, has important implications for autonomous robot navigation and surveillance in dynamic environments. In general, a reliable estimate of motion-in-depth can be helped by considering the dynamic stereo correspondence problem in the stereo image signals acquired by a binocular vision system. Fig. 1 shows the relationships between an object moving in 3-D space and the geometrical projection of the image in the right and left retinas. If an observer fixates at a distance D, the perception of depth of an object positioned at a distance Z_P can be related to the differences in the positions of the corresponding points in the stereo image pair projected on the retinas, provided that Z_P and D are large enough ($D, Z_P \gg a$ in Fig. 1, where a is the interpupillary distance). In a first approximation, the positions of corresponding points are related by a 1-D horizontal shift, the *disparity*, along the direction of the epipolar lines. Formally, the left and right observed intensities from the two eyes, respectively $I^L(x)$ and $I^R(x)$, result related as $I^L(x) = I^R[x + \delta(x)]$, where $\delta(x)$ is the (horizontal) binocular disparity. If an object moves from P to Q its disparity changes and projects different velocities on the retinas (v_L, v_R). Thus, the Z component of the object's motion (i.e., its motion-in-depth) V_Z can be approximated in two ways [1]: (1) by the rate of change of disparity, and (2)

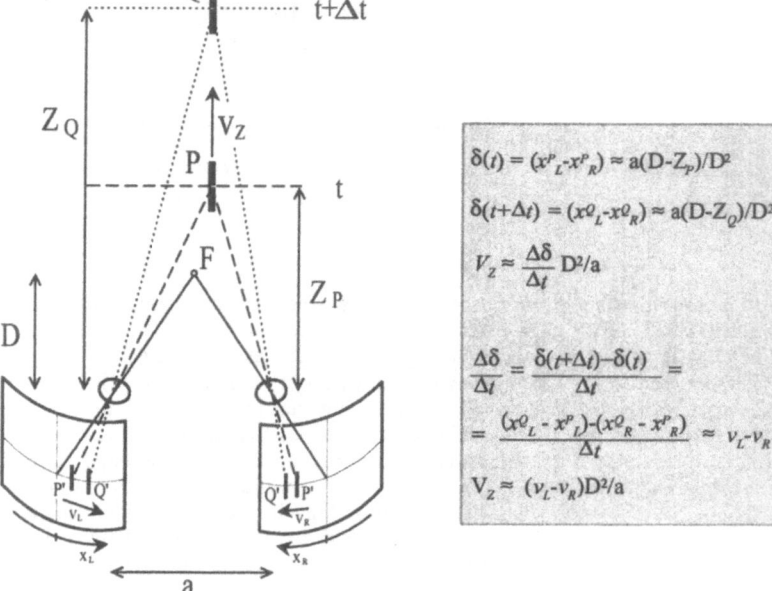

Figure 1: The stereo dynamic correspondence problem. A moving object in the 3-D space projects different trajectories onto the left and right images. The differences between the two trajectories carry information about motion-in-depth.

by the difference between retinal velocities, as it is evidenced in the box in Fig. 1. The predominance of one measure on the other one corresponds to different hypotheses on the architectural solutions adopted by visual cortical cells in mammals. There are, indeed, several experimental evidences that cortical neurons with a specific sensitivity to retinal disparities play a key role in the perception of stereoscopic depth [2][3]. Though, to date, it is not completely known the way in which cortical neurons measure stereo disparity and motion information. In this paper, we show that the two measures can be placed into a common framework considering a phase-based disparity encoding scheme.

2 Phase-based measurements of local disparity

According to the *Fourier Shift Theorem*, the spatial shift δ in an image domain effects a phase shift $k\delta$ in the Fourier domain. On the basis of this property, several researchers (e.g., [4]) proposed phase-based techniques in which disparity is estimated in terms of phase differences in the spectral components of the stereo image pair. Spatially-localized phase measures can be obtained by filtering operations with complex-valued quadrature pair of Gabor filters $h(x, k_0) = e^{-x^2/\sigma^2} e^{ik_0 x}$, where k_0 is the peak frequency of the filter and σ

relates to its spatial extension. The resulting convolutions with the left and right binocular signals can be expressed as $Q(x) = \rho(x)e^{i\phi(x)} = C(x) + iS(x)$ where $\rho(x) = \sqrt{C^2(x) + S^2(x)}$ and $\phi(x) = \arctan(S(x)/C(x))$ denote their amplitude and phase components and $C(x)$ and $S(x)$ are the responses of the quadrature pair of filters. Hence, binocular disparity can be predicted by $\delta(x) = [\phi^L(x) - \phi^R(x)]/k(x)$ where $k(x) = [\phi_x^L(x) + \phi_x^R(x)]/2$ is the average *instantaneous frequency* of the bandpass signal, and can be approximated by the peak of the Gabor filter k_0. Extending to time domain, the disparity of a point moving with the motion field can be estimated by $\delta[x(t), t] = (\phi^L[x(t), t] - \phi^R[x(t), t])/k_0$, where phase components are computed from the spatiotemporal convolutions of the stereo image pair $Q(x, t) = C(x, t) + iS(x, t)$ with directionally tuned Gabor filters with central frequency $\mathbf{p} = (k_0, \omega_0)$.

3 The cortical model

If disparity is defined with respect to the spatial coordinate x^L, by differentiating with respect to time, its total rate of variation can be written as

$$\frac{d\delta}{dt} = \frac{\partial\delta}{\partial t} + \frac{v^L}{k_0}\left(\phi_x^L - \phi_x^R\right) \tag{1}$$

where v^L is the horizontal component of the velocity signal on the left retina. Considering the conservation property of local phase measurements [5], image velocities can be computed from the temporal evolution of constant phase contours, and thus:

$$\phi_x^L = -\frac{\phi_t^L}{v^L} \quad \text{and} \quad \phi_x^R = -\frac{\phi_t^R}{v^R}. \tag{2}$$

Combining Eq. (2) with Eq. (1) we obtain $d\delta/dt = (v^R - v^L)\phi_x^R/k_0$, where $(v^R - v^L)$ is the phase-based interocular velocity difference along the epipolar lines. When the spatial tuning frequency of the Gabor filter k_0 approaches the instantaneous spatial frequency of the left and right convolution signals one can derive the following approximated expressions:

$$\frac{d\delta}{dt} \simeq \frac{\partial\delta}{\partial t} = \frac{\phi_t^L - \phi_t^R}{k_0} \simeq v^R - v^L \tag{3}$$

The partial derivative of the disparity can be directly computed by convolutions (S, C) of stereo image pairs and by their temporal derivatives (S_t, C_t):

$$\frac{\partial\delta}{\partial t} = \left[\frac{S_t^L C^L - S^L C_t^L}{(S^L)^2 + (C^L)^2} - \frac{S_t^R C^R - S^R C_t^R}{(S^R)^2 + (C^R)^2}\right]\frac{1}{k_0} \tag{4}$$

thus avoiding explicit calculation and differentiation of phase, and the attendant problem of phase unwrapping.

Since numerical differentiation is very sensitive to noise, proper regularized solutions have to be adopted to compute correct and stable numerical derivates. As a simple way to avoid the undesired effects of noise, band-limited filters can be used to filter out high frequencies that are amplified by differentiation. Specifically, if one prefilters the image signal to extract some temporal frequency sub-band, $S(x,t) \simeq g * S(x,t)$ and $C(x,t) \simeq g * C(x,t)$, and evaluates the temporal changes in that sub-band, differentiation can be attained by convolutions on the data with appropriate bandpass temporal filters:

$$S'(x,t) \simeq g' * S(x,t) \quad ; \quad C'(x,t) \simeq g' * C(x,t). \tag{5}$$

S' and C' approximate S_t and C_t, respectively, if g and g' are a quadrature pair of temporal filters, e.g.: $g(t) = e^{-t/\tau} \sin \omega_0 t$ and $g'(t) = e^{-t/\tau} \cos \omega_0 t$. By rewriting the terms of the numerators in (4):

$$4S_tC = (S_t + C)^2 - (S_t - C)^2 \quad \text{and} \quad 4SC_t = (S + C_t)^2 - (S - C_t)^2, \tag{6}$$

one can express the computation of $\partial\delta/\partial t$ in terms of convolutions with a set of oriented spatiotemporal filters, whose shapes resemble simple cell receptive fields of the primary visual cortex [6]. Specifically, each square term on the

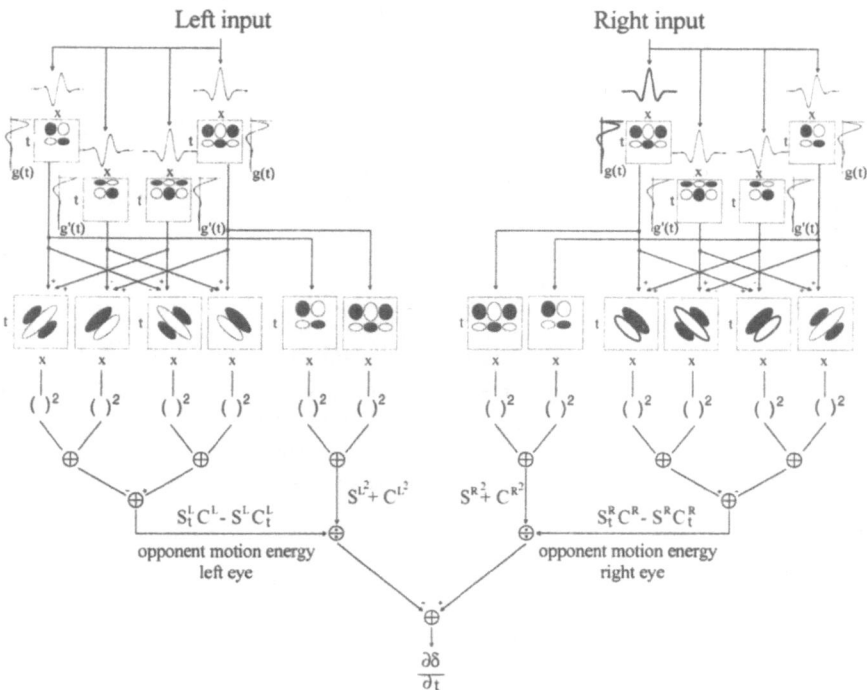

Figure 2: Cortical architecture of a motion-in-depth detector. The rate of variation of disparity can be obtained by a direct comparison of the responses of two monocular units labelled CXL and CXR. Each monocular unit receives contributions from a pair of directionally tuned "energy" complex cells that compute phase temporal derivative $(S_tC - SC_t)$ and a non-directional complex cell that supplies the static energy of the stimulus $(C^2 + S^2)$.

right sides of Eqs.(6) is a directionally tuned *energy detector* [7]. The overall MID cortical detector can be built as shown in Fig. 2. Each branch represents a monocular opponent motion energy unit of Adelson and Bergen's type where divisions by the responses of stationary filters (cf. the denominators of Eq.(4)), yields to measures of velocity that are invariant with contrast. We can extract a measure of the rate of variation of local phase information by taking the arithmetic difference between the left and right channel responses. Further division by the tuning frequency of the Gabor filter yields a quantitative measure of MID. It is worthy to note that phase-independent motion detectors of Adelson and Bergen can be used to compute temporal variations of phase. This result is consistent with the assumption we made of the linearity of the phase model. Therefore, our formulation evidences that formal relationships exist between energy and phase-based approaches to motion modeling.

4 Experimental results

Extensive simulations on both synthetic and real-world image sequences, yield to excellent performaces (see Fig. 3), resulting in correct discrimination between forward and backward movements of objects from the observer. Points where phase information are unreliable are discarded according to a confidence measure that is related to the local energy of the binocular filter output.

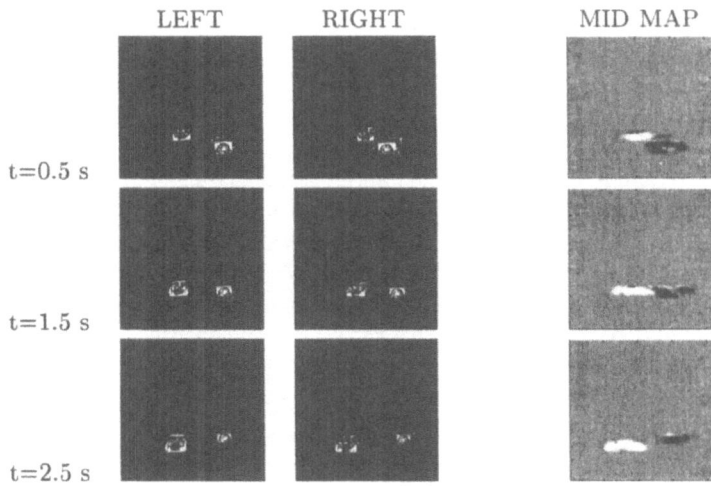

Figure 3: Experimental results on a natural scene. Two toy cars are moving in opposite directions respect to the observer. Left and right frames at three different times are shown. The gray levels in the MID maps code the motion-in-depth of the two cars: the lighter gray blob represents the car moving toward the observer, whereas the darker gray blob represents the car moving away. The background gray level codes all the static elements present in the scene.

5 Discussion and conclusions

There are at least two binocular cues that can be used to determine the motion of an object toward or away from an observer [1]: binocular combination of monocular velocity signals or the rate of change of retinal disparity. Assuming a phase-based disparity encoding scheme [4], we demonstrated that information hold in the interocular velocity difference is the same of that derived by the evaluation of the total derivative of the binocular disparity. The resulting computation relies upon spatiotemporal differentials of the left and right retinal phases that can be approximated by linear filtering operations with spatiotemporal receptive fields. Accordingly, we proposed a cortical model for the generation of binocular motion-in-depth selective cells as a hierarchical combination of monocular spatiotemporal subunits. Each monocular branch of the cortical architecture can be directly compared to the Adelson and Bergen's motion detector[7], thus establishing a link between phase-based approaches and motion energy models.

The algorithmic approach followed is particularly suitable for an "economic" hardware implementation, since such parameters can be gained via a feed-forward computation (i.e., collection, comparison, and punctual operations) on the outputs of a Gabor filtering stage that can be directly implemented in analog VLSI, as demonstrated by recent prototypes of our group [8]. Conversely, the feed-forward computations can be treated in a punctual way, i.e., according to standard computational schemes (sequential, parallel, pipeline). In this way, one can take take full advantage of the potentialities of analog processing together with the flexibility provided by digital hardware.

References

[1] J. Harris and S. N.J. Watamaniuk. Speed discrimination of Motion-in depth using binocular cues. *Vision Research*, 35(7):885–896, 1995.

[2] I. Ohzawa, G.C. DeAngelis, and R.D. Freeman. Encoding of binocular disparity by simple cells in the cat's visual cortex. *J. Neurophysiol.*, 75:1779–1805, 1996.

[3] I. Ohzawa, G.C. DeAngelis, and R.D. Freeman. Encoding of binocular disparity by complex cells in the cat's visual cortex. *J. Neurophysiol.*, 77:2879–2909, 1997.

[4] T.D. Sanger. Stereo disparity computation using Gabor filters. *Biol. Cybern.*, 59:405–418, 1988.

[5] D. J. Fleet and A. D. Jepson. Computation of component image velocity from local phase information. *International Journal of Computer Vision*, 1:77–104, 1990.

[6] G.C. DeAngelis, I. Ohzawa, and R.D. Freeman. Receptive-field dynamics in the central visual pathways. *Trends in Neurosci.*, 18:451–458, 1995.

[7] E.H. Adelson and J.R. Bergen. Spatiotemporal energy models for the perception of motion. *J. Opt. Soc. Amer.*, 2:284–321, 1985.

[8] L. Raffo, S.P. Sabatini, G.M. Bo, and G.M. Bisio. Analog VLSI circuits as physical structures for perception in early visual tasks. *IEEE Trans. Neural Net.*, 9(6):1483–1494, 1998.

Section 6
Image and Signal Processing

A Neural Network-based approach to system identification for whitening interferometer spectra

F.Acernese, L.Milano

Dipartimento di Scienze Fisiche, Università "Federico II" di Napoli
Istituto Nazionale di Fisica Nucleare, sezione di Napoli

F.Barone

Dipartimento di Scienze Farmaceutiche, Università di Salerno
Istituto Nazionale di Fisica Nucleare, sezione di Napoli

A.Eleuteri

Dipartimento di Matematica ed Applicazioni, Università "Federico II" di Napoli
Istituto Nazionale di Fisica Nucleare, sezione di Napoli

R.Tagliaferri

Dipartimento di Matematica ed Informatica, Università di Salerno
Istituto Nazionale di Fisica della Materia, unità di Salerno
IIASS "E.R.Caianiello, Vietri sul mare (SA), Italia

Abstract

In this paper a Neural Network-based approach is presented for the real time noise identification of laser interferometric antennas. The 40-meter Caltech laser interferometer output data, used in our experiments, provides a good testbed of algorithms for noise identification (violin resonances in the suspensions, main power harmonics, ring-down noise from servo control systems, electronics noises, glitches and so on) of the interferometric long GW antennas. The algorithms we propose are quite general and robust, taking into account that they do require neither a-priori information on the data, nor precise model, and constitute a powerful tool for data analysis.

1 Introduction

Gravitational Wave (hereafter GW) detection is certainly one of the most challenging goals for today physics: a very strong proof in favor of the Einstein General Relativity description of phenomena related to the dynamics of gravitation and the opening of a completely new channel of information on astrophysical objects [1] [2]. The VIRGO/LIGO/GEO/TAMA network of ground-based kilometer-scale laser interferometer gravitational wave detectors will be the key to open up that new astronomical channel of information in the frequency band 10 Hz to 10 KHz . The nature of lines affecting the spectra of the output of a GW interferometric antenna like the 40 m proto-type Caltech GW interferometer are connected with mains harmonics, large amplitude coherent lines, highly non-gaussian lines, violin resonances etc. Lines removal reduces data volume, improves gaussianity, permits better matched filters implementation, enables better use of wavelets, permits the use of sub-optimal adaptive filtering algorithms for data triggering. In this kind of data analysis, the most difficult problem is the gravitational signal extraction from the noise due to the intrinsic weakness of the gravitational waves and as a consequence the very poor signal-to-noise ratio. In synthesis that process is part of quality data analysis aimed to obtain robust de-noising and/or whitening filters to the data produced by interferometric detectors of GW before applying any algorithm of detection. To give a contribution to data quality analysis of GW interferometric antennas, we studied the performance of Neural Networks applied to the GW data cleaning problem. We used for identification purpose the real data of LIGO 40 M IFO_DMRO (interferometer differential mode readout; hereafter C40GWO) output data of the 40 m Caltech interferometer obtained in 1994 experiment at Caltech.

2 Neural Networks for non linear system identification

Before the applications of nonlinear techniques, it is necessary to answer this question: is this justified by the data? Too often assumptions about the nature of the data are made without justification. Obviously, this is the case also when linear modeling techniques are applied: the hypotesis of linear Gaussian stochastic processes is often invoked based only on some vague theoretical knowledge of the observed system. But real data is an entirely different matter. According to the results of the experiment performed in 1994 with the 40 m laser interferometer at Caltech we have the proof that, at least in that experiment, the real data are not generated by a linear (possibly rescaled) Gaussian stochastic model. These results pose a serious question to the use of standard linear modeling techniques in the case of GW antennas. From this starting point, we further analyze the problem in search of structure that allows us the creation of a nonlinear model. In any case we followed the principle that the *plus* contains the *minus*. The next step is then the setup of a nonlinear, neural network-based model.

Every discrete-time (or continuous sampled-data, as in our case) dynamical system can be described by a set of difference equations which describe the evolution of the system state [3]:

$$x(t+1) = \mathcal{F}[x(t)]. \tag{1}$$

In general, we do not know the form of the functional $\mathcal{F}(\cdot)$, but we can build an *approximation* to it, given measurements of the state variables $x(t)$.

To create a suitable model, the dynamics of the data-generating process must be understood. The process which generates the observed data $s(t)$ can be described by its state vector $\mathbf{x}(t)$, which usually cannot be observed. It turns out, however [4], that a space formally equivalent to the original state space can be reconstructed using the data sequence $s(t)$. This *phase space reconstruction* provides components of the original space using elements of $s(t)$:

$$x(t) = [s(t), s(t + \tau_1), s(t + \tau_2), \ldots] \tag{2}$$

where each delay τ_k can be thought of as an integer multiple of the sampling time τ_s of the system $(\tau_k = k\tau_s)$.

What value of k should be chosen? In [4] it is suggested, as a prescription, the value k_m where the first minimum of an information-theoretic measure called *average mutual information* (AMI) which gives the amount of information in bits learned about $s(t + k\tau_s)$ from the knowledge of $s(t)$. P is the empirical distribution of the data. k_m is called the *time lag* of the system.

How many delays are necessary to completely describe (*unfold*) the phase space of the system? We must determine a dimension for the space in which neighbor states $\mathbf{x}(t)$ are near because of dynamics and not because we observe them in a low dimensional space. The observed data can be seen as a *projection* of the state space onto a low dimensional space (in our case, the output of the interferometer is a scalar sequence); the effect is that there is an ambiguity because the orbits of the system will intersect. The dimension in which all the orbits of the system unfold is called *embedding dimension*. Having found it, as suggested in [4], then we can describe the state of the system in this way:

$$x(t) = [s(t), s(t + k\tau_s), s(t + 2k\tau_s), \ldots, s(t + (d-1)k\tau_s)] \tag{3}$$

in which d is the embedding dimension.

Note that strictly these results assume a noiseless and infinite-length sequence. Nonetheless, they can be used in practice since the effects of noise and finiteness are mainly an overestimate of the lag and the embedding dimension, leading to an unnecessarily complex description of the dynamics.

Due to its universal approximation capability (see [5]), the Multi-layer Perceptron (MLP) can be used to build a model of the system dynamics. The MLP can be trained by using the reconstructed state space, with pattern-target pairs (to which we will refer from now on as $\{\mathbf{x}, \mathbf{q}\}$):

$$\{[s(t), s(t + k\tau_s), s(t + 2k\tau_s), \ldots, s(t + (d-1)k\tau_s)], s(t + dk\tau_s)\}. \tag{4}$$

The MLP then predicts the evolution of the system one time lag ahead. We used also a criterion to evaluate the goodness of the whitening procedure according to the following performance index, that could be assumed as a comparison performance of all the proposed algorithms of whitening. The spectral flatness measure of a Power Spectral Density (PSD) can be defined as [6]:

$$\xi = \frac{\exp\left(\frac{1}{f_s} \int \ln\left(P(f)\right) df\right)}{\frac{1}{f_s} \int P(f) df} \tag{5}$$

The integrals extend over the Nyquist frequency bandwidth i.e. $-f_s/2 \div f_s/2$, where f_s is the sampling frequency. The ξ parameter varies between 0 and

1 according to the flatness of the spectrum. If P(f) is very peaked then ξ is nearly 0 whilst if the spectrum is flat then $\xi \simeq 1$. It is possible to show that the ratio of ξ indexes before and after the whitening process equals the ratio of the respective autocorrelation functions for zero lags [6].

3 Whitening of the LIGO 40m Interferometer output by Neural Networks

In this section we show how a MLP neural network can be successfully used to whiten the data output by the CalTech LIGO 40m Interferometer. To this aim, the MLP must define a *model* of the dynamics of the interferometer by using only its output.

The approach we followed to build the model is based on sound theoretical foundations. First, the data used were pre-processed using non-linear analysis techniques to extract information on the underlying data-generating process. Then, we followed a probabilistic Bayesian approach to create the model [7], [8]; this allowed the exploration of a *model space*, rather than use a single "optimal" model as usually happens in practice with linear modeling techniques. This learning framework has been chosen following our previous experimental results [9].

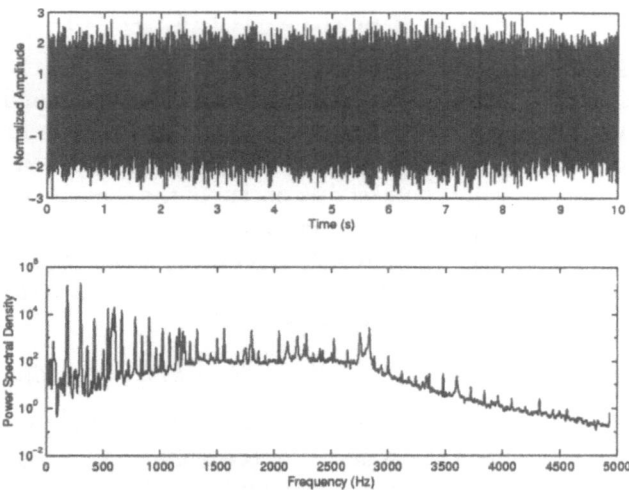

Figure 1: The time evolution and the power spectral density of the data frame used for training.

The data used to train the model is a sequence of 6 seconds sampled at about $5kHz$. The model has then been tested on a different sequence of about 1 minute. Before giving the data to the network, they have been pre-processed

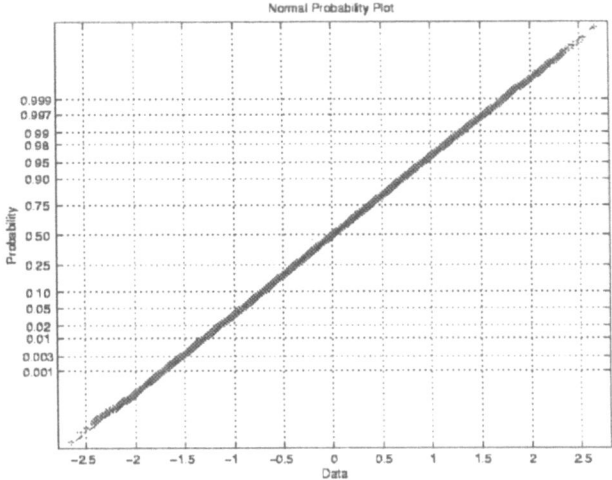

Figure 2: The normal probability plot shows the data corresponding to a Gaussian distribution.

to find suitable time lag and embedding dimension. The results of the analysis are reported: the first minimun of AMI is $2\tau_s$ and the embedding dimension is chosen as $d = 22$.

The trained MLP has the following architecture; 22 input units, one output unit with linear activation function, and 20 hidden units with tanh activation function. Furthermore, 25 regularization parameters have been used: one for every group of connections from each input unit, one for each bias connection for input and hidden units, and one for the group of connections to the output unit.

As can be seen from the figure 1, the problem is rather difficult, since the system has a rather complex evolution. In spite of this, the network accomplishes a rather good job of predicting the system dynamics, also if the network has been trained for only 200 epochs and it is not overly complex.

The normplot of residuals, see figure 2, show that the chosen noise-model is adeguate for the task. Moreover, the network achieves a good predictive performance, see figure 3. This was proved by a quantitative estimation of the capability of the network in predicting the system dynamics: we performed a Kolmogorov-Smirnov test[1] [10] at the 0.05 level to evaluate the difference between the target distribution and that provided by the network. The test gave values of at least 96% in almost all the test cases so that there is not a statistically significant difference at the tested level between them (see tab.1).

---

[1]Modified with the Kuiper probability function which gives a more robust estimation at the tails of the distributions

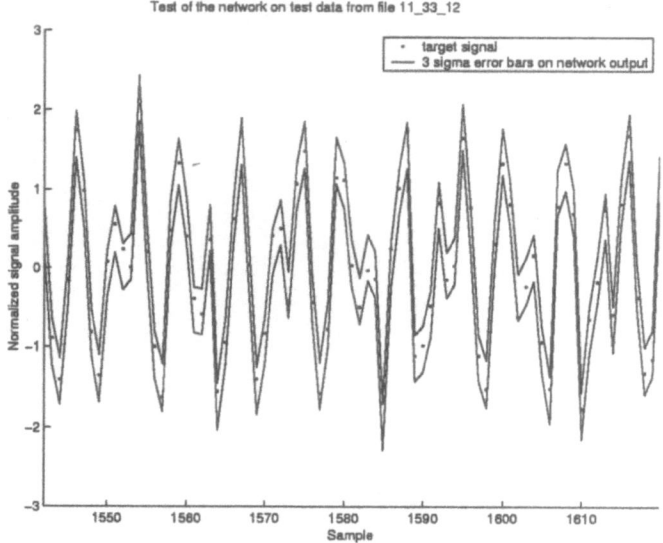

Figure 3: Segment of the test sequence with 3σ error bars.

Note that the model could be made more reliable by using more neurons and/or

data file	test output
11_22_24	0.998
11_27_48	0.932
11_30_30	0.997
11_33_12	0.997
11_35_54	0.963

Table 1: Results of the K-S test on some chunks of data

training for more epochs (and without the risk of overfitting).

All the simulations were made in the MATLAB environment, using the NETLAB Toolbox [11] for the neural network part, and the TSTOOL Toolbox [12] for the non-linear analysis tools. Additional code has been developed by the authors.

4   Conclusions and Perspectives

In this paper we have shown some preliminary tests on the use of a Neural Network for signal processing of gravitational signals. Some observations can be elicited from the experimental results: the proposed methodology has shown good results, also if the network was not very complex and the training runs were few (200 epochs); the use of Bayesian inference has been proved very useful for regularization and model validation; the system works on real data. The next steps in the research are: to test the models with a greater number of samples to obtain a better estimate of the system dynamics; to model the noise inside the system model to improve the system performance and to allow a multi-step ahead prediction (i.e. an output-error model); to use teh error bars like a trigger to detect anomalies in interferometer output.

References

[1] D.G. Blair, The Detection of Gravitational Waves, Cambridge University Press, Cambridge, 1991.

[2] P.R. Saulson, Fundamentals of Interferometric Gravitational Wave Detectors, World Scientific Press, New Jersey, 1994.

[3] S. Chen, S.A. Billings, Modelling and Analysis of Nonlinear Time Series, Int. J. Control, Vol.50, No.6, pp. 2151-2171, 1989.

[4] H.D.I. Abarbanel, Analysis of Observed Chaotic Data, Springer, 1996.

[5] Hornik, K., M. Stinchcombe, and H. White, 1989, Multilayer feedforward networks are universal approximators. Neural Networks, Vol.4 (2), pp.251-257.

[6] S. M. Kay, Modern spectral estimation: Theory and application, Prentice Hall, Englewood Cliffs, 1988.

[7] C. M. Bishop, Neural Networks for Pattern Recognition, Clarendon Press, Oxford, 1995.

[8] D. J. C. MacKay, Hyperparameters: optimise or integrate out ?, Maximum Entropy and Bayesian Methods, Santa Barbara, Dordrecht, 1993.

[9] F. Barone, R. De Rosa, A. Eleuteri, F. Garufi, L. Milano, R. Tagliaferri, A Neural Network-based ARX Model of VIRGO Noise, in Neural Nets WIRN Vietri-99, M. Marinaro and R. Tagliaferri eds., pp. 171-183, Springer-Verlag, London, 1999.

[10] Numerical Recipes in C: The Art os Scientific Computing. 1988-1992, Cambrige University Press, Cambrige, p.575. Available at *www.nr.com*.

[11] C.M. Bishop, I.T. Nabey, Netlab Toolbox, Neural Computing Research Group, Aston University, Birmingham, 1996. Available at *www.ncrg.aston.ac.uk*.

[12] Available at *www.physics3.gwdg.de/tstool*.

A Neural Cursive Character Recognizer

Francesco Camastra

INFM-Computer Science Department (DISI), University of Genoa
Via Dodecaneso 35 - 16146 Genova (Italy)
camastra@disi.unige.it

Alessandro Vinciarelli

Institut Dalle Molle d'Intelligence Artificielle Perceptive - IDIAP
CP 592 - Rue du Simplon 4, 1920 Martigny (Switzerland)
alessandro.vinciarelli@idiap.ch

Abstract

This paper presents a cursive character recognizer embedded in an off-line cursive script recognition system. The recognizer is composed of two modules: the first one is a feature extractor, the second one an LVQ. Experiments are reported on a database of about 58000 isolated characters.

1   Introduction

Off-line Cursive Script Recognition (CSR) has several industrial applications such as the reading of postal addresses and the automatic processing of forms, checks and faxes. Among other CSR approaches [1][2] one attempts to segment words into letters [3]. Since such a task is difficult and error prone, words are usually oversegmented, i.e. the fragments isolated by the segmentation (*primitives*) are expected to be not only characters, but also parts of characters. In order to obtain a letter, it is often necessary to aggregate several primitives. The best complete bipartite match between blocks of primitives and word letters is usually found by applying Dynamic Programming techniques [4].

Given a word, the matching with the handwritten data is obtained by averaging over the costs due to classifying each aggregation of primitives as one of its letters. The word with the best match, i.e. the lowest cost, is selected as the interpretation of the handwritten sample.

A crucial role is then played by the *cursive character recognizer*. This takes as input a pattern composed of one or more aggregated primitives and gives as output a cost for classifying it as any possible letter.

The *Learning Vector Quantizer (LVQ)* was selected as neural classifier because, being a vector quantizer, it yields for each pattern the cost [1] of assigning a pattern to a given letter class.

This paper is organized as follows: in Section 2 the method for extracting features for character representation is presented; Section 3 reports some experimental results; in Section 4 some conclusions are drawn.

---

[1]i.e. the distance from the closest prototype of the class.

2 Feature Extraction

Most character recognizers do not work on the raw image, but on a suitable compact representation of the image by means of a vector of features. Since cursive characters present high variability in shapes, a feature extractor should have negligble sensitivity to local shifts and distortions. The feature extraction process used in our recognizer is described in detail in [5]. The feature extractor, fed with the binary image of an isolated cursive character, generates local and global features. The local features are extracted from subimages (*cells*) arranged in a regular grid covering the whole image. A fixed set of operators is applied to each cell. The first operator is a counter that computes the percentage of foreground pixels in the cell (*gray feature*) with respect to the total number of foreground pixels in the character image. The other operators try to estimate to which extent the black pixels in the cell are aligned along some directions. For each direction of interest, a set of N, equally spaced, straight lines are defined, that span the whole cell and that are parallel to the chosen direction. Along each line $j \in [1, N]$ the number n_j of black pixels is computed and the sum $\sum_j^N n_j^2$ is then obtained for each direction. The difference between

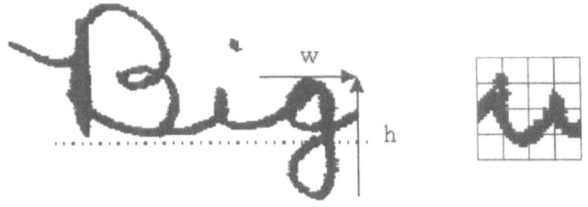

Figure 1: The dashed line is the *baseline*, the fraction of h below is used as first global feature. The second global feature is the ratio w/h.

the sums related to orthogonal directions is used as a feature (*directional feature*). Several directional features were applied and the one having the maximal variance (difference between $0°$ and $90°$ sums) was retained.

We enriched the local feature set with two global features. The first one measures the fraction of the character below the baseline (see fig. 1) and detects eventual descenders, the second one is the *width/height* ratio.

The feature set was tested by changing the number of cells, and the grid giving the best results (4×4) was selected.

In the reported experiments we used a feature vector of 34 elements. Two features are global (*baseline* and *width/height ratio*) while the remaining 32 are generated from 16 cells, placed on a regular 4×4 grid; from each cell, the gray feature and one directional feature are extracted.

3   Experimental Results

The feature set was tested on a database of cursive characters in conjunction with the LVQ classifier. The database contains isolated characters extracted from handwritten words coming from two sources: the first is the database of handwritten words produced by the Center of Excellence for Document Analysis and Recognition (CEDAR) [2] at the State University of New York (SUNY) at Buffalo [6].The second is a database of handwritten postal addresses digitalized by the USPS (United States Postal Service). Word images from which the characters were extracted were all preprocessed according to a scheme that includes morphologic filtering, deslanting and deskewing [7]. The character database contains both uppercase and lowercase letters. Figure 2 shows the percentage distribution of letters in the test set. Since the data is extracted from a database collected by USPS in a real postal plant [6], our database distribution reflects the prior distribution of that site. For this reason some letters are less represented than others or almost absent. Clustering performed with Self-Organizing Maps (SOM) [8] and Neural Gas (NG) [9], showed that, for some letters, the vectors corresponding to the upper and lower case version are distributed in different regions of the feature space. This can happen when upper and lower case characters are different in shape (e.g. g and G). In this case, it was useful to consider the two versions of the letter as separate classes. On the other hand, when the upper case letter is similar to the lower case one except for the dimension (e.g. o and O), the feature vectors are distributed in regions of the feature space neighboring and even overlapping each other. In this case, the two versions of the letter can be joined in a single class. In Table 1 the performances of different SOM and NG maps,

neurons	SOM(q.error)	NG (q.error)
1300	0.197290	0.162117
900	0.204126	0.167981
600	0.209687	0.175800
400	0.217515	0.182672
200	0.227662	0.195116
100	0.242464	0.208706

Table 1: Quantization error of SOM and NG for different neuron numbers.

measured in terms of quantization error, on the whole character database, are reported. Afterwards, the nodes of the best map (NG with 1300 neurons) were labelled with a kNN technique[3]. The neurons were then divided into 26 subsets collecting all the nodes showing at least one version of each letter α among the k classes in the label. For each subset, the percentage η_α of nodes having upper

---

[2]All images belonging to directories train/cities and train/states were used.

[3]Each node is labelled with the classes of the k closest feature vectors

and lower case versions of the letter α in the label was calculated. The results are reported (for every subset) in figure 3. The percentage is an index of the overlapping of the classes of the uppercase and lowercase versions of the letter. This information can be used to represent the data with a number of different classes ranging from 26 (uppercase and lowercase always joined in a single class) to 52 (uppercase and lowercase always in separate classes). For example a class number equal to 46 means that only for six letters (e.g. c,x,o,w,y,z) uppercase and lowercase versions are joined in a single class. Using the percentage η we trained LVQ nets with different number of classes. In each trial, the number of codevectors was selected by means of cross-validation [10]. The number of

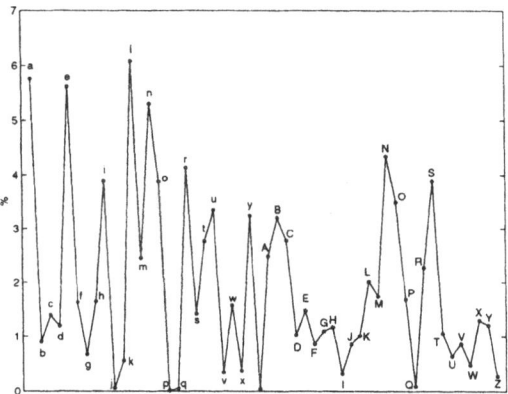

Figure 2: Letter distribution in the test set.

LVQ codevectors, assigned to each class, was proportional to the a-priori class probability. We trained several LVQ nets by specifying different combinations

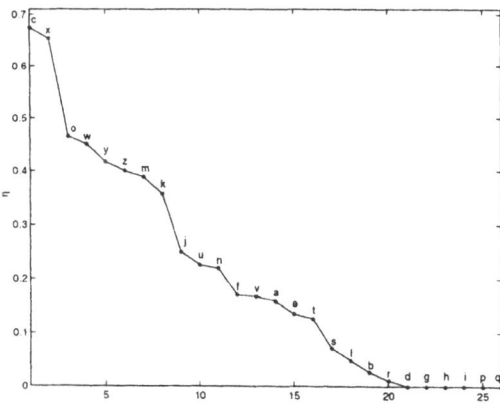

Figure 3: Value of η for each letter.

of learning parameters (different learning rates, and various total number of codevectors). The best LVQ net was selected by means of cross-validation [10]. The experiments were carried out on a training and a test set of 39000 and 19000 characters respectively. In table 2, for different class numbers, the performances

class number	performance
52	83.74
46	83.91
42	84.25
41	84.27
39	84.52
36	84.38
26	84.27

Table 2: Recognition rates on the Test Set, in absence of rejection, for several class numbers.

on the test set, measured in terms of recognition rate in absence of rejection, are reported. Our best result in terms of recognition rate is **84.52%**.
The probabilities of classification of a character correctly top three and top twelve positions are respectively 95.76% and 99.50%.

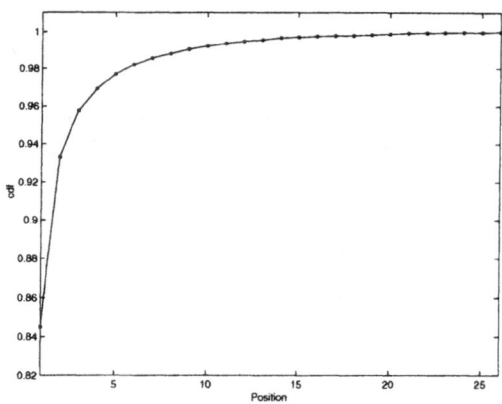

Figure 4: Cumulative probability function of the correct classification of LVQ classifier.

4 Conclusion

We have presented a cursive character recognizer embedded in a offline CSR system. The recognizer is formed by a feature extractor, that performs local averaging, and a LVQ classifier. The cursive character recognizer yielded better recognition results than others previosly reported in literature [11].

References

[1] G. Kim, V. Govindaraju, A lexicon driven approach to handwritten word recognition for real time applications, IEEE Transactions on Pattern Analysis and Machine Intelligence, Vol. 19, No. 4, 366-379, 1997.

[2] A.W. Senior, A.J. Robinson, An Off-Line Cursive Handwriting Recognition System, IEEE Transactions on Pattern Analysis and Machine Intelligence, Vol. 20, No. 3, 309-321, 1998.

[3] T. Steinherz, E. Rivlin, N. Intrator, Off-Line Cursive Script Word Recognition - A Survey, International Journal of Document Analysis and Recognition, Vol. 2, No. 2, 1-33, 1999.

[4] R.E. Bellman, S.E. Dreyfus, Applied Dynamic Programming, Princeton University Press, 1962.

[5] F. Camastra, A. Vinciarelli, Cursive character recognition by Learning Vector Quantization, Pattern Recognition Letters, Vol. 22, No. 6-7, 625-629, 2001.

[6] J.J.Hull, A Database for Handwritten Text Recognition Research, IEEE Transactions on Pattern Analysis and Machine Intelligence, Vol. 16, No. 5, 550-554, 1994.

[7] G. Nicchiotti, C. Scagliola, Generalised Projections: a Tool for Cursive Character Normalization, Proceedings of 5th International Conference on Document Analysis and Recognition, 729-732, 1999.

[8] T. Kohonen, Self-Organizing Maps, Springer Verlag, Berlin, 1997.

[9] T. Martinetz, S. Berkovich, K. Schulten, "Neural Gas" network for vector quantization and its application to time-series prediction, IEEE Transactions on Neural Networks, Vol. 4, No. 4, 558-569, 1993.

[10] M. Stone, Cross-validatory choice and assessment of statistical prediction, Journal of the Royal Statistical Society, Vol. 36, No. 1, 111-147, 1974.

[11] H. Yamada, Y. Nakano, Cursive handwritten word recognition using multiple segmentation determined by contour analysis, IEICE Transactions on Informations and Systems, Vol. 79, No. 5, 111-147464-470, 1996.

Optimal Parameters in Neural Network Models for Speech Phoneme Characterization

A. Esposito[a,b], G. Aversano[b], F. Quek[a]

[a] Department of Computer Science and Engineering, Wright State University
Ohio (US)

[b] International Institute for Advanced Scientific Studies (IIASS)
Vietri sul Mare (SA), Italy

Abstract

A comparison among neural net models (Multilayer Perceptron, Time Delay, and Recurrent neural networks) is proposed. The aim is to evaluate, from a practical point of view, their performance on a problem of classification of phonemes. The efficacy and the limitation of each model will be discussed in the light of their dependence on free parameters like the number of hidden nodes, learning rate and initial weight values.

1 Introduction

In the past decade, several neural net models [Bishop 95] have been proposed in the hope of implementing algorithms which can achieve human-like performance in complex fields such as *speech* and *vision*. All the models were supported, theoretically, by proofs of convergence of the learning rules, thereby ensuring good performance under particular hypotheses. At a practical level, the standard approach to using neural net models requires a finite set of training examples and the setting of a certain number of network parameters which have to be fixed *a priori*. This is the main difficulty for a user of a neural net model, since the theory does not facilitate the choice of optimal values for the network parameters. Such values can only be obtained through a process of trial and error and offer no proof of their optimality for a given problem. Moreover, some of these parameters play primary roles and others secondary ones in the final performance of the net and, so far, theory has little to say about that. Furthermore, the choice of model also plays an important role in the final result.

This work tries to give some practical suggestions on the use of neural net models, reporting a series of experiments on a problem of classification of phonemes, using four different models: Multilayer Perceptron (MLP) [Rummelhart et al. 86], Time Delay Neural Network (TDNN) [Waibel et al. 87, 88, 89] , Simple Recurrent Neural Networks (SRNN) [Elman 90] and Partially Recurrent Networks with only output context (JRNN) [Jordan 86, 86a]. The performance of the various models were evaluated according to the changes of the number of hidden nodes, the learning rate, and the initial weight values.

2 Speech Data Structure and Experiments Set Up

The English phonemes used to train and test the networks were extracted from the TIMIT database [http://www.ntis.gov/fcpc/cpn4129.htm]. This database is composed of English sentences produced by speakers who reside in the US. Each speaker pronounced ten different sentences. Each sentence was segmented by phoneme and labeled. Data was extracted from the sentences according to this segmentation. The phrases for each speaker were different. A total of 253 speakers (181 males and 72 females) produced the audio data used to train and test the nets. These speakers belonged to different US regions (dr1-dr2-dr3 in TIMIT) and consequently adopted different dialectal influences. The phonemes selected for these comparisons were a subclass of the American English vowels and fricatives. The size of the training, validation, and testing sets, and the selected phonemes are reported in Table 1.

Fricatives	#[dh]	#[f]	#[sh]	#[z]	#[v]	#[s]
Training	969	780	739	1233	680	2587
Validation	208	165	158	265	145	554
Testing	208	165	158	265	145	554
Vowels	#[iy]	#[ae]	#[ao]	#[ux]	#[ax]	#[axr]
Training	2028	1168	811	527	1071	1018
Validation	676	389	269	175	357	339
Testing	676	389	269	175	357	339

Table 1: Size of the training, validation and testing sets

The parameters which were regulated during the experiments were the learning rate, the range of values for initializing the weights on the connections and, of course, the global architecture of the net. For all the network models the learning rate was varied within the range [0.2 : 0.0002], whereas the initial weight values were varied within the range [2 : 0.1]. All networks tested had 54 input nodes and 6 output nodes whereas the number of layers and the number of hidden nodes in each layer varied according to the model. For MLPs and TDNNs a two-layered network was used with a number of hidden nodes varied as shown in Table 2. Moreover, shortcut (a node in the layer i is connected to the nodes of any other layer j=1, ..., N, where N is the number of layers in the net) and full connection modalities, and a three layered structure were tested respectively for MLPs and TDNNs.

Although SRNN networks can have more than a single hidden layer and also output context units, these networks were limited to a single-layer test to allow the comparison with JRNNs (which present only output context units and a single hidden layer). SRNNs were tested with or without output context units. The architectural parameters for SRNN and JRNN models are summarized in Table 3. All the experiments were performed using the SNNS simulator [Stuttgart 90-95] and were repeated 5 times for each set-up and for each data set. The subsequent results were obtained by averaging these repetitions.

Network Models	# input nodes	# hidden nodes in the first layer	#hidden nodes in the second layer	# hidden nodes in the third layer	# output nodes
MLP1	54	48	6	-	6
MLP2	54	36	18	-	6
MLP3	54	30	24	-	6
MLP4	54	24	30	-	6
MLP5	54	12	42	-	6
MLP6	54	48	36	-	6
MLP7	54	48	42	-	6
TDNN1	54	45	30	-	6
TDNN2	54	60	40	-	6
TDNN3	54	90	60	-	6
TDNN4	54	70	50	30	6

Table 2: MLP and TDNN architectures

3 The Preprocessing Phase

The speech signal was processed using the Rasta-PLP (Relative Perceptual Linear Prediction) algorithm [Hermansky 90; Hermansky & Morgan 94]. PLP analysis uses know-how from psychoacoustics as a means of estimating the auditory spectrum. Rasta-PLP adds a spectral band-pass operation to PLP analysis resulting in acoustic features which are not only more robust but also have the advantage of greater resistance to distortions. The parameters for this algorithm where adjusted in order to improve reception of the acoustic features of the phonemes. Thus, the speech signal was sampled at 16 kHz, instead of the 20 kHz default setting, and weighted by a Hamming window 10 msec long (the default was 20 msec). Each succeeding frame of a phonetic segment was overlapped with the preceding frame by 5 msec (10 msec by default). This analysis provided nine acoustic features (8 LP coefficients plus gain) at the rate of 200 frames/sec. In the preprocessing phase, a novelty was introduced based on the following considerations: given that the vocal tract is a time varying system producing a non-stationary signal, the speech signal needs to be analyzed on a short-time window, the duration of which is defined by the time constants of the articulatory apparatus (order 10-20 msec). This means that 20 to 30 msec of signal should contain adequate phonemic information apropos to the speech segment under examination. Therefore, only 30 msec of the signal available was used as input into the net. Moreover, the net performance was tested in two different cases: in the first instance, using features obtained from the first 30 msec of the speech segment representing a single phoneme and, in the second, those obtained from the central 30 msec of the same segment. The aim was to discover which part of the signal contains more information on the phoneme identity.

Network Models	# input nodes	# hidden context units	#hidden nodes in the second layer	# output context units	# output nodes
SRNN1	54	24	24	-	6
SRNN2	54	24	24	6	6
SRNN3	54	12	12	-	6
SRNN4	54	35	35	-	6
JRNN1	54	-	48	6	6
JRNN2	54	-	24	6	6
JRNN3	54	-	60	6	6
JRNN4	54	-	16	6	6

Table 3: SRNN and JRNN architectures

4 Results and Discussion

There are no standard rules or well assessed procedures which allow a neural network user to justify the parameter values and the network architecture used for a given application. There are theorems which prove that some neural network models are universal approximators [Renals & Rohwer 89; Hecht-Nielsen, 87,89; Powell, 87; Broomhead & Lowe, 88; Kolmogorov, 57] and there are learning procedures which use heuristics for convergence proofs [Bishop, 95; Haykin 94; Hertz et. al. 91; Williams & Peng, 90; Williams & Zipser, 89; Almeida 87; Pineda 87; Rumelhart et al, 1986, Hopfield 84]. However, none of these theorems and learning procedures are able to give suggestions towards the practical implementation of a neural net. The models exhibit many free parameters and it is still an open question as to how they interact with each other and how these interactions affect the final net performance. The results reported in the present paper permit the behavior of the four neural net models to be summarized, thereby facilitating a practical implementation comparison with theoretical studies. For each of the neural net models reported above (MLP, TDNN, SRNN, JRNN), individual behavior vis-a-vis the problem of phonemes classification is shown (when modifications to the architecture [NA], the learning rate [LR] and the weight initialization values [WI] are applied). It should also be noticed that the number of hidden nodes, even when modified, needs to be limited, since a high number of hidden nodes can produce over-fitting problems [Bishop 95; Haykin 94; Hertz et al 90].

MLP results

The best percentage of correct classification obtained on the test set for an MLP model was 84%. The net architecture and the modalities of connection (shortcut and full) did not play a major role in obtaining this performance.

All seven network architectures reported in Table 3 were tested. Increasing the number of hidden nodes in the different layers did not increase the performance of the network as might be expected from the theory [Bishop 95; Haykin 94; Hertz et al. 90]. This means that the approximation capability of these models is bounded. Ideally, the network output should approximate any given function with infinitesimally small errors [Bishop 95; Haykin 94]. In practice the output performance of such networks provide only a coarse approximation of the target function., no matter how powerful the network architecture.

The range of values used to initialize the network connections did not affect the network performance. The weights of all the MLP architectures reported in Table 2 were initialized within the range values of [-0.1, 0.1], [-0.5, 0.5], [-0.9, 0.9], [-2, 2] but no changes in the net performances were observed. It is expected that greater initial weight values could play a role in the final performance, since, in such a case, a bias is introduced into the learning procedures. However, the theory does not suggest greater initial weight values.

The only parameter which affects the MLPs performance is the learning rate. A very small change in learning rate value (0.0002) increases exponentially the learning time without significantly improving the percentage of correct classification (the improvement obtained was only in the region of 5%), whereas a high learning rate value (0.9, or 0.5) produces oscillations in the learning behavior graph and a significant reduction of the net performance (around the 70% of correct classification on the test set). The best compromise between computational time and net performance (84% of correct classification) was obtained when the learning rate varied within the range of [0.009 : 0.002].

TDNN results

As opposed to MLP, the TDNN performances were very sensitive to modifications in the architecture. The best performances (around 81% of correct classification on the test set) were obtained using the TDNN2 architecture reported in Table 2, whereas, using TDNN1, TDNN3, and TDNN4, the performances were reduced by about 40%. In general, this model requires the identification of an optimal architecture, which strongly depends on the form of application and on the data set. For example, using other speech data sets, some authors [Waibel et al. 87, 88, 89; Esposito & Ezin 98] obtained better results by carefully adjustments of architecture and parameters of TDNN networks. However, there are no theoretical studies - except those resulting from a long process of trial and error - which allow the identification of the optimal architecture. Moreover, the use of delay units makes this model less stable than a MLP, since universal approximation properties cannot be applied.

As for MLP, the net performances are not affected by the range of values used to initialize the weights on the network connections, this suggests that the net behavior is independent from these parameter values. Varying the learning rate values on the same architecture changes the TDNN performances. The efficiency of the model improves when the learning rate changes from 0.0002 (40% of correct classification on the test set) to 0.2 (80% of correct classification on the test set). In general, higher learning rate values give better performances, which suggests that even though the network structure is very similar to an MLP, the net behavior is different. This different behavior can principally be attributed to the presence of delay units which result in significant modifications to the learning process.

JRNN results

Small changes in the number of hidden nodes produce significant variations in the performances of this model. If the implemented architecture is not optimal for a given application, the experimental results may vary from one run to another (for example, the same architecture can give 99in two different runs, both on the same data and the same free parameter values because of the random initial weight assignment). However, as with TDNN, there is not basic theory which can help to discover the optimal network architecture. Thus, a greater number of trial and error processes are needed.

Initial weight and learning rate values also significantly affect net performances. Best results averaged on the testing data (99% of correct classification) were obtained with weights initialized in the range of [-0.1, 0.1] and a learning rate equal to 0.0002. However, changes in the learning rate value require changes in the initial weight values to maintain similar performances. Therefore, it is extremely difficult to establish the initial set-up of this model and also to rely on its final performances given that any small changes made on these free parameters can either improve or significantly reduce the results obtained.

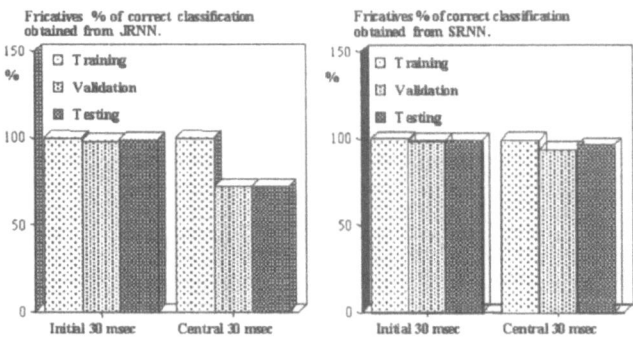

Figure 1: Comparison of JRNN and SRNN performances

SRNN results

The best percentage of correct classification obtained on the test set for this model was 99.3%. These performances were not affected by either the net architecture, the learning rate or the initial weight values.

The model showed a high stability and independence from the free parameters under examination. However, when output context units were introduced the net performances significantly decreased, which raises the question of how this behavior could be explained. The net receives, concurrently, information on its external state through the output context units and also information on its internal representation through the hidden context units. This simultaneous information is conflicting, since one is internal and the other is external. Therefore, the learning process is modified through an attempt to internalize both sets of information. This adds weight to the hypothesis (supported by the experimental data) that this model is stable only when the feedback is relative to a single layer. Only under such conditions could the information supplied to the net be controlled. Augmenting the network complexity through multiple hidden layers and feedback units would require a learning algorithm able to distinguish the information received from the several layers and apply a hierarchical generalization process which would take into account the varying nature of the information. Table 4 shows the better performance obtained with a SRNN and a JRNN on the training, validation and testing set for fricatives. The same data, with Standard Deviation values are plotted in Figure 1.

	SRNN	JRNN
Fricatives (initial 30 msec)		
Training	99.3%	99%
Validation	99%	98.6%
Testing	99%	99%
Fricatives (central 30 msec)		
Training	99.3%	99%
Validation	97%	82%
Testing	99%	82%

Table 4: SRNN and JRNN performances on two different set of fricative data

5 Conclusions

From the data presented it can be concluded that, taking the network models examined, MLP, even when stable and independent from the free parameter setup, is unable to extract temporally correlated information from the data. Its performances are limited and are not improved by increasing the number of hidden nodes or the complexity of the architecture.

TDNNs and JRNNs are unstable models since their behavior is strongly dependent on the net architecture, the learning rate and the initial weight values. However, JRNNs show superior performance to TDNNs under optimal setup conditions.

SRNNs are stable and their performance does not depend on the initial free parameter setups.

It is worth noticing, however, that both JRNN and SRNN performances - due to the implicit sequencing through which data is supplied to the nets - are strongly dependent on the order of the testing patterns. Random ordering significantly affects net performances. To overcome this limitation, tests on dynamic recurrent neural networks (as in [Ström 97]) need to be carried out.

Acknowledgements

We would like to thank Professor Maria Marinario for her helpful comments and suggestions.

This work has been in part supported by the NSF KDI program, Grant No. BCS-9980054, "Cross-modal analysis of speech signal and sense: multimedia corpora and tools for gesture, speech, and gaze research".

References

[1] Bishop C. M., *Neural Network for Pattern Recognition*, Clarendon Press, 1995.

[2] Rummelhart D.E., McClelland J.L., *Parallel Distributed Processing: Explorations*, in the Microstructure of Cognition, MIT Press, 1986.

[3] Waibel A., Hanazawa T., Hinton G.E., Shikano K., Lang K.J., *Phoneme Recognition using Time Delay Neural Networks*, Technical Report TR-1-0006, ATR Interpreting Telephony Research Laboratories, 1987.

[4] Waibel A., Sawai H., Shikano K., *Modularity and Scaling in Large Phonemic Neural Networks*, Technical Report TR I0034, ATR Interpreting Telephony Research Laboratories, July, 1988.

[5] Waibel A., Hanazawa T., Hinton G.E., Shikano K., Lang K.J., *Phoneme Recognition Using Time Delay Neural Networks*, IEEE Trans. Acoust. Speech Signal Process, 1989, 37 (3), 328-339.

[6] Elman J. L., *Finding Structure in Time*, Cognitive Science vol. 14, pag.179-221. 1990.

[7] Jordan M. I., *Attractor Dynamics and Parallelism in a Connectionist Sequential Machine*, Proc. of 8th Ann. Conf. of the Cognitive Science Society, pp. 532-546, Hillsdale NJ, Erlbaum, 1986.

[8] Jordan M. I., *Serial Order: a Parallel Distributed Processing Approach*, Technical Report Nr. 8604, Institute for Cognitive Science, University of California, San Diego, La Jolla, California, 1986a.

[9] Stuttgart Neural Network Simulator (SNNSv4.1), 1990-1995. Institute for parallel and distributed high performance systems, University of Stuttgart.

[10] Hermansky H., *Perceptual Linear Predictive (PLP) Analysis of Speech*, Jour. Acoust. Soc. Am., 1990, 87(4), 1738-1752.

[11] Hermansky H., Morgan N., *RASTA Processing of Speech*, IEEE Trans. On Speech and Audio Processing, 1994, 2(4), 578-589.

[12] Renals S., Rohwer S., *Phoneme Classification Experiments Using Radial Basis Functions*, Proc. of Int. Joint Conf. on Neural Networks, Vol I, pp.461-67, 1989.

[13] Hecht-Nielsen R., *Counterpropagation Networks*, Proc. Int. Conf. on Neural Networks, Vol. II, New York, pp. 19-32,1987.

[14] Hecht-Nielsen R., *Neurocomputing*, Addison-Wesley, Reading, MA, 1989.

[15] Powell M. J. D., *Algorithms for Approximation*, Oxford, 1987.

[16] Broomhead D. S., Lowe D., *Complex Systems* 2, 1988.

[17] Kolmogorov A. N., *On the Representation of Continuous Functions of Many Variables by Superposition of Continuous Functions of One Variable and Addition*, Dokl. Akad. Nauk, USSR, Vol 114, 1957, pp.953-56.

[18] Haykin S. , *Neural Networks - A Comprensive foundation*, IEEE Press, 1994.

[19] Hertz J., Krogh A., Palmer R.G., *Introduction to the Theory of Neural Computation*, Lecture Notes Volume I, Santa Fe Institute Studies in Sciences of Complexity, 1991.

[20] Williams R. J., Peng J., *An Efficient Gradient-Based Algorithm for On-Line Training of Recurrent Network Trajectories*, Neural Computation 2, 490-501, 1990.

[21] Williams R. J., Zipser D., *A Learning Algorithm for Continually Running Fully Recurrent Neural Networks*, Neural Comp., 1, 270-280, 1989.

[22] Almeida L. B., *A Learning Rule for Asynchronous Perceptrons with Feedback in a Combinatorial Environment*, Proc. IEEE First Int. Conf. Neural Networks, II, 609-618, 1987.

[23] Pineda F. J., *Generalization of Back-Propagation to Recurrent Neural Networks*, The American Physical Society, Vol. 59, Number 19, 1987.

[24] Hopfield J. J., *Neurons with Graded Response Have Collective Computational Properties Like Those Two-State Neurons*, Proc. of the National Academy of Sciences, USA, Vol. 81, 1984, pp. 3088-92.

[25] Esposito A., Ezin E. C., *Phoneme Classification using a RASTA-PLP preprocessing algorithm and a Time Delay Neural Network: Performance Studies*, Proc. of WIRN98, M. Marinaro, R. Tagliaferri (eds), pp. 207-217, Springer-Verlag Publisher, 1998.

[26] Ström N., *Sparse Connection and Pruning in Large Dynamic Artificial Neural Networks*, Proc. of EUROSPEECH, vol. 5, 2807-2810, 1997.

Signal classification using Neural Networks

Anna Esposito[a,b]   Mariarosaria Falanga[c,d]

Maria Funaro[c,d]   Maria Marinaro[c,d]   Silvia Scarpetta[c,d]

[a] I.I.A.S.S., Vietri sul Mare, Salerno, IT

[b] Dept.of Computer Science and Engineering,
Wright State University, Dayton (OH) USA

[c] Dipartimento di Scienze Fisiche 'E. R. Caianiello",
Universita' di Salerno (SA), IT

[d] INFM, Sezione di Salerno (SA), IT

Abstract

The aim of this paper is to classify two kind of signals recorded by seismic station: artificial explosions and seismic activity. The problem is approached from both the preprocessing and the classification point of view. For the preprocessing stage, instead of the conventional Fourier Transform, we use a Linear Prediction Coding (LPC) algorithm, which allows to compress the data and extract robust features for the signal representation. For the classification stage, we have compared the performance of several neural models. An unsupervised method, based on the Principal Component Analysis (PCA) and the Mixture of Gaussian (MoG) clustering algorithm, gives a 70% percentage of correct classification. The Elman Recurrent Neural Nets (RNN) is able to reach 91% of correct classification on the test set. However this performance is strongly and critically dependent on the order of presentation of the events. Instead a MLP with a single hidden layer gives the 86% of correct classification on the test set, independently of the order of presentation of the patterns.

1 Introduction

In the Campi Flegrei Area (Napoli, Italy) fishers usually make (illegal) artificial explosions. Since this area is also seismically active, the seismic stations which are monitoring this area should face the problem to distinguish between these two kind of signals: the propagation of the explosions and the seismic activity. Several data are collected of both kinds of events, and the experts can discriminate between them looking to the waveforms. However, an automatic system would be much more practical and useful. To this aim it is necessary both to preprocess the signals, in order to reduce the size of the data, and to identify a good classifier. We approach this problem using a preprocessing stage based on Linear Prediction Coding (LPC) and a second stage of classification based on neural techniques. We discuss the use of Principal Component Analysis (PCA), partially recurrent Elman networks, and Multi-layer Perceptron (MLP) for the classification stage.

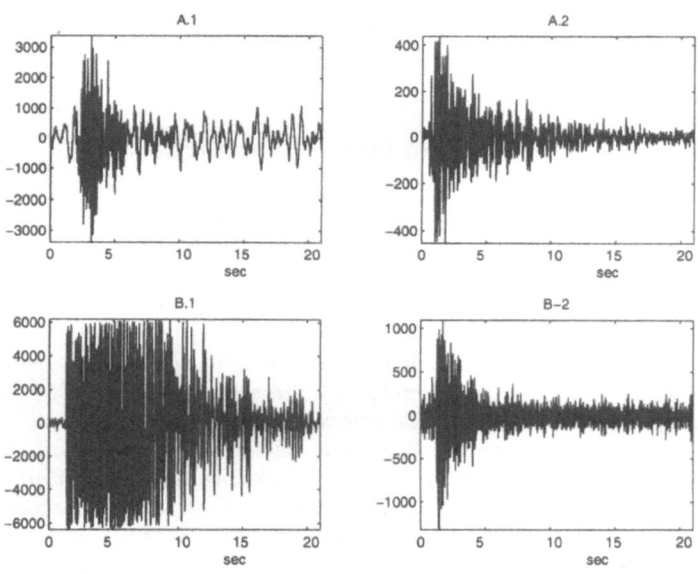

Figure 1: A: Two explosions registrations (vertical components) (Top) and B: Two seismic events registrations (vertical components) (Bottom)

2 Database

The permanent seismic monitoring network set up at Campi Flegrei Area is composed by eight analogic stations: three of them with 3-components and five of them with only vertical components. The seismic signals recorded by the remote stations are transmitted to the Observatory Monitoring Center. Here the analogic signals are sampled at 100 Hz, stored in a PC and made available for the analysis. Available labeled data [2] consists of 15 real seismic events and 15 explosions. Each event (seismic activity or explosion) may be detected by more then one seismic station, so that the total data set available is composed of 280 events (121 explosions and 169 seismic activity). For each event, a registration of 21 sec is taken, starting from the beginning. Since the signal is sampled at 100 Hz, each event is composed of 2100 points. Examples of explosions and seismic events registrations are shown in Fig.1.

3   Preprocessing

In order to classify the signals we should extract the main features from the time-domain signals. A spectrogram may be useful to show the differences between seismic activity and explosions. However, the spectrogram is not a good representation from the point of view of the compression (for example, for our signal of size 2100, a spectrogram on shifted windows of 3 sec would give as output a matrix of size 13x300). Therefore, we preprocess the data using a LPC algorithm [1]. In the LPC technique the signal S is modeled as a linear combination of its past values, $S(n) = \sum_{l=1}^{k} c_l S(n-l)$. In the frequency domain, this is equivalent to modeling the signal spectrum by an all-pole filter. The estimation of the model parameters (predictor coefficients c_l) is derived by the method of least squares. In fig.2 it is shown the residual error as a function of the number k of coefficients. We apply the linear prediction model extracting 8 parameters on each windows of the signal 3 seconds long. Shifting the window along the signal we obtain, for each event, a feature vector of size 8x13.

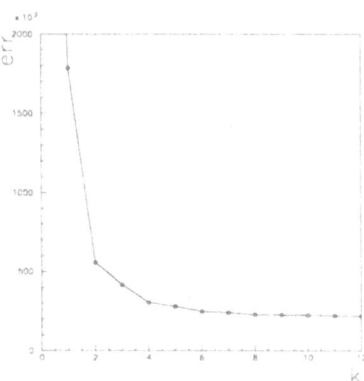

Figure 2: The residual mean square error is shown as a function of the number k of coefficients. The residual error has been averaged over the dataset, i.e. over the 13 windows and over all explosions and seismic registrations.

4 Classification experiments

After the preprocessing stage, our data set is composed of 280 labeled vectors, and each vector has 104 components. We approach the classification task both with an unsupervised strategy and with two kinds of supervised neural network. In order to train and test the supervised neural networks (Elman, and MLP) the data set has been divided in a training set (containing 204 events), a validation set (with 26 events) and a test set (with 50 events). Five different data sets, each composed of training, validation and test set, was obtained by permutation of all the available data, and the networks were trained on each of the five training sets. Each trained network was tested on the corresponding test set, and the average performance was evaluated. The training iterations was stopped at the minimum of the validation error (i.e. just before that the validation error starts to increase, in order to avoid over-fitting).

4.1 Principal Components Analysis

As first data analysis we perform the PCA [3, 4] on the set of data coming from the preprocessing stage. The results shows that the two kind of events are not well separated in the subspace spanned by the first two eigenvectors. Separation does not improve considering also the third and fourth components. We apply a clusterization algorithm (the Mixture of Gaussians algorithm with diagonal variance matrix) in the space spanned by the first 3 eigenvectors, we obtain, using two clusters, a correct classification percentage of 52%, while using 4 clusters (two gaussians for each class) a correct classification percentage of 70%. The two kind of events are not so different to allow a linear unsupervised method to distinguish them clearly. Other kind of differences, i.e. differences in between the seismic activities signals or differences in between explosions signals, may be predominant.

4.2 Elman Network

In the second experiment we uses a supervised partially recurrent neural network introduced by Elman [5]. This network with respect to a simple feed-forward MLP is augmented at the input level by additional units, activated by the previous value of the hidden units, called 'context units'. In this way the context units remember the previous internal representations. We apply the Elman net with an architecture 104-4-2, i.e. 104 input nodes, 4 hidden nodes, 2 output nodes and 4 context units. The learning rate, after a series of trial and error processes, was set to $\eta = 0.002$. This value gives the better net performances in terms of computational time and classification percentage. We obtain, on the average, the 92% of correct classification on the test set. However, we observed that this performance was critically related to the fact that in all the training validation and test set the same order of presentation was kept (i.e., to the net we presented first all the explosions and then all the seismic activities) This situation is not realistic for such kind of events since the explosions and the seismic activities happen without any temporal correlation between them. So, we shuffled the data, mixing the order of explosions and seismic events randomly, and we obtain an averaged correct classification of 62%. This is due to the recurrent structure of the network, since the recurrent connections make the net very sensible to the order of presentation of patterns. At this point we considered the idea to use a neural structure without recurrent connections, as described in the next section.

4.3 Multi-layer Perceptron Network

In the third experiment we used a supervised feedforward network. An MLP with an architecture of 104-8-2 (i.e. 104 input nodes, 8 hidden nodes and 2 output nodes) was trained with the Standard back-propagation algorithm. The learning rate, after a series of trial and error processes, was set to $\eta = 0.002$. The training iterations was stopped at the minimum of the validation error (i.e. just before that the validation error starts to increase, in order to avoid over-fitting). We obtain using this model in average a 86% of correct classification on the test sets. As expected, this results do not depend from the order of presentation of the examples.

5 Conclusions and future work

The reported results offer a solution to the problem of automatically distinguish between explosions and seismic activities using a simple Multilayer Perceptron. This is possible thanks to the preprocessing, which is able to extract robust features which describe very well the differences between the two kind of signals.

Future work can be done in order to optimize the preprocessing stage. By a comparison of the spectra of the signal and the all-pole fit given by the LPC model, the 'optimal' number of predictive coefficients can be estimated. This could improve the performance of the classification stage and further compress the available data.

References

[1] Makhoul J., Linear Prediction: A Tutorial Review. Proceedings of the IEEE, Vol. 63, No. 4 (1975)

[2] Data have been kindly provided by the Prof. del Pezzo at the Vesuvius Observatory (Napoli, Italy).

[3] Oja, E.. Neural networks principal components and subspaces. Int. J. Neural Systems 1, pp. 61-68 (1989).

[4] C. Bishop, Neural Networks for pattern recognition, Oxford University Press 1995.

[5] Elman J.L., Finding structure in time. Cognitive Science. vol. 14, pag.179-221, 1990

We like to thanks Prof. del Pezzo, Prof. de Martino, and their collaborators, for introducing us to the seismic events classification problem, for providing the data and for their fruitful discussions. This work has been in part supported by the NSF KDI program, Grant No. BCS-9980054, 'Cross-modal analysis of speech signal and sense: multimedia corpora and tools for gesture, speech, and gaze research.

Applying LSTM to Time Series Predictable Through Time-Window Approaches

Felix A. Gers   Douglas Eck   Jürgen Schmidhuber

felix@idsia.ch   doug@idsia.ch   juergen@idsia.ch

IDSIA, Galleria 2, 6928 Manno, Switzerland, www.idsia.ch

Abstract. Long Short-Term Memory (LSTM) is able to solve many time series tasks unsolvable by feed-forward networks using fixed size time windows. Here we find that LSTM's superiority does *not* carry over to certain simpler time series prediction tasks solvable by time window approaches: the Mackey-Glass series and the Santa Fe FIR laser emission series (Set A). This suggests to use LSTM only when simpler traditional approaches fail.

1 Overview

Long Short-Term Memory (LSTM) is a recurrent neural network (RNN) architecture that had been shown to outperform traditional RNNs on numerous temporal processing tasks [1–4].

Time series benchmark problems found in the literature, however, often are conceptually simpler than many tasks already solved by LSTM. They often do not require RNNs at all, because all relevant information about the next event is conveyed by a few recent events contained within a small time window. Here we apply LSTM to such relatively simple tasks, to establish a limit to the capabilities of the LSTM-algorithm in its current form. We focus on two intensively studied tasks, namely, prediction of the Mackey-Glass series [5] and chaotic laser data (Set A) from a contest at the Santa Fe Institute (1992) [6].

LSTM is run as a "pure" autoregressive (AR) model that can only access input from the current time-step, reading one input at a time, while its competitors — e.g., multi-layer perceptrons (MLPs) trained by back-propagation (BP) — simultaneously see several successive inputs in a suitably chosen time window. Note that Time-Delay Neural Networks (TDNNs) [7] are not purely AR, because they allow for direct access to past events. Neither are NARX networks [8] which allow for several distinct input time windows (possibly of size one) with different temporal offsets.

We also evaluate stepwise versus iterated training (IT) [9, 10].

2 Experimental Setup

The task is to use currently available points in the time series to predict the future point, $t + T$. The target for the network t_k is the difference between the values $x(t+p)$ of the time series p steps ahead and the current value $x(t)$ multiplied by a scaling factor f_s: $t_k(t) = f_s \cdot (x(t+p) - x(t)) = f_s \cdot \Delta x(t)$. The value for f_s scales $\Delta x(t)$ between -1 and 1 for the training set; the same value for f_s is used during testing. The predicted value is the network output divided by f_s plus $x(t)$. During iterated prediction with $T = n * p$ the output is clamped to the input (self-iteration) and the predicted values are fed back n times. For direct prediction $p = T$ and $n = 1$; for single-step prediction $p = 1$ and $n = T$.

The error measure is the normalized root mean squared error: NRMSE $= \langle (y_k - t_k)^2 \rangle^{\frac{1}{2}} / \langle (t_k - \langle t_k \rangle)^2 \rangle^{\frac{1}{2}}$, where y_k is the network output and t_k the target. The reported performance is the best result of 10 independent trials.

LSTM Network Topology. The input units are fully connected to a hidden layer consisting of memory blocks with 1 cell each. The cell outputs are fully connected to the cell inputs, to all gates, and to the output units. All gates, the cell itself and the output unit are biased. Bias weights to input and output gates are initialized block-wise: -0.5 for the first block, -1.0 for the second, -1.5 for the third, and so forth. Forget gates are initialized with symmetric positive values: $+0.5$ for the first block, $+1$ for the second block, etc. These are standard values that we use for all experiments. All other weights are initialized randomly in the range $[-0.1, 0.1]$. The cell's input squashing function g is a sigmoid function with the range $[-1, 1]$. The squashing function of the output unit is the identity function.

To have statistically independent weight updates, we execute weight changes every $50 + \text{rand}(50)$ steps (where $\text{rand}(max)$ stands for a random positive integer smaller than max which changes after every update). We use a constant learning rate $\alpha = 10^{-4}$.

MLP. The MLPs we use for comparison have one hidden layer and are trained with BP. As with LSTM, the one output unit is linear and Δx is the target. The input differs for each task but in general uses a time window with a time-space embedding. All units are biased and the learning rate is $\alpha = 10^{-3}$.

3 Mackey-Glass Chaotic Time Series

The Mackey-Glass (MG) chaotic time series can be generated from the MG delay-differential equation [5]: $\dot{x}(t) = \frac{\alpha x(t-\tau)}{1 + x^c(t-\tau)} - \beta x(t)$. We generate benchmark sets using a four-point Runge-Kutta method with step size 0.1 and initial condition $x(t) = 0.8$ for $t < 0$. Equation parameters were set at $a = 0.2$, $b = 0.1$, $c = 10$ and $\tau = 17$. The equation is integrated up to $t = 5500$, with the points from $t = 200$ to $t = 3200$ used for training and the points from $t = 5000$ to $t = 5500$ used for testing.

MG Previous Work. In the following sections we list attempts to predict the MG time series. To allow comparison among approaches, we did not consider works where noise was added to the task or where training conditions were very different from ours. When not specifically mentioned, an input time window with time delays t, $t-6$, $t-12$ and $t-18$ or larger was used. Summary of previous approaches:

BPNN [11]: A BP continuous-time feed forward NNs with two hidden layers and with fixed time delays. **ATNN** [11]: A BP continuous-time feed forward NNs with two hidden layers and with adaptable time delays. **DCS-LMM** [12]: Dynamic Cell Structures combined with Local Linear Models. **EBPTTRNN** [13]: RNNs with 10 adaptive delayed connections trained with BPTT combined with a constructive algorithm. **BGALR** [14]: A genetic algorithm with adaptable input time window size (Breeder Genetic Algorithm with Line Recombination). **EPNet** [15]: Evolved neural nets (Evolvable Programming Net). **SOM** [16]: A Self-organizing map. **Neural Gas** [17] : The Neural Gas algorithm for a Vector Quantization approach. **AMB** [18]: An improved memory-based regression (MB) method [19] that uses an adaptive approach to automatically select the number of regressors (AMB). The results from these approaches are found in Table 1.

Table 1. Results for the MG task, showing (from left to right) the number of units, the number of parameters (weights for NNs), the number of training sequence presentations, and the NRMSE for prediction offsets $T \in \{1, 6, 84\}$.

Reference	Units	Para.	Seq.	NMSE		
				$T=1$	$T=6$	$T=84$
Linear Predictor	-	-	-	0.0327	0.7173	1.5035
6th-order Polynom.	-	-	-	-	0.04	0.85
BPNN	-	-	-	-	0.02	0.06
FTNN	20	120	$7 \cdot 10^7$	-	0.012	-
ATNN	20	120	$7 \cdot 10^7$	-	0.005	-
Cascade-Correlation	20	≈ 250	-		0.04	0.17
DCS-LLM	200	200^2	$\approx 1 \cdot 10^5$	-	0.0055	0.03
EBPTTRNN	6	65	-	-	0.0115	-
BGALR	16	≈ 150	-	-	0.2373	0.267
EPNet	≈ 10	≈ 100	$\approx 1 \cdot 10^4$	-	0.02	0.06
SOM	-	10x10	$\approx 1.5 \cdot 10^4$	-	0.013	0.06
	-	35x35	$\approx 1.5 \cdot 10^4$	-	0.0048	0.022
Neural Gas	400	3600	$2 \cdot 10^4$	-	-	0.05
AMB	-	-	-	-	-	0.054
MLP, $p=T$	16	97	$1 \cdot 10^4$	0.0113	0.0502	0.4612
MLP, $p=1$	16	97	$1 \cdot 10^4$	$p=T=1$	0.0252	0.4734
MLP, $p=1$, IT	16	97	$1 \cdot 10^4$	0.0094	0.0205	0.3929
MLP, $p=6$	16	97	$1 \cdot 10^4$	-	$p=T=6$	0.1466
MLP, $p=6$, IT	16	97	$1 \cdot 10^4$	-	0.0945	0.2820
LSTM, $p=T$	4	113	$5 \cdot 10^4$	0.0214	0.1184	0.4700
LSTM, $p=1$	4	113	$5 \cdot 10^4$	$p=T=1$	0.1981	0.5927
LSTM, $p=1$, IT	4	113	$1 \cdot 10^4$	s. text	0.1970	0.8157
LSTM, $p=6$	4	113	$5 \cdot 10^4$	-	$p=T=6$	0.2910
LSTM, $p=6$, IT	4	113	$1 \cdot 10^4$	-	0.1903	0.3595

MG Results. The LSTM results are listed at the bottom of Table 1. After six single-steps of iterated training ($p = 1$, $T = 6$, $n = 6$) the LSTM NRMSE for single step prediction ($p = T = 1$, $n = 1$) is 0.0452. After 84 single-steps of iterated training ($p = 1$, $T = 84$, $n = 84$) the LSTM NRMSE single step prediction ($p = T = 1$, $n = 1$) is 0.0809. Increasing the number of memory blocks did not significantly improve the results.

The results for AR-LSTM approach are clearly worse than the results for time window approaches, for example with MLPs. Why did LSTM perform worse than the MLP? The AR-LSTM network does not have access to the past as part of its input and therefore has to learn to extract and represent a Markov state. In tasks we considered so far this required remembering one or two events from the past, then using this information before over-writing the same memory cells. The MG equation, contains the input from $t-17$, hence its implementation requires the storage of all inputs from $t-17$ to t (time window approaches consider selected inputs back to at least $t-18$). Assuming that any dynamic model needs the event from time $t-\tau$ with $\tau \approx 17$, we note that the AR-RNN has to store all inputs from $t-\tau$ to t and to overwrite them at the adequate time. This requires the implementation of a circular buffer, a structure quite difficult for an RNN to simulate.

MG Analysis It is interesting that for MLPs ($T=6$) it was more effective to transform the task into a one-step-ahead prediction task and iterate than it was to predict directly (compare the results for $p = 1$ and $p = T$). It is in general easier to predict fewer steps ahead, the disadvantage being that during iteration input values have to be replaced by predictions. For $T=6$ with $p=1$ this affects only the latest value. This advantage is lost for $T=84$ and the results with $p=1$ are worse than with $p=6$, where fewer iterations are necessary. For MLPs, iterated training did not in general produce better results: it improved performance when the step-size p was 1, and worsened performance for $p=6$. For LSTM iterated training decreased the performance. But surprisingly, the relative performance decrease for one-step prediction was much larger than for iterated prediction. This indicates that the iteration capabilities were improved (taking in consideration the over-proportionally worsened one-step prediction performance).

The single-step predictions for LSTM are not accurate enough to follow the series for as much as 84 steps. Instead the LSTM network starts oscillating, having adapted to the strongest eigen-frequency in the task. During self-iterations, the memory cells tune into this eigen-oscillation, with time constants determined by the interaction of cell state and forget gate.

4 Laser Data

This data is set A from the Santa Fe time series prediction competition [6][1]. It consists of one-dimensional data recorded from a Far-Infrared (FIR) laser in

---

[1] The data is available from http://www.stern.nyu.edu/~aweigend/Time-Series/SantaFe.html.

a chaotic state [20]. The training set consists of 1,000 points from the laser, with the task being to predict the next 100 points. We run tests for stepwise prediction and fully iterated prediction, where the output is clamped to the input for 100 steps.

For the experiments with MLPs the setup was as described for the MG data but with an input embedding of the last 9 time steps as in Koskela, Varsta and Heikkonen [21].

FIR-laser Previous Work Results are listed in Table 2. Linear prediction is no better than predicting the data-mean. Wan [22] achieved the best results submitted to the original Santa Fe contest. He used a Finite Input Response Network (FIRN) (25 inputs and 12 hidden units), a method similar to a TDNN. Wan improved performance by replacing the last 25 predicted points by smoothed values (sFIRN). Koskela, Varsta and Heikkonen [21] compared recurrent SOMs (RSOMs) and MLPs (trained with the Levenberg-Marquardt algorithm) with an input embedding of dimension 9 (an input window with the last 9 values). Bakker et. al. [10] used a mixture of predictions and true values as input (Error Propagation, EP). Then Principal Component Analysis (PCA) was applied to reduce the dimensionality of the time embedding. Kohlmorgen and Müller [23] pointed out that the prediction problem could be solved by pattern matching, if it can be guaranteed that the best match from the past is always the right one. To resolve ambiguities they propose to up-sample the data using linear extrapolation (as done by Sauer [24]). The best result to date, according to our knowledge, was achieved by Weigend and Nix [25]. They used a nonlinear regression approach in a maximum likelihood framework, realized with feed-forward NN (25 inputs and 12 hidden units) using an additional output to estimate the prediction error. McNames [26] proposed a statistical method that used cross-validation error to estimate the model parameters for local models, but the testing conditions were too different to include the results in the comparison. Bontempi et. al. [27] used a similar approach called " Predicted Sum of Squares (PRESS)" (here, the dimension of the time embedding was 16).

FIR-laser Results The results for MLP and LSTM are listed in Table 2. The results for these methods are not as good as the other results listed in Table 2. This is true in part because we did not replace predicted values by hand with a mean value where we suspected the system to be lead astray.

Iterated training yielded improved results for iterated prediction, even when single-step prediction became worse, as in the case of MLP.

FIR-laser Analysis The LSTM network could not predict the collapse of emission in the test set (Figure 1). Instead, the network tracks the oscillation in the original series for only about 40 steps before desynchronizing. This indicates performance similar to that in the MG task: the LSTM network was able to track the strongest eigen-frequency in the task but was unable to account for high-frequency variance. Though the MLP performed better, it generated inaccurate amplitudes and also desynchronized after about 40 steps. The MLP did however manage to predict the collapse of emission.

Table 2. Results for the FIR-laser task, showing (from left to right): The number of units, the number of parameters (weights for NNs), the number of training sequence presentations, and the NRMSE.

Reference	Units	Para.	Seq.	NMSE stepwise	NMSE iterated
Linear Predictor	-	-	-	1.25056	-
FIRN [22]	26	≈ 170	-	0.0230	0.0551
sFIRN [22]	26	≈ 170	-	-	0.0273
MLP [21]	70	≈ 30	-	0.01777	-
RSOM [21]	13	-	-	0.0833	-
EP-MLP Bakker et. al. (2000) [10]	73	> 1300	-	-	0.2159
Sauer (1994) [24]	-	32	-	-	0.077
Weigend and Nix (1994) [25]	27	≈ 180	-	0.0198	0.016
Bontempi (1999) [27]	-	-	-	-	0.029
MLP	32	353	$1 \cdot 10^4$	0.0996017	0.856932
MLP IT	32	353	$1 \cdot 10^4$	0.158298	0.621936
LSTM	4	113	$1 \cdot 10^5$	0.395959	1.02102
LSTM IT	4	113	$1 \cdot 10^5$	0.36422	0.96834

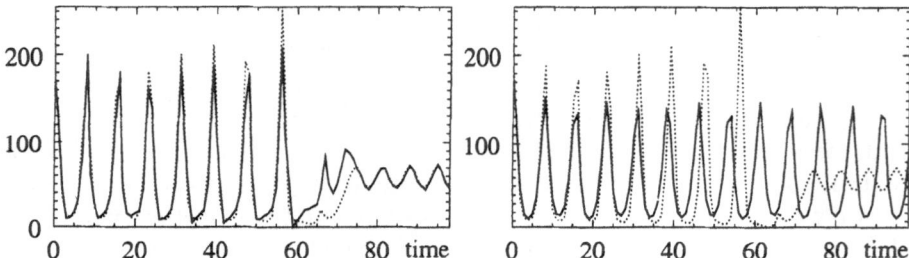

Fig. 1. Test run with LSTM network solution after iterated training for the FIR-laser task. Left: Single-Step prediction. Right: Iteration of 100 steps.

5   Conclusion

A time window based MLP outperformed the LSTM pure-AR approach on certain time series prediction benchmarks solvable by looking at a few recent inputs only. Thus LSTM's special strength, namely, to learn to remember single events for very long, unknown time periods, was not necessary here.

LSTM learned to tune into the fundamental oscillation of each series but was unable to accurately follow the signal. The MLP, on the other hand, was able to capture some aspects of the chaotic behavior. For example the system could predict the collapse of emission in the FIR-laser task.

Iterated training has advantages over single-step training for iterated testing only for MLPs and when the prediction step-size is one. The advantage is evident when the number of necessary iterations is large.

Our results suggest to use LSTM only on tasks where traditional time window based approaches must fail. One reasonable *hybrid* approach to prediction of unknown time series may be this: start by training a time window-based MLP, then freeze its weights and use LSTM only to reduce the residual error if there is any, employing LSTM's ability to cope with long time lags between significant events.

LSTM's ability to track slow oscillations in the chaotic signal may be applicable to cognitive domains such as rhythm detection in speech and music.

Acknowledgment. This work was supported by SNF grant 2100-49'144.96.

References

1. S. Hochreiter and J. Schmidhuber, "Long short-term memory," *Neural Computation*, vol. 9, no. 8, pp. 1735–1780, 1997.
2. F. A. Gers, J. Schmidhuber, and F. Cummins, "Learning to forget: Continual prediction with LSTM," *Neural Computation*, vol. 12, no. 10, pp. 2451–2471, 2000.
3. F. A. Gers and J. Schmidhuber, "Recurrent nets that time and count," in *Proc. IJCNN'2000, Int. Joint Conf. on Neural Networks*, (Como, Italy), 2000.
4. F. A. Gers and J. Schmidhuber, "LSTM recurrent networks learn simple context free and context sensitive languages," *IEEE Transactions on Neural Networks*, 2001. accepted.
5. M. Mackey and L. Glass, "Oscillation and chaos in a physiological control system," *Science*, vol. 197, no. 287, 1977.
6. A. Weigend and N. Gershenfeld, *Time Series Prediction: Forecasting the Future and Understanding the Past*. Addison-Wesley, 1993".
7. P. Haffner and A. Waibel, "Multi-state time delay networks for continuous speech recognition," in *Advances in Neural Information Processing Systems* (J. E. Moody, S. J. Hanson, and R. P. Lippmann, eds.), vol. 4, pp. 135–142, Morgan Kaufmann Publishers, Inc., 1992.
8. T. Lin, B. G. Horne, P. Tiño, and C. L. Giles, "Learning long-term dependencies in NARX recurrent neural networks," *IEEE Transactions on Neural Networks*, vol. 7, pp. 1329–1338, Nov. 1996.
9. J. C. Principe and J.-M. Kuo, "Dynamic modelling of chaotic time series with neural networks," in *Advances in Neural Information Processing Systems* (G. Tesauro, D. Touretzky, and T. Leen, eds.), vol. 7, pp. 311–318, The MIT Press, 1995.
10. R. Bakker, J. C. Schouten, C. L. Giles, F. Takens, and C. M. van den Bleek, "Learning chaotic attractors by neural networks," *Neural Computation*, vol. 12, no. 10, 2000.
11. S. P. Day and M. R. Davenport, "Continuous-time temporal back-progagation with adaptive time delays," *IEEE Transactions on Neural Networks*, vol. 4, pp. 348–354, 1993.
12. L. Chudy and I. Farkas, "Prediction of chaotic time-series using dynamic cell structuresand local linear models," *Neural Network World*, vol. 8, no. 5, pp. 481–489, 1998.
13. R. Bone, M. Crucianu, G. Verley, and J.-P. Asselin de Beauville, "A bounded exploration approach to constructive algorithms for recurrent neural networks," in *Proceedings of IJCNN 2000*, (Como, Italy), 2000.

14. I. de Falco, A. Iazzetta, P. Natale, and E. Tarantino, "Evolutionary neural networks for nonlinear dynamics modeling," in *Parallel Problem Solving from Nature 98*, vol. 1498 of *Lectures Notes in Computer Science*, pp. 593–602, Springer, 1998".

15. X. Yao and Y. Liu, "A new evolutionary system for evolving artificial neural networks," *IEEE Transactions on Neural Networks*, vol. 8, pp. 694–713, May 1997.

16. J. Vesanto, "Using the SOM and local models in time-series prediction," in *Proceedings of WSOM'97, Workshop on Self-Organizing Maps, Espoo, Finland, June 4-6*, pp. 209–214, Espoo, Finland: Helsinki University of Technology, Neural Networks Research Centre, 1997.

17. T. M. Martinez, S. G. Berkovich, and K. J. Schulten, "Neural-gas network for vector quantization and its application to time-series prediction," *IEEE Transactions on Neural Networks*, vol. 4, pp. 558–569, July 1993.

18. H. Bersini, M. Birattari, and G. Bontempi, "Adaptive memory-based regression methods," in *In Proceedings of the 1998 IEEE International Joint Conference on Neural Networks*, pp. 2102–2106, 1998.

19. J. Platt, "A resource-allocating network for function interpolation," *Neural Computation*, vol. 3, pp. 213–225, 1991.

20. U. Huebner, N. B. Abraham, and C. O. Weiss, "Dimensions and entropies of chaotic intensity pulsations in a single-mode far-infrared nh3 laser," *Phys. Rev. A*, vol. 40, p. 6354, 1989.

21. T. Koskela, M. Varsta, J. Heikkonen, and K. Kaski, "Recurrent SOM with local linear models in time series prediction," in *6th European Symposium on Artificial Neural Networks. ESANN'98. Proceedings. D-Facto, Brussels, Belgium*, pp. 167–72, 1998.

22. E. A. Wan, "Time series prediction by using a connectionist network with internal time delays," in *Time Series Prediction: Forecasting the Future and Understanding the Past* (W. A. S. and G. N. A., eds.), pp. 195–217, Addison-Wesley, 1994.

23. J. Kohlmorgen and K.-R. Müller, "Data set a is a pattern matching problem," *Neural Processing Letters*, vol. 7, no. 1, pp. 43–47, 1998.

24. T. Sauer, "Time series prediction using delay coordinate embedding," in *Time Series Prediction: Forecasting the Future and Understanding the Past* (A. S. Weigend and N. A. Gershenfeld, eds.), Addison-Wesley, 1994.

25. A. S. Weigend and D. A. Nix, "Predictions with confidence intervals (local error bars)," in *Proceedings of the International Conference on Neural Information Processing (ICONIP'94)*, (Seoul, Korea), pp. 847–852, 1994.

26. J. McNames, "Local modeling optimization for time series prediction," in *In Proceedings of the 8th European Symposium on Artificial Neural Networks*, pp. 305–310, 2000.

27. B. H. Bontempi G., Birattari M., "Local learning for iterated time-series prediction," in *Machine Learning: Proceedings of the Sixteenth International Conference* (B. I. and D. S., eds.), (San Francisco, USA), pp. 32–38, Morgan Kaufmann, 1999.

Standard Error Estimation in Neural Network Regression Models: the AR-Sieve Bootstrap Approach

Francesco Giordano   Michele La Rocca

Cira Perna

Dipartimento di Scienze Economiche e Statistiche, Università di Salerno

Via Ponte don Melillo, 84084, Fisciano, Salerno - Italy

Abstract

In this paper we investigate the usage of the AR-Sieve bootstrap method to estimate the standard error of the sampling distribution of the neural network predictive values in a regression model with dependent errors. The performance of the proposed approach is evaluated by a Monte Carlo experiment where it is also compared with the classical residual bootstrap scheme.

1   Introduction

Let $\{Y_t\}$, $t \in \{1, \dots, T\}$, a time series modelled as $Y_t = f(\mathbf{x_t}) + Z_t$, where $\mathbf{x}_t = (x_{1t}, \dots, x_{dt})$ is a vector of d non stochastic explanatory variables defined on a compact $\aleph \subset \Re^d$, and $\{Z_t\}$ are (possibly dependent) random variables with zero mean. The function f can be approximated with a *single hidden layer feed-forward neural network* ([3] [6]) of the form:

$$g(\mathbf{x}_t, \theta) = \psi \left(\sum_{k=1}^{m} c_k \phi \left(\sum_{j=1}^{d} a_{kj} x_{jt} + a_k \right) + c_0 \right)$$

where $\theta = (\mathbf{a}_1, \dots \mathbf{a}_m, c_0, c_1, \dots c_k)^T$, with $\mathbf{a}_i = (a_{i1}, \dots, a_{id})^T$, $i = 1, \dots, m$. The term a_{ki} is the weight of the connection between the j-th input neuron and the k-th neuron in the hidden level; c_k, $k = 1, \dots, m$ is the weight of the link between the k-th neuron in the hidden layer and the output; a_k and c_0 are respectively the bias term of the hidden neurons and of the output; $\phi(\cdot)$ and $\psi(\cdot)$ are respectively the activation function of the hidden and of the output layer.

In many statistical applications a key point is the construction of a confidence interval at any input value. Thanks to the increase of computer power, the use of bootstrap methods has improved in the past years as alternative to analytic approaches which are very difficult and complex to derive. In a neural network context some alternative bootstrap proposals have been studied in the case of a regression model with *iid* errors (see [7] [5] [4]) but they are not consistent for a different specification of the error structure. The aim of this paper is to analyze some of the main theoretical and practical issues in the use of the AR-Sieve Bootstrap scheme in neural network regression models with dependent errors. This resampling technique, based on the estimation of a sequence of AR models, gives good performances for linear processes and does not exhibits artefacts in the bootstrap series (see [1] [2]). The paper is organized as follows. In the next section we propose and discuss the use of the AR-Sieve bootstrap technique to evaluate the variance of the neural network fitted values. The results of a Monte Carlo simulation experiment and some concluding remarks are reported in the last section.

2 The residual bootstrap and the AR-Sieve bootstrap for neural network regression models

In the context of neural networks a straightforward bootstrap approach is model based: the dependence structure is modelled explicitly and completely by the estimated neural network and the bootstrap sample is drawn from the fitted model. The procedure can be implemented as follows.

1. Compute the neural network estimates $g(\mathbf{x}_t, \hat{\theta})$ for $t = 1, \ldots, T$.

2. Compute the residuals $\hat{Z}_t = Y_t - g(\mathbf{x}_t, \hat{\theta})$ and the centred residuals

$$\tilde{Z}_t = \hat{Z}_t - \sum_{t=1}^{T} \hat{Z}_t / T.$$

3. Denote by $\hat{F}_{\tilde{Z}}$ the empirical cumulative distribution function (ECDF) of $\tilde{Z}_t$, $t = 1, \ldots, T$ and resample $\{Z_t^*\}$ *iid* from $\hat{F}_{\tilde{Z}}$.

4. Generate a bootstrap series by $Y_t^* = g\left(\mathbf{x_t}, \hat{\theta}\right) + Z_t^*$.

Such model-based approach is designed for application to *iid* data and, of course, it is not consistent if the error terms are dependent. In this case, an effective solution seems to be the AR-Sieve bootstrap which can be implemented in our context as follows. The first two steps are the same as before.

1. Fit an autoregressive model of order p to the residuals $\tilde{Z}_t$ and compute another set of residuals

$$\hat{\varepsilon}_t = \sum_{j=0}^{p} \hat{\phi}_j \tilde{Z}_{t-j}, \hat{\phi}_0 = 1, t = p+1, \ldots, T.$$

2. Compute the centred residuals

$$\tilde{\varepsilon}_t = \hat{\varepsilon}_t - \sum_{t=p+1}^{T} \hat{\varepsilon}_t / (T - p), t = p+1, \ldots, T.$$

3. Denote by $\hat{F}_{\tilde{\varepsilon}}$ the ECDF of $\tilde{\varepsilon}_t$, $t = p+1, \ldots, T$. Resample $\{\varepsilon_t^*\}$, $t = 1, \ldots, T$, from $\hat{F}_{\tilde{\varepsilon}}$.

4. Generate the bootstrap error series $\{Z_t^*\}$, $t = 1, \ldots, T$, defined by

$$\varepsilon_t^* = \sum_{j=0}^{p} \hat{\phi}_j Z_{t-j}^*, \hat{\phi}_0 = 1, t = 1, \ldots, T.$$

Here we start the recursion with some starting value (the initial condition, if available, or some resampled innovations) and wait until stationarity is reached.

5. Generate a bootstrap series by $Y_t^* = g\left(\mathbf{x_t}, \hat{\theta}\right) + Z_t^*$.

The order of the $AR(p)$ model can be considered as a smoothing parameter. A guideline for approximating its value is given by the Akaike information criterion in the increasing range $[0, 10 \log_{10}(T)]$, a default option of many statistical packages. Observe that, even if the AR-Sieve bootstrap is based on a parametric model it is basically non parametric in its spirit since the $AR(p)$ specification is just used to filter the residuals.

The bootstrap series generated with the Residual or the AR-Sieve bootstrap can be used to approximate the sampling distribution, or some particular aspects such as its variability. Given the bootstrap series Y_t^*, $t = 1, \ldots, T$, compute the bootstrap analogue of the neural network parameters and the bootstrap neural network estimates

$$g\left(\mathbf{x_t}; \hat{\theta}^*\right) = \psi\left(\sum_{k=1}^{m} \hat{c}_k^* \phi\left(\sum_{j=1}^{d} \hat{a}_{kj}^* x_{jt} + \hat{a}_k^*\right) + \hat{c}_0^*\right)$$

Then, the standard error of the t-th predicted value

$$s_t = \left\{\text{var}\left[g\left(\mathbf{x_t}; \hat{\theta}\right)\right]\right\}^{1/2}$$

can be estimated by the bootstrap standard error

$$\hat{s}_t = \left\{\text{var}^*\left[g\left(\mathbf{x_t}; \hat{\theta}^*\right)\right]\right\}^{1/2}$$

where $\text{var}^*[\cdot]$ denotes the variance conditional on the observed data $(Y_t, \mathbf{x_t})$, $t = 1, \ldots, T$

As usual the bootstrap variance can be approximated through a Monte Carlo approach by creating many pseudo-replicates of the training set and then re-estimating the neural network on each replicate. So, B bootstrap samples are generated and for each sample $b = 1, \ldots, B$ an estimate, $\hat{\theta}_b^*$, of the parameter vector is computed. The estimate of the bootstrap variance is then given by

$$\text{var}_B^*\left[g\left(\mathbf{x_t}; \hat{\theta}^*\right)\right] = \frac{1}{B-1}\sum_{b=1}^{B}\left[g\left(\mathbf{x_t}; \hat{\theta}_b^*\right) - g\left(\mathbf{x_t}; \cdot\right)\right]^2$$

where

$$g\left(\mathbf{x_t}; \cdot\right) = \frac{1}{B} \sum_{b=1}^{B} g\left(\mathbf{x_t}; \hat{\theta}_\mathbf{b}^*\right).$$

3 Monte Carlo results and some concluding remarks

To study how the proposed bootstrap scheme can be used to produce accurate estimates of sampling variability of the neural network estimates, a Monte Carlo experiment has been performed. The simulated data set has been generated as $Y_t = f\left(x_t\right) + Z_t$ where $f\left(x_t\right)$ is the whabba's function specified as $f\left(x\right) = 4.26\left(e^{-x} - 4e^{-2x} + 3e^{-3x}\right)$ with $x \in [0, 2.5]$. Two different specifications for the noise process Z_t have been considered: a white noise and an ARMA(1,1), specified as $Z_t = 0.8Z_{t-1} - 0.5\varepsilon_{t-1} + \varepsilon_t$ with the innovations ε_t distributed as a Student-t with 6 degrees. To approximate the function $f\left(\cdot\right)$ we use a single input-single output feedforward neural network with two neurons in the hidden layer. The activation functions $\phi(\cdot)$ and $\psi(\cdot)$ are respectively the logistic and the identity function.

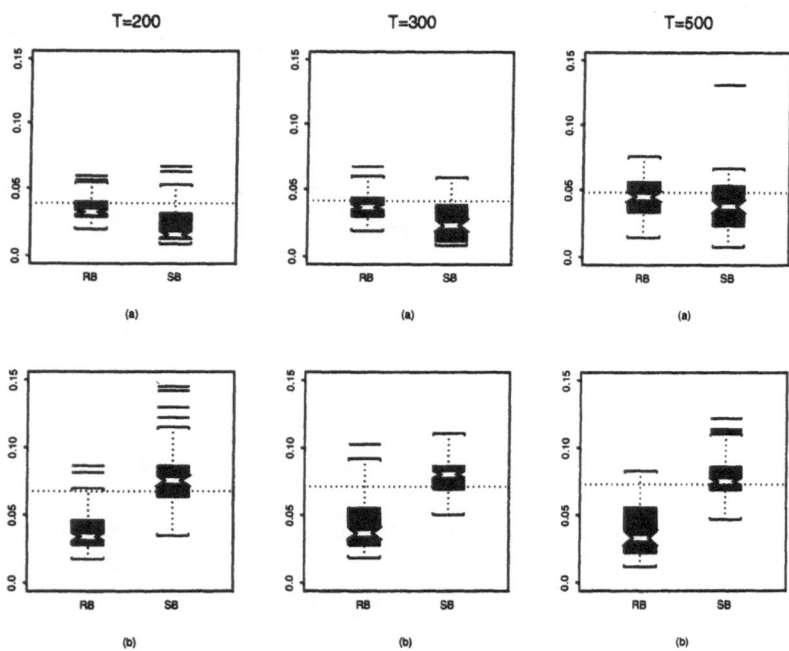

Figure 1: Parallel box- plot of the statistic m_k for different specifications of the error term: (a) Gaussian white noise, (b) ARMA with Student-t innovations

All the simulations are based on 200 Monte Carlo runs and 50 bootstrap replicates. We fixed $T = \{200, 300, 500\}$. As accuracy measure we considered the statistic $m_k = \text{Median}_t\,(\hat{s}_{tk})$ where $\hat{s}_{tk}$ is the estimated standard deviation of $g\left(\mathbf{x}_t; \hat{\theta}\right)$ for the k-th simulated Monte Carlo sample. To measure the absolute error of the estimate over each of the training cases we also considered the statistic $e_k = \text{Median}_t\,(|s_t - \hat{s}_{tk}|)$ where s_t is the actual standard deviation of $g\left(\mathbf{x}_t; \hat{\theta}\right)$. This "true" value is of course unknown and it has been estimated by a Monte Carlo experiment with 2000 runs.

As stressed by Refenes and Zapranis [4] the accuracy of the bootstrap estimates of s_t can be affected by computational problems, such as sensitivity of the learning algorithm to initial conditions. Moreover, when using a resampling algorithm, a strategy for the choice of starting values in each resampling series is needed. In our simulation study, we fixed the starting values in the learning algorithm to the optimal values computed on the observed data. These values are kept fixed for all the B resampled series.

In figure 1 we reported the notched box-plots of the distributions of the statistic m_k for different values of T and for two alternative specifications of the error terms. If the notches on two boxes do not overlap, this indicates a difference in a location at a rough 5 percent significance level. The dotted line refers to the median of the "true" values of the standard errors.

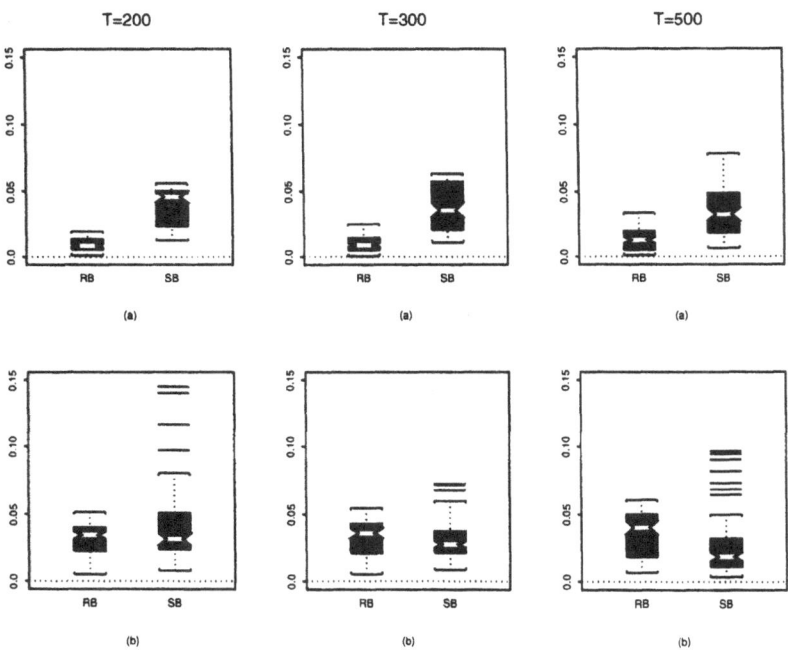

Figure 2: Parallel box-plot of the statistic e_k for different specifications of the error term: (a) Gaussian white noise, (b) ARMA with Student-t innovations

As expected, for Gaussian *iid* innovations the residual bootstrap outperforms the AR-Sieve bootstrap which shows a larger bias and a larger variability. It is interesting to observe that the differences between the procedures, even if evident, are not so marked. In the case of ARMA errors, the improvement over the residual bootstrap, when using the AR-Sieve bootstrap, is considerable: the bias and the variability are both lower. The performances of the AR-Sieve are still better for an increasing sample size. For $T = 500$ in the ARMA case, the differences between the true value and the AR-Sieve estimates are not significant at a rough level of 5 percent. These remarks are basically confirmed looking at figure 2 where we reported the results for the statistic e_k. Again, the AR-Sieve bootstrap outperforms the residual bootstrap in the case of ARMA errors.

Several different aspects should be further explored to get a better insight of the joint usage of neural networks and bootstrap methods. When dealing with dependent data, alternative bootstrap methods have been proposed so it is of interest to evaluate their performances in a neural network framework. Moreover, a comparison with respect to the AR-Sieve used here is also needed.

Acknowledgements. The paper has been supported by MURST 2000 "Modelli stocastici e metodi di simulazione per l'analisi di dati dipendenti".

References

[1] P. Buhlmann. Sieve bootstrap for smoothing in nonstationary time series. *The Annals of Statistics*, 26:48–83, 1998.

[2] P. Buhlmann. Bootstrap for time series. Research report 87, ETH, Zurich, 1999.

[3] K. Hornik, M. Stinchcombe, and H. White. Multy-layer feedforward networks are universal approximators. *Neural Networks*, 2:359–366, 1989.

[4] A. P. N. Refenes and A. D. Zapranis. Neural model identification, variable selection and model adequacy. *Journal of Forecasting*, 18:299–332, 1999.

[5] R. Tibshirani. A comparison of some error estimates for neural network models. *Neural Computation*, 8:152–163, 1996.

[6] H. White. Learning in artificial neural networks: a statistical prespective. *Neural Computation*, 1:425–464, 1989.

[7] H. White and W. G. Baxt. Bootstrapping confidence intervals for clinical input variable effects in a network trained to identify the presence of acute myocardial infraction. *Neural Computation*, 7:624–638, 1995.

Fuzzy Connections in realistic real-time facial animation

Paolo Rigiroli and N. Alberto Borghese

Laboratory of Human Motion Analysis and Virtual Reality, MAVR, Istituto Neuroscienze e Bioimmagini CNR, Scientific Institute HSR, Via f.lli Cervi, 93 - 20090 Segrate (Milano), I – http://www.inb.mi.cnr.it/borghese.html.

Abstract

Real-time realistic reproduction of facial expressions has the potentiality to become a fundamental tool for rehabilitation in psychological and psychiatric disorders. The most accurate techniques are based on biomechanical modelling the face. However, they are inapplicable when real-time is required due to the computational load. An alternative solution pursued here, is to first capture the facial surface by a three-dimensional scanner, and then apply to it the motion of few repere points captured live. In particular, we have implemented a two-layered model, where the connection between the lower layer (control mesh) and the upper layer (topologial model) is realised by fuzzy-connections. This avoids cracks over the surface and gives a smooth deformation of the face.

1 Introduction

Real-time facial animation and the reproduction of facial expression represent one of the frontiers in Computer Graphics. The techniques used can be divided in two main categories: *anatomical synthesis* and *exterior reproduction* techniques. The *anatomical synthesis* techniques [1, 2] are those which are potentially most accurate. They are based on the physical modeling of the face: skeletal and muscular apparatus reconstruction, and cutaneous tissue simulation. Soft tissue simulation largely complicates the model and requires the use of Finite Elements techniques to obtain a 3D animated mesh. However, when real–time animation is required, these methods cannot be applied for the enormous computational load and other techniques should be searched.

The *exterior reproduction* techniques first build a static 3D digital model of the facial surface with its chromatic attributes (by a three-dimensional scanner [3]). Then facial motion is capture live through motion capture instrumentation [4]. These acquire the 3D motion of a set of repere-points indicated on the face by small passive markers. This approach can work in real time provided that the 3D mesh is sufficiently light (constituted of a reduced number of polygons, in the order of 10,000 with actual hardware) and suitable algorithms are developed to transmit the movement of the repere points to the mesh (mapping). We present here a fuzzy technique which guarantees smooth facial animation adopting a simple fuzzy mapping function; and it is therefore suitable to real-time facial animation.

2   Method

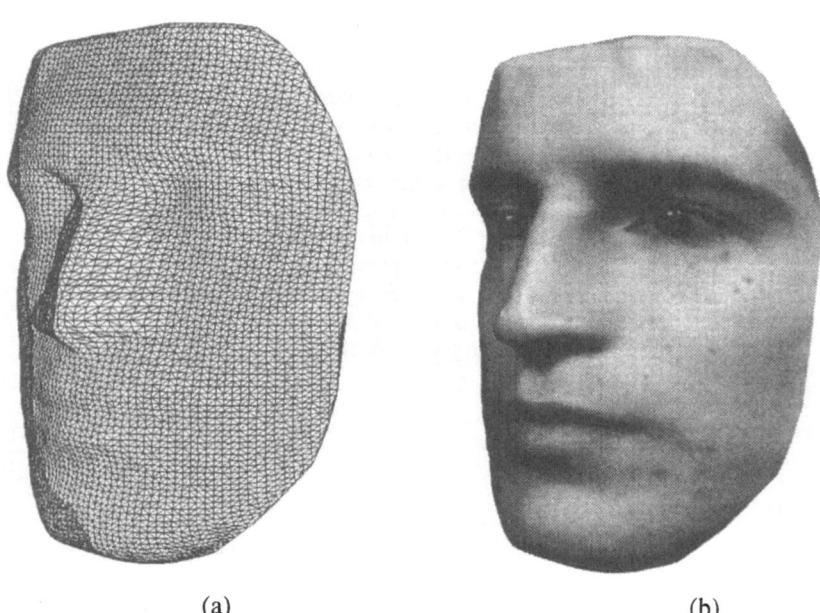

(a)   (b)

Figure 1: The 3D topological mesh to be animated and the same mesh coloured with per-vertex attribute.

The first input to our animation technique is the digital clone of a face. This is constituted of a polygonal (triangular) 3D mesh with the colour field defined as per-vertex attribute [5, 6]. A typical 3D mesh is represented in Figure 1a; and in Figure 1b after colour has been applied to its vertices. The mesh in Figure 1 will be called *topological mesh*.

To give life to the model, the mimic of an actor is captured live. We use here as input a traditional motion–capture system (Elite in our case [5]) to acquire 51 markers positioned on the actor face according to the location points identified in the MPEG-4 standard. A control mesh is created by connecting these points (and some extra virtual markers) each other, to form a control mesh (Figure 2). This is used to dynamically transform in real-time the coloured topological mesh of the same subject (that represents the external aspect of the face) according to the actual expression of the face.

The procedure described here is in three steps: mesh alignment and fuzzy connection, which are done once for each actor, and animation.

After the 3D control and topological meshes have been aligned through custom semi-automatical tool, the mutual interconnections between them can be established. To such purpose we project every vertex of the upper mesh (topological) normally to the nearest face on the control mesh. This has been done through the following algorithm:

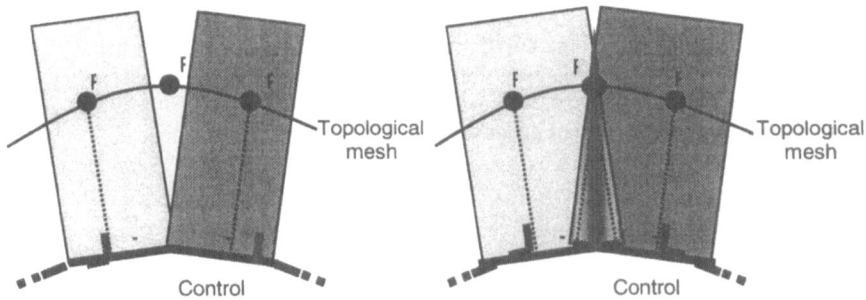

Figure 2. Principle of fuzzy connection. Vertices P1 and P2 of the topological mesh are projected orthogonally to their corresponding faces in the 3D control mesh. The correspondence is unique. Point P3 projects onto two different faces, its motion will be influenced by the motion of both faces.

For every face, F, of the control mesh,

1.   Determination of the rototranslation which makes F to lie on the plane z = 0, through in its centroid (the face is flattened to the ground);

2.   Enlargement of the face F by 5% of its area, obtaining the face F'.

3.   Application of the rototranslation to the entire topological mesh.

4.   Extraction of all the vertices of the topological mesh whose vertical projection lies inside the 2D triangle F'. For each vertex, the number of the triangle and the height over it (z after the rototranslation) are computed;

5.   The 3D coordinates of the vertex are expressed as a linear combination of the 2D co-ordinates of the control triangle in which its principal projections lie, weighted by their height.

6.   If the vertex projects on a boundary region of the control triangle (Figure 3), the 3D point co-ordinates are expressed as a weighted mean of their 3D positions computed for the adjacent faces, the weight is represented by the Gaussian of the distance from the face border (fuzzy membership).

7.   If one vertex projects over more than one face, its height over all the faces is saved (these are the vertices which are close to the boundary of a face).

This exhausts the static phase of mesh alignment and vertex assignment. The model is ready to get life in real-time.

To the scope we monitor the motion of the 3D vertices of the topological mesh and we infer the 3D position of all the vertices of the topological mesh, frame by frame. When a vertex of the topological mesh corresponds to a single face, its 3D position will be updated dynamically by computing its intrinsic coordinates frame by frame. When a vertex of the topological mesh projects onto more than one face of the control mesh, its position is obtained as a weighted mean of the intrinsic coordinates and height over the faces. The weights are the Gaussian of the distance of the projection from the face border. This is exemplified in Fig. 2.

This procedure of fuzzy assignment allows to avoid cracks in the topological surface which do occur during motion when hard correspondence is used. For an expression of smiling, the cracks verify in the region depicted in light grey close to the borders of the control mesh (Figure 3).

3   Conclusion

The method presented is simple, but very powerful. As it involves only local operation in the computation of the 3D vertices of the topological mesh, frame by frame, it allows animation in real-time. The fuzzy assignment allows avoiding cracks, which do occur from different motions of adjacent control faces. More extensive results and videos are reported at the Web page: www.inb.mi.cnr.it/borghese.html.

References

1 Lee Y, Tezopoulos D. and Waters K., Realistic modeling for facial animation. *Computer Graphics* 29(2), pp. 55-62 (1995).

2 Badler, N.I., Animation 2000++. (2000). *IEEE Computer Graphics and Applications* 20(1), pp. 28-29.

3 Borghese N.A., Ferrigno G., Baroni G., Savarè R., Ferrari S. and Pedotti A. (1998) AUTOSCAN: A flexible and portable scanner of 3D surfaces. *IEEE Computer Graphics & Applications*, May/June, pp. 38-41.

4   Borghese N.A., Di Rienzo M., Ferrigno G. and Pedotti A. (1990) - Elite: a goal-oriented vision system for moving objects detection, *Robotica*, Vol. 9, pp 275-282.

5   Borghese N.A. and Ferrari S. (2000), A Portable Modular System for Automatic Acquisition of 3D Objects, *IEEE Trans. Instrumentation & Mesurement*, Vol. 49(5), pp. 1128-1136.

6   Rigiroli P., Campadelli P., Pedotti A and Borghese N.A., (2001), Mesh Refinement with Colour Attributes, *Computer & Graphics.* Vol. 25, No. 3.

Borghese N.A., Ferrigno G. (1990) - An algorithm for 3D Automatic Movement Analysis by means of standard TVcameras - IEEE Trans. on Biom. Eng., Vol. 37 pp. 1221-1225.

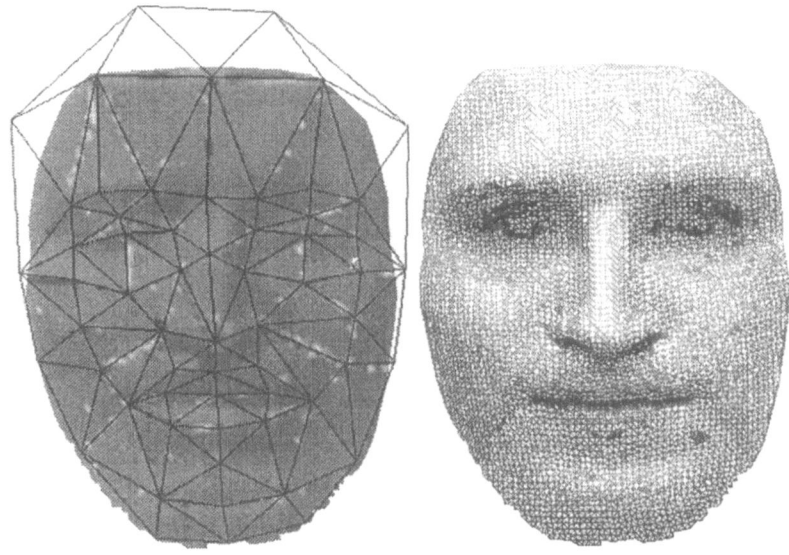

Figure 3. In red the regions where cracks do occur in the topological mesh in a smile expression (a). The same expression with fuzzy association (b).

Section 7
Applications

An Acoustic Passive Detector for Traffic Counts with Neural Networks

Antonino Calabrò, Maria Nadia Postorino, Giuseppe M.L. Sarnè

Facoltà di Ingegneria - Università Mediterranea di Reggio Calabria

Reggio Calabria – Italia

Abstract

Traffic count is fundamental for monitoring traffic flows on a transportation network and for the solution of different problems (as, for example, the estimation of the Origin/Destination demand matrix). Different techniques and instruments, each one with specific advantages and disadvantages, can be used for counting the vehicles on a transportation network. In this paper the use of a passive acoustic detector together with two neural networks working sequentially is proposed for counting the cars on the urban roads. The results obtained with this system are satisfactory and comparable with the existing ones. The proposed system also shows a large improvement of the cost/benefit ratio.

1 Introduction

Automatic traffic counts are an important aspects of the existing traffic control systems, because they provide the input data for resolving a large number of problems as, for example, the analysis of the traffic flow characteristics and the estimation of the Origin/Destination demand matrix. Unfortunately, the high costs of installation and the complex management of the counting systems used at present do not allow having a wide monitoring of the road networks.

The existing detectors [2], [8], [9], [10], [11] are based on different technologies: inductive loops (ILD), microwave, active or passive infrared, ultrasound, passive acoustic and video images. The technology to be used depends on different factors; the most important are the flow of data, the reliability, the accuracy, the time-response, the capability to recognize stopped vehicles or to work in hard atmospheric conditions (fog, rain), the temporal gap between vehicles (≥ 0.5 sec.), the environmental impact and, finally, the number of the necessary detectors (monitoring of more traffic streams and/or zones).

Another distinction among the different detectors can be made in terms of installation modalities. Some detectors, as the ILDs that measure the variations of a magnetic field crossed by the vehicle, need the installation of specific apparatus into the road surface (they are also called "invasive"); this installation is expensive and produces a temporary alteration of the traffic flow conditions during the positioning. Some other detectors are formed only by surface apparatus that do not require specific interventions on the roads and do not modify the circulation (both during the installation and the working stages); furthermore, they often can be used for measuring directly some traffic flow parameters as density, vehicular trajectory and so on. They are also called "not invasive".

Output data provided by the detectors need some specific analyses for obtaining the traffic flow parameters [2], [8]; the algorithms used to this end can be grouped on the basis of the adopted techniques (statistic, adaptable, etc.) and of the efficiency (measured by the values of False Alarm Rate, Detection Rate e Time to Detection).

In order to overcome some of the problems that can arise when invasive detectors are used, a specific tool has been designed and realized for the detection of the traffic flows. It can work both in urban and extra-urban areas, it is cheap and easy to install, can work both in fixed or mobile stations and in all those places where the installation of the invasive detectors is impossible.

The tool consists of an acoustic passive sensor (specifically, a microphone on one side of the road), connected to two artificial back-propagation neural networks (NNs) working sequentially; the system has an optimal rate between costs (hardware, installation, management and data analysis) and benefits (precision).

2 Analysis of the problem

The basic idea underlying the design of the proposed tool is that people can identify a vehicle through the sound it produces during the movement with a good degree of approximation. Then, the corresponding signal contains useful information for its identification. This information can be identified mainly in the frequency spectrum of the produced sound and in the Doppler effect (the frequency of the signal increases when the sound source approaches and decreases when it moves away).

The first variable suggests to use the domain of the frequencies while the second one suggests to analyse spectrum of frequencies in subsequent temporal intervals, t_i (in this work three intervals are used) for each pattern.

The characteristic sound produced in the time domain by a vehicle that moves in front of the sensor, for 3.5 seconds, is depicted in figure 1. As already described, the signal increases when the vehicle approaches the sensor and decreases when the vehicle moves away; this fact allows operating only in those intervals where the signal shows variations of amplitude.

In order to link the produced sound to the vehicle generating it, some transformations of the collected data need. Specifically, the analogical output provided by the microphone is transformed in a digital one by using a Pulse Code Modulation (PCM) transformation, based on a sampling process, quantization on multiple levels and coding. Each one of these phases introduces different error terms; indeed, the sampling process produces loss of information, while the quantization introduces both noise (called quantization noise) and an overload noise. This last term does not exist if the quantizer is well designed.[3].

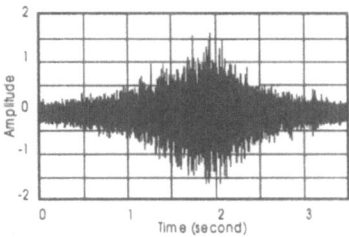

Figure 1

The information loss can be reduced (even eliminated) if the sampling frequency is double compared to the maximum frequency of the examined signal (Nyquist condition); then a great number of samples needs, afterwards provided to the NN as inputs. Because the complexity of a NN increases as the number of input increases, a correct balance has to be find between the two objectives.

The quantization produces a high noise by using a large step, while using a small step it needs a high number of bits and also a large amount of memory to represent and store the amplitude of the signal (if the signal is assumed not bounded in amplitude). For the above reasons a band-pass filter is used. In fact, as observed experimentally, the signal power is gathered on the frequencies less than 5 KHz, even if it is different from zero over all the spectrum. Obviously, there is not an exact agreement between the power of the signal at a fixed frequency and the importance of the information contains. The signal is sampled at 11025 Hz because this is the lowest frequency that the used hardware and the Nyquist condition allowed.

Finally, the coding has been effected with the Gray representation [7] at 16 bits for a greater error reliability.

A change of domain, from time to frequency, is operated on the PCM signal by using the Fast Fourier Transform (FFT), usually employed to obtain a change of domain with PCM signals; it is efficient for sequence of finite lengths and its output is a specular spectrum [5] allowing to halve the data, even if they remain still too many. For this reason, the spectrum is divided in intervals f_j by using one or more functions (maximum, media and so on) that synthesize the relative information.

The sound produced by the vehicles is also significantly affected by different factors; the most important among them are the amount, the composition and the kinematics characteristics of the traffic flow, the road characteristics and the meteorological conditions. From the point of view of the acoustic impact, the first two factors are little significant, while the characteristics of the road are a more important factor. The kinematics of the traffic flow affects both the signal spectrum and the Doppler effect, but the problem can be resolved with an improvement in the NN training. Particularly, the road characteristics to be considered are the road surface, the building presence on one or both the road sides, the ratio building-height/road-width. For the last aspect a further distinction can be made between road U-designed with a close and with an open structure; two types can be considered in the last case: roads with buildings at more than 20 meters from their sides without any obstacle, roads with buildings on one side or with low buildings. Finally, the meteorological conditions affect both the generation and the sound propagation (e.g., the noise level increases on a wet road), while thunder, strong wind and rain can be confused with a vehicle [1].

However, the most important factor that can influence the training of the NN is the reflection of the acoustic waves produced by some surfaces. This condition has been taken into account in the experiment proposed, in fact the traffic detection has been carried out along a road bounded by a high stone-wall (with a high level of acoustic reflection) and some rather low buildings, in order to allow the acoustic waves propagation. In fact, both absence or maximum (Canyon effect) reflections conditions, but little varying, are easily assimilate from a NN, while varying components are not well identified.

3   The proposed technique and results

A NN approach is proposed in this work to resolve the problem of recognizing vehicles by using the sound they produced when they are moving, thanks to the capability of the NNs to resolve mathematical problems when an analytical solution cannot be written or when the complexity of the problem to be resolved is very high.

The supervised back-propagation NN (SBP) is thought to be the most suitable to resolve this problem. The interested reader can refer to the large literature existing about this kind of NN, for example [4] [6] [12].

The data set to be used for the training of the NN has to be sufficiently complete in order to allow the extrapolation of the common elements present in the patterns; such elements are vehicles, restricted in this experiment to cars and identified by their sound other than various noises produced by sources even considerably different. The input data have been collected in different periods of the 1999, by using a condenser microphone situated at 1.2 meters above the ground, on one side of a one-way urban road; the detection has been carried out for different traffic and meteorological conditions. Each sound produced by a car or by a different source has been stored in Wave format (in order to easily modify the data set); at the end, 6026 car sounds and 3184 not-vehicle noises have been collected.

Some preliminary tests showed that only one SBP cannot directly recognize a car transit; for this reason two NNs working sequentially have been considered. The first one can classify cars, rain (together with thunders), background noise, wind, strong wind, voices, chaos (more sources together), various sounds (annoyance elements). The last two classes include critical patterns for the NN training. The second NN is an alternative to a statistical analysis: in fact, it works on the outputs of the first NN, that are not directly interpretable, and provides as its own output a code that identifies the transit of a car or noise.

To arrive at the best configuration, both for the data set and the NN topology, different tests have been carried out. Particular attention has been devoted to the construction of the data set for the first NN (the data set of the second NN is trivial), particularly to the length of the intervals t_i (t_i=0,5 sec.), to the subdivision modality (with a logarithmic function) of their frequency spectrum in shorter intervals f_j to reduce the NN inputs (each input refers to a frequency interval f_j of t_i) and, finally, to the function (the mean value has been used) that has to be applied to each interval for synthesizing the information that it contains.

The tests about the NN have been referred to the number of layers, the activation functions of the neurones, the number of neurones for each layers. These parameters have been valuated both separately and with cross-analysis because, for example, the increase in the number of layers often means a decrease in the number of neurones; similar considerations can be made for the activation functions compared to the number of layers.

The tests carried out showed that the best minimum number of input neurones is 24, with respect to the length of the interval T (T=3 t_i); without the reduction of the signal spectrum the number of f_j in input could be 63. The number of patterns that need for the training is formed by the car and noise transits in equal number; 2600 examples have been considered.

The best pattern composition of noise classes is formed by 200 examples for each class of not-vehicles noise, while only the background noise class has 100 examples because of its homogeneity. Furthermore, in the first NN we triplicated the number of output neurones of the car category for reinforcing the relative learning; as expected, the outputs of this category are the same by threes and then only one is significant and provided as input to the second NN

The input data of the second NN are the outputs provided by the first NN (cars and seven classes of not vehicles), while the output data are −1 or 1 (an output greater than zero means that there is the passage of a car).

The first NN has 24 inputs, two hidden layers with respectively 90 and 40 neurones with hyperbolic tangent activation functions for all the neurones and 10 output neurones in the output layer with hyperbolic tangent as activation functions. The second NN has 8 inputs, one hidden layer with 50 neurones and only one output neurone to identify the car or the noise transit, with hyperbolic tangent as activation function for all the neurones.

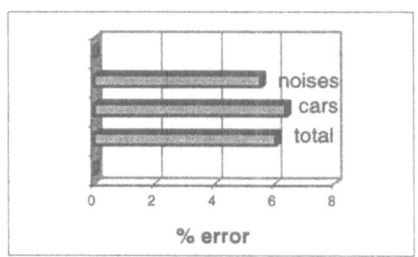 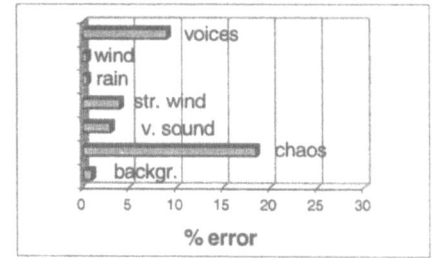

Figure 2 Figure 3

The mean error obtained with the proposed system is 6.04 %, practically equal to that obtained with usual systems, even if the excellence class is less than 5% (the best detection system is the ILD that, if perfectly installed, produce an error near to zero). By following this criterion the proposed system cannot be included in the class of the best detectors, but we think that a large parts of "false detections" caused by different annoyance elements (as voices near to the sensor) can be strongly reduced by using a second microphone, with different orientation, to give more weight to the Doppler effect characteristic of the passage of a moving sound source, in our case a vehicle.

Figure 2 depicts the percentage of error in recognizing cars and noises with respect to the total error; Figure 3 depicts more carefully the percentages of error made on the single classes of noises. In this last case the error of the class "chaos" is more evident, but it is to be reminded that this class, suitably constructed with critical patterns, refers to particular events.

4   Conclusions

The results obtained are widely comparable with those obtained by using the detectors currently on the market, but the proposed tool is more convenient in terms of management and monetary costs (for example, there is a 1:16 ratio with the ILDs in terms of cost). Thus the benefit/cost ratio largely balances the gap due to the small increase of the error with respect to the excellent detectors class.

Further developments, however, have to consider a larger data set than that considered by the authors in this fist stage due to the limited means, possibly extended to all kinds of vehicles.

As a general conclusion, the system proposed in this paper could be usefully employed for the detection of vehicles because, thanks to the use of the NNs, it is cheap and easy to install and it allows monitoring traffic flow on relatively large scale without having significantly reduction of the performances with respect to the commonly used systems.

References

[1] Brown A., Lam K., Urban Noise Survey. Applied Acustics n.20, pp.23-39

[2] Calabrò A., Postorino M.N., Sarnè G.M.L. Uno stato dell'arte dei rilevatori di traffico e degli algoritmi di analisi. Internal report, Università degli Studi di Reggio Calabria, Facoltà di Ingegneria.

[3] Conte E. Lezioni di teoria dei segnali. Liguori editore, 1996.

[4] Hecht–Nielsen R. Theory of back-propagation neural network. IEEE, 1989.

[5] Leon W. Couch II. Digital and analog communication system. Prentice Hall, 1997.

[6] Rumelhart D, McClealland JL and the PDP Research Group. Parallel distributed processing, Vol 1. MIT Press, Cambridge, 1986.

[7] Shannon CE, Weaver W. La teoria matematica delle comunicazioni. ETAS, Milano, 1971.

[8] URL 1: http://www.itsonline.com/index.htm

[9] URL 2: http://www.path.berkeley.edu/~leap

[10] URL 3: http://www.protectiontech.com

[11] URL 4: http://www.rtms-by-eis.com

[12] Wasserman P.D. Neural Computing: theory and practice. ANZA Research, Inc. Van Nostrand Reinhold New York, 1989.

A Fuzzy-G.M.D.H. Approach to V.a.R.

Marco Corazza, Silvio Giove
Dept. of Applied Mathematics, University "Ca' Foscari" of Venice (Italy)
Dorsoduro, n. 3825/E - 30123 Venice (Italy)
E-mails: corazza@unive.it, sgiove@unive.it

1 Introduction

Value at Risk (V.a.R.) is used to measure the possible losses of a stock, a derivative, a portfolio, and so on. Different approaches were proposed to obtain such a value, based on the past history, or on stochastic simulation, or on estimation of the theoretical distributions. We propose a method that empirically reconstructs the conditional distribution of the analyzed financial returns, using two soft-computing techniques based, respectively, on fuzzy estimation and on a polynomial neural network. At first, a non-parametric density estimation is proposed, using a fuzzy *similarity* measure between *k-patterns*, that are sequence of k consecutive values sampled from the considered time series, extending the Nadaraya-Watson approach [7]. Subsequently, the Group Method of Data Handling (on following: G.M.D.H.) neural network is used to compute a polynomial approximation of the unknown relationship between the data. The two-phases algorithm was finally applied to a real financial time series, and the results are used to create a V.a.R. predictor.

2 A fuzzy approach for time series analysis

A non parametric approach is used to estimate the *conditional* V.a.R. for a financial time series; the extension to a mixed portfolio is not considered here. We remark that some dependency between the value at time t and the sampled values was empirically verified and theoretically accepted [10]. The non parametric method that we propose does not require the assumption of a particular stochastic process, and requires the only hypothesis of *mixing conditions* [2], [9], that is, roughly speaking, the underlying stochastic process has *finite memory*. Let us consider the following definitions:

1) $\{x_t\}_{t=1,..,M}$: sampled realisation of a stochastic process Y ;

2) $X_t^k = \{x_{t-k+1}, x_{t\ k+2}, ..., x_t\}$: k-pattern at time t ;

3) $f_{t+T}(z \mid X_t^k)$: the conditional density of Y at time $(t+T)$, conditioned by the last observed k-pattern;

4) $\hat{f}_{t+T}(z \mid X_t^k)$: estimate of $f_{t+T}(z \mid X_t^k)$ at time t.

Then, the conditional probability at time t can be estimated as follows

$$\text{Prob}\left[x_{t+T} \leq \alpha \Big| X_t^k\right] = \int_{-\infty}^{\alpha} f_{t+T}(z \mid X_t^k) dz \tag{2.1}$$

Given a *similarity measure* $\varphi(X_1, X_2)$ between the two vectors $X_1, X_2 \in R^k$, see [4], a consistent and robust estimation of $f_{t+T}(z \mid X_t^k)$ is given by

$$\hat{f}_{t+1}(z \mid X_t^k) = \frac{1}{c} \frac{\displaystyle\sum_{i=k}^{t-1} \varphi(X_t^k, X_i^k) \varphi(z, x_{i+1})}{\displaystyle\sum_{i=k}^{t-1} \varphi(z, x_{i+1})} \tag{2.2}$$

where $c = \int \varphi dz$, and the *kernel* function φ satisfies the following properties:

i) φ is an *exponentially decaying* function;

ii) $\varphi(Y) = \varphi(y_1)\varphi(y_2)...\varphi(y_k)$, $X = [x_1, x_2,..., x_n]$;

iii) φ depends on a positive parameter h called the *bandwidth*.

For T steps ahead, $T > 1$, extending (2.2), we have

$$\hat{f}_{t+T}(z \mid X_t^k) = \frac{1}{c} \frac{\displaystyle\sum_{i=k}^{t-1} \varphi(X_t^k, X_i^k) \varphi(z, x_{i+T})}{\displaystyle\sum_{i=k}^{t-1} \varphi(z, x_{i+T})}, \tag{2.3}$$

with obvious meaning of the symbols introduced. Depending $f_+ (z \mid X^k)$ both on k and h, we write $\varphi_h(X_1, X_2)$ to remark such dependency. The values of h, k, are optimised using a *cross-validation* approach. With this aim, for a desired holding period T, if L the length of the *learning* set (the part of the samples used for the parameter optimisation), the optimal values h, k are determined minimising the average square error

$$\hat{h}, \hat{k} : \arg\min_{h,k} \frac{1}{2} \sum_{i=1}^{M} \{x_{i+T} - \hat{x}_{i+T}\}^2 \tag{2.4}$$

between the samples and the T − steps ahead *predictor* $\hat{x}_{t+T}$, the conditional mean of the density (1.3)

$$\hat{x}_{t+T} = \frac{1}{c} \frac{\displaystyle\sum_{\substack{i \in I_L^* \\ i \neq t}} \varphi (X_t, X_i) x_{i+T}}{\displaystyle\sum_{\substack{i \in I_L^* \\ i \neq t}} \varphi (X_t, X_i)}, \quad t \in I_L^* \tag{2.5}$$

Note that to avoid distorted estimation [1], in the (2.5) the current value is excluded in the summation. The algorithm can be improved, for instance, using *pruning* techniques to determine the optimal set of regressors.

3   The non parametric V.a.R. estimate

The application of the fuzzy approach to the V.a.R. estimation requires the following parameters to be defined
a)   the *holding* period T ;
b)   the *confidence interval* ε (usually from 95% to 99%).
   We compute the following series:

$$\{\Delta x_t\}_{t=1,..,N-T} = \{x_{t+T} - x_t\}_{t=1,..,N-T} \tag{3.1}$$

and then we obtain, using the optimised $\hat{k}, \hat{h}$ values;

i) $Prob\left[x_{t+T} \le \alpha \,\middle|\, X_t^k\right] = \int\limits_{-\infty}^{\alpha} f_{t+T}(z \mid X_t^k) dz$;

ii) $VaR_{t+1}(\Delta \underline{X}_t \mid \underline{X}_t) = \hat{F}_t^{-1}(1-\varepsilon)$, the conditional V.a.R at level ε and holding period T .
   We have tested the algorithm on the Italian *Comit* index time series. The optimised values were $\hat{h} = 8000, \hat{k} = 5$. Figure 1 reports both the conditional probability distribution (tiny line), and the unconditional probability distribution (bold line), at $t = 200$, with $T = 5$. The two graphs in Figure 2 are the two time series of conditional (upper bold line), and unconditional (lower tiny line) V.a.R. estimates for the first 100 data of the test set. The upper bold line is the time series of the conditional V.a.R., while the lowest tiny line is the unconditional V.a.R.. The conditional V.a.R. estimate shows higher values and more irregular dynamic behaviour.

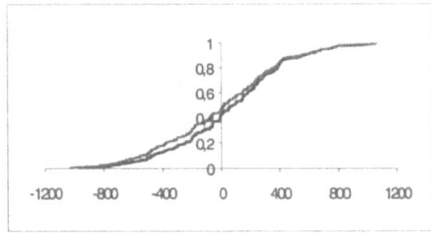
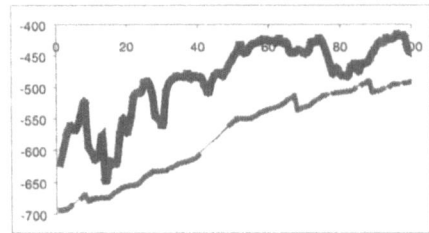

Figure 1   Figure 2

4   The Group Method of Data Handling technique

The basic G.M.D.H. soft-computing technique was created in the sixties by the Ukrainian cybernetist Alexey Grigoryevich Ivakhnenko (see, for more details, [3]). The main target of this scholar in developing such a technique was to realize a non parametric quantitative tool capable of modelling real phenomena when the researcher has not *a priori* either qualitative knowledge or a strong analytical one about them, when the available data sets concerning these phenomena have a small size, and when the same available data sets are highly noise.

All these listed peculiarities are quite close to the ones characterizing the analyses of the economic phenomena; also because of that G.M.D.H.-like techniques seem to be particularly promising tools for investigation in the quantitative finance area (see, for example, [8] and [6]).

In the following of this section we give an outline of the basic G.M.D.H. technique.

Generally, given a variable y representing a phenomenon to be explicated, and given $M \geq 2$ other variables $x_1, x_2, \ldots, x_M$ representing eventually *explicators* for y, the G.M.D.H. technique searches for a "good" *polynomial approximation* of the unknown relationship between y and $x_1, x_2, \ldots, x_M$. Like several other soft-computing techniques, also the basic G.M.D.H. one determines both its "optimal" polynomial structure form and the "optimal" value of the parameters specifying this polynomial form by means of an iterative procedure whose target consists in minimising a predefined cost function.

In particular, this iterative procedure can be synthetically described as follows:

<u>step 1</u>: initialize the iteration counter t to ε, and consider the starting input-output

data set $D(t) = \left\{ \left(x_{1,l}(t), x_{2,l}(t), \ldots, x_{M,l}(t); y_l \right), l = 1, \ldots, L \right\}$, where $x_i(0) = x_i$,

$M(0) = M$, and L indicates the input-output pattern number;

<u>step 2</u>: randomly split $D(t)$ in two not-overlapping sub-sets: a *training* one,

$D_T(t) = \left\{ \left(x_{1,l}(t), x_{2,l}(t), \ldots, x_{M,l}(t); y_l \right), l = 1, \ldots, L_T \right\}$, and a *checking* one,

$D_C(t) = \left\{ \left(x_{1,l}(t), x_{2,l}(t), \ldots, x_{M,l}(t); y_l \right), l = 1, \ldots, L_C \right\}$, with $L_T + L_C = L$;

<u>step 3</u>: for each possible pair of different explicators $x_i(t)$ and $x_j(t)$, with (of course) $i \neq j$, consider the following approximate relationship $y \cong a_{i,j}(t) + b_{i,j}(t) \cdot x_i(t) + c_{i,j}(t) \cdot x_j(t) + d_{i,j}(t) \cdot x_i^2(t) + e_{i,j}(t) \cdot x_j^2(t) + f_{i,j}(t) \cdot x_i(t) \cdot x_j(t)$, in which $a_{i,j}(t), b_{i,j}(t), c_{i,j}(t), d_{i,j}(t), e_{i,j}(t)$, and $f_{i,j}(t)$ are real parameters;

<u>step 4</u>: for each of the previously put in $M(t) \cdot [M(t) - 1]/2$ approximate relationships fit an ordinary least square (on following: OLS) regression by using the sub-data set $D_T(t)$;

<u>step 5</u>: for each of the previously fitted OLS regressions, set an upper bound for the modelling error, $\overline{E}_{i,j}$, to a positive value, and determine the modelling error

$E_{i,j}(t) = \left\{ \sum_{l=1}^{L_T} \left[\hat{y}_{i,j,l}(t) \right]^2 \right\} / L_T$, where $y = \hat{a}_{i,j}(t) + \hat{b}_{i,j}(t) \cdot x_i(t) + \hat{c}_{i,j}(t) \cdot x_j(t) + \hat{d}_{i,j}(t) \cdot x_i^2(t) + \hat{e}_{i,j}(t) \cdot x_j^2(t) + \hat{f}_{i,j}(t) \cdot x_i(t) \cdot x_j(t)$, by using the sub-data set $D_C(t)$; if $E_{i,j}(t) \leq \overline{E}$ then initialize $\hat{x}_k(t+1) = \hat{y}_{i,j}(t)$, where k is a suitable non negative counter lower or equal to $M(t)\cdot[M(t)-1]/2$, and update $\overline{E}$ to $E_{i,j}(t)$;

step 6: if $\max\{k\}\geq 2$ then update t to $t+1$, update $M(t)$ to $\max\{k\}$, update $D_T(t)=\left\{\left(\hat{x}_{1,l}(t),\hat{x}_{2,l}(t),...,\hat{x}_{M(t),l}(t)\right),l=1,...,L_T\right\}$ and go to step 2; else if $\max\{k\}=1$ then $\hat{x}(t+1)$ is the best G.M.D.H. estimation for y; else if $\max\{k\}=0$ the best G.M.D.H. estimation for y is that $\hat{y}_{i,j}(t)$ to which is associated the lowest $E_{i,j}(t)$.

5 Our approach to V.a.R. forecasting

In this section we first sketch an outline of our modified version of the basic G.M.D.H. technique, and secondly we propose a possible application of this methodology to V.a.R. forecasting.

Sample Size	True Value	Estimated Mean value	Confidence Interval $[\mu-2\sigma,\mu+2\sigma]$
	-0.563460000	-0.43033391	[-0.56077956,-0.29988826]
	-0.432530900	-0.43202466	[-0.54065985, -0.32338946] *
15	-0.121972830	-0.40505011	[-0.57600337, -0.23409685]
	-0.028521951	-0.32980960	[-0.55461730, -0.10500190]
	-0.035145824	-0.22609233	[-0.66180748,0.20962282] *
	-0.563460000	-0.45881673	[-0.54572537, -0.37190809]
	-0.432530900	-0.44312850	[-.559470020, -0.32678698] *
25	-0.121972830	-0.28145580	[-0.53854723, -0.32646177]
	-0.028521951	-0.17660178	[-0.58871858, 0.02580670] *
	-0.035145824	-0.24049024	[-0.730984456, 0.3777810] *
	-0.563460000	-0.42549282	[-0.50972179, -0.34126384]
	-0.432530900	-0.41955516	[-0.53335539, -0.30575492] *
35	-0.121972830	-0.40124483	[-0.53843778, -0.26405189]
	-0.028521951	-0.34027446	[-0.53666199, -0.14388694] *
	-0.035145824	-0.29488070	[-0.72754992, 0.13778853] *

Table 1 - The symbol "*" means that the true value belongs to
the corresponding confidence interval.

As for other soft-computing techniques, also for the G.M.D.H. one a well known drawback consists in the fact that such a methodology provides "only" a point estimation of the investigated phenomenon. In order to fill this deficiency, we improve the basic G.M.D.H. technique by implementing a simple *bootstrap-based approach*. In fact, at each utilization of the presented procedure, instead of splitting $D(t)$ only once into a training subset and in a checking one, we split it several times for the purpose of obtaining a population of such not-overlapping sub-sets, respectively $D_{T,n}(t)$ and $D_{C,n}(t)$, with $n = 1, \ldots, N$. So, starting from this population of training and checking sub-sets, we can get a population of "optimal" G.M.D.H. estimations of y by which to determine its confidence interval (see, for more details, [1]).

With regard to the application of the previously sketched modified G.M.D.H. technique, we specify the data set $D(0)$ starting from the output obtained in the first part of this work, that is the V.a.R. time series. In particular, in the previous Table 1 we propose the G.M.D.H. univariate one-step ahead forecasts of the appropriately standardized last five terms of the considered time series, obtained by using five lagged variables, as the sample size of the bootstrap-based population varies.

6 Concluding remarks

In this paper we have presented a two-stage soft-computing approach to V.a.R. calculation and forecasting. As such an approach is only a starting proposal, it offers evidence for possible developments, mainly

- by properly extending this methodology in order to take into account portfolio with nonlinear pay-off;
- and by improving the bootstrap-based technique in order to get "good" confidence intervals for the forecasted values.

References

[1] Efron B. and Tibshirani R.J., *An Introduction to the Bootstrap*, Chapman & Hall, 1993.

[2] Fan J. and Gijbels I., *Local Polynomial Modelling and its Applications*, Chapman and Hall, 1996.

[3] Farlow S.J., The GMDH Algorithm, in Farlow, S.J. (ed.), *Self-Organizing Methods in Modeling*, Marcel Dekker, 1984, 1-24.

[4] Giove S. and Pellizzari P., Time Series filtering and Reconstruction using Fuzzy Weighted Local Regression, in Ribeiro R., Yager R., Zimmermann H.J. and Kacprzyk J. (eds.), *Soft Computing and Financial Engineering*, Physica-Verlag, 1999, 73-92.

[5] Hecht-Nielsen R., *Neurocomputing*, Addison-Wesley Publishing Company, 1990.

[6] Lemke F. and Mueller J.-A., Self-Organizing Data Mining for a Portfolio Trading System, *Journal of Computational Intelligence in Finance*, May/June 1997, 12-26.

[7] Nadaraya E., On Estimating Regression, *Th. Prob. Appl.*, 9, 1964, 141-142.

[8] Ohashi K., GMDH Forecasting of U.S. Interest Rates, in Farlow, S.J. (ed.), *Self-Organizing Methods in Modeling*, Marcel Dekker, 1984, 199-214.

[9] Parzen E., On Estimation of a Probability Density Function and Mode, *Ann. Math. Statist.*, 33, 1962, 196-208.

[10] Scheinkman W. and LeBaron B., Nonlinear Dynamics and Stock Returns, *J. of Business*, 62, 1989, 311-337.

[11] Specht D.F., A General Regression Neural Network, *IEEE Trans. On Neural Networks*, 2 (6), 1991, 299-321.

Self-Organizing Maps for Content-Based Music Clustering

Markus Frühwirth, Andreas Rauber

Department of Software Technology, Vienna University of Technology

Favoritenstr. 9 - 11 / 188, A–1040 Wien, Austria

Abstract

With the increasing amount of music available electronically, methods for organizing these collections to allow intuitive browsing and orientation gain importance. Due to the large amounts of data involved, conventional approaches to organize music by genre or musical style are only of limited applicability, commonly relying on textual descriptions and manual classification. This makes it a particularly challenging application arena for neural networks capable of handling very high-dimensional input spaces and the noisy patterns associated with musical data.

In this paper we present a system based on the *Self-Organizing Map* which automatically organizes a collection of music files according to their musical genre and sound characteristics. Frequency spectra are used to extract feature vectors describing sound and melody characteristics. A two-stage clustering procedure first groups music segments according to their similarity, followed by a clustering of compositions according to the segment similarities. As a result, pieces of music with similar sound characteristics are found in neighboring regions of the resulting map, thus offering a very intuitive interface to unknown music collections.

1 Introduction

The wider availability of cheaper high-tech music recording equipment resulted in a tremendous rise of music data available electronically. Apart from the much-criticized pirated copies of copyrighted labels, many independent composers and smaller bands make their recordings publicly available for little or no fees at all via public domain music libraries such as AudioGalaxy.com. Contrary to well-known composers and bands, where users commonly know the style and characteristics of their favorite stars, finding pieces of music to suit ones taste is rather difficult in this public domain setting. In order to help users in finding their way through the piles of publicly available pieces of music from lesser-known groups, music portals try to provide a manual classification of the titles they offer. This way of organizing and presenting music closely mirrors the way music is presented in conventional stores, where we also frequently find CDs to be organized first by musical genres, within which an alphabetical organization is followed. Yet, providing such a manual classification becomes increasingly difficult with the amount of music submitted every day increasing. Furthermore, the resulting classification into any musical genre hierarchy is highly subjective.

In order to cope with this challenge, methods for automatically organizing music by genre gain importance. Due to the difficulties of analyzing the content of music itself, most approaches reverted to text-based analysis of pieces of music, relying on title and author information, or the lyrics of songs for automatic classification. These features form the core of the search facilities of the MPEG7 standard currently under development [7]. Similar to manual classification, these approaches to finding and organizing music rely heavily on manually created descriptions. A different line of research is constituted by content-based music analysis, trying to organize and locate pieces of music based on the similarity of melodies. The digital music library [4, 1] extracts melody-information from a hummed query and matches it against a database of musical tunes for which the actual scores are available. Similar approaches are reported in [6], using the scores provided by MIDI-files to index and retrieve musical documents, and in [3], focusing on beat detection.

Yet, for the majority of music documents available today, such as the prominent MP3 files, no musical scores are provided. What we would thus like to have is a way to provide content-based organization and retrieval of musical documents based on the actual sound rather than on score transcripts. However, with the huge amounts of data used for describing sound information as well as the inherent noise in musical sound representation, conventional retrieval techniques are of only limited use. This makes it a challenging arena for neural networks, which are particularly suited for generalizing from noisy data and for extracting key features from large datasets.

In this paper we propose a content-based clustering of musical documents based on the actual sound. Rather than trying to extract precise scores, frequency spectra are used to describe the characteristics of a specific piece of music. We then use the *Self-Organizing Map (SOM)* [5], a popular unsupervised neural network, to automatically cluster pieces of music according to their similarity. After the unsupervised training process, similar pieces of music are found in neighboring areas on the two-dimensional map display. This allows a user to easily orient herself within an unknown music collection, by finding, say, classical music in the upper left corner of the map, whereas disco-style music may be found in a different region. Selecting a cluster of music according to ones current preferences, rather than having to specify a list of songs based on textual descriptions provides a more intuitive and direct access to music libraries. These concepts have successfully been applied to text clustering [2, 8].

The remainder of this paper is structured as follows: Section 2 presents the architecture of our system, detailing feature extraction, vector creation and music clustering using the *Self-Organizing Map*. We then provide experimental results using a collection of MP3 files in Section 3 and finally some conclusions as well as an outlook on future work in Section 4.

2 Clustering of Music

Music comes in a variety of file formats such as MP3, WAV, AU, etc., all of which basically store the sound information in the form of pulse code modulation (PCM) using a very high sampling rate of 44.1 KHz. The analog sound signal is thus represented by 44.100 16 bit integer numbers per second, which are interpreted by media players to reproduce the sound signal. To be able to

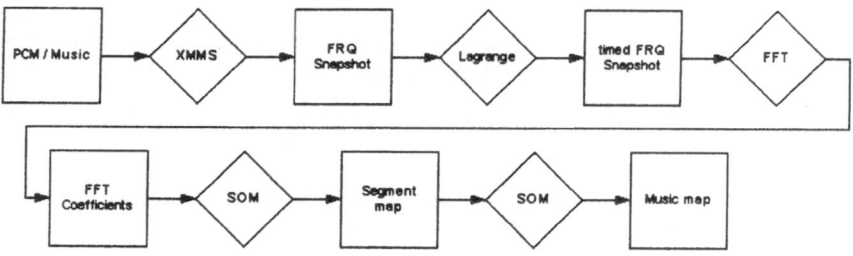

Figure 1: System Architecture: feature extraction, conversion, SOM training

compute similarity scores between musical tunes, a feature vector representation of the various pieces of music needs to be created, which can further be analyzed by the *SOM*. Figure 1 provides an overview of the system architecture.

Starting with any popular music file format, most media players, such as the public domain X Multimedia System (XMMS) are capable of splitting this data stream into several frequency bands. Using the XMMS the signal is split into 256 frequency bands, with approximately one sample value every 20 to 25 ms each. Since not all frequency bands are necessary for evaluating sound similarity and in order to reduce the amount of data to be processed, a subset of 17 frequency bands (i.e. every 15th frequency band) is selected for further analysis, covering the whole spectrum available. In order to capture musical variations of a tune, the music stream is split into sections of 5 seconds length, which are further treated as the single musical entities to be analyzed. While basically all 5-second sequences could be used for further analysis, or even overlapping segments might be chosen, experimental results have shown that appropriate clustering results can be obtained by the *SOM* using only a subset of all available segments. Especially segments at the beginning as well as at the end of a specific piece of music can be eliminated to ignore fade-in and fade-out effects. Specifically, our results show that choosing every second to third segment, i.e. a 5-second interval every 10 to 15 seconds, provides sufficient quality of data analysis.

The intervals between the frequency snapshots provided by the player varies with the system load and can thus not be guaranteed to occur at specified time intervals. We thus have a set of amplitude / timestamp values about every 20 to 25 ms in each of the 17 selected frequency bands. In order to obtain equidistant data points, a Lagrange interpolation is performed on these values as provided in Expression 1, where $f(x_i)$ represents the amplitude of the sample point at time stamp x_i the data points for up to $n + 1$ sample points.

As a result of this transformation we now have equi-distant data samples in each frequency band. The resulting function can be approximated by a linear combination of sinus and cosines waves with different frequencies. We can thus obtain a closed representation for each frequency band by performing a Fast Fourier Transformation (FFT), resulting in a set of 256 coefficients for the respective sinus and cosines parts. Combining the 256 coefficients for the 17 frequency bands results in a 4352-dimensional vector representing a 5-seconds segment of music. These feature vectors are further used for training a SOM.

$$P_n(x) = \sum_{i=0}^{n} \left(\prod_{j=0, j \neq i}^{n} \frac{x - x_j}{x_i - x_j} \right) f(x_i) \tag{1}$$

The *Self-Organizing Map* [5] is one of the most prominent artificial neural network models adhering to the unsupervised learning paradigm. It provides a mapping from a high-dimensional input space to a usually two-dimensional output space while preserving topological relations as faithfully as possible. Input signals $x \in \Re^n$ are presented to the map, consisting of a grid of units with n-dimensional weight vectors, in random order. An activation function based on some metric (e.g. the Euclidean Distance) is used to determine the winning unit (the 'winner'). In the next step the weight vector of the winner as well as the weight vectors of the neighboring units are modified following some learning rate in order to represent the presented input signal more closely. As a results, after the training process, similar input patterns are mapped onto neighboring units of the *Self-Organizing Map*. The feature vectors representing music segments can be thought of data points in a 4352-dimensional space, with similar pieces of music, i.e. segments exhibiting similar frequency spectra and thus similar FFT coefficients, being located close to each other. Using the SOM to cluster these feature vectors, we may expect similar music segments to be located close to each other in the resulting map display.

Using the resulting segment SOM, the various segments are scattered across the map according to their mutual similarity. This allows, for example, pieces of music touching on different musical genres, to be located in two or more different clusters, whereas rather homogeneous pieces of music are usually located within one rather confined cluster on the map. While this already provides a very intuitive interface to a musical collection, a second clustering may be built on top of the segment clustering to obtain a grouping of pieces of music according to their overall characteristics. To obtain such a clustering, we use the mapping of the segments representing a single piece of music to obtain an overall clustering. We thus create a feature vector representation for each piece of music using the location of its segments as descriptive attributes. Given an $x \times y$ SOM we create an $x \cdot y$ dimensional weight vector, where the attributes are the (coordinates of) the units of the segment SOM. Each vector attribute represents the number of segments of a particular piece of music mapped onto the respective unit in the SOM. For example, given a piece of music that has 3 segments mapped onto unit (0/0) in the upper right corner of the map, and 2 segments on the neighboring unit (1/0), the first two attributes of the song's feature vector are basically set to the according values $(3/2/\ldots)^T$, with subsequent norming to unit length to make up for length differences of songs. Training a second SOM using these feature vectors we obtain a clustering where each piece of music is mapped onto one single location on the resulting map, with similar pieces of music being mapped close to each other.

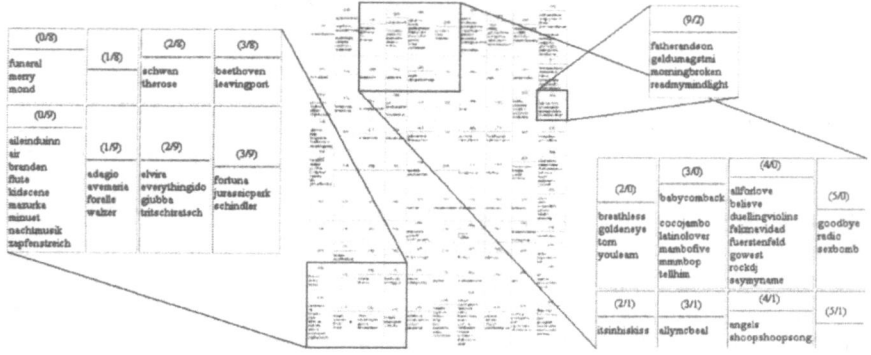

Figure 2: SOM representing 230 pieces of music

3   Experiments

For the following experiments we use a collection of 230 pieces of music, ranging from classical music, such as *Mozart's "Kleine Nachtmusik"*, via some hits from the 1960's such as *Cat Steven's "Father and Son"* or *Queen's "I want to break free"*, to modern titles, e.g. *Tom Jones' "Sexbomb"*.

These songs were segmented into 5-second-intervals, of which every second segment was used for further processing with a total of 17 frequency bands being selected. Following the Lagrange interpolations and FFT we thus end up with 5022 feature vectors representing the 5022 5-second segments of the 230 songs in a 4352-dimensional feature space. These feature vectors were further used to train a 22×22 dimensional *SOM*. Due to space restrictions we cannot provide a representation of the resulting map, yet we will use some examples for more detailed discussion.

For most songs the individual segments are mapped onto a rather small number of neighboring units. For example, we find most segments from classical titles mapped onto the lower right corner of the segment *SOM*. Some titles, such as *"Ironic"* by *Alanis Morissette* contain both rather soft and very dynamic passages and thus have their segments spread across several clusters co-located with segments from other songs of similar characteristics. However, the characteristics of some songs are too fuzzy to allow precise mapping of their segments and are thus spread across larger areas on the map.

In order to obtain a more compact representation of the musical archive, we create new feature vectors for each song based on the location of its segments. This results in a 22×22, i.e. 484-dimensional feature vector for each of the 230 songs. These vectors were used to train the 10×10 *SOM* presented in Figure 2.

Each song is now mapped onto one single position according to its musical characteristics. For example, we find a rather large cluster of classical music in the lower left corner of this map, including, amongst others, *Mozart's "Kleine Nachtmusik"*, *Bach's "Air"* as well as the Andante of his *"Brandenburg Concerto No. 2"* on unit (0/8), next to the *"Moonlight Sonata"* by *Beethoven*. It is important to note, that the *SOM* does not organize the songs according to their melody, but rather according to their musical genre, i.e. their sound characteristics. We thus find mapped onto the same unit both *Tchaikovsky's "Schwanensee"* as well as *Bette Midler's "The Rose"*, a very soft love song with mostly Piano and Violin passages. Another example for this co-location of Pop and classic titles is *Madonna's "Frozen"*, located on the same unit as *Bach's "Fuge in D-Moll"* and the Overture of *Rossini's "Willhelm Tell"*.

To pick just one further example, we find *Cher's "Believe", Robbie Williams' "Rock DJ", The Pet Shop Boys' "Go West"* mapped together on unit (4/0) next to *Lou Bega's "Mambo No. 5"* on unit (3/0) and *Tom Jones' "Sexbomb"* on (5/0).

4 Conclusions

We presented an approach to automatically organize music by content, i.e. based on its genre and sound characteristics. The *Self-Organizing Map*, a prominent unsupervised neural network, is used to cluster feature vectors representing the musical sound based on frequency spectra. In a first step, music segments are organized to obtain a fine-grained representation of segment-wise similarities, based upon which a clustering of the complete songs can be obtained. With this approach similar pieces of music are found in neighboring regions of the map. While the presented approach provides a good organization of music on the two-dimensional map, further improvements may be gained by capturing additional features during the vector creation process. These features may include beat information as well as representations capturing the dynamics of the various frequency bands. Furthermore, weighting functions may be used to assign higher importance to specific frequency bands.

References

[1] D. Bainbridge, C. Nevill-Manning, H. Witten, and R. McNab. Towards a digital library of popular music. In *Proc of the ACMDL'99*, Berkeley, CA, 1999. ACM.

[2] M. Dittenbach, D. Merkl, and A. Rauber. The growing hierarchical self-organizing map. In *Intl Joint Conf on Neural Networks (IJCNN00)*, Como, Italy, 2000. IEEE.

[3] S. Dixon and E. Cambouropoulos. Beat tracking with musical knowledge. In *Proc of the Europ Conf on Artificial Intelligence*, Amsterdam, Netherlands, 2000.

[4] A. Ghias, J. Logan, D. Chamberlin, and S. B.C. Query by humming: Musical information retrieval in an audio database. In *Proc of 3rd ACM Conf on Multimedia*, San Francisco, CA, 1995. ACM.

[5] T. Kohonen. *Self-organizing maps*. Springer-Verlag, Berlin, 1995.

[6] M. Melucci and N. Orio. Musical information retrieval using melodic surface. In *Proc of the ACM Conf on Digital Libraries (DL99)*, Berkeley, CA, 1999. ACM.

[7] F. Nack and A. Lindsay. Everything you wanted to know about MPEG7 – part 1. *IEEE MultiMedia*, pp 65–77, July – September 1999.

[8] A. Rauber. SOMLib: A distributed digital library system based on self-organizing maps. In *Proc 10. Italian Workshop on Neural Nets (WIRN98)*, Vietri, Italy, 1998.

Development of a fuzzy logic control for dialysis application

Silvio Giove[1], Stefano Silvoni
Dept. of Applied Mathematics, University of Venice
Dorsoduro, 3825/E, Venice (ITALY)
E-mail: sgiove@unive.it

Maurizio Nordio
Dept. of Nephrology, Venice Central Hospital
Venice (ITALY)

1 Introduction

Thanks to the high progress in hardware evolution and the consequent economic cost fall-down, in the recent past some automatic systems have been developed to help the clinician during his activity. In this field, fuzzy logic was intensively applied [1], [4], [8], [9], [10], [11], [14]. In this paper, a fuzzy logic hierarchical controller for hemodialysis patients is proposed, with the aim to compute automatically the values of the therapeutic variables used during a dialysis session. The system, now in use in the Venice Central Hospital, showed good performances in the first experimental phase.

2 Automatic control of a dialysis session

Roughly speaking, a dialysis procedure consists in an extra-corporeal filtering of the blood flow. This activity usually requires a strict medical supervision, since it very often produces severe undesired side effects, such as sudden hypotensive collapse. Such episodes are caused by the unbalanced liquid flow between the water flow extraction rate (*Ultrafiltration*, UFR) and the internal liquid flow (plasma *refilling*, PRR) between extra-cellular and cardio-vascular compartments. An excessive sodium extraction or excessive UFR cannot be compensated by an analogous PRR, thus the *volemia* (volume of water in the blood) is reduced, determining hypotension. Conversely, a too high sodium load or a too low UFR can originate a fluid overload followed by heart failure.

---

[1] Corresponding author

Then, it is necessary to obtain the best compromise. Usually, a doctor adjusts the two control variables, the *Ultrafiltration rate* (UFR) and the *sodium concentration* (Na) in the *dialysate*[2], with the aim to satisfy some therapy targets, the most important of which are

a) the decrease of body weight to a pre-defined value
b) the desired sodium balance during and at the end of the session

and also to avoid at the same time collapses and other undesired effects, while guaranteeing the removal of some toxic substances. To avoid the liquid unbalance, the doctor tries to achieve a sufficient PRR [2]. In so doing, medical experience is quite important to obtain the fulfilment of the objectives, on the other side, the manual control is resource consuming, and subject to personal consideration brought to human errors, due for instance to inattention or tiredness. To this aim, some model-based tools were developed to control the process, but the results are not completely satisfactory, because the models are not completely affordable [3]. Conversely our approach based on a fuzzy rule based control system is different and more suitable for real clinical applications [7], [12], [13]. The most important characteristics of this method are

i) even the trend can be taken into account, because a frequent sampling is possible, thus predictive action can be implemented to avoid sudden changes
ii) instead of using a model-based approach our method captures, implements, and replays the medical experience, instead than using a model-based approach
iii) it is almost completely model free, because only a predetermined weight reduction and sodium removal are fixed
iv) the clinical knowledge is implemented using a MIMO fuzzy rule data base
v) it is based on a hierarchical strategy.

3 Data acquisition and pre-elaboration

A dialysis PFD[3] machine has been used to collect the sampled data, namely blood pressure, volemia, sodium conducibility, body weight, recorded in a PC every minute (except for blood pressure, acquired every 10 minutes), and processed every 10 min. The on-line sodium balance is computed by the measurements of plasma conducibility and dialysate conducibility, using a well known mathematical model [5]. A pre-elaboration procedure computes the trend using different methods (least squares, or the average on the last observed values, and other ones), and fuzzify the variables. The trend measures the tendency to increasing or decreasing. For instance, Fig. 1 reports the interpolating line of the sampled volemia values; the trend is nothing else but the linear coefficient of the interpolating line. The variables and the relative trends are fuzzyfied (using *trapezoidal* fuzzy sets). Fig. 2 reports the fuzzy sets for the variables PAS (systolic

---

[2] a solution directly connected with the blood flow.
[3] PFD means *pair filtration dialysis* [13].

blood pressure) and PASt, its trend; the labels "VL, L, G, H, VH", and "N, Z, P", stand for "Very Low", "Low", "Good", "High", "Very High" and "Negative", "Zero", "Positive" respectively. The input variables are (with the number of corresponding fuzzy sets within parenthesis)

1) systolic blood pressure PAS (5) and its trend PASt (3)
2) blood volume changes VVE (3) and its trend VVEt (3)
3) sodium balance error ErNa (3) and weight error ErBW (3)

The output variables are the change of UFR, ΔUFR, and the change of dialysate conducibility, ΔDC, computed by the fuzzy engine, in order to achieve the desired performances.

4 The fuzzy logic control

The fuzzy rule system is a Sugeno-type inference MIMO controller, because it acts on the error and the error trend of several state variables to determine the optimal strategy[4]. It uses a *hierarchical* approach, defined by a fuzzy *meta*-rule data base. To this purpose, 4 sub-systems are defined, one for each controlled variable, and then the supervisory control determines the optimal mix of each sub-module proposed control values, taking the most important control objective into account. The control action is applied every 10 min., when all the state variables are collected, and the control values remains constant within each sampling interval $[T_i, T_{i+1}]$. The output of each rule are crisp singletons, like the ones in Fig. 3 for the variable ΔUFR. All the rules, in the form of an inference "if.. then.." rule are collected in a tabular form, and can be modified by the user (he can also select all other optional parameters and items, like the T-norm). Table 1 reports the rules for pressure control. For instance, the four column-third row rule means "IF PAS is High AND PASt is Positive THEN ΔUFR is Positive Low AND ΔCD is Negative Low". The output of each subsystem are subsequently aggregated by a super-visor rule block, using a defined priority strategy.

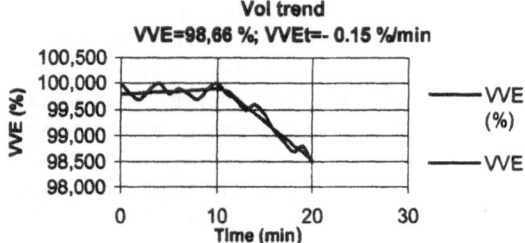

Fig. 1. Volemia trend.

---

[4] In this sense, it is not properly a PID controller, but it is very similar in the conceptual philosophy.

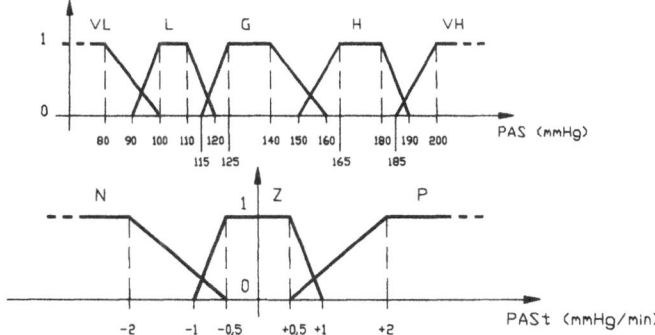

Fig. 2.a-2.b. Fuzzy sets for PAS and PASt.

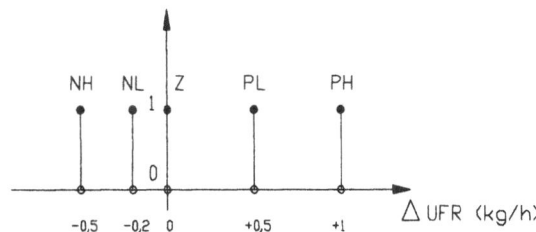

Fig. 3. ΔUFR crisp consequents.

PAS→ PASt↓	Very Low	Low	Good	High	Very High
Negative	ΔUFR=NH ΔCD=PH	ΔUFR=NH ΔCD=PL	ΔUFR=NL ΔCD=Z	ΔUFR=PL ΔCD=Z	ΔUFR=PL ΔCD=NL
Zero	ΔUFR=NH ΔCD=PH	ΔUFR=NL ΔCD=PL	ΔUFR=Z ΔCD=Z	ΔUFR=PL ΔCD=Z	ΔUFR=PH ΔCD=NL
Positive	ΔUFR=NH ΔCD=PL	ΔUFR=NL ΔCD=Z	ΔUFR=PL ΔCD=Z	ΔUFR=PL ΔCD=NL	ΔUFR=PH ΔCD=NH

Tab. 1. PAS and PASt rule table.

5 The management of priorities and the integrated system

The priority of the actions to be performed was given by a set of weights computed using, again, a decision table of fuzzy rules. When both PAS and VVE were satisfactory, the tables for NaBe and We were used to gain the objectives of the correct Na balance (predetermined by the doctor) and the dry weight of the patient. If PAS or VVE were not good, their proper actions were preferred. Anywise SBP had the maximal priority, followed, in order, by, VVE, ErNa, and ErBW. For instance, referring to ErBw (characterised by the lowest priority), its weigh is negligible if at least one of the other variables (PAS, VVE, ErNa) has a high weight. The aggregation of the outputs was obtained using a weighted sum:

$$\Delta UFR = \sum_{i=1}^{4} w_i \Delta UFR(i), \quad \Delta DC = \sum_{i=1}^{4} w_i \Delta CD(i)$$

where $\Delta UFR(i)$ and $\Delta CD(i)$ are the output of each rule table and w_i are the weights calculated by the priority table Tab. 2. The values PAOB, PAOG, VVEB, VVEG, stand for "PAS is Bad", "PAS is Good", and so on, and are computed from the relative sub-module decision tables. For instance, the value PAOB is the maximum activation degree of the rules implemented in the Tab.1, except the element in second row and third column (corresponding to "PAS is Good, PASt is Zero"). The system was tested in 10 sessions, and all the patients gained the prescribed dry weight with a correct sodium balance. No hypotension episode was observed. In four cases the dry weight and a correct sodium balance were obtained reducing the dialysis time without significant changes in blood pressure.

Pressure	Volemia	Output weighs	Output
PAOB		$W_1=$ PAOB	TabP
PAOG	VVEB	$W_2=$ min{PAOG,VVEB}	TabV
PAOG	VVEG	$W_3=$ min{PAOG,VVEG}	TabNa
PAOG	VVEG	$W_4=$ min{PAOG,VVEG}	TabDBW

Tab. 2. Priority management table.

6 Conclusion

We have proposed a fuzzy experience-based control system for dialysis application, using a modular architecture and a hierarchical control strategy. The first tests have showed good performances, while the complete results will be presented in a next study, together with statistical indexes that will be used to improve the global performance of the controller. Moreover, we are developing an adaptive action to personalise the system and adapt it to different patient typology.

REFERENCES

[1] Bellazzi R., et al., Adaptive drug dosage in long term treatment by using fuzzy controllers and bayesian networks, *Proceedings of IFAC Symposium*, Galveston, 1994, 202-203.

[2] Churchill D.N., Sodium and water profiling in chronic uremia, *Nephrol. Dial. Transplant.*, 11, Suppl. 8, 38-41.

[3]   Daugirdas J.T., Dialysis hypotension: a hemodynamic analysis, *Kidney Int.*, 39, 1991, 233-246.

[4]   Degani R., Pacini G., Fuzzy classification of electrocardiograms, *Optimization of Computer ECG Processing*, North-Holland Publishing Company, 1980.

[5]   Di Filippo S., Corti M., Andrulli S. , Manzoni C., Locatelli F., Determining the adequacy of sodium balance in hemodialysis using a kinetic model, *Blood Purif.* vol. 14, pp. 431-436, 1996.

[6]   Giove S., Fuzzy control for medicine: state of the Art and New Perspectives, in *New Trends in Fuzzy Systems*, World Scientific, 1998 (invited paper), 235-252.

[7]   Giove S., Nordio M., Zorat A., An adaptive fuzzy control module for automatic dialysis, *Proceedings of F.L.A.I. 1993*, Linz, 1993, 146-156.

[8]   Kageyama S., et al., Blood glucose control by a fuzzy control system, *Proceedings of the Int. Conf. on Fuzzy logic & Neural Networks*, Iizuka, 1990, 557-560.

[9]   Linkens D.A., Shieh J.S., Peacock J.E:, Hierarchical fuzzy modelling for monitoring depth of anaesthesia, *Fuzzy Sets and Systems* 79, 1, 1996, 43-58.

[10] Mitra S., Fuzzy MLP based expert system for medical diagnosis, *Fuzzy Sets and Systems* 65, 2-3, 1994, 285-296.

[11] Moller D. P.F., Fuzzy logic and its impact for medical applications, *Proceedings of EUFIT '93*, Aachen, 1993.

[12] Nordio M., Giove S. et al., A new approach to blood pressure and blood volume modulation during hemodialysis: an adaptive fuzzy control module, *The International Journal of Artificial Organs*, 18, 1995, 513-517.

[13] Nordio M., Giove S., Silvoni S., A decision support system to prevent hypotensive episodes during dialysis, *Proceedings of EMBEC'99*, Graz, 1999.

[14] Roy M.K., Biswas R., I-v fuzzy relations and Sanchez's approach for medical diagnosis, *Fuzzy Sets and Systems*, 47, 1992, 35-38.

Evaluation of Teaching Activity through a Fuzzy System[1]

Michele Lalla
Gisella Facchinetti
Giovanni Mastroleo

University of Modena and Reggio Emilia

Modena - Italy

Abstract

Student evaluations of teaching staff are compulsory in Italian universities. The Ministry of University and Scientific and Technological Research proposed a questionnaire with items based on the four-point Likert scale and a traditional item-by-item analysis. A fuzzy inferential system is proposed to analyze the data collected through this questionnaire, for items with a four/five-point Likert scale. Fuzzy evaluation was set up with the support of "fuzzyTECH" by INFORM.

1 Introduction

The evaluation of university research and teaching activities was established by Law no. 370 (of 19/10/1999, Official Gazette, General Series, no. 252 of 26/10/1999) and administrations failing to comply will be excluded from some grants. The Ministry of University and Scientific and Technological Research (MURST) recently founded an Observatory (now, a Committee) for University System Evaluation,[2] which created several research groups on various topics. One of the latter [5] proposed a course-evaluation questionnaire with items using a four-point Likert scale: ①*Definitely no*, ②*No rather than yes*, ③*Yes rather than no*, ④*Definitely yes* (MURST scale). They also suggested using means and variances to analyze data, translating the categories (or labels) into a *ten-point scale* as follows: ①=2, ②=5, ③=7, ④=10. On the one hand, for this ordinal scale, the absence of a middle position could violate the linearity assumption. On the other hand, mean and variance cannot validly be used. Furthermore, the meaning of the labels is not

---

[1] This paper is a reduced version of a chapter in a report (in progress) prepared for the Local Research Project "Metodi e tecnologie per innovare e riorganizzare la didattica", approved and financed in 2000 through reserved quota intended for use in oriented research at the University of Modena and Reggio Emilia.

[2] It was established by a Ministerial Decree of 22.02.1996, but its tasks were established by article 5 of Law no. 537 of 24/12/1993 (S.O. no. 121, Official Gazette no. 303 of 28/12/1993) and subsequently by articles 9, 15, and 19 of the Decree of the President of the Republic (D.P.R.) of 30/12/1995 (Official Gazette no. 50 of 29/02/1996).

clear to all students and their intensities could be marked by a high level of uncertainty. A set of categorical alternatives could be: ①*Very insufficient*, ②*Insufficient*, ③*Sufficient*, ④*Good*, ⑤*Very good* (mark scale) because it seems more suited to the evaluation procedure as it is fairly similar to the score system used at previous school levels. Each item score could be translated into a ten-point scale by multiplying by two the numerical label of the category, making any evaluation more interpretable. The elimination of the middle position was based on the assumptions that: (1) it attracts people who are careless or lazy or have no opinion, (2) respondents tend toward one of the two nearest alternatives, (3) respondents really in the neutral position randomly choose a polar alternative [10]. The mark scale would avoid these issues, as there is no truly neutral category.

The local Committee for Technical Evaluation adopted the questionnaire proposed by MURST, with slight modifications and a mark scale. This paper presents a fuzzy system to evaluate teaching activity showing that it is more flexible to handle data and presents no problems as to measurement methodology, such as the four- or five-point Likert scale. In fact, both scales could be used without difficulty. Paragraph 2 illustrates the fuzzy model built up to generate the numerical evaluation on a ten-point scale for some conceptual domains of teaching activity. Paragraph 3 concludes with some comments and remarks.

2 The fuzzy system for teaching evaluation

The questionnaire provided by the local Committee for Technical Evaluation was based on the one proposed by Chiandotto and Gola (1999) and it had five sections for a total of twenty-four items. **Section I**, *lecture room and resource room*, contained three items: (1) Adequacy of the Lecture Room, ALR, (2) Adequacy of the Resource Room, ARR, (3) Adequacy of the Resource Equipment, ARE. **Section II**, *work load and teaching organization*, included four items: (4) Adequacy of the Work Load requested, AWL, (5) Adequacy of the Work Load requested by other Current Courses, AWLCC, (6) Adequacy of the Scheduling for other Current Courses, ASCC, (7) Adequacy of Exam Scheduling for other Current Courses, AESCC. **Section III**, *lectures*, included eight items: (8) Correspondence between Actual and Planned lectures, CAP, (9) Correspondence of the number and duration of the Lectures with respect to Official Schedule, CLOS, (10) Adequacy of the Teaching Materials —course books, handouts, *etc.*—, ATM, (11) Notification of the Form and rules of the Exams, NFE, (12) In-depth Study of the Lecture subjects, ISL, (13) Clarity of the Teacher's Presentations, CTP, (14) Motivation and Interests aroused by Teacher, MIT, (15) Teacher Availability during Office hours, TAO. Item (16) was discarded because it merely requested a global evaluation of the lecture domain and it was judged as redundant. **Section IV**, *teaching-support*, presented four items: (17) Usefulness of Teaching-Support Activities — seminars, workshops, *etc.*—, UTS, (18) Adequacy of the Teaching-Support Level of difficulty, ATS, (19) Completeness of the Answers given by Tutors, CAT, (20) Correspondence of the number and duration of the Tutors' Lectures with respect to the official Schedule, CTLS. **Section V**, *further information*, (21) Level of Background Knowledge of the subject, LBK, (22) Level of Interest in the Subject matter, LIS, (23) Level of Overall Satisfaction with the course, LOS, (24) Attendance and Study planned (by students) to pass the Exam the first time, ASE.

The evaluation of a single item or domain is conventionally made by an average of the numerical label or the values corresponding to a ten-point scale. The items included in a domain have the same importance, while it is easy to note that there are variables indicating the efficiency of the course better than others. The categories of the scales adopted were labeled by linguistic terms and their translation into the corresponding numeric values could be completely arbitrary. Furthermore, there was controversy concerning the middle position. An interesting solution is given by a fuzzy expert system to generate the evaluation of a single item or specific domain. In fact, the fuzzy set theory represents an ideal tool to handle this kind of data, as it was originally proposed as a means to represent the indeterminacy and to formalize qualitative concepts that generally have no precise boundaries. An expert system allows for the possibility to use the single inputs at different levels of importance through the decision tree and rule-blocks, where the place of entry and the combinations of the alternatives indicate the most important variables.

The fuzzy expert system had 23 inputs (or items) and it produces many different outputs: see Figure 1, where the final evaluation of the total decision tree is the most important, but many other partial outcomes are yielded as pieces of branches (intermediate outputs) up to the translation of a single fuzzy variable in a crisp value obtained in a new way. These partial outcomes permits teachers and the local Committee to have an evaluation not only of a course as a global entity, but also of a group of variables (such as lectures, logistics, teaching-support) and single items (such as ALR, AWL, CAP, CTP). The production of a crisp value for a single fuzzy variable represents a new procedure with the respect to the usual application of a fuzzy expert system, which needs at least two inputs to be able to function.

The essential steps in designing a fuzzy system ([1], [8], [11]) are: (*i*)identification of the problem and the selection of the type of fuzzy system that best suits the decision-tree, (*ii*)definition of the input and output variables, their fuzzy values, and their membership function —termed the *fuzzification* step (of input and output)—, (*iii*)construction of blocks of control rules and the translation of the latter into a fuzzy relation, (*iv*)treatment of any input information to select the fuzzy inference method, (*v*)translation of the fuzzy output into a crisp (numerical) value —termed the *defuzzification* step (of the output).The complete system is reported in Figure 1. Its structure consisted of several fuzzy modules linked together step by step and the input variables were introduced at different levels of importance, depending on the distance of the input node from the last output node (Evaluation in Figure 1) along the decision-tree: the weight increases as this distance decreases. Each single aggregation produced intermediate variables that had a particular meaning. The fuzzification, (*ii*), and the construction of blocks of control rules, (*iii*), are the main problem in building a fuzzy expert system. These two steps could be performed in several ways. In this study, a sample of students, constituting the target population, and a group of teachers were interviewed as experts on the problem because it was impossible to use methods like machine-learning, neural networks, and genetic algorithms, for two reasons: (a)the past data on the numerical values for the mark scale categories were not available; (b)the mathematical model underlying the procedures to yield the traditional scores was known and it was that alone that made it more in keeping with reality. The fuzzification of input variables, (*ii*), was carried out by using the answers collected by the corresponding questionnaire [9] using a mark scale. For example, LIS offered the alternatives: ①*Very insufficient*, ②*Insufficient*, ③*Sufficient*, ④*Good*, and ⑤*Very good*. The students numerically evaluated these labels on a ten-point scale. The scores collected for each term for each question were analyzed in order to identify the form, peak, and amplitude of the corresponding fuzzy number. The relative frequency distributions had been normalized at one to be comparable and to derive the membership function of the relative linguistic attributes. Almost all the terms were represented by piece-linear functions. Figure 2 illustrates the fuzzification for this variable, as an example.

Figure 1 – *Fuzzy inference system for teacher and course evaluation*

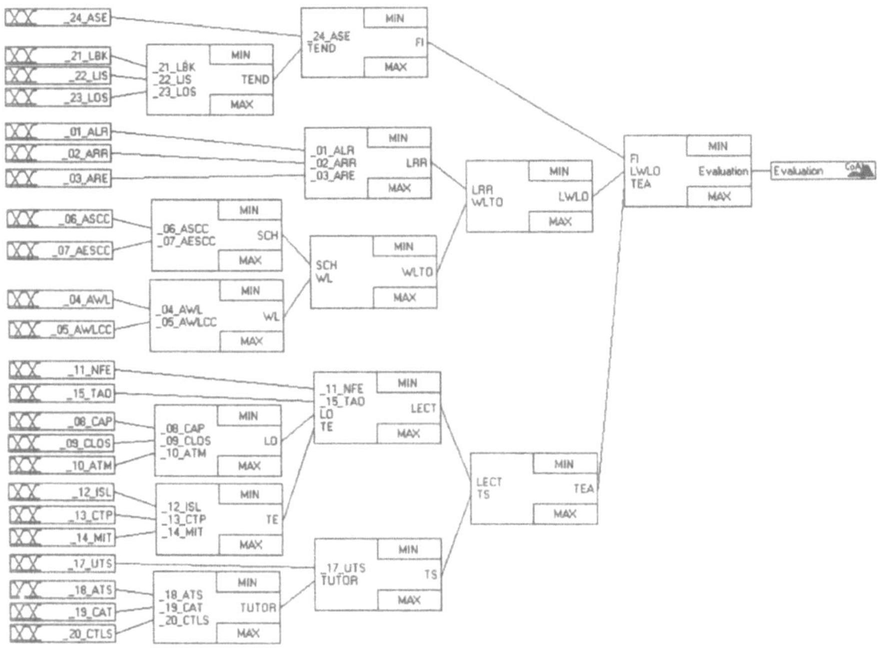

The rule-blocks, (*iii*), were set up through the experts' opinions, *i.e.*, the experiences of teachers and students. The MIN Operator was the aggregation operator, selected for the precondition (*iv*). The linguistic output resulting for each module (intermediate inputs) was also the (linguistic) input for the next module. Therefore, its function permitted the connection between the rule-blocks. Defuzzification, (*v*), was carried out for each respondent after having inserted the data in the system [12]. The crisp value, corresponding to the best representation of the fuzzy value of the linguistic output, was obtained by the "Center of Area"

(CoA) method.

Figure 2 – *Fuzzification of the LIS variable*

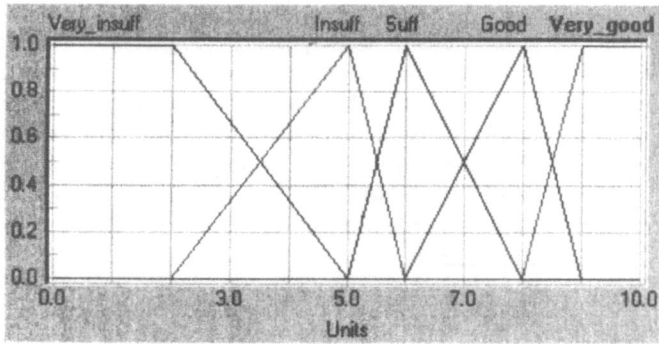

To obtain information about the domains, the partial outputs were produced with respect to single items and groups of variables. For example, the aggregation {21_LBK, 22_LIS, 23_LOS} generated a partial output (see Figure 1) which may be considered as a new variable, which was termed Tendency (TEND). Using this aggregating strategy, 7 new systems were built up to produce the first partial outputs, and so on until the end of the tree. However, the specificity of teaching evaluations requires the analysis of the single item, as the teachers should know the particular domain where it failed or judgment was not positive. Therefore, a new unprecedented procedure was implemented to yield the fuzzy output for a single input variable. For example, the input variable {22_LIS} contained the answers of students to this item referring to the Level of Interest in the Subject: each answer consisted in a selected label on the mark scale corresponding to an integer value of the set $A = \{2,4,6,8,10\}$ expressed on a ten-point scale. The fuzzy inference system for LIS is reported in Figure 3. The input is a value in the set A, while the output is the defuzzification of the single fuzzy set corresponding to $a \in A$.

Figure 3 – *Fuzzy inference system for LIS: input and output variable*

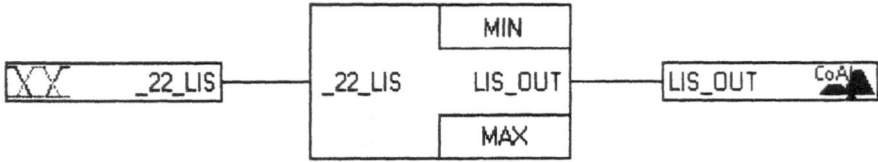

As all the linguistic terms are overlapped in some regions, the fuzzy representation of each crisp input value, a, attributable to a response given by a student, always produces a new figure built by the union of the two linguistic attributes that the crisp value fires, with cut-off at the level of activation of the single attributes. This fuzzy set is not normalized, but its center of gravity can be calculated. An example, if a student response is $a=4$, this value will activate two membership functions: one corresponding to "Very insufficient", up to about the level of 0.35, and another corresponding to "Insufficient", up to about the level of 0.65, as illustrated in Figure 4. The firing output is the polygon blackened in Figure 4 and the CoA method will be applied to it to determine the crisp value.

Figure 4 – *Block of the LIS output variable and firing output*

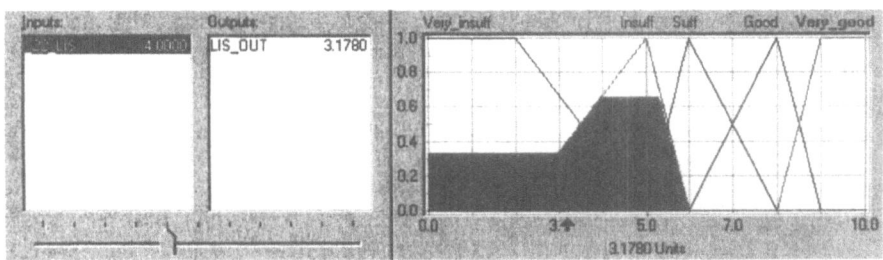

The crisp input $a=4$ involved a fuzzy translation with an attribution value equal to 3.178. The translations from the five possible LIS labels to their corresponding crisp values, determined through the defuzzification (v), are reported in Table 1.

Table 1 – *Translations from the LIS labels to fuzzy evaluations*

	LIS				
Input	2	4	6	8	10
Output	1.86	3.18	6.33	7.67	9.22

Set A will have a corresponding fuzzy set, $A_F = \{1.86, 3.18, 6.33, 7.67, 9.22\}$. Applying this procedure to the 22 remaining items, 22 transformation fuzzy sets, $A_{F;i}$ ($i=1,\ldots,22$) were obtained. Although some problems involving the measurement of concepts could be overridden, this result did not so differ much from that achieved through the mean of the evaluation carried out by a sample of students drawn from the target population, as the latter values correspond to an interval scale level. Therefore, the powerfulness of a fuzzy system is not exploited fully, as it is only from the aggregation of more than one input variable that a global score is obtained, as well as and an aid in making a decision, if this is the case. However, the evaluation of teaching activity through a fuzzy system is effective in obtaining scores on concepts determined by more than one item, as designed in Figure 1 and it is necessary in local and national scoring of teaching efficiency. Furthermore, the fuzzy score for each item was attained through an average of the crisp values, as reported in Table 2 ("Fuzzy") and compared with the averages of the label values of the ten-point scale ("T-P S"), but it could represent a sort of restriction. A possible extension is to use the fuzzy system through the individual respondents, which could lead to a model similar to a "fuzzy regression". This is beyond the scope of this paper, but it is an interesting field for our work in the future.

Some empirical results obtained by the two procedures are shown in Table 2, as an example of student evaluations at the end of the first semester in the Faculty of Economics of the University of Modena and Reggio Emilia. The means of fuzzy scores were generally lower than those of the ten-point scale, but the differences were limited to about half of a point. The ten-point scale values and fuzzy values showed correlation coefficients varying by teacher and subject, and ranged from 0.95 to 1. Therefore, these differences often proved to be statistically significant at the level of 0.05 in a t-paired test, which is sensitive to strong correlations.

Table 2 – *Means of the ten-point scale and of fuzzy evaluations by item and course*

	Mathematics		Mathematics for Financial Market		Political Economy		Public Economics	
	T-P S	Fuzzy	T-P S	Fuzzy	T-P S	Fuzzy	T-P S	Fuzzy
ALR	7.94	7.58	8.02	7.68	8.27	7.81	8.31	7.94
ARR	5.90	5.53	6.12	5.76	5.86	5.62	7.77	7.33
ARE	6.34	5.92	6.54	6.08	6.11	5.68	7.38	6.99
AWL	7.41	7.55	6.87	7.04	7.45	7.83	7.05	7.34
AWLCC	6.16	6.00	6.24	6.22	6.23	6.16	7.00	7.29
ASCC	6.22	5.80	6.07	5.66	5.86	5.49	7.09	6.83
AESCC	5.81	5.44	6.40	6.02	6.32	5.89	6.93	6.62
CAP	7.52	7.36	7.88	7.70	7.86	7.80	8.33	8.12
CLOS	8.11	8.00	8.02	7.85	7.50	7.52	7.73	7.66
ATM	7.16	6.95	6.27	6.03	7.64	7.51	8.00	7.74
NFE	7.09	6.94	6.77	6.68	6.64	6.51	7.07	6.99
ISL	6.62	6.45	6.42	6.25	6.59	6.43	7.09	6.87
CTP	7.52	7.21	7.92	7.52	6.59	6.40	7.85	7.52
MIT	6.99	6.76	6.87	6.65	6.91	6.71	7.77	7.43
TAO	7.33	6.92	6.75	6.34	8.27	7.74	7.93	7.43
UTS	5.13	5.03	5.35	5.22	5.89	5.67	7.15	6.86
ATS	5.20	5.13	5.21	5.09	6.45	6.23	7.44	7.12
CAT	5.16	5.07	5.54	5.43	7.22	6.93	7.99	7.64
CTLS	5.36	5.16	5.07	4.83	6.70	6.33	7.82	7.43
LBK	6.74	6.57	5.82	5.69	6.17	6.09	6.67	6.62
LIS	7.19	6.99	6.81	6.66	8.23	7.87	7.27	7.09
LOS	7.24	7.20	6.99	6.94	7.18	7.07	7.23	7.16
ASE	7.41	7.28	7.63	7.42	6.77	6.67	7.00	7.01
Total	6.68	6.47	6.59	6.38	6.90	6.69	7.47	7.26

3 Conclusions

A fuzzy inferential system easily overcomes the dispute over the four- or five-point Likert scale. However, the fuzzy approach offers the possibility to use values that are more flexible and proximate to those students really want to attribute to them. The rule-blocks set up accounted for links between the inputs and the importance that teachers and students attributed to the single input (item), although this is a critical step, as it is affected by an extremely subjective point of view. Moreover, a new target was examined: the transformation of a single label value, corresponding to the student responses, into a single crisp (fuzzy) value. The suggested procedure uses a fuzzy expert system with only one input to obtain a crisp translation of the single fuzzy number and the evaluation of a single concept was given by an average (mean) of these values, *i.e.*, a "fuzzy average of fuzzy numbers" which requires further in-depth study. There are a lot of definitions of the Fuzzy average value such as those introduced by Dubois and Prade [7], Campos and Gonzales ([3], [4]), and Detyniecki and Yager [6] for ranking fuzzy numbers [2], either dependent on additive measure or fuzzy measure using the Choquet integral. The use of these definitions will lead to interesting results in the future.

References

[1] Bandermer H., Gottwald S. (1996). *Fuzzy Sets, Fuzzy Logic, and Fuzzy Methods*, John Wiley & Sons, New York.
[2] Bortolan G, Degani R. (1985). A review of some methods for ranking fuzzy numbers, *Fuzzy Sets and Systems*, 15, 1-19.
[3] Campos L.M., Gonzales A. (1989). A subjective approach for ranking fuzzy numbers, *Fuzzy Sets and Systems*, 29, 145-153.
[4] Campos L.M., Gonzales A. (1994). Further contributions to the study of the Average Value for ranking Fuzzy Numbers, *International Journal of Approximate Reasoning*, 10, 135-153.
[5] Chiandotto B., Gola M..M. (1999). Questionario di base da utilizzare per l'attuazione di un programma per la valutazione della didattica da parte degli studenti, sito MURST (di allora): *http://www.murst.it/osservatorio/attivnuc.htm*
[6] Detyniecki M., Yager R.R. (2000). Ranking fuzzy numbers using α-Weighted Valuations. *International Journal of Uncertainty, fuzziness and Knowledge-based Systems*. Vol.8, n° 5, 573-592.
[7] Dubois D., Prade H. (1983). Ranking fuzzy numbers in the setting of possibility theory, *Information Sciences*, 30, 183-224.
[8] Kasabov N.K. (1996). *Foundations of Neural Networks, Fuzzy Systems, and Knowledge Engineering*, MIT Press.
[9] Lalla M., Facchinetti G., Mastroleo G. (2001). A Fuzzy Expert System for Evaluating University Teaching Efficiency, *IFAC Symposium on Modelling and Control of Economic Systems SME 2001*.
[10] Schuman H., Presser S. (1996). *Questions and Answers in Attitude Surveys: Experiments on Question Form, Wording, and Context*; Sage Publications, Thousand Oaks, CA.
[11] von Altrock C. (1997). *Fuzzy Logic and Neurofuzzy Applications in Business and Finance*, Prentice Hall.
[12] Yager R.R, Filev D.P. (1993). On the issue of defuzzification and selection based on a fuzzy set. *Fuzzy Sets and Systems*, 55, 255-272.

A NEURAL SOLUTION TO THE SYMBOL GROUNDING PROBLEM

Eliano Pessa   Graziano Terenzi

Dipartimento di Filosofia – Sezione Psicologia
Università degli Studi di Pavia
Piazza Botta, 6 (Palazzo S.Felice)
27100 Pavia, Italy
e-mail: eliano.pessa@unipv.it ; g.terenzi@inwind.it

Abstract

The Symbol Grounding Problem has been dealt with through a neural network architecture based on two interconnected modules: one deputed to symbol categorization, and another deputed to associate thematic roles to phrase components. The operation of the latter was implemented through the FGREP method (Forming Global Representations through Extended backPropagation), already introduced by Miikkulainen and Dyer [6]. Differently from what proposed by these authors, we used, as subvectors of vectors representing single phrase components, suitable codings of the categories to which the components themselves were associated by the categorization module. Such a modification let us obtain an improvement of performance of our architecture, with respect to the original Miikkulainen-Dyer model, in a task consisting of finding out the correct thematic roles of single components of phrases given as inputs.

1.Introduction

The *Symbol Grounding Problem* (SGP) [3] is one of the more pressing problems within the field of natural language processing. As generally acknowledged, it is tied to the lack of understanding of the relationship holding between symbols and environmental states. Whereas the search for a solution of SGP appears as unfeasible within the standard symbolic computational approach adopted by 'strong' Artificial Intelligence, a connectionist approach based on neural networks seems the best candidate for building a theory of the interconnection between symbols and external physical inputs. The main idea underlying the neural solution to SGP can be summarized as follows: the 'natural' association between symbols and physical inputs results from a suitable *adaptation* process in which a neural network architecture learns to perform a semantic task by progressively adjusting the form of the relationship between symbols and inputs as a function of the success obtained in performing the task itself. In this paper we will try to implement such an idea, and to solve SGP, within the particular context of a task of association between thematic roles (like *actor*, *patient*) and phrase components. To this regard, we will introduce a neural architecture which generalizes a proposal already made by Miikkulainen and Dyer [6]. The main novelty of our architecture consists in using vector representations of each phrase component, made by two different subvectors: one whose elements are initially randomly chosen (as happens in many connectionist codings of symbolic entities); another one whose elements code the semantic category in which the given phrase component was placed by a suitable categorizing module. Such extended representations are used to set the initial structure of a *Global Symbol Lexicon* (GSL), which undergoes successive modifications, through a supervised learning procedure, as a function of the output error made by a Multilayer Perceptron (MLP), deputed to associate representations of input phrase components to their thematic roles. Numerical experiments showed that our architecture, consisting of a MLP, a GSL, and a categorizing module, was effectively able to perform the aforementioned association task. Besides, its performance was mainly dependent on the particular form of the relationship holding between external inputs and their inner (symbolic) representations. Such a form was obtained as a consequence of a learning procedure, based on a suitable training set, so that we are authorized to assert that our architecture gave a neural solution to SGP. The most important result, obtained from computer simulations, has been that the highest performance in the association task was achieved when the semantic categories used to determine the subvector 2) of each representation were chosen from low-level categories, instead that from high-level categories. Such a circumstance could provide us with a general heuristic for designing neural architectures deputed to solve SGP, and whence to find the 'natural' associations between symbols and meanings.

2. Symbol categorization

A number of studies, belonging to a research tradition dating back to De Saussure [2], evidenced how the symbolic function, within the context of natural language, is based on a complex relationship between a class of auditory representations of linguistic stimuli, and a class of mental representations, relative to (or triggered by) suitable physical events. Such representations could be identified with the *meanings* of the corresponding linguistic stimuli. The situation, however, is complicated by two circumstances: (a) there are, at least, two different kinds of mental representations: the low-level *perceptual categories* to which physical events belong, and the *higher-order categories*, capturing correlations between different low-level categories; (b) the relationship between auditory representations of linguistic stimuli and mental representations isn't *topology-preserving*: this means that two linguistic stimuli very close one to another from the auditory point of view can be related to two mental representations very different one from another; this implies that the mapping from linguistic stimuli to mental representations cannot be identified with a *linear mapping*.

In order to take into account such circumstances, we introduced, within our neural architecture, a *categorizing module*, deputed to (1) associate to each physical stimulus (here identified with a visual image) both the code of a suitable linguistic stimulus (i.e. a word), and the low-level and high-level category to which the physical stimulus itself is belonging and (2) associate to each code of a linguistic stimulus (word) the low-level and high-level category (mental representation) of the related physical event.

The categorizing module is composed by three different sub-modules: 1) the *main categorizer*, associating visual images to low-level categories, and, in turn, associating these latter to high-level categories, 2) the *encoder*, associating input words to low-level categories, and 3) the *decoder*, associating low-level categories to output words. The main categorizer was implemented through a

RBF network, inspired by ALCOVE model [4, 5]. Its input layer is activated by a grey-level coding of the pixels of a visual image of physical input stimulation, whereas each hidden layer unit corresponds to a particular (low-level) perceptual category. For this reason each hidden unit is associated to a particular prototype visual image, and its output h_i is given by:

$$h_i = F(P_i - S_i)$$

where F denotes a suitable radial basis function, P_i is the prototype visual image associated to the i-th hidden unit, and S_i denotes the actual input image. In turn, each unit of the output layer is associated to a particular high-level category. The output u_i of the i-th output unit is given by:

$$u_i = \sum_j w_{ij} h_i \ ,$$

where, as customary, $_j$ w_{ij} are the connection weights from hidden to output units. These outputs are converted to choice probabilities Pr_i using standard Luce rule:

$$Pr_i = u_i / (\sum_j u_j) \ .$$

As regards the encoder and the decoder, both are implemented through simple two-layer Perceptrons (one input and one output layer), whose output units have sigmoidal activation functions. The connection weights of the symbol categorization module were determined through a supervised learning procedure consisting of two successive phases. In the first one, the main categorizer was trained, on a set of 32 different visual images (each one coded through 30x20=600 pixels), to associate each image to its correct high-level category. The hidden layer contained 32 units and the prototype of each unit was just one image of the training set. The output layer contained 12 units. Widrow-Hoff rule was used to find the values of connection weights from hidden to output layer. In the second learning phase the encoder and the decoder were trained separately. More precisely, the encoder was trained to associate to the input vector coding a particular word (like *dog*) the correct pattern of activation of the hidden units of the main categorizer, corresponding to the presentation as input to this latter of a particular image (the image of a *dog*). In turn, the decoder was trained to associate to a particular pattern of activation of the hidden units of the main categorizer (like the one resulting from the input presentation of the image of a *dog*) an output vector coding a particular word (*dog*). Again, Widrow-Hoff rule was used. In our implementation both encoder input layer and decoder output layer contained 32 units (the length of the vector chosen to code a single word).

3. Semantic Processing and FGREP method

Whereas the symbol categorization module is deputed essentially to fix the initial structure of a Lexicon containing the words to be used in the subsequent semantic processing, we need a method to connect such a structure with the performance in a particular semantic task. To this regard, we adopted the so-called FGREP method, first proposed by Miikkulainen and Dyer [6]. FGREP (*Forming Global Representations through Extended backPropagation*) is based on two main components: a three-layer Perceptron, and a Global Lexicon containing explicit vector representations of the symbolic entities to be used (words, in our case). The system is trained to perform a specific semantic processing task typically by taking as external input the surface vector coding of the symbolic entities being used throughout the task. Within the Lexicon, such a coding gets associated with vectors of initially randomly set values. Later on, representations of the same items are taken out of Lexicon and possibly given as input and as target to the Perceptron, in a way dependent on the task; error signal is then backpropagated to the input layer, changing, along the path, both weights and input representations as if they were an extra layer of weights. The resulting representations replace the old ones in the Lexicon. Thus, as regards the case-roles mapping task to be discussed, the operation of the system during the training phase can be sketched as given by the following sequence of steps:

1) *forming input representations*: for each component of the input sentence, *get* the associated representations from Lexicon and *concatenate* them within a single input vector

2) *forming target representations*: for each component of the target sentence, *do* the same as in 1) except for concatenating representations within a single target vector

3) *learning the processing task*: for each couple of vectors in the training set, *propagate* input , *back-propagate* target and *update* weights

4) *updating representations in Lexicon*: (see [6], pp. 349-350) *compute* error signal for units in input layer

$$\delta^{(l)}_i = \sum_j \delta^{(2)}_j w^{(l)}_{ij} \ ,$$

where $\delta^{(k)}_i$ stands for the error signal relative to the i-th unit in k-th layer (as a convention, we will adopt the value $k = 1$ to denote the input layer, $k = 2$ to denote the hidden layer, and so on) and $w^{(l)}_{ij}$ is the weight of the connection from i-th unit in the input layer to j-th unit in the first hidden layer;

then, *compute* the following quantity, on which the updating of representations is based:

$$\Delta r^{(a)}_i = \eta ' \delta^{(l)}_i \ ,$$

where $r^{(a)}_i$ is the i-th element of vector representation of the symbolic item a, $\delta^{(l)}_i$ is the error signal of the corresponding input layer unit and $\eta '$ is the Lexicon learning rate, chosen as different from the learning rate η of the three-layer Perceptron; finally, *update* the representation vectors through the:

$$r^{(a)}_i (t + 1) = clip(r^{(a)}_i (t) + \Delta r^{(a)}_i) \ ,$$

where:

$$clip(activity) = \begin{cases} activity & for \ activity > 1 \\ 0 & for \ activity < 0. \end{cases}$$

4. A Neural Architecture for Symbol Processing

By coupling the Symbol Categorizer with the FGREP module, we obtained a neural architecture for performing the task of associating thematic roles to grounded phrase components. We choose, to perform our association task, of having to do with a simplified situation, in which all phrases are endowed with the same syntactic structure, consisting of 4 elements: a subject, a verb, an object, and a with-clause. Such a choice let us deal with a FGREP module in which, once fixed the number of elements of the vector coding a single symbolic entity, the dimensions of input and output layer remained fixed and given in advance. To this regard, we remind that the input layer was subdivided into 4 slots, corresponding to the 4 phrase components, whereas the output layer was subdivided into 5 slots, corresponding to the 5 possible thematic roles (agent, patient, instrument, action, modificator).

5. Numerical Experiments

By using the previously described architecture, we performed a number of different experiments, based on a training set of 1439 different phrases. Within the test phase, we made use of two different validation sets: one containing 38 familiar phrases, already contained within the training set, and another containing 38 unfamiliar phrases, not belonging to the training set. The experiments can be grouped into three categories:
a)   experiments with an initially randomly chosen coding of phrase components;
b)   experiments in which phrase components were initially coded through the high-level or low-level categories corresponding to them, as determined by the Categorizer module;
c)   experiments in which phrase components were initially coded both in a random way and through the categories corresponding to them.

In the first experiment of group a) each phrase component (word) was randomly coded through a 12-elements vector. The learning phase of FGREP module was carried out for 600 epochs, with fixed values of learning parameters ($\eta = 0.1$, $\eta' = 0.0005$). The average performance on the two validation sets was 77.5%. However, a Hierarchical Cluster Analysis, done through Nearest Neighbor method on representation vectors obtained at the end of learning phase, evidenced a categorical structure very different from the 'natural' one relative to the words used. The responsible for this effect could be the too low value of η', precluding from a serious modification of representations during learning, and whence from their departure from randomness. Unfortunately, an increase of η', introduced in further experiments, gave rise to a marked worsening of performance. For example, when $\eta' = 0.001$, the average performance was only 57%. We tried to compensate for this effect by increasing the number of elements of vectors used to represent the single words. In a first simulation with 18-elements vectors, carried out for 300 epochs with $\eta = 0.1$, $\eta' = 0.001$, we obtained an average performance of 80.5%. In a second simulation with 32-elements vectors, we used for the first 50 epochs the values $\eta = 0.1$, $\eta' = 0.001$, and for the subsequent 600 epochs the values $\eta = 0.1$, $\eta' = 0.05$. At the end we obtained an average performance of 84%.

As regards the experiments of group b) we studied two different possibilities: either to utilize high-level categories, or to utilize low-level categories. In the first case we used 12-dimensional vectors, obtained from activation patterns of the output layer of main categorizer. 100 training epochs with $\eta = 0.1$, $\eta' = 0.0005$ gave rise, however, to a FGREP performance of only 57%. It is to be remarked, on the other hand, that a Hierarchical Cluster Analysis done on final representation vectors showed a more 'natural' grouping of them in categories more easily recognizable by a human subject. An improvement of performance, up to 65%, was obtained by adopting the strategy of starting the learning phase with high values of learning parameters ($\eta = 0.4$, $\eta' = 0.4$), by lowering them subsequently ($\eta = 0.4$, $\eta' = 0.01$). In the case, instead, of low-level categories we used 32-dimensional vectors, corresponding to activation patterns of hidden layer of main categorizer. In this case, with $\eta = 0.5$, $\eta' = 0.05$ and only 30 learning epochs we obtained an average performance of 88.5%. A further prolongation of learning phase for other 600 epochs didn't gave rise to an improvement of performance.

In the experiments of group c) we introduced word representations based on 18-dimensional vectors: 12 elements coding high-level categories corresponding to single words, and other 6 elements initially chosen at random. A typical experiment with $\eta = 0.1$, $\eta' = 0.001$, carried out for 300 epochs, gave rise to an average performance of 83%. Further experiments showed that the latter value could be increased by increasing the dimensionality of representation vectors.

6. Discussion and conclusions

The results so far obtained showed that the introduction of categorical representations can give rise to an improvement of performance, with respect to the original FGREP model with initially random representations, in two ways: 1) by reducing learning times, 2) by increasing performance level in the semantic association task. These advantages, however, are present only when using low-level categories. This is connected to the circumstance according to which the best performances are associated to an absence of confusion between semantically related words. Such a situation is most likely to occur with low-level categories (where virtually each word is associated to a different visual image or to a different pattern of activation of allowable visual images) than with high-level categories (where different words could belong to the same category).

Even if our architecture gave a partial solution to SGP, we must, however, remember that it doesn't take into account many other circumstances, holding in natural language processing, such as the hierarchical structure of categories used by human subjects, and the existence of an *internal grounding* [1], besides the *external* one considered in this paper. Notwithstanding these difficulties, we feel that our study showed the feasibility and the usefulness of a neural-network-based approach to SGP and, more generally, to the problem of individuating the relationships between symbols and meanings.

Bibliography

[1] D. Chalmers, Subsymbolic Computation and the Chinese Room. In J. Dinsmore (Ed.) *The Symbolic and Connectionist Paradigms: Closing the Gap*, 25-48, Lawrence Erlbaum Associates, Hillsdale NJ, 1992.

[2] F. De Saussure, *Cours de Linguistique Générale*. Editions Payot, Paris, 1922.

[3] S. Harnad, The Symbol Grounding Problem. *Physica D*, 42, 335-346, 1990.

[4] J. K. Kruschke, ALCOVE: An Exemplar-based Connectionist Model of Category Learning. *Psychological Review*, 99, 22-44, 1992.

[5] J.K. Kruschke, Human Category Learning: Implications for Backpropagation Models. *Connection Science*, 5, 3-36, 1993.

[6] R. Miikkulainen & M.G. Dyer, Natural Language Processing with Modular Neural Networks and Distributed Lexicon. *Cognitive Science*, 15, 343-399, 1991.

Hole Identification System in Conducting Plates by using Wavelet Networks

Giovanni Simone[1]
Francesco Carlo Morabito[2]

Università "Mediterranea" di Reggio Calabria - Facoltà di Ingegneria
Via Graziella, Loc. Feo di Vito - I-89100 Reggio Calabria , Italy
Phone: +39 0965 875 224   Fax: +39 0965 875 220
e-mail: [1]simoneg@ing.unirc.it, [2]morabito@unirc.it
Web: http://neurolab.ing.unirc.it

Abstract

In this paper, we propose a wavelet network (WN) approach to the identification of holes in conducting plates, in the context of a Non Destructive Evaluation (NDE) signal processing system, based on the eddy currents inspection. The system aims to locate holes in the specimen under inspection by using a two-stage approach, namely, a WN followed by a least squares post-processing block. The WN stage estimates the distances between the hole and the sensor probes; the least squares stage identifies the hole on the basis of the distances computed by the previous neural block. The efficacy of the proposed approach is tested on artificial data and compared with different approaches based on feedforward multilayer perceptron (MLP) and on radial basis function neural network. The robustness of the system has been tested: the effects of the white noise and of the lift-off noise at different signal-to-noise ratios have been inspected.

1 Introduction

In order to improve manufacturing quality and ensure public safety, components and structures are inspected for defects or faults which may reduce their structural integrity. Among the methods of testing developed for maintenance and inspection purposes, Non-Destructive Evaluation (NDE) techniques present the advantages of leaving the specimens undamaged after inspection [1]. The NDE inspection method, applied throughout this paper, is the Eddy Current Testing (ECT) [1]. A magnetic sensor, scanning the surface of the metallic specimen to be inspected, produces a time-varying magnetic field, that induces electrical currents on the material (eddy currents). The presence of a flaw affects the formation of eddy currents, and this perturbation is measured by the sensor to locate and characterize the defect. The same sensor is successively located in different positions: the sensor, used in this case, consists of an exciting probe and 4 measuring probes. The same sensor is moved in 8 different locations: this situation is equivalent to the case where 8 sensors of the same nature are present. Consequently, 32 measured samples are available in the measurement database (4 measures for each position of the sensor). The most important issue in this context is to develop efficient signal processing techniques, hopefully completely automated [2,3,6], which allow to decide about the integrity of the inspected specimen. The information about the defect in the testing signals is unavoidably corrupted by noise and/or other undesired signals (e.g. lift-off variations, probe angle errors, edge effects, junction of structures, ...) [1], and signal processing techniques are requested in order to be able to detect defects also at low SNRs. In this paper, we propose a two-stage scheme based on a wavelet network and on a least squares block that aims to identify the location of a hole in a conducting plate. By using a set of magnetic measurements, a wavelet network estimates the distances between the center of the hole and M measuring probes: the wavelet network is able to provide as output M distances, that are the distances between the hole and the M nearest sensors to the hole; the least squares approach, typically used in Global Positioning System (GPS) receivers [7,8], estimates the hole location on the basis of the M distances computed by the previous step. The number of the computed distances (M) is varied in order to optimize the system in terms of root mean square errors for the x-location and y-location of the hole; this implies that both the structure of the wavelet network and the least squares block are varied, in order to find the more suitable architecture. We compared our system with different approaches based on typical NNs [2,3,6], where the G.P.S. based scheme has not been used; in these cases, it has been applied only a NN having as input the magnetic measurements and as output the hole parameters; the considered neural architectures are: a feed-forward MLP with fast back-propagation training algorithm; a feed-forward MLP with Levenberg-Marquardt training algorithm; a radial basis function neural network; a wavelet neural network. The action of the gaussian noise has been inspected. Furthermore, the effects produced by the variation of the distance between the sensor and the plate (lift-off distance) have been examined, in both cases of the RBFNN and of the WN.

2 Radial Basis Function Neural Networks (RBFNN) and Wavelet Networks (WN)

Two different kinds of neural approaches have been exploited to locate the hole on the basis of the eddy current measurements; these networks will estimate the distances between the hole and the sensors. The applied structures are a radial basis function neural network and a wavelet network: the outline similarities and the differences among these two structures have been carried out in [10]; in the present paper, we examine the differences between these different neural approaches in terms of the ability of the systems to locate the hole.

A RBFNN [4,5,10] is a network with three layers: a input layer, a hidden layer with radial basis neurons and an output layer of linear neurons. The weights and biases of each neuron in the hidden layer define the location and width of a radial basis function. Each linear output neuron forms a weighted sum of these radial basis functions. By determining the suitable set of weight and bias values for each layer, and providing a sufficient number of hidden neurons, a radial basis network can fit any function with any desired accuracy. The basis function that we employed is a Gaussian function.

When the training database is affected by noise phenomena due to varying sampling times, sparse and dense data in different operating regions and the inherent presence of both large and small dynamics, the multiple resolution learning can be a way to overcome these problems. TheWNs, introduced by Zhang [9] combines the concept of neural network with the wavelet transform, by using dilation and translation parameters to fit the data at different resolution scales. In order to represent the information carried by the data, simultaneously in time and frequency, the wavelet transform has been proposed. In practice, $f(x)$ has to be recovered from a finite number of wavelet coefficients, and, therefore, we will obtain just an approximation of the input function:

$$\hat{f}(x) = \sum_{i=1}^{N} w_i \cdot \psi(D_i \cdot x - t_i) + \mu. \tag{3.1}$$

where N is the number of the retained wavelet coefficients, $\psi(\cdot)$ is the wavelet, D_i and t_i are the dilation and translation parameters, and μ is the parameter to be added to approximate non-zero mean functions. This reconstruction formula can be emulated by using a multiplayer perceptron, consisting of one hidden layer of "wavelons", i.e. units with activation $(D_i \cdot x - t_i)$ and transfer function $\psi(\cdot)$, and one output with inner product activation and linear transfer function. The μ bias term has to be also considered. To train the networks we use a noiseless database of 200 patterns; the training database is obtained from the field database, by exploiting the field magnitude for each pattern, and sorting the 32 obtained samples by decreasing magnitude. It is important to note that just M samples are used as input of the NN, that computes M distances between the hole and the M sensors at the largest field magnitude. Since the locations of the EC sensor is *a priori* known, the output distances can be exploited to locate the hole.

3 The least squares (G.P.S. receiver) approach (L.S.A.)

The basic principle used by a Global Positioning System (G.P.S.) receiver to determine its position involves the measurement of range to several satellites [7,8]; in this sense, if we look at our sensors as the satellites of the G.P.S. system, and at the hole in the conducting plate as the G.P.S. receiver, we can convert the G.P.S. navigation solution into the hole location estimation based on the magnetic measurements. In principle, if we can make a range measurement to two different magnetic sensors, it should be possible to fix the hole location in the plate; however, due to the noise effects, we need a number greater then two to estimate the hole location. If we denote the hole location to be estimated as $\hat{h} = (\hat{h}_x, \hat{h}_y)$, then the problem is solved by the following equation:

$$\hat{h} = b + \Delta X \tag{4.1}$$

where b is the barycentre of the nearest estimated sensors, $\Delta X = (H^T \cdot H)^{-1} \cdot H^T \cdot \Delta\rho$, $H = [-\hat{r}_1, -\hat{r}_2, ..., -\hat{r}_m]^T$, $\hat{r}_i$ is the line of sight unit vector from the current estimate of the hole location to the i-th sensor, $\Delta\rho$ is the vector of the distances estimated by the NN.

Neural Architecture	ε_x [%]	ε_y [%]
FF- Fast BP	34.51	30.17
FF – Lev. Mar.	20.53	25.84
RBFNN	17.80	15.76
RBFNN – LSA	0.51	1.19
WN	13.40	17.34
WN-LSA	0.31	0.87

Table 1: Comparison between different neural architectures.

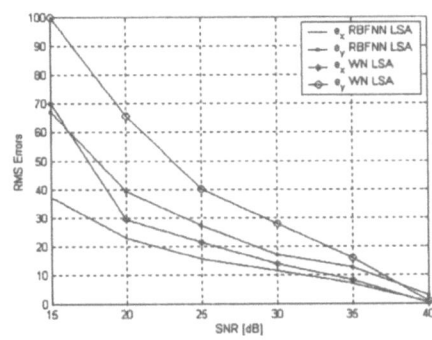

Fig.1: Performances of the RBFNN-LSA and WN-LSA systems for the database affected by gaussian noise.

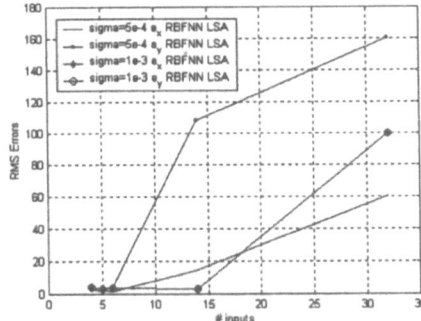

Fig.2: Performance of the RBFNN-LSA for the database affected by lift-off noise.

Fig.3: Performances of the WN-LSA systems for the database affected by lift-off noise.

4 A comparison with other neural architectures

In order to test the performance of our system, we compared it with other neural architectures [4]; nevertheless, in these last cases, we did not employ the least squares approach, but only a neural network that we trained to locate the hole on the basis of the magnetic field magnitude. We tested a feed-forward network (Multilayer Perceptron) with the fast back-propagation training algorithm, with 3 layers, where the middle layer consists of 16 neurons with a sigmoidal transfer function and the output layer is linear; the second architecture is the same neural network, but we employed the Levenberg-Marquardt training algorithm. We considered also a RBFNN and a WN that locate the hole without the use of the least squares block. Furthermore, the matched exploitations of the RBFNN and of the LSA, and of the WN and of the LSA have been considered. These neural systems have been compared by considering the full-scale root mean square errors, for the x and y hole locations, on the testing noiseless database. Table 1 shows the results. In terms of root mean square errors, the best performances are obtained by the joint use of the Wavelet Network and of the least squares technique; whereas, in this last case, with respect to the RBFNN approach, the floating point operations number is obviously greater, since the architecture of the network in this case is more complex. The RBFNN-LSA and the WN-LSA systems have to be compared in the case where the noise affects the testing databases, to choice the architecture that performs the best results in terms of rms-errors: the following Section will describe the performances of the proposed techniques in the presence of white noise and lift-off noise at different signal-to-noise ratios.

5 Noise effects on the system performance

An important test on the system performance is the action of the noise on the root mean square errors for the x-location and y-location of the hole. A white noise has been considered, by adding this zero-mean gaussian noise to the magnetic measurements: the standard deviation has been varied to obtain different signal-to-noise ratios. Thus, we simulated 6 different testing databases, at 6 different SNRs (15, 20, 25, 30, 35, 40 dB): after the training on the noiseless database, the performances of the RBFNN-LSA and of the WN-LSA systems have been evaluated in terms of the percentage root mean square errors, $\varepsilon_x [\%]$ and $\varepsilon_y [\%]$. The structure of the neural architectures has been changed by optimizing the number of the magnetic field samples, inputs of the NNs. The performances of the RBFNN-LSA and WN-LSA and WN-LSA schemes are represented in Fig. 1, at different SNRs: the value of 14 for the number of inputs offered the best values of rms-errors for both the RBF and WN based systems. By observing the values reported in the Fig.1 obtained with this value $N=14$, the RBFNN-LSA and the WN-LSA offer performances very similar at high SNRs, that are the most usual cases; for very low SNRs, that are almost unusual, the RBFNN-LSA offered rms-errors lower than the WN-LSA values. However, a test based on databases affected by gaussian noise is not enough to reliably evaluate the system performance; for this reason, we also considered the most common case where the measurements are affected by variation of the distance between the moving sensor and the surface. Usually, these variations can be modeled by using a gaussian distribution for this distance, called lift-off: in our simulations, two different values of standard deviation have been considered, and both the systems have been tested by changing the number of input measurements, and by computing the rms-errors for the x and y hole locations. The results are summarized in Figs. 2,3. The usefulness of the WN-LSA is evident: for the RBFNN-LSA in the worst case $\varepsilon_x = 100\%$ $\varepsilon_y = 160\%$, in the best $\varepsilon_x = 4.8\%$ $\varepsilon_y = 5.2\%$; for the WN-LSA in the worst case $\varepsilon_x = 4.3\%$ $\varepsilon_y = 4.3\%$, in the best $\varepsilon_x = 0.5\%$ $\varepsilon_y = 1\%$.

6 Conclusions

In this paper, we compared different neural architectures to automatically locate holes in conducting plates, on the basis of eddy current measurements; we proposed a novel approach based on the matched exploitation of two systems: the first one, based on a wavelet network, estimates the distances between the hole and a set of sensors that are ranked by the value of the measurement magnitude; the second one consists of a least squares technique that, like a global positioning system, locates the hole on the plate by using the estimates computed by the previous neural step. The results, carried out by the proposed system, have been compared with that provided by standard neural architectures like MLP and RBFNN and WN, where the LSA has not been used; furthermore, the WN-LSA have been compared with the RBFNN-LSA, where we used a RBFNN instead of the WN, to estimate the distance between the hole and the sensors. The robustness of the proposed system has been tested in different contexts: noise free measurements, white noise at different signal-to-noise ratios, and lift-off noise at different signal-to-noise ratios. Even if at low SNRs the RBFNN-LSA shows better results for the databases affected by white noise, when the more usual case of the lift-off noise is considered, this system gives poor results with respect to the rms-errors estimated for the WN-LSA system. In fact, WN-LSA is able to minimize the percentage root mean square error for the x-location and for the y-location of the hole, by providing optimal performances also in the worst case of lift-off noise in the measurements.

References

[1] J. Blitz, "Electrical and Magnetic Methods of Non-destructive Testing", *Chapman & Hall*, Second Edition, 1997;

[2] F.C.Morabito, A.Gasparics, "A Wavelet Neural Network Processor of Eddy Current NDE Data", *Electromagnetic Nondestructive Evaluation (III)*, Lesselier and Razek Eds., IOS Press, 1999, pp.108-116;

[3] L.Udpa, S.S.Udpa, "Application of Signal Processing and Pattern Recognition Techniques to Inverse Problems in NDE", *International Journal of Applied Electromagnetics and Mechnaics*, Vol.8, 1997, pp.99-117;

[4] S.Haykin, "Neural Networks, A Comprehensive Foundation", *Macmillan, New York*, 1994;

[5] C.Bishop, "Pattern Recognition and Neural Networks", *Oxford University Press*, 1995;

[6] F.C.Morabito, M.Campolo, "A Task Decomposition Neural Network Approach to Non-Destructive Testing Problems", *Proc. of World Congress on Neural Networks*, 1994, Vol.1, pp.566-571;

[7] B.W. Parkinson, F. Van Graas, P.K. Eng, et al., "Global Positioning System: Theory and Applications", *American Institute of Aeronautics and Astronautics*, Vol.1 and 2, 1994;

[8] M.P.Green, "Extended Kalman Filter for Integrating Tracking Data from Ground-Based Radar and Airborne Global Positioning System", *Master Thesis, M.I.T.*, 1998;

[9] Q.Zhang, "Using Wavelet Networks in Non-parametric Estimation", *IEEE Trans. on Neural Networks*, Vol.8, No.2, March 1997, pp.227-236;

[10] L.M.Reyneri, "Unification of Neural and Wavelet Networks and Fuzzy Systems", *IEEE Trans. on Neural Networks*, Vol.10, No.4, July 1999, pp.801-814.

Neuro-Fuzzy Techniques to Estimate and Predict Atmospheric Pollutant Levels

Mario Versaci

University "Mediterranea" of Reggio Calabria,
Faculty of Engineering, DIMET
Via Graziella, Loc. Feo di Vito, Reggio Calabria, Italy
e-mail: versaci@ing.unirc.it

Abstract

The main goal of this work is to supply the directives for the design of an environmental monitoring system able to estimate and predict the pollutant values of Villa San Giovanni, an important town on the Messina channel (Italy). For this purpose, neuro-fuzzy inference techniques are exploited. In particular, by using a MatLab® Toolbox, sophisticated Fuzzy Inferece Systems (FISs) were carried out. The inference engine is a bank of fuzzy rules. Each rule is of the IF... THEN structure in terms of linguistic frameworks in which the easy understanding due to the open box structure can help the politicians to take decisions about the urban traffic. In addition, a comparisons with "black box" techniques as Neural Networks (NN) are taken into account.

1 Introduction

Villa San Giovanni is important town subordinate to periodicals and accidental acute episodes of pollution. Villa San Giovanni is encircled from hills, except for the side that shows oneself on the Messina's channel. The urban environmental of the city is subject every day to slow changes which had to human activities and natural processes reported to the development of the city, movements of traffic, ferry boats terminal that connect Villa San Giovanni towards the Sicily. In addition, the city is subject to very high levels solar radiations during the summertime, when the temperature often catches up the 40 °C, increasing effect of photochemical phenomena to compromise the quality of the air. All these weather conditions contribute to the creation of very strong pollution episodes. Fig. 1 visualizes the area of Messina channel. The main characteristic of this paper regards the estimation and the prediction of pollutant levels in the atmosphere of a strategic city area due to the urban traffic. This work takes place inside of SMAURN Project (Sistema di Monitoraggio Ambientale Urbano mediante lUtilizzo di Reti Neurali) whose purpose is to design an on-line monitoring system by a set of sensors that estimate the air quality in the area. The optimal location of the sensors in the interest area is sure output the more interesting of the model and is correlated to the geomorphologic characteristics of the area under study. The design use a network of terminals to study the parameters and the temporal prediction of their evolutions. This network makes biological, chemical, physical and meteorological investigations of the air, by examination of the urban environment and the air quality. The measurements are automatically transfer from the station to central database. After calibration and controls, data are stocked in a final database where statistical and visualization data systems control the data. A central system of acquisition works from collector and manages the data in arrival from the stations. The installation of three monitoring stations in different situations are also previewed. The necessity of an environmental monitoring system appears clearly in order to supply to the politician an instrument of aid to the decisional power. Neural Networks (NN) were employed to estimate and predict the pollutant levels with encouraging results [1, 4]. On the other hand, their "Black Box" structure do not give helps about political decisions. In this context, FISs can be useful because their "*IF... THEN*" structure in terms of linguistic frameworks in which the easy understanding due to the no black box structure helps the politicians to take decisions about the urban traffic. In addition, the uncertainty of the data and the non linearity of the posed problem justify the choosing for these systems.

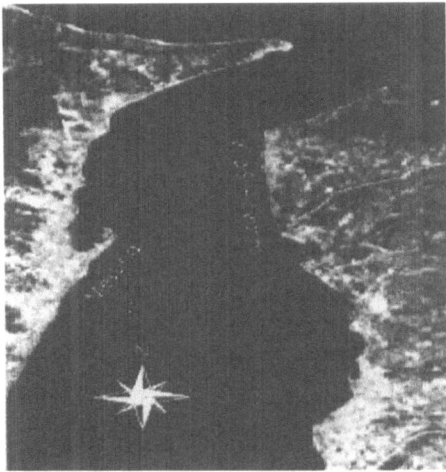

Fig.1: The study area of the Messina Channel.

2 The Experimental Database Exploited

The database contain hourly readings for various environmental and pollutant factors. The measured pollutants concentrations and the meteorologica parameters are reported in Table I. The analyzed data in this paper refers to a station (Archimede's station) located downtown, along an important way which collects the vehicular traffic from peninsular Italy. The covariance is an important factor in the study of the interrelations between pollutants and weather conditions at a measurement location as well as the correlation between stations pairs. In the case a data sequence includes empty data cells, due to missed measurements, the system disregards them from the calculations. Wind analysis plays a relevant role for the study of natural conditions occurring during the development of an air pollution episode as well as for the extraction of long term meteorological features. The correlation with other meteorological variables, as temperature and solar radiations, explain the need of fuzzifying the map. The study of each pollutant in connection with the wind speed and directions in the area are carried out. Some wind direction with medium speed may transport pollutants towards selected areas thus creating pollution problems. The wind in this area blows mostly along the NE / SW axis with the prevailing wind directions being simila in summer, fall, winter and spring. The prediction RMS error improves to about the 5 % by using these evidences. The database is composed by 12 columns and 714 rows. Its structure is reports in Table II. In addition, another database (350 rows) has been used in order to carried out testing evaluation.

Table I. Structure of Database

column	variable	column	variable
1	SO_2 ($\mu g/m^3$)	7	TSP (total suspended particulate) ($\mu g/m^3$)
2	CO ($\mu g/m^3$)	8	PM10 ($\mu g/m^3$)
3	O_3 ($\mu g/m^3$)	9	Speed of the wind (m/sec)
4	NO ($\mu g/m^3$)	10	Direction of the wind (degrees)
5	NO_2 ($\mu g/m^3$)	11	temperature (°C)
6	HCNM ($\mu g/m^3$)	12	Atmospheric pressure (mbar)

3 Neuro-Fuzzy Inference Systems: an Overview

The problem to estimate the polluting level can be formulated as the search of a suitable mapping between the set of available measurements and the selected set of pollutant parameters [4]. This approach falls in the category of database manipulation tools where the unknown set of shaping parameters is derived by means of a suitable multi-dimensional interpolation procedure on a data-set covering the expected range of inputs/outputs. On the other hand, model-based schemes using an optimisation approach where the search for the solution implies the iterative minimization of a cost function can be take into account. The first approach requires the availability of a data base of simulated and/or experimental cases that is used to 'learn" the mapping. For this goal, fuzzy systems are very good tools as they hold the non-linear universal approximation property, and they are able to handle experimental data as well as a priori knowledge on the unknown solution, which is expressed by inferential linguistic rules in the form of IF-THEN whose antecedents and consequents utilise fuzzy sets instead of crisp numbers. Independently from the technique that is used to solve the identification problem, our purpose is anyway to associate to a particular pattern of measurements, the pollutant level in the air. Fuzzy Neural models are basically feedforward networks that use a Fuzzy Inference Systems (FIS) as a first guess model of the dynamic process and then tune the initial choice of the model's parameters in accordance with the available input-output pairs. The inputs of the procedure are interpreted as fuzzy variables. Each fuzzy value carried out by a fuzzy variable is characterised by a fuzzy membership function (FMF). Each FMF is expressing a membership measure to each of the linguistic properties. FMFs are usually scaled between zero and unity, and they overlap. The choice of these FMFs as well as the optimisation of their parameters is a matter of design. The typical FMFs are trapezoidal or triangular-shaped functions but other function can be used. More recently, FMFs have been designed using optimisation procedures, including NN learning methods. To improve the flexibility of our model, we have used Gaussian FMFs. By considering the output variable as a fuzzy variable, one can characterise the relationship between two fuzzy variables (one of input, the other one of output) as a conditional statement of the form IF A THEN B, where A and B are labels of fuzzy sets representing the values of input and output respectively. A FIS is designed according to the following procedure: fuzzification of the input-output variables; fuzzy inference through the bank of fuzzy rules; defuzzification of the fuzzy output variables. In our test problem, the inputs of the procedure are the measurements, while the outputs are some pollutant. The most simple FIS model exploits known constraints from a very limited number of inputs. This model is very parsimonious with respect to both NNs as well as model based approaches. In the FIS generation we have used the input-output pairs without exploiting the concept of learning: as a result, the estimation accuracy is invariably not quite good. However, the design of such a "naïve" FIS can turn out to be useful as a first guess model and for real time systems. The result can be improved either by using an algorithm of automatic extraction of FIS from numerical data (MATLAB® GENFIS System) and possibly by introducing learning (MATLAB® ANFIS) [5]. A network FIS scheme facilitates the computation of the gradient vector for computing the parameter corrections. Once the gradient vector is obtained, a number of optimization routines can be applied to reduce the error. The extraction of fuzzy rules is what politicians ask. They express concepts as:

IF *the concentration of CO is large and the wind speed is small*
THEN *the traffic must be reduced*.

This fact helps them in order to take decisions.

4 Summary of Results

In the past, NN models were used to predict the time evolution of the pollutants basically of the feed-forward multi-layer perceptron type [2, 4]. The inputs of the models were samples of the measured concentrations and the outputs were the predicted concentrations for the next hours and for the following days. The RMS error was acceptable for predictions which uses not only the last hours concentrations but also an additional set of inputs representing the measured concentration value at the same hour in recent days and in days with similar meteorological conditions. The errors are increased for one-week prediction but are always within 10%. The conceived fuzzy system can be useful in order to estimate on-line the pollutant values in the air and to predict the levels of polluting in function of the levels estimated in the previous hours. For this purpose, two FISs . The first one estimates the pollutant levels. In this case, the structure has been conceived by means of system Matlab GENFIS system using, as inputs, some pollutant ones with to the relative atmospheric parameters while, as output, we consider a pollutant. The system has been improved by ANFIS routine in order to optimize the position of the membership functions.

The on-line system uses a pattern of measurements as inputs and his output is the dangerous pollutant estimation. Table II shows the best results obtained for training and testing evaluation. By using FIS approach, we are able to write rules of behavior.

The final purpose is to predict the pollutant concentration some hours after the last estimation.

Table III reports structure of predicting database.

In this paper, the prediction has been carried out until four hours after the last estimation.

Table II. Results by FIS

#inputs	Output	#rules	RMSE (training)	RMSE (testing)
12	SO_2	65	2.60%	5.2%
12	CO	59	3.01%	4.21%
12	O_3	64	2.8%	4.0%
12	NO	50	4.0%	4.4%
12	NO_2	53	3.91%	4.51%
12	PM10	59	3.02%	3.72%
12	HCNM	55	3.70%	4.28%
12	TSP	66	2.95%	3.5%

Tale III. Structure of predicting database

estimations of the same pollutant in the previous hours										Four hours later
1	2	3	4	5	6	7	8	9	10	14
2	3	4	5	6	7	8	9	10	11	15
3	4	5	6	7	8	9	10	11	12	16
4	5	6	7	8	9	10	11	12	13	17
...	...	...	...	...	...	...	...	...	...	...

The relevant result regard the prediction of O_3: for this case the number of rules is 51 and the RMSE is 4.09%.

5 Conclusions and Perspectives

a) In this paper a preliminar design of an environmental monitoring system able to estimate and predict the pollutant values of Villa San Giovanni is proposed.

b) By using a MatLab® Toolbox, Fuzzy Inferece Systems (FISs) were carried out in order to estimate and predict atmospheric pollutant levels.

c) The fuzzy approach is very efficient in order to identify and to predict pollutant levels.
d) The extraction of FISs from the database allows us to carry out the non-linearity of the problem.
e) The reduced computational complexity is very well for online applications.
f) Finally, the linguistic structure of FISs can be exploited by politicians in order to take decisions about the reduction of pollutant levels.
g) In addition, the reduced number of rules can be used to take into account human decisions.
h) Finally, the performance of the systemscan be improved by using expert's knowledge.
i) In the future, the results can be increased by using special fuzzy systems (for example, fuzzy ellipsoidal systems).

6 References

[1] C. M. Roadknight, G.R. Balls, et al, Modeling Complex Environmental Data, IEEE Transactions on Neural Networks, Vol. 8, No.4, p. 852, July 1997;
[2] D. Marino, B. Ricca, Neural Networks for Econometric and Environmental Models for Territory Management, Proceedings of the XVII Italian Congress on Regional Sciences, Sondrio, Italy, 16-18 Oct 1996;
[3] B Kosko, "Fuzzy Engineering" Prentice Hall International, 1997;
[4] D. Marino, F.C. Morabito, "A Fuzzy Neural Network for Urban Environment Monitoring System: the Villa San Giovanni Study Case", Neural Nets, Wirn Vietri-99, p 323, May 1999;
[5] R. Jang, "ANFIS: Adaptive –Network-based Fuzzy Inference Systems", IEEE Transaction on Systems, Man, and Cybernetics, Vol. 23, N. 3, May 1993.

Section 8

Special Session: From Synapses To Rules

On connectionism and rule extraction

Asim Roy

School of Information Systems

Arizona State University, Tempe, AZ 85287-3606

USA

1.   On connectionism and rule extraction

There are two major motivations for rule extraction from trained artificial neural networks. First, some of the proposed neural network architectures, like multiplayer perceptrons, are so complex that that it is difficult to understand the logic behind any decision or inference made by such a network. So from an engineering standpoint, rule extraction from such a complex network provides a way to understand and explain the logic behind any decision made by it. By the way, [11] define the rule extraction from neural networks task as follows: "Given a trained neural network and the examples used to train it, produce a concise and accurate symbolic description of the network." So the objective of rule extraction is to provide a certain type of symbolic description of the network. A second major motivation for rule extraction is to bridge the divide between symbolic AI and connectionism; that is, to show that connectionist subsymbolic systems are just an implementation of higher-level symbolic systems. Thus rule-extraction and rule-insertion, whereby a connectionist network is created from a set of symbolic rules [16,17], provides a seamless integration between these two levels, the symbolic and the subsymbolic.

After a brief review of some work in the area of rule extraction, both symbolic and fuzzy types, this paper examines a few issues that relate to rule extraction. In section 2, it looks at the issue of whether there is any rule extraction in the brain itself. In section 3, it argues that there is an inherent conflict between rule-extraction and connectionism and that rule extraction procedures require control theoretic notions. In section 4, the paper argues that connectionism also uses control theoretic notions and thus connectionism is not a new kind of computing mechanism. Hence both rule extraction and connectionism are depended on control theory principles.

1.1   Rule extraction – a brief review

After the advent of connectionism and artificial neural networks, the predominant belief among scientists in the brain-related sciences is that the symbolic and fuzzy rules are actually embedded in the networks of neurons in the brain - that these rules exist in the connection weights, the node functions and in the structure of the network [1, 2, 3, 4, 5, 6, 8, 9, 10, 11, 14, 15, 16, 17, 18, 22, 24, 25, 30, 31, 32, 36,

47, 48, 49, 51, 53, 54, 55, 56, 57 and others]. It is also believed that when humans verbalize or externalize these rules in some other form, they simply "read" the rules from the corresponding neural networks in their brains. So the theories of symbolic and fuzzy logic were combined with the theories of neural network and connectionism to develop the computational structures and algorithms that can emulate the "processes" by which humans learn, use and express both the symbolic (crisp) and fuzzy (imprecise and vague) rules.

Significant work has been done over the years in the area of fuzzy neural networks. [27] was one of the first ones to propose adding fuzzy membership functions to perceptrons. [1, 4, 8, 10, 22, 30, 32, 36, 54, and 56] survey and present new models and learning methods for fuzzy neural networks. There is also a significant body of work on extracting symbolic rules from artificial neural networks [2, 5, 6, 9, 11, 14, 15, 16, 17, 18, 24, 25, 31, 47, 48, 51, 53, 55 and others]. [3] present an overall taxonomy for categorizing techniques for extracting symbolic rules from artificial neural networks.

2. Is there rule extraction in the brain?

This part of the paper questions whether there is any rule extraction in the human brain. It argues that the brain is unable to extract rules from biological networks that are actually used to perform a given task. Behavioral evidence is used to argue for the case.

This section therefore postulates that the brain might not be performing any rule extraction at all. It argues for this possibility by examining behavioral evidence for some very simple cases of human learning. Section 2.1 discusses the existence of two separate systems in the brain for some common supervised learning situations – a non-operational component that simply stores instructions and rules in pure memory form for a certain cognitive/analytic or motor task, and an operational component that actually learns through practice how to operationalize those rules and perform the task. In section 2.2, it is argued that the brain is never able to extract rules from the operational component that has learned to do the task when the non-operational component is lost due to non-use or when it didn't exist in the first place.

2.1 On the existence of two systems in the brain

Assume a person has never played soccer and never even heard about the game. So, as far as the brain of this person is concerned, there is not an iota of information there about the game. In order to teach soccer to this person, suppose he or she is confined to a place for a month or so (or for any other appropriate amount of time necessary for proper instructions) with soccer coaches, books and video about soccer, and everything else that might be needed to provide proper instructions on soccer, including say players to provide actual demonstrations of the game. (Here, one can substitute the learning of soccer with the learning of any other motor or cognitive/analytic task, including the learning of a language or mathematics for that matter.) Suppose, however, in this process of teaching the game, the person is never allowed to touch a ball or perform any actual practice of the game. So, hopefully, after a month or so of soccer instructions through this process, this person should have stored in the brain a substantial amount of information about soccer, including many images of actual soccer plays. But can this person really play soccer well, or at least reasonably well, even after a month or so of intensive instructions, if the person had never been allowed to touch a ball and practice the game during that time? Perhaps not. So the question is, why not? Obviously something is lacking in the brain of that person that is derived from the practice of that game. In other words, some component or mechanism in the brain is missing, the one that is created and developed through actual practice of the game. And this is true for learning of any skill, be it cognitive/analytic or motor. That missing component must be the one that encodes and operationalizes the high-level instructions and rules into detailed decisions and signals for various parts of the brain and the body. And that component can be created and developed (learned) through actual practice only; it cannot be constructed directly from the high-level instructions that are provided. Let this component be called the operational component or subsystem. So the person learning to play soccer without any actual practice cannot develop this operational subsystem in the brain simply through the instructions that are provided, even though the instructions may occur over a prolonged period of time. There is nothing new in these behavioral observations, no profound new discoveries about human behavior. They are a simple restatement of some ordinary facts about human learning.

This made-up scenario illustrates very clearly that there are two component systems in the brain in this mode of teaching or learning: the one that stores in pure memory form all the instructions and rules about the task to be learned (call this the non-operational component or subsystem, since it is not encoded for an operational role as explained above), and a second one that operationalizes for the body and the brain all those rules and instructions (this the operational component or subsystem). The above case is an illustration of training that produces persons who might know the rules of the task very well, but may not be able to perform the task well or at all. So these people would have the non-operational subsystem in the brain, but would lack the operational one.

The existence of these two component systems within the brain perhaps could be verified through many of the current techniques of brain imaging [26]. It should show a certain area or areas being active when performing the task after a prolonged period of instructions on the task that included no practice, and a different area or areas being active when performing the task after a period of actual practice.

A recent study by [47] may lend some insight on the issue. In this study, a positron emission tomography (PET) device was used to monitor neural activity in the brain as subjects were taught and then retested on a motor skill. The task required them to manipulate an object on a computer screen by using a motorized robot arm. It required making precise and rapid reaching movements to a series of targets while holding the handle of the robot. And these movements could only be learned through practice. During practice, the blood flow was most active in the prefrontal cerebral cortex of the brain. After the practice session, some of the subjects were allowed to do unrelated routine things for five to six hours and then retested on their recently acquired motor skill. During retesting of this group, it was found that they had learned the motor skill quite well. But it was also found that the blood flow now was most active in a different part of the brain, in the posterior parietal and cerebella areas. Hence it clearly shows that the encoding of the operational subsystem, by means of practice, is in a different part of the brain.

An obvious question is, what is the role of the non-operational subsystem in the creation and development of the operational part? In other words, what role does the non-operational subsystem play in the process of practice of a task? When one practices a given task based on a set of instructions and rules, one obviously has to exercise those rules and instructions to generate actual training examples for the operational subsystem in the brain to learn from. So the non-operational subsystem basically has to generate training examples for the operational subsystem to learn from. There is no other mechanism in the brain that can produce the training examples appropriate for a given task. In the case of soccer or any such physical game, the non-operational subsystem in the brain is used to generate actual movements in various organs of the body during practice and those movements are then gradually encoded in the second subsystem to produce an operational system. So, as stated before, the operational subsystem actually learns from data generated by the non-operational subsystem. At the end of practice, one might have both the subsystems, but they would clearly be separate. And, as stated earlier, the existence of these two separate subsystems could be verified through brain imaging techniques [26].

Note that the notion of operational and non-operational subsystems in the brain, in this kind of supervised learning situation, is different from the notion of memory and learning subsystems of [34]. They, in particular, suggest that, in the process of learning, the hippocampus and the neocortex may play complementary roles as memory and learning subsystems. This is based on experimental findings that show that the neocortex uses a very gradual learning process that exploits the structure of the training inputs in the memory subsystem. And they found that the hippocampus complements the neocortex by providing the mechanism for rapid acquisition of memories (training examples) that are used for subsequent learning by the neocortex. Thus an "off-line" process of integration, generalization, and consolidation in the neocortical system follows the rapid acquisition of memories in the hippocampus. But the notion of operational and non-operational subsystems in the brain is different from this notion of memory and learning subsystems. The non-operational subsystem, as explained earlier, is simply the generator of memories (training examples, training data) that are used to train the operational subsystem. So the non-operational subsystem is not the actual memory, but its generator. Second, it should be noted that the memory and learning subsystems of [34] could very much be part of the process by which the operational subsystem is created. So there is no conflict here between these two notions. This paragraph was somewhat off a detour from the main argument, but perhaps was required for the purpose of clarification.

2.2   Is there rule extraction in the brain?

Now to the real question: Is there rule extraction in the brain? Consider the following facts. It indeed is quite normal for people to forget the original instructions on any task after a while. For example, nobody remembers the original soccer, swimming, mathematics, or grammar instructions after a few years. They might remember some bits and pieces of instructions here and there, particularly the memorable ones that become good stories afterward, but perhaps nothing more than that. But that does not mean that one forgets how to swim, play soccer, do mathematics, or use the rules of grammar, particularly if one is using or doing them on a regular basis. One can conclude from this behavioral evidence that the operational subsystem survives in the brain as long as it is used, but a substantial part or all of the non-operational subsystem (that is, the memory of the actual instructions) disappears over time. In other words, the original information about the task (statements of rules, instructions, images and so on) is lost.

But how does this behavioral evidence relate to the question of whether there is rule extraction in the brain? Consider the scenario presented above and consider what happens when one is asked to restate the rules of soccer, swimming, mathematics, or grammar many years after the initial learning took place. If there was rule extraction in the brain, one should simply be able to extract those rules from the operational subsystem and state them as needed. <u>But that does not happen</u>. For example, many persons, including the present author (who certainly has no claims to writing perfect or even good English), have great difficulty recalling the various rules of English grammar even though they might write in English on a regular basis using the same rules of grammar. <u>So, evidently, the rules are there in the operational subsystem and are being used regularly, but the brain is unable to extract those rules from that subsystem and restate them verbally or in some other form</u>. The brain, therefore, is unable to extract and restate rules from an operational subsystem that actually encodes those same rules inside it.

One might argue that in the case of soccer, swimming, and similar motor skills, people can indeed describe the rules of the game at some level. So aren't they extracting the rules from the operational subsystem in that case? Perhaps not. Here are some arguments to consider. First, many people who have never practiced the motor skill or played the game, and therefore don't have an operational subsystem, can also describe the rules of the game at some level. And this is possible even when they never had any kind of instructions on the game or had it a very long time ago. So they are obviously not accessing and extracting rules from an operational subsystem in their brain. Second, the human ability to restate the rules of games involving motor skills may depend very much on the ability to recreate mental images of such games in the brain and then interpreting and recalling rules based on those mental images. So, again, there would be no rule extraction from the operational subsystem in that case. To verify this fact, the reader is welcome to try the following exercise: try stating the rules of any game without mentally creating an image of the game. It would be impossible to do. So the point is, the rules expressed in such cases come from a source different from the operational subsystem, a source that perhaps states rules by creating mental images of the game on the fly.

It may be appropriate to examine other possible rule extraction scenarios. Imagine there is indeed a module in the brain that can read and extract rules from different operational subsystems within the brain. Now consider the situation of a child who has just learned to recognize a few objects (e.g. humans, cats, dogs, water, clothes, different types of food and so on) and associate sounds, emotions and meaning with those objects. Can this child extract and express the rules involved in distinguishing those objects since the operational system is already in place in the brain? Perhaps not. Suppose now the child has learned to put together some simple sentences in some language. So a rudimentary language subsystem is in place in the brain. Can the child now extract the rules of the language learned so far? Again, perhaps not. These examples can go on and on.

The final blow to the idea of rule extraction in the brain comes from the very idea that there is a module or subsystem in the brain (call it the "rule extractor" for convenience) that can access, read and extract rules from any network in the brain. There is no evidence for it in neuroscience and no such empowering module is conceived in connectionism either. If it did exist, humans wouldn't have any trouble extracting and stating rules from any of the networks in the examples discussed above.

2.3   A summary of this section

This section has argued that there is no rule extraction in the brain. It did so mainly by examining behavioral facts about human learning and the ability of humans to extract and express rules from the operational subsystems of their brains. The section did not get into the architectural details of the operational subsystems (the biological networks), but only assumed that the biological networks existed in some operational form. So it did not get into the symbolic/subsymbolic issue.

3.   On the conflict between rule extraction and connectionism

This section points out a basic conflict between the idea of rule extraction, both symbolic and fuzzy types, and connectionism. In section 4 it shows how control theoretic ideas can resolve this problem and how connectionism itself uses such control theoretic ideas without explicitly acknowledging it.

The general idea of reading (extracting) rules from a neural network has a fundamental conflict with the ideas of connectionism. This is because the connectionist networks by "themselves" are inherently incapable of producing the "rules," that are embedded in the network, as output, since the "rules" are not supposed to be the outputs of connectionist networks. And in connectionism, there is no provision for an external source (a neuron or a network of neurons), in a sense a third party, to read the rules embedded in a particular connectionist network. Some more clarification perhaps is needed on this point. The connectionist framework [12, 13, 33, 44, 45, 50] in the use mode, has provision only for providing certain inputs (real, binary) to a network through the input nodes and obtaining certain outputs (real, binary) from the network through the output nodes. That is, in fact, the only "mode of operation" of a connectionist network. In other words, that is all one can get from a connectionist network in terms of output - nothing else is allowed in the connectionist framework. So no symbolic or fuzzy rules can be "output" or "read" by a connectionist network. The connectionist network, in a sense, is a "closed entity" in the use mode; no other type of operation, other than the regular input-output operation, can be performed by or with the network. There is no provision for any "extra or outside procedures" in the connectionist framework to examine and interpret a network, to look into the rules it's using or the internal representation it has learned or created. So, for example, the connectionist framework has no provision for "reading" a weight from a network or for finding out the kind of rule/constraint learned by a node. The existence of any "outside procedure" for such a task, in existence outside of the network where the rules are, would go against the basic connectionist philosophy. Connectionism has never stated that the networks can be "examined and accessed in ways" other than the input-output mode. So the connectionist network is a fairly "sealed" system.

So there is nothing in the connectionist framework that lets one develop procedures to read and extract rules from a network. So a rule extraction procedure's first major violation of the principles of connectionism is in invoking a means of extracting the weights and rules and other information from a network. There is no provision/mechanism in the connectionist framework for doing that. Second, the rule extraction algorithms often do some refinements of the networks "directly", by changing some of the weights and other parameters of the network, without using a local learning law [3, 7, 15, 18, 25, 26, 31, 47, 48, 51, 52, 53 and others]. So a second major violation of the connectionist principles is in storing the modified weights and other parameters back on the network by "means" other than what is allowed by connectionism. The connectionist framework has a specific, well-defined mechanism for changing weights and other parameters: only the nodes of a network can change the connection weights and other parameters through their local learning laws. But that is the only means allowed - it does not allow a separate means (an external agent) to change those weights or any other parameters. So any algorithmic process or operation that uses such extra means to change the weights and other parameters of a network would be in complete violation of the principles of connectionism.

So the whole notion of rules existing in a network, which can be accessed and verbalized as necessary, is contradictory to the connectionist philosophy. There is absolutely no provision for "accessing rules" in the connectionist framework. Connectionism forgot about the need to extract rules.

As is obvious from the above discussion, the connectionist ideas do not permit the reading of rules from a network or the adjustment of networks by means other than local learning laws. So, if the rules are to be read and the networks are to be adjusted by means other than local learning laws, then some alternative ideas about how the brain works and learns are required. One such alternative is the control theoretic framework proposed recently in [38, 43]. A new body of arguments has been presented to support the control theoretic notion. The control theoretic framework postulates that there are parts of the brain that control other parts and it allows for greater freedom in constructing learning algorithms and other procedures, such as rule extraction and network adjustment algorithms. So, under the control theoretic framework, "direct" adjustment and reading of network parameters (connection weights, node parameters and so on), by agents external to a particular network, would be acceptable. But beware that having said that the control theoretic framework would allow for such rule extraction procedures, there is still doubt whether the brain actually does any rule extraction of this type.

It is perhaps important to note at this point that connectionist systems are not supposed to have controllers in them. Here is a John Haugeland characterization of connectionist networks (from "What is Mind Design" by John Haugeland in [23]: "There is no central processor or controller, and also no separate memory or storage mechanism." So the proposed control theoretic paradigm for the brain is in direct conflict with connectionism. But the next section shows that connectionism itself uses control theoretic ideas without explicitly acknowledging it.

4.   Connectionism is nothing but control theory

It has been argued by connectionists [2, 13, 19, 20, 21, 28, 29, 44, 45 and many others] that their methods do not embody standard control theory concepts, that they have introduced a qualitatively new set of concepts and mechanisms. This section argues that connectionist systems are indeed based on control theoretic notions. It makes this argument by first examining the basic control theory concepts and then showing that some of the simplest connectionist learning methods - like back-propagation, adaptive resonance theory (ART), reduced coulomb energy (RCE), and radial basis function (RBF) - are actually based on those standard control theoretic notions. More complex connectionist systems, such as those that are either similar in structure to those simple systems or are based on those simple systems, are also, by extension, based on standard control theoretic notions. This section, therefore, refutes the claim of connectionism that their methods do not embody standard control theory concepts. This implies that standard control theoretic notions should be applicable to developing systems similar to the brain and in understanding how the brain works and learns [38, 40, 41, 42, 43].

The section is organized as follows. Section 4.1 characterizes the notion of control and controllers in any system. In section 4.2, it is argued that some of the simplest connectionist systems are actually based on standard control theory concepts. This is followed by a summary in section 4.3.

4.1 Standard Control Theory - What are controllers? What are their characteristics?

In general, most complex systems can be decomposed into various subsystems according to their functionality. Controller-based systems are characterized by the presence of one or more controllers in them, controllers that control one or more subsystems within the system. In other words, in a controller-based system, there might be one or more subsystems in control of other subsystems that are subservient to them in some sense. Thus, in this case, the controlling subsystem can be called the "master" subsystem.

The main function of a controller is to supply certain operating parameters to the subservient subsystem. And that can be done in a variety of ways. Perhaps some examples will clarify this notion. For example, many man-made devices are generally operated by humans - e.g. a car, an airplane, or a TV. In these overall systems, the car, the airplane or the TV is the "subservient" subsystem and the human is the controller, the "master" subsystem. The overall system consists of both the man-made device (the car, the airplane, or the TV) and the human. The human in these systems supplies the operating parameters to the subservient subsystems. For example, the human uses the accelerator of a vehicle to set its speed, its steering wheel to determine its direction of movement, and the buttons of a remote control to control a TV. In subsequent discussions, the subservient subsystem, without its controller, will simply be called the "system" and the subservient system plus the controller will be called the "overall system."

4.1.1 The argument against the notion of a controller in any system

Before proceeding further, one has to deal with the arguments against the very notion of a controller, because the notion of a controller in any system is very much disputed by many in brain-related sciences. Dealing with this issue also brings out a very important property of controllers. The standard argument against controllers runs as follows: The car, the airplane or the TV that is operated by a human is actually a feedback system. In a feedback system, a subsystem receives inputs (feedback) from the other subsystems, and these inputs (feedback) are then used to determine its output(s), its course of action. Thus these subsystems are completely dependent on each other (co-dependent) for their outputs and, therefore, there is no subsystem controlling another subsystem in these overall systems. Thus, the argument goes, it is not proper to characterize the human as the controller in any of the above-mentioned systems - the car, the airplane, or the TV – because the human determines the course of action based on information (feedback) from these subsystems. Thus, it is further argued, if one is intent on claiming that the human is the controller in these overall systems, then the system itself (the car, the airplane, or the TV) can also be claimed to be the "controller," the one that controls the human. So, by these arguments, there are no controllers (central or distributed) in any system, natural or man-made.

On the surface, the above arguments seem to be correct, because in a feedback system, as in the examples above, the so-called controller's actions depend on the state of the subsystem it is trying to control. So the output of any subsystem, including the controller, is a function of the inputs (feedback) received by it from the other subsystems. So one is back to ground zero in trying to characterize controllers and distinguish them from the subsystems they control.

4.1.2 Back to square one – So who is a controller? What are its characteristics?

This "no controller in any system" argument has to be dealt with first before proceeding any further. A fundamental characteristic of a controller, unlike the system that it controls, is that it can determine its course of action (its output signals, that is) without considering the state of the system it is trying to control. In other words, the controller can also operate in a non-feedback mode. That means, it can operate with other types of inputs for the generation of its control signals and it is thus not necessarily dependent on feedback from the system it is trying to control. So a controller, by its very nature, is capable of operating in a manner independent of the system it is trying to control. Some examples will clarify this notion. For example, a person who is operating a TV with a remote control can simply close his or her eyes and turn the TV ON or OFF at random or in some predetermined fashion without considering what is being shown on the TV. Thus turning the TV ON or OFF is no longer depended on what is on the TV; the TV no longer has any influence on the controller - that is, the person with the remote control. But the operation of the system itself (the TV) still depends on the ON/OFF signal from the controller, that can't be or has not changed. In the case of a heating/air conditioning system, the thermostat can be set to turn the heating/cooling system ON or OFF every minute, or on the basis of any other predetermined time intervals, without any consideration of the actual temperature. Similarly, a driver can operate a car in a non-feedback mode by driving with the eyes closed and ears blocked, cutting-off all feedback through those channels, although the risk of an accident would increase substantially.

Thus the basic nature of a controller in any system is that it can operate in many different modes, with a different set of inputs, and therefore it's operation is not necessarily based on feedback from the system it is trying to control. The controller can still send different operating instructions to the subsystem it is controlling, but those operating instructions no longer depend on feedback of information from that subsystem. In contrast, the basic system itself is still dependent on operating instructions from the controller for its operation, that can't be changed. This is the main distinguishing character of a controller. And this is the character that entitles it to be called the "master" subsystem, because it can send signals (inputs) to the basic system and operate it in any arbitrary manner, even though other inputs to the basic system have not changed. In other words, the basic system is "depended" on the controller for its operations, but there is no such dependency the other way round.

It is important to clarify here that "controllers" can exist in other types of systems; they are not limited to being components of continuous, interactive feedback systems only. For example, many "master" subsystems have no continuous contact with their "subservient" subsystems. For instance, consider a doctor who provides treatment and medication to a person who is ill. After a certain treatment or medication, the doctor may not have any contact with the actual biological processes of the patient for a while, unless there is some kind of continuous monitoring system used to monitor the patient. Suppose, the doctor monitors the condition of the patient daily and tries other medication or treatment if something doesn't work. In this situation, the doctor is not in continuous contact with the subservient system (the patient), but only has intermittent contact. The doctor, however, is still the controller in this situation, since he or she can be arbitrary in the treatment of the patient. So this is a type of system where the controller can be "out-of-contact" with the subservient system for some period of time. In other systems, the controller can be the source of a single, one-time signal or decision, instead of multiple signals or decisions being provided in continuous feedback systems. Examples of such situations include 1) starting a random fire in a forest, and 2) spreading a bad rumor that starts a riot in some place. One might claim that the controller in this case loses control of the subservient system. But despite the subsequent "out-of-control" character of the subservient system, there is no question about the controlling nature of the "master" subsystem that starts the process. So, the "master" subsystem in all of these different systems are still "controllers" because of the arbitrary way in which they can determine the signals being sent to the "subservient" subsystems, whether it is one-time or multiple times.

4.2 Is connectionism based on standard control theory notions?

To answer the question "Is connectionism based on standard control theory notions?" one has to establish that connectionist systems either have controllers inside them or use outside controllers or both. To establish this, all one needs to do is examine some of the simpler connectionist learning systems and show that they use controllers. Once that is established, it then follows by logical extension that more complex connectionist systems, those that in turn use these simpler learning mechanisms or are similar in structure, also use controllers, and thus are based on control theory notions. The logical analysis of the simpler connectionist learning systems is based on the following determination: (1) what decisions are being made by the individual subsystems, (2) whether those decisions are being conveyed from one subsystem to another, (3) whether those decisions can potentially be arbitrary, and lastly, (4) what decisions are being conveyed to these systems from the outside by external sources. In general, if a potentially arbitrary decision made in one subsystem A is conveyed to and used by another subsystem B, then it means that subsystem A controls subsystem B. The key test here for a subsystem to be characterized as a controller is its "potential to be arbitrary." In the normal mode of operation, a controller might very well operate on the basis of certain rules, but that does not negate the fact that it is still a controller with the "potential to be arbitrary." For example, the motor control portion of the brain operates on the basis of some rules acquired over time, but that does not mean that it can't control the various limbs of the body in an arbitrary manner without following those rules. Similarly, the central bank in a country might operate on the basis of some economic models and rules, but that does not mean it "potentially" can't set the interest rates in an arbitrary manner ignoring those models and rules, although that might never happen.

It would be appropriate at this time to examine a few simple connectionist systems and establish that they use standard control theory notions. Here some standard connectionist learning methods are examined and it is shown that they employ controllers in their operation and thus they, in turn, use standard control theory concepts. As stated earlier, larger and more complex connectionist systems, those that employ these simple learning mechanisms or are similar in structure to them, would also be using control theory notions, because the subsystems embedded in them do or because of their similarity in structure to these simpler systems. It might be appropriate to start with the best-known connectionist learning method: the back propagation algorithm [44]. For algorithms like back-propagation, including any variations of it, an external agent (perhaps a human, perhaps another module in an overall connectionist system) supplies from the outside the design of a network and the values for the various learning parameters that are necessary for it to learn. Since the outside agent can determine the network design and the various learning parameters potentially in an arbitrary fashion (this arbitrary nature of the agent can be verified with certainty when a human is the external agent and is providing the information to back-propagation), the outside agent is therefore a controller for the back-propagation method. Thus the back-propagation learning method employs an external controller, much like a driver in a car or a pilot in an airplane. The back propagation algorithm, therefore, is based on standard control theory notions.

For other connectionist learning methods like adaptive resonance theory (ART) [19, 20, 21], the reduced coulomb energy (RCE) [37], the radial basis function (RBF) networks [35] and the like, the network design module is inside the algorithm. So where is the controller in them? The usual design task in ART, RBF, RCE and the like is to add a new prototype or exemplar (a center and a radius or width) to the network. The design task, therefore, is to expand the size of the network as and when necessary. The training task is to make adjustments to all those prototypes or exemplars – that is, to adjust their centers and widths or radii. So, logically, the design and training functions are housed in separate modules in these learning schemes. So, as before, the design module supplies to the training module the design of a network. So the logical structure of these algorithms is similar to back-propagation - the network design and training modules are decoupled and the design module supplies design decisions to the training module. Therefore, since the network design decisions and decisions about the various learning parameters come from one or more outside sources to the training module (the network design from the design module; the various learning parameter values provided by sources external to the algorithm, perhaps a human or another module within an overall system), these outside sources act as controllers to the training module in algorithms like ART, RBF, RCE and the like. Thus these learning methods (ART, RCE, RBF, and the like) employ one or more controllers (internal and external) in order to work. These learning methods, therefore, are based on standard control theory notions.

Again, if these methods are embedded and used in more complex connectionist systems, then they too, by extension, are based on standard control theory notions.

For the algorithms discussed here, and for other connectionist systems with similar structures or connectionist systems that embed these algorithms within them, the interaction between the training module and the controlling source(s) (human outside agents, internal modules) is not just a one-time affair. In fact, the training modules of these algorithms come back to the controlling sources over and over again with their results and the controlling sources then, if not satisfied with the results, provide new network designs and new sets of parameter values and orders the training modules to get new solutions on that basis. This is much like a doctor trying a particular medication or treatment on a patient, waiting to see the outcome after such a treatment, and if the outcome is not satisfactory, trying a different medication or treatment and so on. So the interaction between the training modules and the controlling sources in these algorithms, like the doctor case, is not just a one-time affair; it happens continually. However, the controlling sources are out-of-contact with the training modules for the time during which they are getting a solution, much like the doctor and patient case.

Note that the use of control theoretic concepts is part of the conceptual structure of these learning systems, independent of how they are implemented and, in particular, whether or not a neurocomputer, with parallel computation capabilities, is used for implementation. Also note that the foregoing analysis of the learning methods was based strictly on their logical structure and nothing else.

4.3   A summary of this section

This section proposed to show that standard control theory concepts are used in connectionists systems. It has done this in two parts. First, it examined the notion of control and controllers in any system and characterized controllers as subsystems in an overall system that can operate in an arbitrary manner. Using this characterization, it then performed a logical analysis of the structure of some core connectionist learning systems - like back-propagation, adaptive resonance theory (ART), reduced coulomb energy (RCE), and radial basis function (RBF) - and showed that they have and do use controllers in them. Sometimes these controllers are housed within the learning system, sometimes they are external to the learning system (like back-propagation and the like), and sometimes it is a combination of the two (like ART, RCE, RBF and the like). But the section clearly establishes that controllers do exist in these systems and thus these systems are based on control theory concepts. By logical extension, the more complex connectionist systems, the ones that use these simpler learning mechanisms inside them or rely on them in some other manner or are similar in structure, also use controllers and are, in turn, based on standard control theory notions. This refutes the claim in connectionism that their methods do not embody standard control theory concepts, that they have introduced a qualitatively new set of concepts and mechanisms. This implies that control theory concepts can indeed be used to construct brain-like systems and in understanding how the brain works and learns [38, 40, 41, 42].

5. Conclusions

This paper has questioned whether there is any rule extraction in the human brain. It has also argued that there is an inherent conflict between rule-extraction and connectionism and that rule extraction procedures require control theoretic notions. It has further argued that connectionism uses control theoretic notions and thus connectionism is not a new kind of computing mechanism. Hence both rule extraction and connectionism are depended on control theory principles.

References

[1]   Abe, S. and M.-S. Lan (1995). *Fuzzy Rule Extraction Directly from Numerical Data for Function Approximation*. IEEE Trans. Systems, Man & Cybernetics, 25:119--129.

[2]   Alexander, J. A. & Mozer, M. C. (1995). *Template-based algorithms for connectionist rule extraction*. In Tesauro, G., Touretzky, D., & Leen, T., editors, Advances in Neural Information Processing Systems (volume 7). MIT Press.

[3]   Andrews, R., Diederich, J. and Tickle, A. B. (1995). *A survey and critique of techniques for extracting rules from trained artificial neural networks*. Knowledge-based Systems, 8, 6, 373-389.

[4]   Andrews, R. and J. Diederich, eds, (1996). *Proceedings of the NIPS'96 Workshop on Rule Extraction From Trained Artificial Neural Networks*. NIPS Foundation.

[5]   Apolloni, B., Malchiodi, D., Orovas, C., and Palmas, G. (2000a). *Learning rule representations from data*. Under review.

[6]   Apolloni, B., Malchiodi, D., Orovas, C., and Palmas, G. (2000b). *From synapses to rules*. In Foundations of Connectionist-symbolic Integration: Representation, Paradigms, and Algorithms – Proceedings of the 14th European Conference on Artificial Intelligence.

[7]   Boden, M. (1994). Horses of a Different Color? In: Honavar, V. and Uhr, L. (Ed.)
Artificial Intelligence and Neural Networks: Steps Toward Principled Integration. New
York: Academic Press.

[8] Buckley, J. J. and Hayashi, Y. (1994). *Fuzzy neural networks*. In: Yager, R. and Zadeh, L. (Ed.) Fuzzy Sets, Neural Networks and Soft Computing. New York: Van Nostrand Reinhold.

[9] Carpenter, G.A. and Tan, A.-H. (1995). *Rule extraction: From neural architecture to symbolic representation*. Connection Science, 7, 3--27.

[10] Carpenter, G. A. and Grossberg, S. (1994). *Fuzzy ARTMAP: A synthesis of neural networks and fuzzy logic for supervised categorization and nonstationary prediction*. In: Yager, R. and Zadeh, L. (Ed.) Fuzzy Sets, Neural Networks and Soft Computing. New York: Van Nostrand Reinhold.

[11] Craven, M. W. and Shavlik, J. W. (1994). *Using sampling and queries to extract rules from trained neural networks*. Machine Learning: Proceedings of the Eleventh International Conference, San Francisco, CA.

[12] Fahlman, S. E. and Hinton, G. E. (1987). Connectionists Architectures for Artificial
Intelligence. *Computer*, 20, 100-109.

[13] Feldman, J. A. and Ballard, D. A. (1982). Connectionists Models and Their Properties. *Cognitive Science*, 6, 205-254.

[14] Frasconi, P., Gori, M., Maggini, M., and Soda, G. (1995). *Unified integration of explicit rules and learning by example in recurrent networks*. IEEE Transactions on Knowledge and Data Engineering, vol. 7, no. 2, pp. 340-346.

[15] Fu, L. M. (1994). *Rule generation from neural networks*. IEEE Transactions on Systems, Man and Cybernetics, 24 (8), pp. 1114-1124.

[16] Giles, L. and C.W. Omlin (1993). *Extraction, insertion and refinement of symbolic rules in dynamically-driven recurrent neural networks*. Connection Science, 5(3,4):307--337, Special Issue on Architectures for Integrating Symbolic and Neural Processes.

[17] Giles, L. and Christian W. Omlin (1994). *Extraction and insertion of symbolic information in recurrent neural networks*. In V. Honavar and L. Uhr, editors, Artificial Intelligence and Neural Networks: Steps toward Principled Integration, pages 271--299. Academic Press.

[18] Goonatilake, S. and S. Khebbal (Ed.), (1995), *Intelligent Hybrid Systems*. New York: Wiley.

[19] Grossberg, S. (1982). Studies of Mind and Brain: Neural Principles of Learning Perception, Development, Cognition, and Motor Control. Boston: Reidell Press.

[20] Grossberg, S. (1987). Competitive learning: From interactive activation to adaptive
resonance. Cognitive Science, 11, 23-63.

[21] Grossberg, S. (1988). Nonlinear neural networks: principles, mechanisms, and architectures. *Neural Networks*, 1, 17-61.

[22] Gupta, M. M. and Rao, D. H. (1994). *On the principles of fuzzy neural networks*. Fuzzy Sets and Systems, 61, 1, 1 – 18.

[23] Haugeland, J. (1996). What is Mind Design. Chapter 1 in Haugeland, J. (ed), Mind
Design II, 1997, MIT Press, 1-28.

[24] Honavar, V. and Uhr, L. (Ed.), (1994), *Artificial Intelligence and Neural Networks: Steps Toward Principled Integration*. New York, NY: Academic Press.

[25] Honavar, V. and Uhr, L. (1995). *Integrating Symbol Processing Systems and Connectionist Networks*. In: Goonatilake, S. and Khebbal, S. (Ed.) Intelligent Hybrid Systems. New York: Wiley.

[26] Horwitz, B., Friston, K. J., and Taylor, J. G. (2000). *Neural modeling and functional brain imaging: an overview*. Neural Networks, Vol. 13, No. 8-9, 829-846.

[27] Keller, J. M. and Hunt, D. (1985). *Incorporating fuzzy membership functions into*
the perceptron algorithm. IEEE Trans. Pattern Anal. Machine Intelligence, 7, 693-699.

[28] Kohonen, T. (1988). An introduction to neural networks. *Neural Networks*, 1, 3-16.

[29] Kohonen, T. (1989). Self-organization and associative memory. 3rd ed. Berlin, Heidelberg: Spriger-Verlag.

[30] Kosko, B. (1992). *Neural Networks and Fuzzy Systems*. Prentice Hall, Englewood Cliffs, NJ.

[31] Levine, D. and Apariciov, M.. (Ed.) (1994). *Neural Networks for Knowledge Representation*. New York: Lawrence Erlbaum.

[32] Lin, C. T. and Lee, C. S. G. (1994). *Supervised and unsupervised learning with fuzzy similarity for neural network-based fuzzy logic control systems*. In: Yager, R. and Zadeh, L. (Ed.) Fuzzy Sets, Neural Networks and Soft Computing. New York: Van Nostrand Reinhold.

[33] McClelland, J. L. (1985). Putting knowledge in its place: A scheme for programming
parallel processing structures on the fly. *Cognitive Science*,9,113-146.

[34] McClelland, J.L., McNaughton, B.L., and O'Reilly, R.C. (1995). *Why there are complementary learning systems in hippocampus and neocortex: Insights from the successes and failures of connectionist models of learning and memory.* Psychological Review. 102: 419-457.

[35] Moody, J. & Darken, C. (1989). Fast Learning in Networks of Locally-Tuned Processing Units, *Neural Computation*, 1(2), 281-294.

[36] Pal, S. K. & Mitra, S. (1992). *Multi-layer perceptrons, fuzzy sets and classification.* IEEE Transactions on Neural Networks, NN-3, 683-697.

[37] Reilly, D.L., Cooper, L.N. and Elbaum, C. (1982). A Neural Model for Category
Learning. *Biological Cybernetics*, 45, 35-41.

[38] Roy, A. (2000). *On Connectionism, Rule Extraction and Brain-like Learning.* IEEE Transactions on Fuzzy Systems, Vol. 8, No. 2, pp. 222-227.

[39] Roy, A., Kim, L.S. & Mukhopadhyay, S. (1993). *A Polynomial Time Algorithm for the Construction and Training of a Class of Multilayer Perceptrons.* Neural Networks, Vol. 6, No. 4, pp. 535-545.

[40] Roy, A., Govil, S. & Miranda, R. (1995). *An Algorithm to Generate Radial Basis Function (RBF)-like Nets for Classification Problems.* Neural Networks, Vol. 8, No. 2, pp. 179-202.

[41] Roy, A., Govil, S. & Miranda, R. (1997a). *A Neural Network Learning Theory and a polynomial Time RBF Algorithm.* IEEE Transactions on Neural Networks,8, 6, pp. 1301-1313.

[42] Roy, A. & Mukhopadhyay, S. (1997b). *Iterative Generation of Higher-Order Nets in Polynomial Time Using Linear Programming.* IEEE Transactions on Neural Networks, 8, 2,402-412.

[43] Roy, A. (1999). *Brain's internal mechanisms – a new paradigm.* Proceedings of the International Joint Conference on Neural Networks (IJCNN'99), Washington, D.C., paper no. 259.

[44] Rumelhart, D.E., and McClelland, J.L.(eds.) (1986). Parallel Distributed Processing:
Explorations in Microstructure of Cognition, Vol. 1: Foundations. MIT Press, Cambridge,
MA., 318-362.

286

[45] Rumelhart, D.E. (1989). The Architecture of Mind: A Connectionist Approach. Chapter 8 in Haugeland, J. (ed), Mind Design II, 1997, MIT Press, 205-232.

[46] Shadmehr, R. and Holcomb, H. (1997). *Neural correlates of motor memory consolidation.* Science, Vol. 277, pp. 821-825.

[47] Setiono, R. and Liu, H. (1996). *Symbolic Representation of Neural Networks.* IEEE Computer, 29(3), pp. 71-76.

[48] Setiono, R. and Liu, H. (1997). *NeuroLinear: From neural networks to oblique decision rules.* Neurocomputing, 17, pp. 1-24.

[49] Simpson, P. K. (1992). *Fuzzy min-max neural networks – part I: Classification.* IEEE Trans. On Neural Networks, 3, 5, 776-786.

[50] Smolensky, P. (1989). Connectionist Modeling: Neural Computation/Mental Connections. Chapter 9 in Haugeland, J. (ed), Mind Design II, 1997, MIT Press, 233-250.

[51] Sun, R. (1994). *Logic and Variables in Connectionist Networks: A Brief Overview.* In: Honavar, V. and Uhr, L. (Ed.) Artificial Intelligence and Neural Networks: Steps Toward Principled Integration. New York: Academic Press.

[52] Sun, R. (1994). *Integrating Rules and Connectionism for Robust Commonsense Reasoning.* John Wiley and Sons, New York, NY.

[53] Sun, R. and Bookman, L. (Ed.) (1995), *Computational Architectures Integrating Symbolic and Neural Processes.* New York: Kluwer.

[54] Takagi, H. & Hayasi, A. (1991). *NN-driven fuzzy reasoning.* Int. J. Approximate Reasoning. 5, 191-212.

[55] Towell, G. and Shavlik, J. (1993). *The extraction of refined rules from knowledge-based neural networks.* Machine Learning, 13, 1, 71-101.

[56] Yuan, F., Feldkamp, L.A., Davis, L.I., & Puskorius, G.V. (1992). *Training a hybrid neural-fuzzy system.* Proceedings of IJCNN'92, Baltimore, Vol. II, pp. 739-744.

[57] Yager, R. R. (1993). *Generalized fuzzy and matrix associative holographic memories.* J. of Int. and Fuzzy Systems, 1, 1, 43-53.

[58] Zadeh, L. A. (1965). *Fuzzy Sets.* Information and Control, 8, 338-353.

[59] Zadeh, L. A. (1973). *Outline of a new approach to the analysis of complex systems and decision process.* IEEE Trans. Systems, Man and Cybernetics, 3, 1, 28-44.

Beyond Simple Rule Extraction: Acquiring Planning Knowledge from Neural Networks

Ron Sun

CECS Department, University of Missouri
Columbia, MO, USA

Todd Peterson

Computer Science Department, Brigham Young University
Provo, Utah, USA

Chad Sessions

Computer Science Department, University of Alabama
Tuscaloosa, AL, USA

Abstract

This paper discusses learning in hybrid models that goes beyond simple classification rule extraction from backpropagation networks. Although simple rule extraction has received a lot of research attention, we need to further develop hybrid learning models that learn autonomously and acquire both symbolic and subsymbolic knowledge. It is also necessary to study autonomous learning of both subsymbolic and symbolic knowledge in integrated architectures. This paper will describe planning knowledge extraction from neural reinforcement learning that goes beyond extracting simple rules. It includes two approaches towards extracting planning knowledge: the extraction of symbolic rules from neural reinforcement learning, and the extraction of complete plans. This work points to a general framework for achieving the subsymbolic to symbolic transition in an integrated autonomous learning framework.

1 Introduction

This paper will discuss learning in hybrid models that goes beyond simple classification rule extraction from backpropagation networks. Although simple rule extraction has received a lot of research attention (Fu 1991, Towell and Shavlik 1993, Tickle et al 2000), we need to further develop hybrid learning models that learn autonomously and acquire both symbolic and subsymbolic knowledge. It is necessary to study autonomous learning of both subsymbolic and symbolic knowledge from scratch, without requiring a priori domain knowledge to begin with, in integrated architectures. In this regard, this paper will describe planning knowledge extraction from neural reinforcement learning (see Sun 1997, Sun and Peterson 1998, Sun et al 2000, Sun and Sessions 1998). It includes two approaches towards extracting planning knowledge: the extraction of explicit, symbolic, planning rules from neural reinforcement learners, and the extraction of complete explicit plans from such learners. The advantages of symbolic knowledge extraction include (1) the improvement of learning (especially with the rule extraction approach), and (2) the improvement of the usability of results of neural reinforcement learning. Theoretically speaking, this work points to a general framework for achieving the subsymbolic to symbolic transition in an integrated autonomous learning framework (Sun 2000).

2 Hybrid Learning through Knowledge Extraction

We will first review reinforcement learning. Then we will detail rule extraction and plan extraction in turn.

2.1 Sequential Decision Tasks and Reinforcement Learning

In sequential decision tasks, an agent needs to perform a sequence of actions to reach some goal states. It learns autonomously to perform such tasks, from scratch, without teacher input. The characteristics of such a setting, which is the most essential in the real world, include: autonomous and on-line learning, non-stationary environments (revision of knowledge), no external teacher input (no known correct output), and so on.

One possible algorithm for dealing with this type of setting is Q-learning (Watkins 1989). A Q-value is an evaluation of the "quality" of an action in a given state: $Q(x,a)$ indicates how desirable action a is in state x (which consists of sensory input). One easy way of choosing an action is to choose the one that maximizes the Q-value in the current state; that is, we choose a if $Q(x,a) = \max_i Q(x,i)$. To ensure adequate exploration, a stochastic decision process, for example, based on Boltzmann distribution, can be used, so that different actions can be tried in accordance with their respective probabilities to ensure various possibilities are all looked into. That is,

$$p(a|x) = \frac{e^{Q(x,a)/\alpha}}{\sum_i e^{Q(x,a_i)/\alpha}}$$

Here α controls the degree of randomness (temperature) of the decision-making process.

To acquire the Q-values, we use the *Q-learning* algorithm (Watkins 1989). In the algorithm, $Q(x,a)$ estimates the maximum discounted cumulative reinforcement that the agent will receive from the current state x on:

$$\max(\sum_{i=0}^{\infty} \gamma^i r_i),$$

where γ is a discount factor that favors reinforcement received sooner relative to that received later, and r_i is the reinforcement received at step i (which may be 0). The updating of $Q(x, a)$ is based on minimizing

$$r + \gamma e(y) - Q(x, a)$$

where γ is a discount factor, $e(y) = \max_a Q(y, a)$, and y is the new state resulting from action a. Thus, the updating is based on the *temporal difference* in evaluating the current state and the action chosen. Through successive updates of the Q function, the agent can learn to take into account future steps in longer and longer sequences notably without explicit planning (Watkins 1989). The agent may eventually converge to a stable function and find an optimal sequence that maximizes the reinforcement received. Hence, the agent learns to deal with sequential decision tasks, in an autonomous, on-line fashion, without requiring any a priori domain-specific knowledge. Note that Q-learning can be implemented in a backpropagation network.

2.2 Rule Extraction

A two-level model (the CLARION model) was developed for extracting rules and using them along with neural reinforcement learning (Sun 1997, Sun and Peterson 1997, 1998, Sun et al 2000). In the model, the bottom level is a backprop net implementing Q-learning (Watkins 1989, Lin 1992, Tesauro 1992) and the top level is a localist rule net (Sun 1992; see details later).

2.2.1 The Algorithm

A high-level pseudo-code algorithm that describes the operation of the model is as follows:

1. Observe the current state x.
2. Compute in the bottom level the Q-values of x associated with each of all the possible actions a_i's: $Q(x, a_1)$, $Q(x, a_2)$, ..., $Q(x, a_n)$.
3. Find out all the possible actions $(b_1, b_2, ..., b_m)$ at the top level, based on the input x and the rules in place.
4. Compare the values of a_i's with those of b_j's, and choose an appropriate action b
5. Perform the action b, and observe the next state y and (possibly) the reinforcement r.
6. Update the bottom level in accordance with *Q-Learning*.
7. Update the top level with *Rule-Extraction-Revision*.
8. Go back to Step 1.

The Bottom Level. It implements Q-learning. To implement Q-learning, we chose to use a four-layered network, in which the first three layers form a backpropagation network for computing Q-values and the fourth layer (with only one node) performs stochastic decision making. The output of the third layer (i.e., the output layer of the backpropagation network) indicates the Q-value of each action (represented by an individual node), and the node in the fourth layer determines probabilistically the action to be performed based on a Boltzmann distribution (Watkins 1989).

The learning of the network is based on minimizing the following:

$$err_i = \begin{cases} r + \gamma e(y) - Q(x,a) & \text{if } a_i = a \\ 0 & \text{otherwise} \end{cases}$$

where i is the index for an output node representing the action a_i.

Q-learning allows autonomous learning (without any a priori domain knowledge) of closed-loop action policies in sequential decision tasks, from which symbolic rules and plans can be extracted. The use of neural networks in implementing Q-learning is due to the need to deal with huge state spaces in many tasks (Lin 1992, Tesauro 1992, Sutton 1996).

The Top Level. We devised a novel rule learning algorithm based on neural reinforcement learning. The basic idea is as follows: the agent performs rule learning (extraction and subsequent revision) at each step, which is associated with the following information: (x, y, r, a), where x is the state before action a is performed, y is the new state entered after an action a is performed, and r is the reinforcement received after action a. If some action decided by the bottom level is successful then the agent extracts a rule that corresponds to the decision and adds the rule to the rule network. Then, in subsequent interactions with the world, the agent verifies the extracted rule by considering the outcome of applying the rule: if the outcome is not successful, then the rule should be made more specific and exclusive of the current case; if the outcome is successful, the agent may try to generalize the rule to make it more universal. Rules are in the following form: *conditions* $\longrightarrow$ *action*, where the left-hand side is a conjunction of individual conditions each of which refers to a primitive: a value range or a value in a dimension of the (sensory) input state.

At each step, the agent updates the following statistics for each rule condition and each of its minor variations (i.e., the rule condition plus/minus one value), with regard to the action a performed: that is, PM_a (i.e., Positive Match) and NM_a (i.e., Negative Match). Here, positivity/negativity is determined by the following inequality: $\max_b Q(y,b) - Q(x,a) + r > threshold$, which indicates whether or not the action is reasonably good. Based on these statistics, the information gain measure is calculated; that is,

$$IG(A, B) = log_2 \frac{PM_a(A) + 1}{PM_a(A) + NM_a(A) + 2} - log_2 \frac{PM_a(B) + 1}{PM_a(B) + NM_a(B) + 2}$$

where A and B are two different conditions that lead to the same action a. The measure compares essentially the percentage of positive matches under different conditions A and B (with the Laplace estimator; Lavrac and Dzeroski 1994). If A can improve the percentage to a certain degree over B, then A is considered better than B. In the algorithm, if a rule is better compared with the match-all rule (i.e, the rule with the condition that matches all inputs), then the rule is considered successful (for the purpose of deciding on expansion or shrinking operations).

The agent decides on whether or not to extract a rule based on a simple success criterion which is fully determined by the current step (x, y, r, a):

- *Extraction*: if $r + \gamma e(y) - Q(x, a) > threshold$, where a is the action performed in state x and y is the resulting new state (that is, if the current step is successful), and if there is no rule that covers this step in the top level, set up a rule $C \longrightarrow a$, where C specifies the values of all the input dimensions exactly as in x.

The criterion for applying the *expansion* and *shrinking* operators, on the other hand, is based on the afore-mentioned statistical test. Expansion amounts to adding an additional value to one input dimension in the condition of a rule, so that the rule will have more opportunities of matching inputs, and shrinking amounts to removing one value from one input dimension in the condition of a rule, so that it will have less opportunities of matching inputs. Here are the detailed descriptions of these operators:

- *Expansion*: if $IG(C, all) > threshold1$ and $max_{C'} IG(C', C) \geq 0$, where C is the current condition of a matching rule, *all* refers to the match-all rule (with regard to the same action specified by the rule), and C' is a modified condition such that $C' = C$ plus one value (i.e., C' has one more value in one of the input dimensions) (that is, if the current rule is successful and the expanded condition is potentially better), then set $C'' = argmax_{C'} IG(C', C)$ as the new (expanded) condition of the rule.

- *Shrinking*: if $IG(C, all) < threshold2$ and $max_{C'} IG(C', C) > 0$, where C is the current condition of a matching rule, *all* refers to the match-all rule (with regard to the same action specified by the rule), and C' is a modified condition such that $C' = C$ minus one value (i.e., C' has one less value in one of the input dimensions) (that is, if the current rule is unsuccessful, but the shrunk condition is better), then set $C'' = argmax_{C'} IG(C', C)$ as the new (shrunk) condition of the rule. If shrinking the condition makes it impossible for a rule to match any input state, delete the rule.

The Combination. In the overall algorithm, Step 4 is for making the final decision of which action to take by incorporating outcomes from both levels. The agent combines the corresponding values for an action from the two levels by a weighted sum; that is, if the top level indicates that action a has an activation value v (which should be 0 or 1 as rules are binary) and the bottom level indicates that a has an activation value q (the Q-value), then the final outcome is $w_1 * v + w_2 * q$. Stochastic decision making with Boltzmann distribution based on the weighted sums is then performed to select an action out of all the possible actions. Relative weights or percentages of the two levels are automatically set based on the relative performance of the two levels (Sun and Peterson 1998).

2.2.2 Advantages of Rule Extraction

Extracting rules has some advantages that make it indispensable:

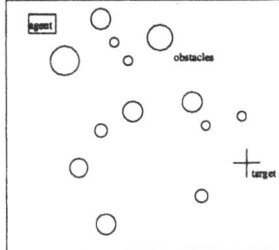

Figure 1: Navigation through a minefield

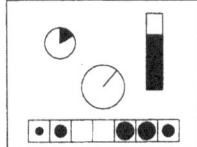

Figure 2: The Navigation Input

The display at the upper left corner is the fuel gauge; the vertical one at the upper right corner is the range gauge; the round one in the middle is the bearing gauge; the 7 sonar gauges are at the bottom.

- Extracted rules can help to speed up learning. If properly used, rules that are extracted on-line during learning can help to facilitate the learning process itself.

- Rules can help to improve the performance of learned systems.

- Rules help to guide the exploration of new situations, and reduce the time necessary to learn in new situations.

- Rules can also help in comprehending and communicating learned skills.

Such advantages have been demonstrated (Sun and Peterson 1998).

For example, we tested CLARION on the simulated navigation task as shown in Figure 1. The agent has to navigate an underwater vessel through a minefield to reach a target location. The agent receives information only from a number of instruments. As shown in Figure 2, the sonar gauge shows how close the mines are in seven equal areas that range from 45 degrees to the left of the agent to 45 degrees to the right. The fuel gauge shows how much time is left before fuel runs out. The bearing gauge shows the direction of the target from the present heading of the agent. The range gauge shows how far the target is from the current location. Based only on such information, the agent decides on (1) how to turn and (2) how fast to move. The time allotted to the agent for each episode is 200 steps. The agent, within an allotted time period, can either (1) reach the target (a success), (2) hit a mine (a failure), or (3) run out of time (a failure).

Mine Density During Training: 10

	Train 10	B+T 10	B 10	T 10	B+T 30	B 30	T 30	B+T 60	B 60	T 60
CLARION	651.8	63.5	6.5	4.5	35.5	1.5	0.5	11.5	1.0	0.0
s.d.	31.3	34.4	4.5	6.9	21.0	2.3	1.5	9.5	2.0	0.0
Q	645.7	82.0			42.0			14.5		
s.d.	86.9	14.2			24.5			18.1		

Figure 3: Learning and transfer from 10-mine minefields

Q refers to the bottom level used alone with Q-learning as the sole learning method. *Train* indicates the total numbers of successful episodes during training. The next three blocks contain performance data (in percentage), in three different mine densities (10, 30, and 60) using the trained models with either the top level, the bottom level, or both together.

Learning speed. Figures 3, 4, and 5 show the data of CLARION. In terms of learning effectiveness, which is measured by the number of successful episodes out of a total of 1000 episodes of training (averaged over 10 runs), the "train" columns of these figures show the difference between CLARION and the bottom-level neural net alone (trained with only Q-learning). It appears that at higher mine densities (that is, in the more difficult settings), CLARION performed significantly better compared with the bottom-level neural net alone. In the 30-mine and 60-mine cases, the superiority of CLARION (over the neural net alone with Q-learning) is statistically significant (with t tests, $p < 0.05$).

Transfer. The right three blocks of Figures 3, 4, and 5 show the transfer data, where transfer is measured by the percentage of successful episodes in new settings by the trained models (each trained model is applied to minefields that contain a *different* number of mines for a total of 20 episodes; the data is averaged over 10 runs). As indicated by the tables, CLARION outperforms the bottom-level neural net alone (trained with Q-learning) in transfer at higher mine densities; the higher the mine density, the more pronounced the difference is. The differences are statistically significant in the 30-mine and 60-mine cases (using t tests, $p < 0.05$). Finally, comparing the transfer performance of the top level, the bottom level, and the whole system, after they are trained together, we notice that the whole system always performs much better than either level alone. Learning rules does help to improve transfer performance.

Trained performance. The right three blocks of Figures 3, 4, and 5 also contain the trained performance data. Trained performance is defined to be the percentage of successful episodes in the *same* settings as used in training by the trained models (each trained model is tested for a total of 20 episodes; the data is averaged over 10 runs). At higher mine densities, the trained performance of CLARION is better than the bottom-level neural net alone (trained with Q-learning). Comparing the performance of the whole system and the two levels separately after the two levels are trained together, we again notice that the whole system performs much better than the bottom level and the top level alone. The differences are statistically significant.

Rules Extracted. Here is a small subset of rules to give an idea:

Bearing: straight ahead

Mine Density During Training: 30

	Train 30	B+T 10	B 10	T 10	B+T 30	B 30	T 30	B+T 60	B 60	T 60
CLARION	663.8	89.0	5.0	1.0	75.0	7.0	0.0	47.5	2.5	0.0
s.d.	48.4	26.5	3.2	2.0	23.6	5.6	0.0	24.9	2.5	0.0
Q	539.1	77.0			68.0			35.5		
s.d.	105.6	17.5			20.4			20.7		

Figure 4: Learning and transfer from 30-mine minefields

Mine Density During Training: 60

	Train 60	B+T 10	B 10	T 10	B+T 30	B 30	T 30	B+T 60	B 60	T 60
CLARION	581.4	99.5	9.5	2.0	96.0	8.5	0.0	76.0	6.0	0.0
s.d.	79.0	1.5	6.5	3.3	3.7	4.5	0.0	15.9	6.6	0.0
Q	495.8	71.5			67.5			47.5		
s.d.	137.9	11.6			16.8			24.3		

Figure 5: Learning and transfer from 60-mine minefields

```
LeastDense: center and right
FurthestMine: center
LeftAvgMineDistance: close
CenterAvgMineDistance: very far
RightAvgMineDistance: very far
Direction: go straight, Speed: very fast


Bearing: far right
LeastDense: left
FurthestMine: left
LeftAvgMineDistance: far
CenterAvgMineDistance: close
RightAvgMineDistance: very close
Direction: turn left, Speed: very fast


Bearing: straight ahead, right, far right, right behind
LeastDense: right
FurthestMine: right
LeftAvgMineDistance: very close or close
CenterAvgMineDistance: close
RightAvgMineDistance: far
Direction: turn right, Speed: very fast
```

2.3 Plan Extraction

The above rule extraction method generates isolated rules, bearing in mind individual states, but not the chaining of these rules in accomplishing a sequential decision task. In contrast, the following plan extraction method generates a complete explicit plan that can by itself accomplish a sequential task. By an *explicit plan*, we mean an action policy consisting of an explicit sequence of action steps, that does not require (or requires little) environmental feedback during execution (compared with a completely closed-loop action policy as generated by Q-learning).

2.3.1 The Algorithm

The PlanExtraction algorithm (Sun and Sessions 1998) turns a set of Q-values (and the corresponding closed-loop policy resulting from these values) into a plan that is in the form of a sequence of steps (in accordance with the traditional AI formulation of planning). The basic idea is that we use beam search, to find the best action sequences (or conditional action sequences) that achieve the goal with a certain probability. The search is based on the insight that the optimal Q-value learned through Q-learning represents the total future probability of reaching the goal (Sun and Sessions 1998). Thus Q-values can be used as a guide in searching for explicit plans.

The algorithm employs the following data structures for plan extraction. The *current state set, CSS*, consists of multiple pairs in the form of $(s, p(s))$, in which the first item indicates a state s and the second item $p(s)$ indicates the probability of that state. For each state in CSS, we find the corresponding best action. In so doing, we have to limit the number of branches at each step, for the sake of time efficiency of the algorithm as well as the representational efficiency of the resulting plan. The set thus contains up to (a fixed number) n pairs, where n is the branching factor in beam search. In order to calculate the best default action at each step, we include a second set of states CSS', which covers a certain number (m) of possible states not covered by CSS.

Set the current state set $CSS = \{(s_0, 1)\}$ and $CSS' = \{\}$
Repeat until the termination conditions are satisfied (e.g., *step > D*)
- For each action u, compute the probabilities of transitioning to each of all the possible next states (for all $s' \in S$) from each of the current states ($s \in CSS$): $p(s', s, u) = p(s) * p_{s,s'}(u)$
- For each action u, compute its estimated utility with respect to each state in CSS: $Ut(s, u) = \sum_{s'} p(s', s, u) * \max_v Q(s', v)$. That is, we calculate the *probabilities* of reaching the goal after performing action u from the current state s.
- For each action u, compute the estimated utility with respect to *all* the states in CSS': $Ut(CSS', u) = \sum_{s \in CSS'} \sum_{s'} p(s) * p_{s,s'}(u) \max_v Q(s', v)$
- For each state s in CSS, choose the action u_s with the highest utility $Ut(s, u)$: $u_s = argmax_u Ut(s, u)$
- Choose the best default action u with regard to all the states in CSS': $u = argmax_{u'} Ut(CSS', u')$
- Update CSS to contain n states that have the highest n probabilities, i.e., with the highest $p(s')$'s: $p(s') = \sum_{s \in CSS} p(s', s, u_s)$, where u_s is the action chosen for state s.
- Update CSS' to contain m states that have the highest m probabilities calculated as follows, among those states that are not in the new (updated) CSS: $p(s') = \sum_{s \in CSS \cup CSS'} p(s', s, u_s)$, where u_s is the action chosen for state s (either a conditional action in case $s \in CSS$ or a default action in case $s \in CSS'$), and the summations are over the old CSS and CSS' (before updating). [1]

---

[1] For both CSS and CSS', if a goal state or a state of probability 0 is selected, we may remove it and, optionally, reduce the beam width of the corresponding set by 1.

297

Action	Description
0-	left
1-	slightly left
2-	straight
3-	slightly right
4-	right
-5	0 knots
-6	10 knots
-7	20 knots
-8	30 knots
-9	40 knots

Figure 6: The possible actions in the Navigation task.

In the measure Ut, the agent takes into account the probabilities of reaching the goal in the future from the current states (based on the Q-values; see Theorem 1 in Sun and Sessions 1998), as well as the probability of reaching the current states based on the history of the paths traversed (based on $p(s)$'s). This is because what we are aiming at is the estimate of the overall success probability of a path. The basic idea, combining measures of past history and future possibilities, is essentially the same as the A* algorithm. However, instead of an additive combination, we use a multiplicative combination, because probabilities require such a combination. In the algorithm, the agent selects the best actions (for $s \in CSS$ and CSS') that are most likely to succeed based on these measures.

2.3.2 Advantages of Plan Extraction

The advantages of plan extraction lie in improving the usability of results and in compressing action policies. Instead of closed-loop policies resulting from Q-learning that have to rely on moment-to-moment sensing, some extracted plans can be run with little (or even no) sensing of the environment, and thus they are useful in situations where there is little or no environmental feedback, or where there is only unreliable feedback. Even when reliable feedback is available, they are beneficial in terms of saving sensing costs. Furthermore, usually extracted plans are much smaller than the original action policies represented by Q-values; that is, they achieve policy compression. Thus, extracting plans also saves representational cost (Sun and Sessions 1998).

Minefield navigation. An an example, in this task, based on the results of Q-learning, plans were extracted. One example plan is shown in Figure 7. The plan indicates what to do in different circumstances, that is, a strategy for navigating through the minefield that avoids mines and goes in the general direction of the target. The plan is basically a sequence of zigzagging actions. The plan is much smaller than the corresponding action policy in the form Q-values (which has 10^{12} entries) from which the plan was extracted, and thus achieves policy compression.

Tower of Hanoi. Another example is the Tower of Hanoi task, which produces easily interpretable plans and is thus used here for illustration. It consists of three pegs, with peg 1 starting with the three discs. The goal of the task is to get the three discs from peg 1 to peg 3. Only the top disc on a peg can be moved. The three discs are of three different sizes and a larger

```
Step 1: [(2, 9)]
Step 2: [(6, 49) (3, 49) (27, 9) (24, 9) (33, 49)]
Step 3: [(19, 9) (2, 9) (4 49)]
Step 4: [(6, 49) (5, 9) (3, 49) (24, 9)]
Step 5: [(19, 9) (6, 49) (4, 49) (2, 9)]
Step 6: [(19, 9) (6, 49) (5, 9) (3, 49)]
Step 7: [(6, 49) (19, 9) (4, 49)]
Step 8: [(19, 9) (6, 49) (5, 9)]
Step 9: [(6, 49) (19, 9)]
Step 10: [(19, 9) (6, 49)]
Step 11: [(6, 49) (19, 9)]
Step 12: [(19, 9) (6, 49)]
Step 13: [(6, 49) (19, 9)]
Step 14: [(19, 9)]
Step 15: [(6, 49)]
Step 16: [(19, 9)]
```

Figure 7: A conditional plan extracted for the Navigation task. $n = 5, m = 8$. In each pair of parentheses, the first number is an (aggregated) state, and the second is an action. Actions are numbered as indicated in Figure 6. No default action has a utility value above zero and thus none is included. The plan is a sequence of zigzagging actions for avoiding mines.

Action	Description
A0	Peg 1 to Peg 2
A1	Peg 1 to Peg 3
A2	Peg 2 to Peg 1
A3	Peg 2 to Peg 3
A4	Peg 3 to Peg 1
A5	Peg 3 to Peg 2

Figure 8: The possible actions in the Tower of Hanoi task

disc may not rest on a smaller disc. There are six possible actions (as shown in Figure 8), although at most only three can be performed at each step (due to the relative size constraint). These moves generate 27 allowable states (see Figure 9).

Q-learning was applied to learn an action policy. Plan extraction was then applied. The plan steps are as follows:

Step 1: moving the top disc from peg 1 to 3 (action 1). Step 2: from peg 1 to 2 (action 0). Step 3: from peg 3 to 2 (action 5). Step 4: from peg 1 to 3 (action 1). Step 5: from peg 2 to 1 (action 2). Step 6: from peg 2 to 3 (action 3). Step 7: from peg 1 to 3 (action 1).

The goal can be reached by an extracted plan with a 100% probability. The plan is much smaller than the corresponding action policy in the form of Q-values (which requires at least 54 entries), and achieves policy compression. This plan does not require step-by-step sensing of the environment, and thus plan extraction enhances usability as well.

3 Concluding Remarks

Both subsymbolic and symbolic knowledge are needed for intelligent agents. They both can and should be learned on-line, autonomously, starting with no

State Number	Description
0	(123,0,0)
1	(23,1,0)
2	(23,0,1)
3	(13,2,0)
4	(13,0,2)
5	(12,3,0)
6	(12,0,3)
7	(3,12,0)
8	(3,0,12)
9	(3,1,2)
10	(3,2,1)
11	(2,13,0)
12	(2,0,13)
13	(2,1,3)
14	(2,3,1)
15	(1,23,0)
16	(1,0,23)
17	(1,2,3)
18	(1,3,2)
19	(0,123,0)
20	(0,23,1)
21	(0,13,2)
22	(0,12,3)
23	(0,3,12)
24	(0,2,13)
25	(0,1,23)
26	(0,0,123)

Figure 9: The possible states in the Tower of Hanoi task

State 0 is the starting state. State 26 is the goal state. In the description, pegs are separated by commas. "1" indicates the smallest disc, "2" the median-sized, and "3" the largest.

a priori domain knowledge, although different algorithms may be used to learn them. Hence, we need to explore hybrid learning frameworks for agents. In accordance with the characteristics of autonomous, sequential learning agents (Sun 2000, Sun et al 2000), we developed learning methods that perform neural reinforcement learning first and extraction of symbolic rules and plans later on its basis, in an integrated hybrid learning framework. The extraction of symbolic planning knowledge enhances the overall hybrid system in various ways.

Acknowledgements: This work was supported in part by Office of Naval Research grant N00014-95-1-0440.

References

L.M. Fu, (1991). Rule learning by searching on adapted nets, *Proc.of AAAI'91*, pp.590-595.

N. Lavrac and S. Dzeroski, (1994). *Inductive Logic Programming*. Ellis Horword, New York.

L. Lin, (1992). Self-improving reactive agents based on reinforcement learning, planning, and teaching. *Machine Learning*. Vol.8, pp.293-321.

R. Maclin and J. Shavlik, (1994). Incorporating advice into agents that learn from reinforcements. *Proc.of AAAI-94*. Morgan Kaufmann, San Meteo, CA.

R. Sun, (1992). On variable binding in connectionist networks. *Connection Science*, Vol.4, No.2, pp.93-124. 1992.

R. Sun, (1997). Learning, action, and consciousness: a hybrid approach towards modeling consciousness. *Neural Networks*, 10 (7), pp.1317-1331

R. Sun, (2000). Symbol grounding: a new look at an old idea. *Philosophical Psychology*, Vol.13, No.2, pp.149-172.

R. Sun, E. Merrill, and T. Peterson, (2000). From implicit skills to explicit knowledge: a bottom-up model of skill learning. *Cognitive Science*. in press.

R. Sun and T. Peterson, (1997). A hybrid model for learning sequential navigation. *Proc. of IEEE International Symposium on Computational Intelligence in Robotics and Automation (CIRA'97)*. Monterey, CA. pp.234-239. IEEE Press.

R. Sun and T. Peterson, (1998). Autonomous learning of sequential tasks: experiments and analyses. *IEEE Transactions on Neural Networks*, Vol.9, No.6, pp.1217-1234.

R. Sun and C. Sessions, (1998). Extracting plans from reinforcement learners. *Proceedings of the 1998 International Symposium on Intelligent Data Engineering and Learning (IDEAL'98)*. pp.243-248. eds. L. Xu, L. Chan, I. King, and A. Fu. Springer-Verlag.

R. Sutton, (1996). Generalization in reinforcement learning. *Advances in Neural Information Processing Systems 8*. MIT Press. Cambridge, MA.

T. Tesauro, (1992). Practical issues in temporal difference learning. *Machine Learning*. Vol.8, 257-277.

A. Tickle, J. Diederich, et al, (2000). Lessons from past, current issues, and future research directions in extracting knowledge embedded in artificial neural networks. In: S. Wermter and R. Sun, (eds.) *Hybrid Neural Systems*, Springer-Verlag, Berlin.

G. Towell and J. Shavlik, (1993). Extracting refined rules from Knowledge-Based Neural Networks, *Machine Learning*. 13 (1), 71-101.

C. Watkins, (1989). *Learning with Delayed Rewards*. Ph.D Thesis, Cambridge University, Cambridge, UK.

Twisting Features with Properties

B. Apolloni,[*] D. Malchiodi, I. Zoppis

Dip. di Scienze dell'Informazione, Università degli Studi di Milano
Via Comelico 39/41, 20135 Milano, Italy

S. Gaito

Dip. di Matematica *F. Enriquez*, Università degli Studi di Milano
Via Saldini 50, 20133 Milano, Italy

Abstract

We provide three steps in the direction of shifting probability from a descriptive tool of unpredictable events to a way of understanding them. At a very elementary level we state an operational definition of probability based solely on symmetry assumptions about observed data. This definition converges, however, to the Kolmogorov one within a special *large number law* fashion that represents a first way of twisting features observed in the data with properties expected in the next observations. Within this probability meaning we fix a general *sampling mechanism* to generate random variables and extend our twisting device to computing probability distributions on population properties on the basis of the likelihood of the observed features. Here the randomness core translates from the above symmetry assumptions in a generator of unitary uniform random variables. Willing discovering suitable features (which are classically defined as *sufficient statistics*), we refer directly to the notions of Kolmogorov complexity and *coding theorem* in particular. This is to connect the features to the inner structure of the observed data in terms of concise computer codes describing them in a well equipped computational framework.

This new statistical framework allows us to recover and improve results on computational learning at both subsymbolic and symbolic stages, figuring a unique shell where the full trip from sensory data to their conceptual management might occur.

Key words: Computational learning, Learning rules, PAC learning, Algorithmic inference, Kolmogorov complexity.

1 First step

The estimate $\widehat{p}$ for the mean p of a random variable X distributed according to a Bernoulli law upon the presentation of a sample $\mathbf{X}_M = (X_1, \ldots, X_m)$ is usually derived counting the number $k = \sum_{i=1}^{m} X_i$ of 1's in the observed sample and then setting $\widehat{p} = k/m$. An alternative way for *appreciating* it can be found by considering that $\widehat{p}$, referring to the probability that the next observed bit X_{m+1} will assume the value 1, can be found through analysing the fact that for such X_{m+1} we would observe exactly $k+1$ ones within a $m+1$ sized sample.

---

[*]Corresponding author: e-mail apolloni@dsi.unimi.it.

Assuming that the sequencing of zeroes and ones in the sample is inessential to the observed phenomenon, we appreciate $p_1 = P[X_{m+1} = 1]$ as the ratio between the number of those permutations of the sampled values having the last element equal to one and the number of all permutations. Namely

$$\widehat{p}_1 = \frac{m!(k+1)}{(m+1)!} = \frac{k+1}{m+1}$$

Analogously, we appreciate $p_0 = P[X_{m+1} = 0]$ through

$$\widehat{p}_0 = \frac{m!(m-k+1)}{(m+1)!} = \frac{m-k+1}{m+1}$$

Note that $\widehat{p}_0 + \widehat{p}_1 = \frac{m+2}{m+1}$; that is, the estimated probabilities do not sum up to 1: this is due to the fact that they refer to different probability spaces. To put this idea in a more rigorous form, first we introduce an incremental definition for the sample space:

Definition 1.1. The *symmetric sample space* for a statistical experiment providing a sample $\mathbf{X}_m = (X_1, \ldots, X_m)$ is a pair $(\Omega_m, \mathscr{B}_m)$ where Ω_m is the set of all the *allowed* permutations of the m-tuplet $(X_1, \ldots, X_m)^1$ and $\mathscr{B}$ is a σ-field of subsets of Ω_m.

In this context we define the probability measure P on $(\Omega_m, \mathscr{B}_m)$ per usual as the ratio between the number of interesting sample points and the number of the possible ones. Given $\mathbf{X}_m$ as a sequence of independent bits (i.e. all permutations are allowed), in this framework the above alternative estimation of probability that the next observed bit will assume the value 1 has its natural environment in the probability space $(\Omega^1_{m+1}, \mathscr{B}_{m+1}, P)$, where Ω^1_{m+1} is the set of all the permutations of the $(m+1)$-tuplet $(X_1, \ldots, X_m, 1)$, while $\mathscr{B}_{m+1}$ and P are defined, as above described, over Ω^1_{m+1}.

Analogously, the probability that the next observed bit will assume the value 0 has to be calculated in the measurable space $(\Omega^0_{m+1}, \mathscr{B}_+)$, where now Ω^0_{m+1} is the set of all the permutations of the $(m+1)$-tuplet $(X_1, \ldots, X_m, 0)$.

More in general, the probability that K of the following M bits will assume the value 1 will be estimated through

$$\widehat{p}_{(K;M,k,m)} = \frac{\binom{m}{k}\binom{M}{K}}{\binom{m+M}{k+K}} = \frac{\binom{k+K}{k}\binom{m-k+M-K}{m-k}}{\binom{m+M}{m}} \tag{1}$$

computed in the space $(\Omega_{m+M}, \mathscr{B}_{m+M}, P)$, where $(\Omega_{m+M}$ is the set of all the permutations of the $(m + M)$-tuplet $(X_1, \ldots, X_m, X_{m+1} \equiv 1, \ldots, X_{m+K} \equiv 1, X_{m+K+1} \equiv 0, \ldots, X_{m+M} \equiv 0)$.

The links between this inference of the empirical probability and the Kolmogorov one [1] arise asymptotically:

---

[1] i.e. those permutations that do not change the meaning of the sequence.

- When $m \to \infty$, the Kolmogorov sample space is the set of all possible values which can be assumed by the elements of the strings which constitute our sample space.

- When $m \to \infty$, the two definitions of estimated and appreciated probability converge to the same value.

- When $M, K \to \infty$, $\widehat{p}_{(K;M,k,m)} = p_{(k;m,M,K)}$ tends to the Binomial distribution law $p_{(k;m,K/M)}$ with the sample size and the asymptotic 1's frequency in the population for parameters.

To appreciate the relationship between the two definitions for small sample and small population (as usual we denote by this term the subsequent M bits) we generated a variety of pairs (sample, population) from a Bernoulli variable with p ranging from 0 to 1 under the constraint of both $k + K$ and $m + M$ as in (1) being constant. In Figure 1 we see that, as expectable, probabilities appreciated through (1) go around, but do not coincide with those classically estimated through frequency. The reasons why we prefer this new inferential

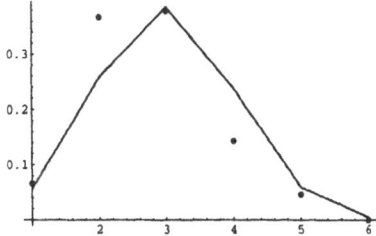

Figure 1: Relationship between appreciated and estimated probability in 60 families of pairs (sample, population), each obtained by sampling from a Bernoulli variable where p rises from 0 to 1 with step 0.01. With reference to Equality 1, $m = 20$, $M = 5$, $k + K = 9$. Horizontal axis: K, vertical axis: both frequencies (bullets) and companion values of $\widehat{p}_{(k;M,K,M)}$ (line).

way of finding the empirical probability are the following: (i) We don't need to suppose the existence of an intrinsical probability, but we can perform our inferential method only on the basis of the observed data, (ii) it makes sense also for small size samples and populations, and (iii) future and past play the same role because the above defined space is made of the global strings of data.

2 Second step

The typical inference framework is met when $M \to \infty$ and m is small. In this case the object of our inference is a (possibly infinite) string of data X that we partition in a prefix which we assume to be known at the current time (and therefore call sample), and an infinite suffix of unknown data which concerns the future that we call population (see Figure 2). All these data share the feature of being independent observations of a same phenomenon. Therefore, in the limit of the convergence of the probability to the target of large number law, without loss of generality we assume these data as the output of a same function g_ϑ having input from a set of independent random variables U uniformly distributed in the unitary interval – effectively, the most essential source of randomness[2].

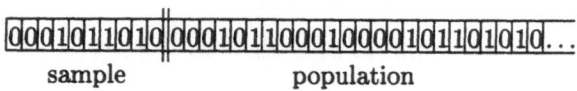

sample   population

Figure 2: Sample and population of random bits.

We will refer to $\mathscr{M} = (U, g_\vartheta)$ as a *sampling mechanism* and to g_ϑ as an *explaining function*, and this function is precisely the object of our inference. Let us consider, for instance, the sample mechanism $\mathscr{M} = (U, g_p)$, where

$$g_p(u) = \begin{cases} 1 & \text{if } u \le p \\ 0 & \text{otherwise} \end{cases} \tag{2}$$

explains sample and population distributed according to a Bernoulli law of mean p like in Figure 2. As shown in Figure 3, for a given sequence of U's we obtain different binary strings depending on the height of the threshold line corresponding to p. Thus it is easy to desume the following implication chain

$$(K_{\widetilde{p}} \ge k) \Leftarrow (p < \widetilde{p}) \Leftarrow (K_{\widetilde{p}} \ge k + 1) \tag{3}$$

and the consequent bound on the probability

$$P[K_{\widetilde{p}} \ge k] \ge P[p < \widetilde{p}] \ge P[K_{\widetilde{p}} \ge k + 1] \tag{4}$$

which characterizes the cumulative distribution function (c.d.f.) F_p of the parameter p. In our statistical framework indeed, the unknown p is a random variable in $[0, 1]$ representing the asymptotic frequency of 1 in the populations that are compatible, as a function of U suffix of the sample, with the number k of actually observed 1. Here $K_{\widetilde{p}}$ denotes the random variable counting the number of 1's in the sample if the threshold in the explaining function switches to $\widetilde{p}$ *for the same realizations* of U.

Note the asymmetry in the implications. It derives from the fact that raising the threshold parameter in g_p cannot decrease the number of 1 in the observed sample, but we can recognize that such a rise occurred only if we really see a number of ones in the sample greater than k.

We will refer to every expression similar to (3) as a *twisting argument*, since it allows us to exchange events on parameters with events on statistics.

---

[2]Such a g_ϑ always exists by the probability integral transformation theorem [2]. By default capital letters will denote random variables and small letters their corresponding realizations.

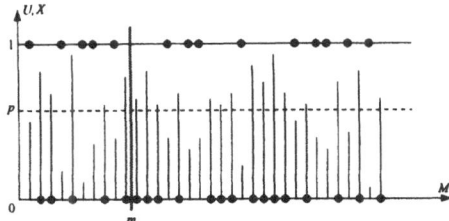

Figure 3: Generating a Bernoullian sample. Horizontal axis: index of the U realizations; vertical axis: both U (lines) and X (bullets) values. The threshold line p realizes a mapping from U to X through (2).

Twisting sample with population properties is our approach to statistical inference, which we call *algorithmic inference*. Its general framework is depicted in Figure 4. For any sampling mechanism, we have on the one hand the *world*

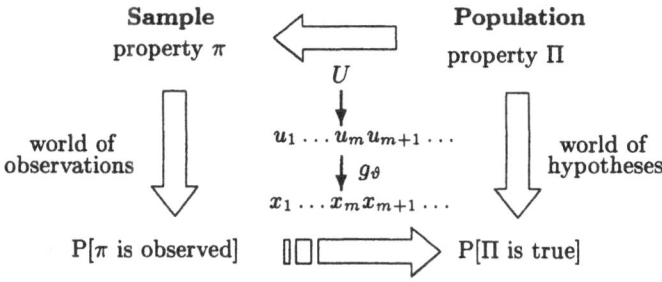

Figure 4: Twisting properties between sample and population.

of hypotheses about g_ϑ that results in special properties of the population, which we call Π; on the other, the *world of actual observations* where – as g_ϑ is the same – the above hypotheses result in corresponding properties π on the sample. So we can use the likelihood of the actual sample in respect to π, a quantity that in principle can be easily computed when the hypotheses are fully specified, to get the probability that the corresponding Π are satisfied.

In this inferential approach we recover the key notion of $1 - \delta$ confidence interval for the parameter ϑ, intended as the pair of values (L_i, L_s) such that:

$$P[L_i < \vartheta < L_s] \geq 1 - \delta$$

Confidence intervals for a Bernoulli distribution
In particular, from (4), to compute confidence intervals for p we choose (L_i, L_s)

such that

$$\sum_{i=k+1}^{m} \binom{m}{i} L_s^i (1 - L_s)^{m-i} = 1 - \frac{\delta}{2} \tag{5}$$

$$\sum_{i=k}^{m} \binom{m}{i} L_i^i (1 - L_i)^{m-i} = \frac{\delta}{2} \tag{6}$$

Here the random variable is exactly p, and the confidence refers to the possible suffix of a given sample observed on X. This is highlighted in Figure 5, where we considered a string of $20 + 200$ unitary uniform variables representing, respectively, the randomness source of a sample and a population of Bernoulli variables. Then, according to the explaining function (2) we computed a sequence of Bernoullian 220 bits long vectors with p rising from 0 to 1. The pairs $k/20$ and $h/200$, computing the frequency of ones in the sample and in the population respectively, are reported along one fret line in the figure. We repeated this experiment 20 times (using different vectors of uniform variables). Then we drew on the same graph the solutions of equations 5 and 6 with respect to p with varying k and $\delta = 0.1$. As we can see, for a given value of k the intercepts of the above curves with a vertical line with abscissa $k/20$ determine an interval containing almost all intercepts of the frets with the same line. A more intensive experiment would show that, in the approximation of $h/200$ with the asymptotic frequency of ones in the suffixes of the first 20 sampled values, on all samples, and even for each sample if we draw many suffixes of the same one, almost $100(1 - \delta)$ percent of the frets fall within the analytically computed curves.

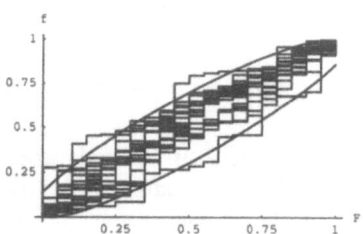

Figure 5: Generating 0.9 confidence intervals for the mean p of a Bernoulli random variable with population and sample of $n = 200$ and $m = 20$ elements, respectively.
$F = k/m =$ frequency of ones in the sample; $f = h/n =$ frequency of ones in the population.
Fret lines: trajectories described by the number of ones in sample and population when p ranges from 0 to 1, for different sets of initial uniform random variables. Curves: trajectories described by the confidence interval extremes when the observed number k of 1 in the sample ranges from 0 to m.

PAC learning

A special issue of the above inferential problem is represented by the typical learning target of Probably Approximately Correct (PAC) learning theory [3]. Here the parameter to be investigated is the probability that an inferred function will compute erroneously on next inputs (will not explain new sampled points). In greater detail, the general form of the sample is:

$$\mathbf{Z}_m = \{(X_i, b_i),\ i = 1, \ldots, m\}$$

where b_i are Boolean variables. If we assume that for every M and every $\mathbf{Z}_M$ an f exists in a Boolean class $\mathbf{C}$, call it *concept* c, such that $\mathbf{Z}_M = \{(X_i, c(X_i)), i = 1, \ldots, M\}$, then we are interested in the right sided confidence interval of the measure $U_{c \div h}$ of the symmetric difference between another function computed from $\mathbf{Z}_m$, that we denote as *hypothesis* h, and any such c [3]. We use the following twisting argument for $U_{c \div h}$

$$\left(T_\varepsilon \geq t_{U_{c \div h}} + 1\right) \Leftarrow (U_{c \div h} < \varepsilon) \Leftarrow \left(T_\varepsilon \geq t_{U_{c \div h}} + \mu\right) \tag{7}$$

where $t_{U_{c \div h}}$ is the number of actual sample points falling in $c \div h$, i.e. points X_i where either $c(X_i) = 1$ and $h(X_i) = 0$ or vice versa. T_ε is the analogous statistic for an enlargement of $c \div h$ of measure ε, and μ the *detail* of the class $\mathbf{C} \div h$ of symmetric differences, for short the witness of an $U_{c \div h}$ increase (see [4] for a formal definition).

The companion probabilistic inequality allows us to recover many results from PAC learning theory. The main theorem is the following:

Theorem 2.1. *[5] For a given probability space $(\mathfrak{X}, \mathscr{B}, \mathrm{P})$ where $\mathscr{B}$ is a σ-algebra on $\mathfrak{X}$ and P is a possibly unknown probability measure defined over $\mathscr{B}$, assume we are given*

- *a concept class $\mathbf{C}$ on $\mathfrak{X}$ with detail $\mathrm{D}_{\mathbf{C},\mathbf{C}} = \mu$;*

- *a sample $\mathbf{Z}_m$ drawn from the fixed space and labeled according to a $c \in \mathbf{C}$ labeling an infinite suffix $\mathbf{Z}_M$ of it as well;*

- *a fairly strongly surjective function [4] $A : \{\mathbf{z}_m\} \mapsto \mathbf{C}$ misclassifying at most $t \in \mathbb{N}$ points of total probability no greater than $\rho \in (0, 1)$.*

Consider the family of sets $\{c \div h\}$ with $c \in \mathbf{C}$ labeling $\mathbf{z}_m$, $h = A(\mathbf{z}_m)$ and detail $\mathrm{D}_{\mathbf{C},h} = \mu_h$, misclassifying t_h points of probability ρ_h, and denote with

---

[3] Note that in classic scenarios we look for a c that labels points of every $\mathbf{Z}_M$ and try to discover it (rather, its approximation h) in spite of the sample $\mathbf{Z}_m$'s variability. Here we assume a dual perspective: according to our algorithmic inference paradigm, for fixed sample $\mathbf{Z}_m$ we can have different populations $\mathbf{Z}_M$, hence different c's explaining them. These are related, however, to the explanation h we found for the sample, and we work precisely on this relation.

[4] A usual regularity condition, resulting as a counterpart of the *well behaved* function [6] request. For formal definitions see [4].

$U_{c \div h}$ the random variable given by the probability measure of $c \div h$ and by $F_{U_{c \div h}}$ its c.d.f. Then for a given $(\mathbf{z}_m, h)$ and each $\beta \in (\rho_h, 1)$

$$I_\beta(1 + t_h, m - t_h) \geq \mathrm{P}^{(m)}[U_{c \div h} \leq \beta] =$$
$$F_{U_{c \div h}}(\beta) \geq I_\beta(\mu_h + t_h, m - (\mu_h + t_h) + 1) \quad (8)$$

and for each $(\mathbf{z}_m, h)$ and $\beta \in (\rho, 1)$

$$I_\beta(1 + t_h, m - t_h) \geq F_{U_{c \div h}}(\beta) \geq I_\beta(\mu + t, m - (\mu + t) + 1) \quad (9)$$

where $\mathrm{P}^{(m)}$ refers to the m product space of $(\mathfrak{X}, \mathscr{B}, \mathrm{P})$ and $I_\beta(\mu + t, m - (\mu + t) + 1) = 1 - \sum_{i=0}^{\mu+t-1} \binom{m}{i} \beta^i (1 - \beta)^{m-i}$ is the incomplete Beta function (i.e. the c.d.f. of the Beta random variable with parameters $\mu + t$ and $m - (\mu + t) + 1$ evaluated in β).

Subsymbolic learning

At a subsymbolic level, when working with neural networks, with reference to relation (7) we check inequalities on statistics just by changing the parameters of the network. A main problem is to check whether the error function which drives the visit of the parameter space is a suitable statistic or not [5]. If it is, we can assume this statistic as a reliable indicator of the closeness of the current parametrization of the neural network to the function to be learnt. Otherwise, we incur the usual drawbacks such as relative minima of the statistic, overfitting and so on.

3 Third step

The twisting argument leaves us with the crucial problem of finding sufficient statistics. This problem finds a straighforward solution through the factorization lemma [1] when we work with easy probabilistic models. On the contrary, the same lemma does not enjoy manageable results when the distribution law in hands is explained by complex functions, for instance computing the solution of NP-hard problems [6]. In this section we give a dual issue of the factorization lemma in our statistical framework. It sheds light on new methods for finding sufficient statistics or approximations of them. Let us start from an algorithmic issue of the definition of sufficient statistics:

Definition 3.1. [2] For a given parameter set Θ, and explaining function g_ϑ with $\vartheta \in \Theta$, let X be the output random variable, $f_X(.; \vartheta)$ its probability density, and $\mathbf{Z}_m$ a sample of size m drawn from X within a space $\mathfrak{X}$. A statistic $S : \mathfrak{X}^m \mapsto \mathbb{R}$, inducing on $\mathfrak{X}$ the partition $\mathfrak{U}(S)$, is said to be *sufficient* with reference to the parameter ϑ if the ratio $f_{\mathbf{Z}_m}(\mathbf{x}^1; \vartheta)/f_{\mathbf{Z}_m}(\mathbf{x}^2; \vartheta)$ does not depend on ϑ when $\mathbf{x}^1$ and $\mathbf{x}^2$ belong to a same element of $\mathfrak{U}(S)$;

---

[5] Elsewhere we show that every twisting argument must be grounded on functional modifications of a sufficient statistic [7].

[6] This is the case of the distribution law of pairs of random instance and solution of a knapsack problem [9].

The definition simply says that, when looking at a useful sample property (a statistic indeed) we must focus on properties that remain unchanged on samples having the same occurrence probability of the observed one. If we do not know this probability we can estimate it through a maximum likelihood principle as follows.

Consider the following lemma putting in relation probability with complexity of a string.

Definition 3.2. [10] Let $\mathfrak{X}$ be the set of all binary strings and $|x|$ the length of the string x. Denote with $f(x) < \infty$ the fact that f is defined on x. A partial recursive function (prf) $\phi : \mathfrak{X}^* \to \mathfrak{X}$ is said prefix if $\phi(x) < \infty$ and $\phi(y) < \infty$ implies that x is not a proper prefix of y. Fixed a universal prefix prf U [7], the conditional Prefix (or Levin's) Complexity $K(x|y)$ of x given y is defined as

$$K(x|y) = \min_{p \in \mathfrak{X}} \{|p| \text{ such that } U(p, y) = x\}, \tag{10}$$

and the unconditional Prefix Complexity $K(x)$ of x as $K(x) = K(x|\lambda)$, where λ is the empty string.

Lemma 3.1. *[10] The probability measure* P *of any string* $x \in \mathfrak{X}$ *explained by the function* g_ϑ *is related to the prefix complexity* K *of* x *and* g_ϑ *through the following equation:*

$$P(x) \leq 2^{-K(x)} 2^{K(g_\vartheta)} \tag{11}$$

The lemma comes from the fact that $-\log(P(x))$ can be used as a prefix code of x in a prefix machinery having the description of g_ϑ in its library, and this machinery can be simulated by a universal prefix machinery U by running a code of length $K(g_\vartheta)$. Thus, a sequence of length $-\log(P(x)) + K(g_\vartheta)$ can be used to code x in the reference machinery U of Definition 3.2. Of course, in respect to this machinery the shortest code of x has a length $K(x)$ no greater than the above.

Though both $K(x)$ and $K(g_\vartheta)$ are not computable in general by definition[8] [10], we will use the upper bound in Equation 11 as a *maximum likelihood* estimate [1] of P(x). Therefore, our problem of finding a consistent statistic approximately coincides just with the one of reading the upper bound on the probability of a sample and identifying the function of the sampled data on which the upper bound depends. Disregarding for a moment the term $2^{K(g_\vartheta)}$, we isolate within the other upper bound factor the part we assume to be independent on the unknown aspects of the population (which are synthetized by the parameter ϑ) from the part depending on them (the wanted statistics). Of course, samples with this same statistic have the same probability, apart from coefficients independent on ϑ; hence these statistics result sufficient. Therefore a second approximation (an estimate indeed) consists in writing the second

---

[7]i.e. a machinery capable of computing any computable function according to the Church thesis [11].

[8]This negative result is a variant of the well-known Turing machine *halting lemma* [12].

member of (11) in such a readable form. As mentioned before, we cannot write the minimal codes ϕ underlying $K(x)$; however we can look for very efficient programs π as estimates $\widehat{\phi}$ of ϕ that we split as follows:

$$\widehat{\phi}_x = \pi_{\widetilde{g}}((\pi_{h(x_1)}, ..., \pi_{h(x_m)}), \pi_{t(x_1, ... x_m)}) \tag{12}$$

with $g_\vartheta \equiv \widetilde{g}(\vartheta)$, where the allotment of the computational tasks is aimed at minimizing the total π_is' length. Namely, we recognize in the efficient compression of property t of the sample the sufficient statistic evoking a general property of the whole population, while the remnant part h of x_i must be computed singularly on each variable. $\widetilde{g}$ is the part of the envisaged population property that we already know. It is a cognitive constraint that generally makes $\widehat{\phi}_x$ longer, but also a useful help in devising it. We can easily recognize in the first argument of $\pi_{\widetilde{g}}$ the $-\log$ of the first factor of the likelihood factorization when a sufficient statistic exists:

$$P(x) = f_1(x_1, ..., x_m) f_2(t(x_1, ..., x_m), \vartheta) \tag{13}$$

Here we further split f_2 in the π_t and $K(g_\vartheta)$ contributions. This allows a balancing of description complexities of statistics, constraints, and residual unknown parts of a sample (which looks for an enlarged issue of the structural risk minimization task introduced in [13]); these are stemmed by $\widehat{K}(t)$, $K(g_\vartheta)$ and $\{\widehat{K}(h(x_i))\}$, in an approximated issue of Equation 11, that reads

$$\widehat{P}(x) = 2^{-\sum_{i=1}^{m} \widehat{K}(h(x_i)) - \widehat{K}(t(x_1, ..., x_m)) - \widehat{K}(\widetilde{g})} 2^{K(g_\vartheta)} \tag{14}$$

Here $2^{K(g_\vartheta)}$ is a sort of rewarding factor allowing us to assume great probability in case of complex explaining functions. However neither the true ϑ nor the true complexity value is known; thus the maximum likelihood principle requires us to give a very short global description of the sample by minimizing the total length of π as in Equation 12.

In line with current thread on hybrid systems [14, 15, 16] we may imagine fulfilling this task in a subsymbolic and a symbolic step. The latter accounts for what we formally know about the string sampling mechanism. The subsymbolic part must supply what still remains unknown. This a typical job of a neural network for instance. In this case a subsidiary inference task arises to estimate the parameters of this device. Thus another (hopefully sufficient) statistic joins the previous one; in other words, we realize that the global inference problem needs a pair of sufficient statistics. Learning a neural network is a non easy problem supported by an actually poor theory. In the previous section we got some insights from the twisting argument theory, but we can enjoy still poorer intuition about the joint estimation of the pair of statistics. Rather, still in the aim of minimizing our sample description, we enunciate the following "don't cheat" principle:

Principle 1. *Given a computational framework (machine, language, ...), for suitably describing a function on a training set, a formula beats a neural network only if its description length, including observed statistics for free parameters, is shorter than the neural network's.*

Example 3.1. In force of the above principle,

1. The symbolic description of the XOR function, for instance through the formula "$1 - x_1 x_2 - (1 - x_1)(1 - x_2)$", beats its description through a neural network described by a $2-2-1$ MLP, namely "$\sigma(5.52(\sigma(-1.49x_1 + 1.48x_2 - 0.53)) + 5.52(\sigma(-1.48x_1 - 1.49x_2 - 0.53)) - 3.27$" where σ denotes a sigmoidal activation function, learnt from the sample $(1,1,0),(1,0,1),(0,1,0),(0,0,0)$ through the usual backpropagation algorithm [17].

2. In classifying emotions in a phonetic database, a C4.5[18] decison tree consisting of 64 If-Then-Else rules on 74 features is beaten by a Support Vector Machine [13] with linear kernel on the same variables [19].

4 Conclusions

We moved from a first model based on a random bit generator where the sole knowledge we can extract is the frequency of ones in the next bits, to a second model where the random source is coupled with a computing machinery and we observe properties about the latter, up to the last model where the random source disappears in favor of a prefix machinery coupled with the unfeasible job of computing the shortest descriptions. We realize that the inference goal is to compute properties that could be ascertained in terms of occurrence frequencies in the future observations of a phenomenon, and conclude that these properties have nothing to do with the mysterious operation of tossing a coin; rather, they merely represent a correct synthesis of what we have already observed or know about the phenomenon. This approcah, whose ultimate randomness source lies in some uncomputable strings, ϕ's in the last section, allows us to deepen a minimal structural risk minimization principle shedding some light on the designing of hybrid subsymbolic-symbolic learning paradigms.

References

[1] S. S. Wilks, Mathematical statistics, Wiley publications in statistics, John Wiley, New York, London, 1965.

[2] V. K. Rohatgi, An Introduction to Probability Theory and Mathematical Statistics, Wiley series in probability and mathematical statistics, John Wiley & Sons, New York, Chichester, Brisbane, Toronto, Singapore, 1976.

[3] L. Valiant, A theory of the learnable, Communications of the ACM 27 (11) (1984) 1134–1142.

[4] B. Apolloni, S. Chiaravalli, Pac learning of concept classes through the boundaries of their items, Journal of Theoretical Computer Science 172 (1997) 91–120.

[5] B. Apolloni, D. Malchiodi, Gaining degrees of freedom in subsymbolic learning, Journal of Theoretical Computer Science 255 (2001) 295–391.

[6] A. Blumer, A. Ehrenfreucht, D. Haussler, M. Warmuth, Learnability and the vapnik-chervonenkis dimension, Journal of the ACM 36 (1989) 929–965.

[7] B. Apolloni, D. Iannizzi, D. Malchiodi, Algorithmically inferring functions, Tech. rep., Università degli Studi di Milano (2000).

[8] S. Zacks, The Theory of Statistical Inference, Wiley series in probability and mathematical statistics, John Wiley & Sons, New York, London, Sydney, Toronto, 1971.

[9] S. Martello, P. Toth, The 0–1 knapsack problem, in: Combinatorial Optimization, Wiley, 1979, pp. 237–279.

[10] M. Li, P. Vitànyi, An Introduction to Kolmogorov Complexity and its Applications, Springer, Berlin, 1993.

[11] A. Church, Introduction to Mathematical Logic I, Vol. 13 of Annals of Mathematics Studies, Princeton University Press, Princeton, NJ, 1944.

[12] H. Roger, Theory of recoursive functions and effective computability, Mc Graw-Hill, 1967.

[13] V. Vapnik, The Nature of Statistical Learning Theory, Springer, New York, 1995.

[14] B. Apolloni, D. Malchiodi, C. Orovas, G. Palmas, From synapses to rules, in: Foundations of Connectionist-symbolic Integration: Representation, Paradigms, and Algorithms - Proceedings of the 14th European Conference on Artificial Intelligence, 2000.

[15] M. Hilario, An overview of strategies for neurosymbolic integration, in: F. Alexandre (Ed.), Connectionist-Symbolic Processing: From Unified to Hybrid Approaches, Lawrence Erlbaum, 1998.

[16] R. Sun, Integrating rules and connectionism for robust commonsense reasoning, Wiley, New York, 1994.

[17] D. E. Rumelhart, G. E. Hinton, R. J. Williams, Learning internal representations by error propagation, in: Parallel Distributed Processing, Vol. 1, MIT Press, Cambridge, Massachusstes, 1986.

[18] J. Quinlan, Comparing connectionist and symbolic learning methods, in: Computational Learning Theory and Natural Learning Systems. Volume I. Constraints and Prospects, MIT Press, Cambridge, 1994, pp. 445–456.

[19] W. A. Fellenz, G. J. Taylor, C. R., E. Douglas-Cowie, F. Piat, S. Kollias, C. Orovas, B. Apolloni, On emotion recognition of faces and speech using neural networks, fuzzy logic and the assess system, in: S. Amari, C. Lee Giles, M. Gori, P. V. (Eds.), Proceeding of the IEEE-INNS-ENNS International Joint Conference on Neural Networks - IJCNN 2000, IEEE Computer Society, Los Alamitos, 2000, pp. II–93,II–98.

Neural nets and the puzzle of intentionality

Gianfranco Basti
IRAFS – International Research Area on Foundations of the Sciences, Pontifical
Lateran University, Rome, Italy

Antonio Luigi Perrone
PUL-ReLab – Pontifical Lateran University Research Laboratory,
Rome, Italy

Abstract

In this work, we ask epistemological questions involved in making the intentional behavior the object of physical and mathematical inquiry. We show that the subjective component of intentionality can never become object of scientific inquiry, as related to self–consciousness. On the other hand, the inquiry on objective physical and logical components of intentional acts is central to scientific inquiry. Such inquiry concerns logical and semantic questions, like reference and truth of logical symbols, as well as their relationship to the "complexity" of brain networking. Such metalogical inquiry suggests indeed some hypotheses about the amazing "parallelism", "plasticity" and "storing capacity" that mammalian and ever human brains might exhibit.

1. Introduction

Our work is divided into two main sections. In the *First Section*, we deal with the study of intentionality, as characteristic of intelligent life, in the framework of *functionalism* in classic AI research program. We show the logical and meta–logical limitations of this approach to the problem of intentionality. In the *Second Section*, we discuss the relevance of a particular approach to the problem of logical foundations after the *Gödel incompleteness theorems* and its relevance for the problem of intentionality. The only way to avoid such limitation theorems is to allow a change of axioms in the logical system concerned, so to make the same representation space of the system "dynamic" in a deeply new sense. We suggest the relevance of such an approach of Computational Intelligence (CI) for a logically consistent theory of intentionality, as well as for the solution of cognitive neuroscience problems related to neural dynamics and neural computations relationships. Namely, the question of "*true parallelism*" in brain computations, as well as the "plasticity" and the "memorization capabilities" of brain computations, with respect to their artificial simulations. This approach constitutes the *logical* counterpart of the well–known *epistemological* theory of true knowledge as continuous *self–conforming* (*adaequatio*) of the mind to singular realities in their unending becoming.

2. Intentionality and Cognitive Neuroscience

It is hard to defend the functionalist pretension [1] of using Tarski's formal semantics [2] for dealing with psychological intentionality, overall in the study of perception. Indeed, what we mean by "intentionality" is not only the act of *reflexive thought* of formal manipulation of logical symbols and relations already otherwise constituted in our mind. In this sense intentionality could be in agreement with the *methodological solipsism* of functionalist theory [3], as well as with nominalism of Tarski's formal semantics. On the contrary, intentionality essentially means the act of *productive thinking* of new logical symbols and hence of new logical relations. In short, intentionality is essentially related to the act of *constitution of symbols,* and in the case of constitution of *true* symbols, intentionality is essentially related to the problem of constitution of symbols always *adequate* to the singular context of their use. So, any scientific theory of intentionality must deal with the problem of intentionality at the *pre–symbolic level,* i.e., at the level of the unending process of *symbol constitution and modification.*

This criticism against the functionalist approach to intentionality has been developed in the last twenty years. In this regard, two other counterexamples of the famous "Turing room" metaphor have been proposed: the "Searle room" and, more recently, the "Putnam room". These two metaphors exemplify indeed two main criticisms that can be posed to the symbolic treatment of the intentionality problems in the functionalist approach. These criticisms are, respectively:

1. from the standpoint of the *intensional* (with *s*) *logic* approach to the theory of intentionality;
2. from the standpoint of the *theory of coding* in the logical *foundations of computability theory.*

Let us begin with J. Searle's criticism.

2.1 John Searle: intentionality and the intensional logic

In order to exemplify in which sense the Turing test fails in proposing a valid proof of the equivalence between a mind and a computer, J. Searle proposed the counterexample of his "Chinese room" [4]. Even though a Turing test satisfies the criteria of an extensional approach to the problem of meaning, nevertheless it is impossible to affirm that this approach can be considered as a satisfying operational translation of what we designate as an intentional act of knowing. The "relation to a content" as characteristic of any intentional act implies not only the *extensional* reference to names of objects, but also the *intension* of a conscious significance by which we associate names and objects in different contexts. *Intending* a meaning and by it *referring* to an object are not the same thing, even though they are effectively always together in any conscious intentional act [5].

This reciprocal irreducible character of the intensional and of the extensional components of any intentional act is evident also in the logic of their linguistic expression. In the intensional logic indeed the *extensionality* axiom and the related *substitution* axiom do not hold [6]. For instance, from the extensional standpoint, the notion of "water" and the notion of "H_2O" are to be considered as synonyms, since they apply to the same collection of objects. From the intensional standpoint, however, they do not have the same meaning; just substitute the term "water" with the scientific term "H_2O" in some poetic or religious discourse. The result is meaningless. Owing to the exclusively extensional character of the treatment of the semantic content in the functionalist approach, this approach is thus absolutely not sufficient for cognitive psychology.

Unfortunately, the constructive part of Searle's theory of intentionality is void of any theoretic and scientific significance. Nevertheless, what Searle's criticism rightly emphasizes is that the functionalist approach to the study of mind cannot be at all adequate owing to its exclusively extensional approach to semantic problems.

For these very same reasons W. V. O. Quine stated that the mind–body problem is essentially a *linguistic* and not ontological problem [7]. It is ultimately the problem of the non-reducible character of intensional to extensional statements. So, because of the extensional character of any scientific language, for him intentionality cannot be at all object of scientific inquiry [8]. This reductionism, typical of the logical empiricism of Quine's philosophy is typical also of Patricia and Paul Churchland interpretation of the connectionist approach to cognitive neuroscience [9].

On the other hand, it is evident that the role of intensional logic is at the level of *productive thinking* and not of *reflexive thought*, i.e., at level of logical symbol *constitution* and not at level of their *formal manipulation*. The recovering of intensional component of mind operation has thus to be related with the recovering in logic of the *analytic method* (induction, generalization, analogy) as the method of new hypothesis *discovery* against the modern reduction of logic to the only *axiomatic method* as the method of hypothesis *proof* [See Sect 3]. A further step in this direction, is the discussion on the relationship between intentionality and the problem of information *coding*.

2.2 Hilary Putnam: intentionality and the problem of coding

One of the most exciting events in the brief history of cognitive sciences is the abandonment of the functionalist approach by its supporter who introduced it into the scientific and philosophical debate: the mathematician and philosopher Hilary Putnam. This is related to the unsolvable problems of *reference and truth* characterizing any intentional act, when approached from the standpoint of the computability theory [10].

As we can expect from a cultivated logician and mathematician as Putnam is, his complete theoretical conversion form the early functionalism posed the intentionality question at the right place, both from the computational and from the logic points of view. As we know since Tarski's seminal work, any formal theory of reference and truth is faced with the Gödelian limits, making impossible a recursive procedure of satisfaction in a semantically closed formal language. Effectively, the core of the problem is that such a recursive procedure for being complete would imply the solution of the *coding* problem through a diagonalization procedure; that is, the solution of the so–called "Gödel numbering" problem. In computational terms, the impossibility of solving the coding problem through a diagonalization procedure means that no TM can constitute by itself the "basic symbols", the primitives, of it own computations. For this reason Tarski rightly stated that, at the level of the propositional calculus, the semantic theory of truth has nothing to say about the conditions under which a given simple ("atomic" in L. Wittengstein's terms) proposition can be asserted. And for this very same reason, in a fundamental paper about *The meaning of "meaning"* [11], Putnam stated that no ultimate solution exists either in extensional logic both of the problem of *reference* and, at the level of linguistic analysis, of the problem of *naming*.

In this sense, Putnam stated, we would have to consider ultimately names as *rigid designators* "one - to - one" of objects in S. Kripke's sense [12]. But no room exists both in intensional and in extensional logic for defining this natural language notion of *rigid designation* in terms of a logical relation, since any logical relation only holds among terms and not between terms and objects, as Tarski reminded us. Hence a formal language has always to suppose the existence of names as rigid designators and cannot give them a foundation.

To explain by an example the destructive consequences of this point for a functionalist theory of mind, Putnam suggested a sort of third version of the famous "room – metaphor", after the original "Turing test" version of this metaphor and J. Searle's "Chinese – room" version of it. Effectively, Putnam proposed by his metaphor a further test that a TM cannot solve and that, for the reasons just explained, has much deeper implications than the counterexample to the Turing test proposed by Searle. For instance, Putnam said, if we ask "how many objects are in this room?", the answer supposes a previous decision about which are to be considered the "real" objects to be enumerated — i.e., rigidly designated by numerical units. So, one could answer that the objects in the room are only three (a desk, a chair and a lamp over the desk). However, by changing the enumeration axiom, another one could answer that the objects are many billions, because we have to consider also the molecules of which the former objects are constituted.

Out of metaphor, any computational procedure of a TM (and any computational procedure at all, if we accept Church's thesis) supposes the determination of the basic symbols on which the computations have to be carried on. Hence, from the semantic standpoint, any computational procedure supposes that such numbers are *encoding* (i.e., unambiguously naming as rigid designators) as many "real objects" of the computation domain (See [10], p. 116). In short, owing to the coding problem, the determination of the *basic symbols* (numbers) on which the computation is carried on, *cannot have any computational solution* at the actual state of development of the formal computability theory.

In other words, neither the problem of real reference nor of inductive schematism, essential for a scientific theory of human and animal perception, have in principle any solution from the functionalist approach to cognitive science.

3. Intentionality and the foundations of logic

3.1 Analytic versus axiomatic method in logic after Gödel

The preceding discussion about the core of the human intentionality is expressed in the language of cognitive science as the capability of human mind of re–defining the basic symbols of its computations. The double opposition between *inductive* versus *deductive* schematism and *productive* versus *reflexive* thought in cognitive science, has a logical counterpart in the opposition between *analytic* and *axiomatic* method in logic. Namely, in the opposition between a logic defining its own role also as *logic of discovery* of new hypotheses, and a logic reducing its role to the simple *logic of justification,* the logic of proving statements by deductive procedures, starting from fixed premises or *axioms.* Effectively, after Gödel — and, more recently, in the heterogeneous universe of the computer sciences — the necessity of studying logical procedures allowing change in axioms during calculations is an argument of ever growing importance. The notions of *soft-computing* as opposed to symbolic computations and of CI modeling of cognitive processes as opposed to AI modeling goes in the same direction [13]. In fact, for contemporary logic, computer science and cognitive sciences there is the shared necessity of avoiding the multifarious limitation theorems which have their formal origins in Gödel's [14-16].

The interest for recovering to modern logic and modern sciences *the analytic method[1] of classical, pre-modern logic* depends on the fact that it is in principle impossible to allow axiom changes within formal systems. Following Cellucci's reconstruction, the historical origin of the analytic method is in Plato's logic and it consists in affirming that the premises of any deductive procedure consist in pure *hypotheses,* since it is impossible to attain the truth of any mathematical entity. Each hypothesis consists thus in a "step" toward the further one in a never ended bottom-up process. The aim of logic would consist in the continuous progress toward ever more general principles, without the possibility of stopping such a process[2].

The historical origin of the *axiomatic method* is in Greek geometry and namely in the prototype of any axiomatic system: Euclid's *Elements.* It is based on the supposition that we can attain self-evident principles, without developing research toward ever more fundamental hypotheses. Further, Aristotle's logic transformed the axiomatic method into the proper object of logic, and proposed the axiomatic method in mathematics as a model for any other science. On the other hand, he refused the idea of a mathematical science of nature, typical of Pythagorean and Platonic traditions. Nevertheless, for Aristotle, the analysis still plays an important role as method of discovery of the so-called "middle-term" in any syllogistic procedure, that is the term connecting the "major premise" of the syllogism to its "conclusion"[3]. The construction of a deduction system following the axiomatic method in its syllogistic version within each scientific discipline constitutes the deductive "synthetic" moment, after the "analytic" one, devoted to the principle discovery. In this sense, the synthetic component has functions to make scientist's discoveries *rigorously expressible and profitable for all.* So, for Aristotle cannot exist one only axiomatic system for expressing all the mathematical truths or the true contents of any science. The analytic method for discovering new principles and finding new truths plays thus an essential, though subordinate, role in Aristotle's logical and epistemological theory.

---

[1] As we explain after, "analytic" has here to be intended in a radically different way as to its modern sense, the sense used by Pappo, Descartes, Newton and Leibniz.
[2] See, for instance Plato, *Parmenides,* 136c,1-7, *Letters,* VII, 342a-343c. The necessity of an *infinite* character of this bottom-up process is however negated in *Republic,* VI, 511b6-8 where it is said that knowledge is a sort of ascension-descent through a sort of universal deduction tree. That is, knowledge is intended in *Republic,* before as a bottom-up process by the *resolution* (finitely *analytic*) method toward a final not-hypotetical principle, for re-descending thereafter to all the consequences through a top-down process by the *synthetic* (deductive) method. This program, at least for geometry, was effectively implemented in Euclid's *Elements.*
[3] See Aristotle, *Post. An.,* I, 22, 83b,39-84a,2.

In the modern age, the axiomatic method was established with important differences from Aristotelian teaching. The most important one was the rejection of axioms as "real definitions" or essence definitions, because of Galileian science self–limitation to *quantitative properties* of the physical things. This rejection was confirmed by Newtonian physics, vindicating *the absolute phenomenal character* of the new physics, and the *purely formal character* of the three laws of dynamics, as conditions for justifying the calculus and geometrical predictability of quantitative phenomena. The *Logique* of Port–Royal, re–proposing former reflections of B. Pascal, asserted the necessity for mathematics of using only "nominal definitions", by a separation between "definitions" and "existence assertions".

In modern mathematical logic and in Hilbert's formalism, the nominal character of definitions implied the rejection of Frege's logicism, by renouncing the necessity of supposing "truth" and "meaningfulness" of formal system axioms for maintaining only their *coherence*. "Truth", "meaningfulness", as well as "coherence" are metalogical properties of formal systems and must be metalogically checked by algorithmic procedures. According to Hilbert, a set of axioms is not *coherent* because it is *true* and *existent the objects* to which these axioms refer. On the contrary, because the set of axioms is coherent and its coherence can be proved by a finite recursive (algorithmic) procedure, they are also *true* and *existent* their objects. On this basis, Hilbert pursued the possibility of constructing one only formal system for all mathematics. He stated also the possibility of using the axiomatic method for the "logic of discovery", by supposing the possibility of an algorithm able to determine, for each statement expressible in a given formal language, whether is it demonstrable or not within this language. Church–Rosser theorem denies such an algorithm can exist in formal systems. Moreover, Gödel's incompleteness theorems for arithmetic and their extension to all formal systems in the work of Turing and Tarski, ruled out the idea that the notion of mathematical truth can be exhausted by any formal system.

In this sense it has been asserted that logic and mathematical systems must be *open* systems in which the analytic method must recover its ancient role as logical method of new axiom discovery [14-19][4]. In other words, the incompleteness destiny for logical systems is unavoidable only *iff* we want to maintain *fixed* principles of demonstration, affirming that the formal systems are the *only* logical systems and the axiomatic method is the *only* method of logic. The *logic of discovery,* the logical method for new principle detection for the continuous construction of scientific (demonstrative) procedures, is the most important part of logic, *since only this type of non–determinism can avoid undecidability spectres.*

According to Cellucci, the reasons for which the discovery of limitation theorems for formal systems can be interpreted as a necessity for recovering the analytic method in its early Platonic version (see note 4) against the monism of the axiomatic method are very deep. They are essentially three:

1. *For avoiding the incompleteness,* it is not sufficient to construct a series of formal systems, each obtained by adding as new axiom the undecidable proposition of

---

[4] This is true, though some distinctions have to be made with respect to the difference between: 1) Plato's and Aristotle's definition of the analytic method as bottom–up process for the definition of new hypotheses and/or as process for the definition of new axioms for making possible a demonstration; and 2) the modern definition of analysis, all depending on Pappo's definition of it, as top–down process of decomposition of a compound in its parts. Of course (2) cannot be reduced to (1). See [16], pp. 292-299 and pp. 349-351.

the precedent one. Indeed the main question is whether there are complete formal systems successions obtained in such a way. The answer is very limited and substantially negative. Formulas of the type $\forall x\, A(x)$, where $A(x)$ is *a decidable* property, are demonstrable, even though there cannot be an algorithmic (finite) procedure for deciding the truth of the formula $\forall x\, A(x)$. On the contrary, formulas of the type $\forall x\, \exists y\, A(x, y)$, where $A(x, y)$ is a decidable relation, are not demonstrable, though they are true in the system [19]. More generally, the solution to Gödel's incompleness theorems for formal systems cannot consist in a series of systems chosen through an effective procedure. Some sort of non–determinism is necessary in the construction of the systems and hence in the construction of the axioms.

2. *The only non–determinism sufficient for avoiding Gödel's incompleteness* in formal systems consists *in the introduction of new axioms* and not in the simple possibility of non–deterministic multiple choices [20]. "The non–determinism required by Gödel result is the non–determinism related to the possibility of introducing at each step new axioms in a non algorithmic way" (See [16], p. 326). This denies that the system might be considered "formal" in classical sense and that the method used might be axiomatic — or "analytic" in modern sense (Gentzen's natural deduction methods included. See note 4).

3. *Turning to "mathematical intuition"* for justifying the discovery of new axioms, as Gödel himself did, implies a double unpleasant consequence. Before all, it means that there must exist ultimately in logic and mathematics (and hence in any science, metaphysics included) an irrational, subjective component [21-22]. "Here we are not in the realm of science, but of poetry". On the other hand, also if we intend the "intuition" in the strong sense of Gödel's "ideal intuition" of abstract concepts — that would be relative to infinite mathematical objects and that would be the result of a difficult training of the mathematician — we are faced with unavoidable limitations. The certainty thus obtained is unusable for granting that *certainty* in concrete mathematical choices we are searching for. For instance, let us suppose that in the system S there exists a true formula A, undecidable (i.e., both A and non-A cannot be demonstrated in this system) and a given abstract concept of set, $\mathfrak{S}$, known for intuition and for which the axioms of S are equally true. For a corollary of the first incompleteness theorem of Gödel, there must exist also another formula B and another intuitive notion of set, $\mathfrak{S}'$, for which the axioms of S are equally true, but such that B is *true* for $\mathfrak{S}'$ and false for $\mathfrak{S}$ (it is sufficient that we pose as B the statement not-A). In this case the ideal intuition cannot be used for deciding whether $\mathfrak{S}$ or $\mathfrak{S}'$ is the correct set notion. An examplification of such a case is whether we pose S as the Zermelo-Franklin set theory (ZF), $\mathfrak{S}$ as ZF notion of set and $\mathfrak{S}'$ as Cohen notion of set, after his demonstration of the independence of continuum hypothesis from the axiom of choice [23]. It is thus evident that ideal intuition, in spite of its implicit reference to infinitary method of demonstration[5], cannot grant that absolute mathematical certainty which formal systems are searching for (See [16], p. 254).

---

[5] It is to be remembered that G. Gentzen demonstrated the coherence of number theory by extending the mathematical induction till ε_0 [24]. In this way he explained why Hilbert's finitary arithmetic cannot give a similar demonstration of number theory coherence, so to satisfy Gödel's second incompleteness theorem.

However, the reference to *infinitary methods* in mathematics, which can abstractly grant coherence and truth but with weak effectiveness, can offer another contribution to a better understanding of Plato's analytic method limitations. Plato's impossibility of reaching mathematical truth and his preference for hypotheses and not for self-evident axioms are both based on an *ontological assumption*. This assumption is in many senses equivalent to the core of Tarski's demonstration of impossibility of defining semantic notions such as truth, coherence, reference, etc. by a purely formal recursive procedure of satisfaction, without attaining formal languages of ever higher logical types. The common ontological assumption here concerned is summarized in the following quotation from Plato's Dialogue, *Parmenides*:

> (If you pose the essence and the existence of a given object), you have to examine *simultaneously all* the consequences of such a hypothesis, both with respect to the object itself, and with respect to each other object individually considered, as well as with respect to whichever collection of these objects and with respect to the other objects considered all together. (...) This task is *never ending* (*Parmenides* 136c, 1-6).

It is evident that this is the same problem identified by Tarski for demonstrating the undecidabilty of semantic notions in formal systems because of the necessity of posing "infinitely many notions of satisfaction that must be introduced simultaneously because they cannot be defined independently" [2].

The solution suggested by Cellucci for avoiding this limitation would recover in a post–modern (post–Gödel) way the core of Plato's analytic method. Effectively it results very close to M. Minsky's "society of mind". It consists in supposing many systems connected together in a *continuously variable way*, without, of course, because of Gödel's, Church's and Turing's limitation theorems, any possible formal rule and/or algorithmic procedure governing this variation and/or the choice among the systems.

In other words, Cellucci concludes, we are faced today with a constraining alternative.

1. From one side, there is logic following *the axiomatic method* that not only gives no knowledge amplification, but it is no longer able, after Gödel, to grant absolute certainty. So, to avoid contradictions, this approach weakens the strength of logical implications (See, for instance, P.J. Cohen's "generic set" theory [23]), demonstrating only generic and therefore propositions *useless* for solving specific, concrete problems.
2. On the other side, we have *the analytic method* that, without granting certainty, is able at least to amplify knowledge by providing, new hypotheses for demonstrating useful propositions.

It may be obvious that post–modern logic has to choose the second alternative: if it is possible to have logical systems only with a local and limited demonstrative power, at least they showed be able to demonstrate useful propositions! This is the reason for Cellucci's preference for the analytic method.

It is useful to conclude this subsection by recalling the result of this overview about the opposition of the two logical methods (the analytic one and the axiomatic one), in the light of Gödel's theorems. This result is that the true problem is only the following: how to grant an "open character" to logical systems, that is, *a controlled proce-*

dure making a logical system able to change its axioms, in order to avoid undecidable situations typical of formal (i.e., closed) systems. In this light it is easy to understand that this is the same problem we faced in cognitive science, discussing H. Putnam's approach to intentionality problem (See § 2.2).

3.2 Connectionist *vs.* unstable and non-stationary (chaotic) NN

From the logic and computational standpoint, a connectionist NN after the learning is equivalent to a TM, reproducing in itself all the theoretical limitations we discussed above, with respect to *reference* and *truth*. Of course, the novelty with respect to classical symbolic methods of AI is the pre–symbolic task of the learning phase by which a NN *seems* to constitute by itself the logical symbols of its predicate calculus.

The theoretical problem is however the following: is a connectionist NN in learning a computational architecture able to constitute formally its own basic symbols intended as *rigid designators* of changing objects of the real world? The answer is evidently negative. A NN could be effectively able to constitute its own basic symbols *iff*, it was in a continuous learning. I.e., if it was able to modify, *depending on input,* not the statistical weights of its *fixed* topology of connections, but the same geometrical topology of the connections, so to lock dynamically itself "onto" the external object modifications . On the other hand, only in this case a NN will assume the typical *dynamic* and *computational* characteristics of biological networking. That is:

1. From the *dynamic standpoint,* it will assume the characteristics of an *unstable* and even *non–stationary* dynamics. Indeed, in the connectionist NN's, despite the non–linear character of such dynamic systems, the information (e.g., a pattern) is stored in each stable final state (fixed point attractor) of its dynamics. That is, it is stored in some absolute minimum of the "energy" landscape (i.e., of some complex function measuring the distance between the actual state and some target state) of the dynamics. On the contrary, what is typical of real brain networking is the *unstable* character of the signal transmission and processing among neurons. For instance, in real brains, the firing rate of neuron spikes is continuously changing. In this way, it becomes despairing any attempt to interpret in a frequentistic way the learning rule for weight connections as, on the contrary, the Hebbian rule pretends to do. Moreover, there is evidence in real brains of more complex oscillatory and even chaotic (i.e., unstable in itself, even though pseudo–stable or pseudo–periodic with respect to a properly chosen interval ε) global dynamic behaviors [25-28].

    The informational advantages of chaotic behavior in neural dynamics, become evident as soon as we consider the information richness hidden in the pseudo–cycles of a chaotic dynamics. Roughly speaking, in the energy landscape of a classical non-linear neural net, such as a Hopfield net, it is possible to memorize less than one pattern for each of the n minima [29]. In a chaotic memory it would be possible to profit *in real time*[6], on a deterministic basis, of all the cyclic com-

---

[6] Because a chaotic net does not memorize patterns "statically" into fixed points of the dynamics but into unstable cycles that can be recovered on a deterministic basis, it is not necessary to reset the net after a recognition for the next one, as with static nets. It is sufficient to change a parameter value for switching from a cycle into another.

binations of these minima, with an exponential increment of the memory capability (theoretically it is possible to improve the memory capacity till 2^n patterns. See Figure 1). In our view, in this dynamic use of the brain dynamic instability is hidden the secret of straightforward memorization capacity of the biological and specifically the human brain. Computationally, the main difficulty is that till now there were no effective computational techniques of pseudo–cycle extraction of any length, because of the complexity of chaotic behavior. This complexity indeed makes inapplicable to deterministic chaos classical statistical methods of signal analysis. In the last four years, however, one of us, developed a new effective technique of pseudo–cycle extraction of any length, with a computation time growing only linearly with the cycle length [30]. We have the definitive experimental evidence that this method, based on the new foundational ideas discussed in the next Section, can extract practically *all* the pseudo–cycles of a chaotic dynamics [31].

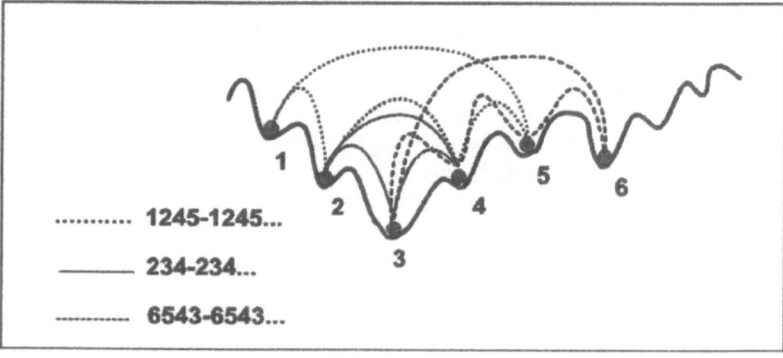

Figure 1. Intuitive representation (effectively it is not possible to define a Ljapunov function of a chaotic system) of the storing capacity of a chaotic dynamics into the 2^n pseudo–cycles among the n minima of its energy landscape. For instance, if we imagine that each minimum corresponds to a feature of a visual object, it is easy to understand that each class of object corresponds to a cycle, i.e., a given combination of features (see Figure 2). Moreover, by a simple phase change (e.g., a change in the ordering of minima within a given cycle) the net could easily recognize the sameness of the object also under three-dimensional rotation in the space. Finally, because we are faced here with pseudo–cycles and not with cycles, it becomes easy to explain also the physical basis of the analytic procedures of *induction, generalization* and *analogy* through such a dynamic structure of recognition as object–reconstruction locked onto real object modifications.

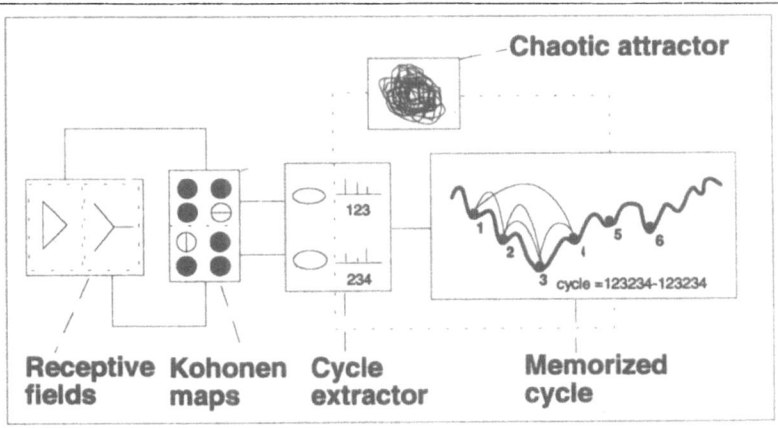

Figure 2. Intuitive representation of a chaotic NN scheme

Finally, there is an amazing *evidence* of the *non – stationary character* of real brain networking. For instance, Positron Emission Tomography (PET) techniques of inquiry give a sort of biological evidence of what logicians intend with the notion of names as *dynamic rigid designators* of objects. Namely, in cognition tasks, such as attention focusing or moving object tracking, completely different neuron networks are excited to designate the very same object [32]. It is as if the real brain is continuously modifying the geometrical connection topology of its computation network, to match the object modifications. On the other hand, this sort of accommodation of the basic symbol space for matching varying objects is precisely what is needed from a NN for being able of performing *really parallel computations*. Let us illustrate briefly this essential point.

2. *From the computational standpoint,* a connectionist NN cannot be considered as a really parallel computational architecture, because the inner units are *fully connected* with the input units x_k (see Figure 3 (a)). A really parallel computation implies that the inner units compute functions $p_i (X)$ defined only on some subset of the input units [33]. For considering such functions as rigid designators of varying external objects it is thus necessary that the supports $S_{p_i}(X)$ of these functions are varying with the objects (See Figure 3(b)). The non–stationary character of brain networking displays all its intrinsic computational value, if interpreted in this sense. Such a neural net model, $\Psi^D (X)$, is called *dynamic perceptron* (See Figure 3(b_1-b_2)). It is characterized by an automatic pre–processing devoted to modify the net connection geometry, depending on the correlations of each singular input — practically it is in continuous learning, not on the weights, but on the connection topology. This architecture was developed by A. L. Perrone, as a partial implementation of the previous ideas on cognitive intentionality, to solve real pattern recognition problems [34]. In any case, there are straightforward neurophysiological evidences of the so–called "dynamic receptive field" of neurons belonging to different sensory systems of mammalians that could find by the notion of "dynamic perceptron" their computational model, showing the informational

324

relevance of such a strange behavior[7]. The dynamic receptive field has been observed in mammalian retina [35], auditory cortex [36-37]; primary visual cortex [38-39]. It was found that there exist subfields, some of which are activated only during 20-50 msec for a continual presentation of stimuli, and the combination of activated subfields varies even for a static presentation of stimuli. In primary visual cortex, it is well known that there exist neurons with orientation specificity. Another type of neurons, whose orientation specificity — i.e., a tuning — is dynamically changeable, was found in relation to the dynamic receptive field [38]. In this context, a classical receptive field can be reformulated as a spatio-temporal summation of dynamic receptive fields. The spatial summation is taken over an entire receptive field, and the temporal summation over a few hundreds miliseconds. Since the time scale 20-50 msec is almost equal to a "unit" of psychological time, the dynamic receptive field may be considered as a neural correlate of internal dynamics for the reorganization of mental space. Namely, the presence of dynamic receptive field suggests the presence of the process of dynamic re-modelling due to dynamic interactions between higher and lower levels of information processing [38-39].

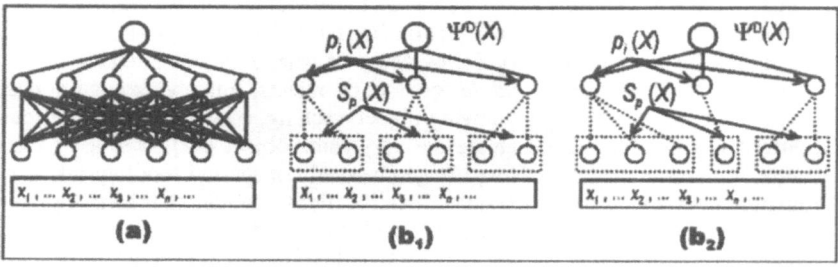

Figure 3.

3.3   Conclusion

In cognitive neuroscience it is generally held that a given neural circuitry is a *code* of some given intentional *belief*. However, in the light of all the precedent discussion, we feel that any honest computational approach to the study of mind cannot limit itself to state simply that a given brain circuitry is a "code" of a "belief", i.e., of a mental representation of a given thing. At the actual state of development of the computability theory, *there is not* and *cannot be* any formal demonstration of this *threefold correspondence* among the *referential thing*, the *neural code* and the *belief*.
This sort of correspondence can be only a *matter of convention*, depending on the meta-language we choose to define this correspondence. Namely, this correspondence is only an *interpretation* in the technical sense of the model theory, just as to

[7] We thank prof. I. Tsuda of the Dept. Of Mathematics of Hokkaido University in Sapporo (Japan) for this personal communication about the relationship between the pre-processing of our "dynamic perceptron" and the neurophysiological evidence of the "dynamic receptive field" in sensory cortex. We are preparing with prof. Tsuda a specific paper on this topics.

say that a given activated circuitry in a computer or a sequence of signals in a telegraph corresponds to the letter "A".
However, a distinction is necessary.

1. The problem of formally defining the *coreference* (i.e., to have the same reference) between a belief statement, expressed in intentional language (*I-talk*, e.g.: "I (believe to) see a red colour") according to intensional logic, and a related observation statement (*O-talk*), of some neurological (e.g.: "a modification in the variable y is measured at time t in the brain location z as a response to a given input x"), computational, psychological etc. theory, according to extensional logic, *is not a solvable problem* (See § 3.1).
2. On the contrary, to solve the problem of the *real reference*, that is the problem of the correspondence between *a neural code* – not necessarily constituted according to a Hebbian law – and an *external thing*, it is sufficient to demonstrate that a biological brain is able to compute functions not computable for a TM, as opposed to Church's thesis. In other words, to solve the real reference problem for a scientific theory of perception it is sufficient to demonstrate that what characterizes a biological brain (and more generally any biological organism) is its *capability of dynamically redefining the basic symbols*, the codes, of its own computations, in dependence of singular different occurrences of their own objects.

To understand this point, we need a completely different approach to the real reference problem in the light of the pre–modern analytic method in logic and particularly in the light of the classical theory of intentionality as its cognitive basis.

References

[1] J.A. Fodor, «Fodor's guide to mental representation: the intelligent auntie's vademecum», *Mind* 94:76-100 (1985); J.A. Fodor, *Psychosemantics. The problem of meaning in the philosophy of mind*, Cambridge, MA, MIT Press (1987).
[2] A. Tarski, «The semantic conception of truth and the foundations of semantics», in: *Readings in philosophical analysis*, H. Feigl, ed., New York, Cambridge University Press, pp. 52-84 (1944, 1949).
[3] J.A. Fodor, «Methodological solipsism considered as a research strategy in cognitive psychology», *The Behavioral and Brain Sciences* 3:63-109 (1980).
[4] J.R. Searle, «Mind, brains and programs. A debate on artificial intelligence», *The Behavioral and Brain Science* 3:128-135 (1980). ID., *Intentionality. An essay in the philosophy of mind*, New York, Cambridge University Press (1983); ID., *Mind language and society*, New York, Basic Books (1999).
[5] R. McIntyre, «Intending and referring», in: *Husserl, intentionality and cognitive science*, H.L. Dreyfus and H. Hall, eds, Cambridge MA., MIT Press, pp. 219-235 (1982).
[6] E. Zalta, *Intensional logic and the metaphysics of intentionality*, Cambridge, MA, MIT Press (1988).
[7] W.V.O. Quine, *Quiddities. An intermittently philosophical dictionary*, Cambridge, MA, Harvard University Press (1987).
[8] W.V.O. Quine, *Word and object*, Cambridge, MA, MIT Press (1960).

326

[9] P.S. Churchland, *Neurophilosophy. Toward a unified science of the mind-brain*, Cambridge MA, MIT Press (1986); P. Churchland, *The engine of reason, the seat of the soul*, Cambridge MA, MIT Press (1996).

[10] H. Putnam, *Representations and reality*, Cambridge, MA, MIT Press (1988).

[11] H. Putnam, «The mening of 'meaning'». In: *Philosophical papers: mind, language and reality*, New York, Cambridge University Press (1972), pp. 215-271.

[12] S. Kripke, *Naming and necessity*, Cambridge MA, Harvard University Press (1972, 1996).

[13] A. Clark, *Being there. Putting brain, body and world together again*, Cambridge MA, MIT Press (1998).

[14] I. Lakatos, *Mathematics, science and epistemology*, Cambridge, Cambridge University Press (1978).

[15] D. R. Hofstadter, *Fluid concepts and creative analogies*, New York, Harper Collins Publ. (1995).

[16] C. Cellucci, *Le ragioni della logica*, Roma–Bari, Laterza (1998).

[17] G. Basti, «Per una lettura tomista dei fondamenti della logica e della matematica», in: Basti G. and Perrone A.L., *Le radici forti del pensiero debole: dalla metafisica, alla matematica, al calcolo*, Padova-Roma, Il Poligrafo e Pontificia Università Lateranense, pp. 19-254 (1996).

[18] G. Basti «L'approccio aristotelico-tomista alle aporie dell'induzione». In: *Il fare della scienza. I fondamenti e le palafitte*, F. Barone, G. Basti, C. Testi eds., Padova, Il Poligrafo, pp. 41-95 (1997).

[19] S. Feferman, «Transfinite recursive progressions of axiomatic theories», *The Journal of symbolic logic* 27, pp. 259-316 (1962).

[20] T. G. McCarthy, «Self–reference and incompleteness in a non–monotonic setting», *The Journal of philosophical logic* 23, pp. 423-449 (1994).

[21] J.-Y. Girard, «Le champ du signe ou la faillite du réductionisme», in: E. Nagel and J. R. Newmann, *Le théorème de Gödel*, Paris, Editions du Seuil, p. 161 (1989).

[22] K. R. Popper, *Logic of scientific discovery*, London, Routledge and Keegan P. (1959).

[23] P.J. Cohen, *Set theory and the continuum hypothesis*, New York (1966).

[24] G. Gentzen, «Die Wiederspruchsfreiheit der reinen Zahlenthorie», in *Mathematische Annalen*, 112, pp. 439-565 (1936).

[25] C.M. Gray, P. Koenig, A.K. Engel and W. Singer «Oscillatory responses in cat visual cortex exhibit inter-columnar synchronization which reflects global stimulus properties», *Nature* **338**, pp. 334-337 (1989).

[26] R. Eckhorn, H.J. Reitboeck, M. Arndt and P. Dicke «Feature linking via synchronization among distributed assemblies: simulation of results from cat visual cortex», *Neural Computation* 2:293-307 (1990).

[27] A.K. Engel, P. Koenig, C.M. Gray and W. Singer «Synchronization of oscillatory responses: a mechanism for stimulus-dependent assembly formation in act visual cortex», in: *Parallel processing in neural systems and computers*, R. Eckmiller, ed., Amsterdam, Elsevier, pp. 212-217 (1990).

[28] C.A. Skarda, and W.J. Freeman «How brains make chaos in order to make sense of the world», *Behavioral and Brain Sciences* 10:161-195 (1987).

[29] G. Parisi, «Asymmetric Neural Nets and the Process of Learning», *Journ.of Phys. A: Math.Gen*, 19, L675-680 (1986).

[30] A.L. Perrone, «A formal scheme to avoid undecidabilities: an application to chaotic dynamics characterization and parallel computation» in: *Cognitive and dynamical systems. Lecture Notes in Computer Science*, S.I. Andersson, ed., 888:9-52 (1995); ID., «Verso una teoria dinamica della computazione», in: G. Basti and A.L. Perrone, *Le radici forti del pensiero debole: dalla metafisica, alla matematica, al calcolo*, Padova-Roma, Il Poligrafo e Pontificia Università Lateranense, pp. 255-332 (1996); ID., «Applications of chaos theory to lossy image compression», *Nuclear Instruments and Methods in Physics Research. Section A.*, 389, pp. 221-225 (1997) ; ID., «The cognitive role of chaos in neural information processing». In: *Proceedings of the International School of Biocybernetics: «Processes in the perception representation mechanisms»*, C. Taddei-Ferretti and C. Muzio eds., Singapore-London, World Scientific (1999).

[31] A.L. Perrone, «A new approach to chaotic systems characterization and its implications for biology», *Aquinas* XLIII-2:381-409 (2000).

[32] M.I. Posner, and M.E. Raichle *Images of mind*, New York, Scientific American Library (1994).

[33] M. Minsky, and S. Papert *Perceptrons*. Second Edition, Cambridge Mass., MIT Press (1988).

[34] A.L. Perrone, Basti G., Messi R., Pasqualucci E., Paoluzi L. «Offline Analysis of HEP events by the 'dynamic perceptron' neural network», *Nuclear Instruments and Methods in Physics Research. Section A.*, 389, 210-213 (1997).

[35] M. Tsukada, (1998). Private communication for his experimental findings in late 1970s on dynamic receptive field in cat retinal ganglion cells.

[36] J. J. Eggermont, A. M. Aertsen, H. J. Hermes, and P.I.M. Johannesma, «Spectro-Temporal Characterization of Auditory Neurons: Redundant or Necessary?», *Hearing Research* 5, pp. 109-121 (1981).

[37] M. P. Kilgard and M. M. Merzenich, «Cortical map reorganization enabled by nucleus basalis activity», *Science* 279, pp. 1714-1718 (1998).

[38] H. Dinse, «A Temporal Structure of Cortical Information Processing», *Concepts in Neuroscience* 1, pp. 199-238 (1990).

[39] H. Dinse, «A time-based approach towards cortical functions: neural mechanisms underlying dynamic aspects of information processing before and after postontogenetic plastic processes», *Physica D* 75, pp. 129-150 (1994).

Where thought lives: place or palace?

Gabriele E. M. Biella

Istituto Neuroscienze e Bioimmagini CNR and Dipartimento di Scienze e Tecnologie Biomediche, Università Statale di Milano-Via Fratelli Cervi, 93- 20090 Segrate (Milan) Italy

Abstract

Localistic versus distributive processing are seemingly antagonistic views of the central nervous system general function. The issue gives rise to complex philosophical debates that, stemming from the monistic-dualistic everliving debate, invocate justification from anatomical, functional and psychological observations. A brief sketch of the current debates is given.

1. Introduction

The title represents an iteration theme of the overdisputed challenge between mechanistic decomposition and localization vs dynamical (process) modeling in cognitive systems and, more generally, in neuroscience.

The mechanistic description allows for naming and taxonomy of components, meeting under rules in a "complex" system. Here I use naively the term complex as 'not simple' or monadic and composed by congruous parts.

The dynamics approach implies a system integration, that takes places under most different conditions, a composite position combining proposals of widely different hypotheses and solutions.

The choice between the mechanistic vs dynamic (or process based) premise is the counterpart to the dualism-physicalism (or materialism) alternative, that shall be discussed under a weak but general and ontological materialist drive.

The premise shall give us the access to an overview of the neural correlates of consciousness (NCC), pointing on theoretic localization of different experimental explanations of consciousness. This description is made subordinate to the aforementioned topic of localistic vs dynamic processes.

2. Conditionally weak materialism: oblige to fragile position

2.1 The dualistic issues

In the manifold versions of dualism [1, 2, 3, 4], stepping from the starting position of the cartesian Méditation on disparity of res extensa and res cogitans, mind can exist without matter and matter can exist without mind. The interactionst dualism of Descartes depicts the classic mind-body problem with the epitome of dualistic choice. In stronger terms how a spatially extended item can interact with a non-spatially extended one? W.D. Hart [1988] in "The Engines of the Soul", disclosing the modern appeal to the dualistic modal problem, shifts the position of the quest: the interaction problem is not a problem with a dualist ontology but a problem on the assumption of causation. The assumption that a mental state is caused by matter is reduced to the relativistic physical problem of the conversion from energy to matter. Causation is suspended or transformed into irrelevant notion as in the context of energy-matter mutual dependence issues. This is an active, modern dualistic position less extremely committed to the critical (passive) position of the New Mysterian philosophy (NM), this last denying the even remote possibility of scientific reductionism.

2.2 The materialistic issues

The interchangeability of material and physical renders some irregularity in the conceptual development of a materialistic view [5].
Along several philosophers' view factual and real world knowledge are a set of statements on physical elements (objects or actions). This attributes physicalism a reductive front to the physical immediateness that however permits objectivism and third part consent. [6,7,8,9,10,11].

2.2.1 Supervenience
Non reductive physicalism necessitates of the intervention of corollary issues like token identity thesis and supervenience. Most important in mind and cognition phylosophy, supervenience was introduced by Donald Davidson in 1970 "....there can not be two events alike in all physical respects but differing in some mental respect, or that an object cannot alter in some mental respect without altering in some physical respect" [12]. Strict physicalism could not overcome the obstacle of the improper identity between mental and physical properties. Supervenience eludes the problem of that identity yet mantaining the physical determination of the mental with equally strong restrictions condensed in the statement 'no mental differences without physical differences' (and vice-versa). In the mind-body context mental properties and facts supervene on physical properties and facts without the necessity of identity.

2.2.2 The mind-body pair

As for the relation of the mind-body pair, hard (reductive) materialists assume the equivalence of their physical properties [13, 14] while non reductive materialists consider that psychological properties have an acceptable matter-segregated life but with different hints among functionalists or behaviorists or eliminativists.

Functionalists seem to advocate the "multiple realizability" issue, a crucial request for cognitive science coming from the topics generated by the Turing machine protocols [15] saying that tokens of the same mental type can be instantiated on tokens of different physical type [16].

2.2.3 Type-type identity – Token-token identity

There is however a poor evidence of the consistent, true correspondence between psychological facts and physical neural facts. However, type-type identity requires that correspondence. Then, flecting to a weaker choice, the token-token identity, functionalists materialists skip for that difficulty and adopt a deconstructivist turn: in keeping with this choice whichever token (from a specific molecule up to a specific cultural expression) is composed by physical phenomena. The final step is done with compositional materialism, the weakest and my preferred (current) position denying the token-token complete identity and supporting that physical-psychological events are not type identical to their constituent elements or events (two objects can be made by diverse atoms and in the meantime display an objectual sameness, thus opening a comparable explanation for psychological events). This allows for smoothed emergentism, a circumnavigation around the explanatory gap with the aware, almost deliberate recognition of the opacity of the original problem of the rise of subjective psychologically identified event from physical event [17].

Being impossible in these short description a sound attribution of every finely tuned materialistic position to each author a list of papers (and authors) is reported all belonging to the "materialistic side", all differentiating crucially for some of the issues noted above [18, 19, 20, 21]. Other less precisely describable postions are the evolutionary aspects of consciousness or 'Consciousness is a virtual machine which evolved' [22, 23]).

3. Philosophical extensions from anatomo-functional observations

3.1 The NCC problem

After this introductory remarks we can stipulate a more complete appeal of the NCC problem.

David Chalmers, philosopher and director for the studies on consciousness at the University of Arizona, a NCC "is a minimal neuronal system such that there is a minimal mapping of states of that system to states of consciousness" given for understood the adequacy or sufficiency of the neural system to the corresponding state of consciousness. It is evident here that I shift from the previous allegiance in psychological events to the, however composite, specific theme of consciousness. But the current research doesn't allow for an available psychophilosophical description of thought. Quoting a NCC leads to our original question on the physical source of consciousness that beyond the dualistic-physicalist dialectic poses a further, topologic problem on localization or distribution of the source.

3.2 Topologic issues

There are several functional or structural interpretations on the topologic issue. As Chalmers has already pointed out: G. Edelman in the eighties developed the hypothesis of reentrance (or reciprocal signalling in the thalamo-cortical circuits, [24]), F.Crick and C.Koch identified a oscillatory frequence of 40 Hz [25, 26], and those hypotheses have been amplified by Llinas, Ribary and coworkers into the concept of the brain as a closed system, due to the fact that the cortical input to the thalamus is tenfold that coming to the thalamus from the periphery [27]. In this view Llinas holds the the Central Nervous System (CNS) is a 'reality emulating system and that the parameters of the emulated reality are delineated by the senses'. This emulation can happen thanks to recurrent circuitry of the thalamo-cortico-thalamic loop. Minor far reaching and pretty neurological or biochemical essence hypotheses are based on a reticular-thalamic activation, the different area binding by NMDA coactivation, specific neurochemical levels of activation [28]. Specific form of consciousness (visual awarness) has been ascribed to certain neuronal populations in the extrastriate cortex projecting to the pre-frontal cortex and to processes of the visual input into the ventral stream [29].

3.3 Input information processing

The general feature common to all the current theories on consciousness is founded on modulation of input and on input information processing [30].
Just to join to our main discussion the problem has developed in two main topics, the one on the particular way an information is processed, the other on the particular type of input represented by information relative to consciousness. Thus a modal vs type (or 'process vs representation') postition is discussed on the background of specialized vs non-specialized supporting mechanism [31]. Thus, as Atkinson and colleagues have already discussed, consciousness can be diversely described as generated by special process type running on specialized pathways (a consciousness dedicated processing on dedicated structure), or as special mode to represent an otherwise general information through a specific 'consciousness pathway, or again as the result of modally specific processes irrespective of the supporting neural network and as modally irrespective process irrespective of the specific neural substrate.

3.4 Theoretic neuroanatomy

Examples of the four addresses in neuroscience and neuropsychology can be described as follows:

Specialized anatomical substrates have relied on memory functions. One of the first models is that of Atkinson and Shiffrin [32] that proposed that a short term memory-like mechanisms (Short Term Store) contains only those representations that overcame a threshold controlled by STS processes. Those contents represent the subject consciousness. This model, though reduced to 'local memories', insists on consciousness representational competence of a memory mechanism itself.

In the second type of mechanism, consciousness can arise only in specific circuits running specific processes. One of the most representative theories is the higher order thought consciousness of Edmund Rolls. Rolls actually proposes that higher order thoughts about a state is given by the fact that the subject can have higher order thoughts on that state: the crucial localization of this specific competence is provided by language brain structures and by their interconnection to other brain areas [33].

Theories assuming a non specialised neural substrate for otherwise representational specific processes have been proposed by several groups. A paradigm is represented by O'Brien and Opie, indicated as 'connectionist theory of phenomenal experience'. It endorses also the theoretical environment introduced in the neural networks by Parallel Distributed Processing (PDP). This tells that consciousness is maintained and composed by multiple, diverse and simultaneous tokens. These in addition must display stable behavior because only under stability regimen it is conceivable a coherent and effective communication among PDP modules [34, 35, 36].

Among the most powerful and significant models of the NCC is the last in this list. It provides a theoretical substrate to the theory that consciousness depends on specific processes widely distributed in diverse (any?) areas of the brain.

This most powerful (and the most recent) proposal come from Giulio Tononi and Gerald Edelman [37, 38].

The proposal by Tononi and Edelman is defined 'dynamic core hypothesis'. The theory holds that the neural processes that endorse and sustain consciousness are represented by stable and very efficient patterns of reciprocal signalling that represent the 'core'. This stable core integrates informations (by complex neural dynamics as the re-entrance mechanism) from a, continuosly changing, neuronal grouping in diverse brain areas, distributed over the entire brain.

The model thus appeals for consciousness to be a process (constituted by the core integration) and not a mechanism, without any anatomically defined localization. However, a special role is played by the re-entrant circuits of the thalamo-cortico-thalamic circuits. The variety of the conscious experience is however due to the different integration of the activated areas. The dynamic core is efficient enough to bind together all the activated areas involved in time developing consciousness.

Now it is necessary to grasp some concept of what a cerebral circuit is as the laying basis of the neurally based models of consciousness, of their philosophical pretensions and the rations startpoint for every discussion on brain and thought..

4. The very anatomy

The cerebral cortex (covering the white matter) is a 2 mm (or so), six layered structure. Every layer has a strctural identity and often single layers are subdividible in further sublayers; As a principle of functional segregation, neurons with functional analogy are clustered in homogeneous areas. The organization is conserved in vertical extension to form cylinder-like patterns known as cortical column. Single comumn have a 30-60 μm diameter. Clusters of hundreds of minicolumns are bounded in macrocolumns up to 1 mm across. Both minicolumns and macrocolumns have an overall hexagonal shape in planar sections. The shape is an emergent property that indicates the cellular the darwinistic border competition for each functional unit, the best spatial compromise between units numerosity and efficiency. The competition on the borders is a continuous, all the life long process with a mobile mosaic involved in a task (sensory, motor or associative).

4.1 Columns, blobs and patches

The cortical organization is not a mere repeats of columns. In the posterior (occipital) regions of the primary visual cortex in primates (the area V1) there are regions or patches of neurons. Some of these patches, called blobs, contain specifically color-sensitive neurons. There are blobs sensitive to shape. Blobs are segregated one from the other by macrocolumnar distances. Color sensitive blobs in V1 project to color sensitive stripes (elongated areas in V2 the proximate cortical area to V1). Other cortical patterns are divided in barrels. These regionalizations are specific for sensory cortices with peculiar structures linked to highly space organized (somatotopic) projections from the thalamus.
Dale Purves [39] defined all the structures discussed above as cortical modules and this term is applied to every segregated cortical pattern or 'patchiness'. However strong discussions arose on this loose semantic choice, indicating an undefined black box with suggestion for functional insights.
A general wiring plan of the cortex shows that cortical layer IV is the input station from the thalamus, while layer VI integrates the outputs back to the thalamus. The Vyh layer sends messages to deep structures beyond the thalamus. Superficial layers are mainly (not exclusively!) devoted to near and far cortico-cortical connections.
Several uncertainties are also related to the extension of "sensory cortices", "motor cortices" or "associative cortices". Most authors agree that on the whole hemisferic aggregate of 52 sudivisided areas, the association cortex is extended for up the 90% of the entire cortical surface, while Irvin Diamond assumed that every fifth lyer has to be understood like a motor cortex and every IV layer like a

sensory cortex, while, simultaneously and concurrently, every second and third layer is an association cortex.

These are not mere opinions in that synchrony and delayed synachronies can be assumed to entrain diverse cerebral areas with diverse strategies and to shape the problem of "thought" or the conscious process undelying it

4.2 Connections

Basic issues come from deeper anatomic details like the lateral connections in the cortical structure. Recurrent inhibitions and excitations are basic circuit elements enriching the overall syntaxis of the structure. Recurrent excitations come often from the superficial layers of the cortex and going through the white matter to other cortical regions. They feedback originally incoming signls to other homologous superficial layers while send new messages when they reach layer IV. There are more subtle and finer wiring details that shall be discussed more properly. It is however important to consider that recurrent excitations can induce synchrony and it is known that cells in minicolumns often fire synchronously when involved in a task and that the extension of synchrony. A diffuse synchrony wave is wider and wider as tasks become more requiring. Several neurochemical details are also known combined to these anatomo-functional issues. In some way some long-range fiber endorsed, simultaneous synchrony in the thalamo-cortical network can be indicated as the core of the conscious process.

Is in these models an adherence to a weak materialistic identifiable with compositional materialism or token-token identity?

All the spectrum of answers can be sanctioned.

A brain distributive hypothesis for consciousness seems more proper even on the basis of clinical reports. This is the functional side of the original question.

But, as for the matter of consciousness the final question remains unanswered

References

[1] Popper, K. R. (1977). Some remarks on panpsychism and epiphenomenalism. Dialectica 31:177-86.

[2] Popper, K. & Eccles, J. (1977). *The Self and Its Brain: An Argument for Interactionism.* Springer Verlag, Berlin Heidelberg New York.

[3] Eccles, J. 1987. Brain and mind: Two or one? In (C. Blakemore & S. Greenfield, eds) *Mindwaves.* Blackwell.

[4] Hart, W. D. (1988). *The Engines of the Soul.* Cambridge University Press.

[5] Nagel, T. (1993). What is the mind-body problem? In *Experimental and Theoretical Studies of Consciousness* (Ciba Foundation Symposium 174). Wiley. New York, Chichester.

[6] Chalmers, D. J. (1996). Can consciousness be reductively explained? In The Conscious Mind. Oxford University Press.

[7] Chalmers, D. J. (1996). *The Conscious Mind: In Search of a Fundamental Theory.* Oxford University Press, Oxford

[8] Chalmers, D. J. (1997). Availability: The cognitive basis of experience? In (N. Block, O. Flanagan, and G. Guzeldere, eds) *The Nature of Consciousness.* MIT Press.

[9] Chalmers, D.J. (1999) What is a neural correlate of consciousness? In Neural Correlates of Consciousness: Conceptual and Empirical Questions (Metzinger, T., ed.), MIT Press

[10] Levine, J. (1983). Materialism and qualia: the explanatory gap. Pacific Philos. Q. 64, 354–361

[11] Kim, J. (1997). The mind-body problem: Taking stock after forty years. Philosophical Perspectives 11:185-207.

[12] Davidson, D. (1970) Mental Events. (reprinted in Davidson, D. (1980). Essays on actions and Events. Oxford University Press, Oxford.

[13] Feinberg, T. E. (1997). The irreducible perspectives of consciousness. Seminars in Neurology 17:85-93.

[14] Kirk, R. (1982). Physicalism, identity, and strict implication. Ratio 24:131-41.

[15] Fodor, J. (1983). The modularity of mind, Bradford Books, MIT Press, Cambridge, Mass.

[16] Hill, C. S. (1991). *Sensations: A Defense of Type Materialism.* University Press.Cambridge. Cambridge, Mass.

[17] Levine, J. (1983). Materialism and qualia: the explanatory gap. Pacific Philos. Q. 64, 354–361

[18] Block, N. (1995) On a confusion about a function of consciousness. Behav. Brain Sci. 18, 227–287

[19] Block, N. & Stalnaker, R. (1999). Conceptual analysis, dualism, and the explanatory gap. Philosophical Review.

[20] Chalmers, D. J. (1995). Facing up to the problem of consciousness. Journal of Consciousness Studies 2:200-19.

[21] Robinson, H. (ed) (1993). *Objections to Physicalism.* Oxford University Press, Oxford.

[22] Dennett, D. C. & Kinsbourne, M. (1992). Time and the observer: The where and when of consciousness in the brain. Behav. Brain Sci. 15:183-201.

[23] Dennett, D.C. (1991). Consciousness Explained, Little, Brown

[24] Edelman, G. M. (1987). Neural Darwinism: The Theory of Neuronal Group Selection (Basic, New York).

[25] Crick, F. and Koch, C. (1990) Towards a neurobiological theory of consciousness. Semin. Neurosci. 2, 263–275

[26] Crick, F. and Koch, C. (1995). Why neuroscience may be able to explain consciousness. Sci. Am. 273(6):84-85.

[27] Llinas, R.R. et al. (1994). Content and context in temporal thalamocortical binding. In *Temporal Coding in the Brain* (Buzsaki, G. et al., eds), Springer Verlag, Berlin Heidelberg New York.

[28] Flohr, H. (1995) Sensations and brain processes. Behav. Brain Res.71, 157–161.

[29] Hobson, J.A. (1997) Consciousness as a state-dependent phenomenon. In *Scientific Approaches to Consciousness* (Cohen, J. and Schooler, J., eds), pp. 379–396, Lawrence Erlbaum

[30] Kurthen, M. et al. (1998) Will there be a neuroscientific theory of consciousness? Trends Cognit. Sci. 2, 229–234.

[31] Atkinson, A. P. Thomas M.S.C. and Cleeremans, A.(2000) Consciousness: mapping the theoretical landscape.TICS, 4: 372-382.

[32] Atkinson, R.C. and Shiffrin, R.M. (1971) The control of short-term memory. Sci. Am. 224, 82–90.

[33] Rolls, E.T. (1998) *The Brain and Emotion*, Oxford University Press, Oxford.

[34] O'Brien, G. & Opie, J. (1997). Cognitive science and phenomenal consciousness: A dilemma, and how to avoid it. Philos. Psychol. 10:269-86.

[35] O'Brien, G. and Opie, J. (1999) A connectionist theory of phenomenal experience. Behav. Brain Sci. 22, 127–196

[36] Sperry, R. W. (1992). Turnabout on consciousness: A mentalist view. J. Mind Behav. 13:259-80.

[37] Tononi, G. and Edelman, G.M. (1998) Consciousness and complexity. Science 282: 1846–1851

[38] Edelman, G.M. and Tononi G. (2000). A universe of Consciousness. Basic Books, New Tork.

[39] Purves, D., Riddle, D.R. and LaMantia, A.S (1992). Iterated patterns of brain circuitry (or how the cortex gets its spots). TINS 15: 362-368.

Author Index